Critical Thinking and Writing
A DEVELOPING WRITER'S GUIDE WITH READINGS

Critical Thinking and Writing

A DEVELOPING WRITER'S GUIDE WITH READINGS

Kristan Cavina
Mount San Antonio College

WADSWORTH PUBLISHING COMPANY

I(T)P™ AN INTERNATIONAL THOMSON PUBLISHING COMPANY

Belmont • Albany • Bonn • Boston • Cincinnati • Detroit • London • Madrid • Melbourne
Mexico City • New York • Paris • San Francisco • Singapore • Tokyo • Toronto • Washington

English Editor: Angela Gantner Wrahtz
Assistant Editor: Lisa Timbrell
Editorial Assistant: Kate Peltier
Production: Robin Lockwood
Text and Cover Designer: Christy Butterfield
Print Buyer: Barbara Britton
Permissions Editor: Robert Kauser
Copy Editor: Steven Gray
Cover and Interior Photographer: Nick Pavloff © 1994
Compositor: Thompson Type
Printer: Courier Companies, Inc.

Printed in the United States of America

1 2 3 4 5 6 7 8 9 10—01 00 99 98 97 96 95

For more information, contact Wadsworth Publishing Company:

Wadsworth Publishing Company
10 Davis Drive
Belmont, California 94002, USA

International Thomson Editores
Campos Eliseos 385, Piso 7
Col. Polanco
11560 México D.F. México

International Thomson Publishing Europe
Berkshire House 168-173
High Holborn
London, WC1V7AA, England

International Thomson Publishing GmbH
Königswinterer Strasse 418
53227 Bonn, Germany

Thomas Nelson Australia
102 Dodds Street
South Melbourne 3205
Victoria, Australia

International Thomson Publishing Asia
221 Henderson Road
#05-10 Henderson Building
Singapore 0315

Nelson Canada
1120 Birchmount Road
Scarborough, Ontario
Canada M1K 5G4

International Thomson Publishing Japan
Hirakawacho Kyowa Building, 3F
2-2-1 Hirakawacho
Chiyoda-ku, Tokyo 102, Japan

Library of Congress Cataloging-in-Publication Data
Cavina, Kristan.
    Critical thinking and writing : a developing writer's guide with
readings / Kristan Cavina.
        p.   cm. — (Developmental writing series)
    Includes index.
    ISBN 0-534-24294-4
    1. English language—Rhetoric.   2. English language—Grammar.
3. Critical thinking.   4. College readers. I. Title. II. Series.
PE1408.C3926 1995
808'.042—dc20   94-43830
                                                                CIP

This book is printed on acid-free recycled paper.

To Dan Cavina in appreciation of his frequently needed help, technical and otherwise. To Yolanda Cavina for her ever-present student's perspective. To my good friends, whose support helped to make this book possible.

Brief Contents

Contents

Preface

Critical Thinking and Writing presents a new approach to the teaching of writing. In this textbook, designed to prepare students for college writing, the connection between thinking and writing is followed through all phases of the writing process. Student work, both effective and ineffective, has inspired this textbook. Consequently, the text focuses on the creation of meaning as well as on students' real problems in expressing that meaning accurately.

Both current and earlier writing texts have presented isolated examples of critical thinking methodologies and materials. *Critical Thinking and Writing* appears to be the first comprehensive composition textbook to present the writing process systematically in harmony with the concepts of critical thinking.

Important features of the text are the following:

- Emphasis is on those concepts that are of the greatest use to students who are attempting to improve their writing.
- Concepts are carefully sequenced to maximize student understanding. Moreover, major concepts, including topic, controlling idea, topic sentence and thesis statement, key supporting ideas, logical order of information, transitions, types of supporting information answering specific questions, strategies for conclusions, and ideas for revision are introduced very early in the text so that students can begin to apply them in their writing, and they are later treated systematically so that students can gain an in-depth understanding of each concept. In addition, concepts and terms are recycled to facilitate retention of them by students.
- Explanations in the text are concise. Extensive space has been devoted, rather, to examples and practice material.
- An answer key has been provided so that students can work with greater independence and responsibility and instructors can have more flexibility in structuring class time.
- Current issues are emphasized in the examples, exercises, readings, and writing assignments. In this way, students can work with information that is meaningful to them and is of value in their academic, professional, and personal lives.
- Multifaceted reality is stressed. Different possible points of view and degrees of validity are presented. Students are discouraged from habitually looking for answers that are simply right or wrong.
- Skill development in a cooperative rather than competitive learning environment is encouraged.

Critical thinking has been defined by scholars in the field in a number of different yet meaningful ways. Richard Paul and Michael Scriven, in a statement prepared for the National Council for Excellence in Critical Thinking, have defined critical thinking as *"the intellectually disciplined process of actively and skillfully conceptualizing, applying, analyzing, synthesizing, and/or evaluating information gathered from, or generated by, observation, experience, reflection, reasoning, or communication, as a guide to belief and action."* Focusing on critical thinking as it directly relates to writing, I define it as *"a reasoning process through which one clarifies ideas, supporting them with relevant facts, taking into account the assumptions on which they are based, and assessing their implications."*

Expanding on this definition, I have prepared, as part of my Statement on Critical Thinking and Writing for the National Council for Excellence in Critical Thinking, a series of objectives for students who are taking a writing class in which emphasis is on critical thinking as the basis of effective writing. These students should learn to

Formulate a clear statement of the thesis.

Support that statement by giving adequate, relevant, accurate information, evaluating the credibility of the sources of the information.

In providing the support for the thesis statement, understand and take into consideration arguments from other points of view.

Take into consideration the assumptions on which the ideas expressed in writing are based.

Take into consideration the implications of ideas expressed in writing.

Avoid unwarranted inferences.

Provide necessary explanations and clarifications.

Identify relationships between ideas, arranging ideas logically and providing transitions to clarify the relationships between ideas.

Express ideas in precise language, with grammatically correct sentences and appropriately chosen words.

Avoid irrelevant information, contradictions, oversimplifications, and unsupported general statements.

Read and listen critically, understanding the purpose of each writing assignment.

This textbook also makes systematic use of the critical thinking principle of having students discover on their own what concepts and strategies they need to learn, why they need to learn them, and how they can go about learning them. The text provides very carefully sequenced material so that students can discover and then practice the concepts and strategies they should master in order to be effective writers. Those using this text will also achieve a greater awareness of the principle that real learning comes from understanding ideas rather than memorizing information.

Still in harmony with critical thinking principles, this text will enrich students' college years by providing them with a highly positive learning experience, acquainting them with concepts and strategies that they can apply in other classes as well, and giving them encouragement to be responsible to a great extent for their own learning.

A writing class conducted according to critical thinking principles brings students other benefits as well. Critical thinking is appropriate outside the classroom in more and more situations. The ability to think effectively, evaluating ideas from different perspectives, is becoming increasingly important in today's multicultural, interdependent world. When we refine students' thinking skills, we empower them as individuals. In this way, we are helping them to become responsible and productive members of society.

More specific teaching strategies are detailed in the *Instructor's Manual*.

ACKNOWLEDGMENTS

I wish to thank the following reviewers for their excellent advice and suggestions: Kathleen Beauchene, Community College of Rhode Island; Kelly Belanger, Youngstown State University; Alan Belsches, Troy State University; Patricia

Buckler, Purdue University, North Central; Linda Daigle, Houston Community College; Linda Eastburn, Linn-Benton Community College; Nancy J. Eaton, Westfield State College; Deborah James, University of North Carolina, Asheville; Francine Jamin, Montgomery College, Tacoma Park; Jodi Jarvis, Salem State College; Kathleen Krager, Walsh College; Sandra Lee Tompkins, Hiwassee College; Lawrence Lewis, University of Texas, Brownsville; Robert McEachern, University of Louisville; Beatrice Mendez-Egle, University of Texas, Pan American; Paul Perry, Palo Alto College; James Runnels, Inver Hills Community College; Linda Spain, Linn-Benton Community College; Caroline Stern, Ferris State University; and R. J. Willey, Oakland Community College.

I would also like to thank Angie Gantner Wrahtz, Lisa Timbrell, Kate Peltier, Robin Lockwood, Christy Butterfield, and Nick Pavloff for their valuable contributions.

To the Student

Critical Thinking and Writing is a user-friendly book intended to guide you through the process of writing. This student-oriented text is based on real student work. It will help you understand what you are doing right when your writing is effective as well as what is happening when your communication in English is not effective. By following this text carefully, you will be able to make real improvement in your writing.

SOME SUGGESTIONS

Give yourself an opportunity to discover each concept on your own. Experiment with the discovery material until you come up with some possible answers before you read the explanations in the text.

Carefully go over each principle and the examples before you try the practice material.

Unless your instructor indicates otherwise, begin with Chapter 1, then continue with Chapter 10, then Chapter 2, and so forth, alternating between Part 1 and Part 2.

Part One

PARAGRAPHS AND ESSAYS

Students frequently prefer an oral presentation or even a test to a written composition assignment. When they are given a composition to write, they foresee having to spend long hours working on a paper that may not turn out well in spite of all the time they have invested. In addition, students are hesitant about writing because they suppose that being able to write effectively is a gift that only certain people possess. In other words, they do not realize that many writers, without being particularly gifted, are quite competent simply because they have learned to use the various principles and strategies essential to the writing process. The purpose of this book is to enable college writers to discover those principles and strategies and put them into practice.

When we write, our primary purpose in transferring our thoughts to paper is to communicate them to others. But since we are usually not present when our message is actually read, we cannot see the reactions of our readers or clarify something that they do not understand in the writing. For this reason, our intended meaning needs to be communicated clearly and accurately through our written message; and in order for communication to be effective, the message must be both carefully thought out and suitably structured.

It is possible for you to discover on your own a great deal about how to communicate meaning that is well thought out and effectively structured. First of all, you can discover the structure of a carefully organized composition by reconstructing one.

E X E R C I S E

Try arranging the following sentences so that they make a paragraph. There is one best order; see if you can discover it. Then go back over the sentences to find out why it makes sense to put them in a certain order. Once you have drawn your conclusions, compare your findings with the information in the answer key.

1. These writers can then structure their ideas and write a coherent composition.

2. And they also hope, all too frequently, that by simply going back and making a few corrections and changes, they can produce good writing.

3. Finally, there are those who list ideas in order to gather a body of relevant information.

4. People approach the task of writing a composition in different ways.

5. Next, there are those who "just start writing."

6. The blank page stifles their creative powers.

7. First of all, there are those who panic.

8. These writers often feel that they only lose time if they try to organize their ideas first.

9. As a result, they find it difficult to get any words on paper.

10. They take time to think about their subject and write down everything that comes to mind about it.

E X E R C I S E

Once you have formed the paragraph, consider the following questions, one at a time. Compare your findings for each question with the information provided in the answer key before you go on to the next question.

1. What is the writer discussing?

2. What statement is made (what point does the writer make) about people's approaches to writing?

3. Which sentence expresses both the idea of "approaches to writing" and the idea of "different"?

4. What else makes sentence 4 stand out?

5. What exactly is developed in the other sentences?

6. What different approaches are discussed?

7. Which sentences bring up, or announce, these different approaches?

8. What is the best order for these three sentences?

9. How does the wording indicate that particular order?

10. What else distinguishes these three sentences from the others?

11. Is there any logic in the arrangement of the three different approaches?

12. What other information is provided on the different approaches to writing?

13. What does "The blank page stifles their creative powers" tell us about the panic that many writers feel?

14. What does "they find it difficult to get any words on paper" explain about the panic?

15. What do the explanations in sentences 8 and 2 tell us about the "just start writing" approach?

16. What do sentences 10 and 1 tell us about the "list ideas" approach?

17. Why does sentence 2 follow sentence 8?

18. What is the function of the word *these* at the beginning of sentences 1 and 8?

There is no separate concluding statement in this paragraph, but sentence 1 (the final sentence of the reconstructed paragraph) ends with the idea of writing "a coherent composition"—the final goal of a writer.

The Paragraph: A Short Composition

The preceding sentences, when rearranged, form a short composition on a very narrow topic. Such a limited topic can be developed in a **paragraph**.

THE TOPIC SENTENCE: TOPIC + CONTROLLING IDEA

As you read through the sentences the first time, you probably asked yourself, perhaps without realizing it, what they could be about. As you went through the sentences, instinctively trying to discover what they were about, you were looking for one of the fundamental elements of the unit we call a paragraph: the **topic**. A composition is about something, and *topic* is the term we use for what the writer is discussing in the composition—in other words, for what the writing is about.

Your second step in analyzing the sentences was probably to look for what the writer was saying about the topic, in other words, what statement, or assertion, was being made about the topic. You were actually searching for the second fundamental element of the paragraph: the **controlling idea**. We write in order to make a statement or to express ourselves about something, and *controlling idea* is the term we use for the statement the writer is making about the topic of the composition.

The sentence in a paragraph that contains both the topic and the controlling idea, in the form of a statement, is called the **topic sentence**. The topic sentence is the general statement that covers the more specific information included in the rest of the paragraph.

DEVELOPMENT OF A PARAGRAPH: DEVELOPMENT OF THE CONTROLLING IDEA

When we write, we use some **key ideas** to develop the controlling idea. In the paragraph on approaches to writing, the key ideas are the "panic" approach, the "just start writing" approach, and the "list" approach. These ideas are introduced in the form of **main supporting sentences**.

The ideas in the main supporting sentences are then developed further: additional sentences provide the explanations and illustrations that readers need in order to understand each key idea.

In this way, the entire paragraph, directly or indirectly, develops the controlling idea.

PARAGRAPH STRUCTURE

The structure of a typical expository paragraph can be shown in outline form:

Topic sentence
  I. Main supporting sentence
      A. Explanations and illustrations
 II. Main supporting sentence
      A. Explanations and illustrations
III. Main supporting sentence
      A. Explanations and illustrations
 IV. (Concluding statement)

The preceding outline shows **levels of support:** each set of explanations and illustrations helps the reader understand a key idea as it is expressed in a main supporting sentence. The main supporting sentences, in turn, develop and clarify the topic sentence.

The outline shows typical—not absolute—paragraph structure. The actual number of main supporting sentences in a paragraph varies, and the number of sentences that are used to explain and illustrate depends on how much the writer needs to clarify.

In this outline of a typical expository paragraph, the conclusion appears in parentheses because a paragraph that is not part of a longer composition generally needs a conclusion, but one that is part of a longer work usually does not.

Each part of this structure fulfills an important purpose. Readers do not take in the meaning of each word as they read unless they are reading slowly. They tend, rather, to focus on key points. Therefore, effective writing is structured so that the reader can readily find the key points but also take in additional information. In this way, a well-structured paragraph facilitates comprehension and, therefore, communication.

SAMPLE PARAGRAPHS

1 Many educators feel that there are several important reasons for bringing Latin back into the school. First, a knowledge of Latin is extremely helpful for anyone wishing to build a better vocabulary in English. Over half of the words in English come directly or indirectly from Latin. In addition, new words are created primarily from Latin roots, prefixes, and suffixes. Second, an understanding of Latin's more complex grammar can help make English grammar more meaningful. For example, a student who has worked with the Latin

noun cases can more easily distinguish a subject from an object in English and therefore make the verb agree properly with the subject. Finally, a knowledge of Latin helps students acquire greater language awareness. Different levels of language are appropriate in different situations, and a sense of words is developed with the study of a related language such as Latin. Thus, Latin, although "dead" itself, is very much alive in English, and it should have its place in the classroom.

EXERCISE

Consider the following questions about the preceding paragraph, one at a time.

1. What is the topic of the paragraph?
2. What is the controlling idea?
3. What reasons are given for bringing Latin back into the school?
4. Does the conclusion simply restate the topic sentence?
5. How would you outline this paragraph?

2 There are three types of TV shows I especially dislike. First are the violent police dramas. Next are the soap operas. Last are the game shows involving couples.

EXERCISE

Consider the following question about the preceding paragraph.

1. What do you find unsatisfactory about the paragraph?

3 There are three types of TV shows I especially dislike. First are the violent police dramas. There is no valid reason for the senseless violence in these shows. Moreover, children who watch these programs may come to accept fierce, unrestrained behavior as a normal part of real life. Next are the soap operas. The situations are forced, and the actors and actresses do not appear capable of having genuine human emotions. The viewer is dragged along through never-ending, pointless stories. Last are the game shows involving couples. The contestants are baited, and in their reactions they reveal facts and opinions that are too personal for public consumption. These programs are degrading to the individuals who participate and insulting to the viewers. When any of these shows come on, I change channels.

EXERCISE

Consider the following questions about the preceding paragraph, one at a time.

1. How does this paragraph compare with the one before it?
2. How would you evaluate this paragraph as an example of college writing?
3. How does the conclusion relate to the rest of the paragraph?

4. How would you outline this paragraph?

5. How could this paragraph be revised so that it would be more convincing?

---

4 Students who are about to enroll in college should become familiar with the college catalog. It gives detailed descriptions of all the courses offered by the school. These are very
helpful to the students because they need to make choices about subjects. I was able to
find out what subjects I would be interested in, not just those I had to take. The catalog
also indicates prerequisites and course sequencing. It is possible to put together from the
catalog an entire four-year program before enrollment time. I quickly realized I didn't want
to waste time taking the wrong things. Time wasted is also money wasted. College can be
expensive enough even when all goes well. For example, a dorm room can easily run $400
a month. My older sister is paying over $500, but she intends to move out as soon as she
finds another place. In addition, the college catalog contains a wealth of other information
about the institution. The student who knows what is in the catalog and plans carefully at
the beginning will save a lot of frustration later.

EXERCISE

1-6

Consider the following questions about the preceding paragraph.

1. How would you evaluate this paragraph as an example of college writing?

2. What do the sentences that need to be eliminated have in common?

3. For what audience, or readers, would the sentences about the writer be appropriate?

4. After eliminating the inappropriate sentences, can we make sense of the remaining ones?

5. How does the concluding statement relate to the topic sentence and the rest of the paragraph?

6. How could this paragraph be revised so that it would be more convincing?

AUDIENCE, PURPOSE, AND POINT OF VIEW IN COLLEGE WRITING

Very informal writing like that in sample paragraph 4 is usually not appropriate
for college purposes, but it is suitable for an entirely different audience—that is,
someone who knows the writer personally. The personally oriented sentences
would have meaning for readers who are acquainted with the writer. However,
they communicate very little to strangers. To be meaningful, writing must be appropriate for the intended **audience**—the person or persons who will read what
is written. Consequently, the writer needs to be aware of who those readers are.
For most college writing, the specific audience is the instructor of the class, and the
general audience is the college-educated public.

The **purpose** of most writing assignments in college—essays, essay examinations, reports, and research—is to have the students generate relevant information
about topics and add explanations, illustrations, or arguments to show readers that
their statements are valid. Thus, most college writing involves a certain amount of
persuasion. In paragraph 4, however, the writer does not convince the reader of
anything by stating that he or she was able to find interesting subjects from the

descriptions in the catalog because anyone reading the catalog would be likely to have the same experience. In fact, a sentence such as "Students are able to find out from these descriptions what subjects they are interested in, not just what subjects they have to take" would provide much more convincing support.

The sentences in sample paragraph 4 that fail to support the statement that students should become familiar with the college catalog are *I* oriented. The first person **point of view** is not advantageously used here because the writer's own experiences do not make any real contribution to this statement. Describing personal experiences that are essentially similar to the experiences of many others is not usually helpful, and anything that does not contribute to the writer's intended meaning should be left out of the composition.

Most college writing, in order to be convincing, needs to be as objective as possible. For that reason, the third person—*he, she, it,* and *they*—point of view is usually used. The first person—*I* and *we*—is appropriate primarily in the narration of a personal experience. Similarly, the second person—*you*—is used mainly in the description of a process. And because *you* refers to the reader, it should not be used in college writing to mean people in general, as it frequently is in conversational English.

MORE SAMPLE PARAGRAPHS

5   Many people who have access to good public transportation prefer not to own a car for a number of important reasons. First, it is expensive to have a car. The purchase price of even a basic transportation vehicle amounts to several months' wages for most people. Gas for the car is also a major expense, as are routine maintenance and unforeseen repairs. In addition, there is the cost of insurance for the vehicle, which over the lifetime of the car may total more than the original purchase price. Another problem that vehicle ownership brings is legal liability. Anything that happens to the car or to anyone in it is ultimately the owner's responsibility. This liability can involve some real risks, too. For example, in an automobile accident, a person who was in no way at fault may still lose both money and a good driving record. Last, a person who has a car must put up with requests for rides from friends and relatives who do not have their own transportation. The problem is that others often expect favors at any hour of the day or night without seeming to understand that the driver also has a life to attend to. All of these inconveniences can make owning a car a mixed blessing indeed.

E X E R C I S E

1-7

Consider the following questions about the preceding paragraph, one at a time.

1. What is the topic of this paragraph?
2. What is the controlling idea?
3. What are the key supporting ideas?
4. What transitions highlight the main supporting sentences?
5. What kinds of explanations are given for the first key idea?
6. What kinds of explanations are given for the second key idea?

7. What kinds of explanations are given for the third key idea?

8. What do the words "these inconveniences" in the final sentence refer to?

9. What is the result of "these inconveniences," according to the concluding statement?

---

6 The overcrowding of classes due to budget cuts in education is having some negative effects on student learning. Overcrowded classes, first of all, are more difficult to teach. Discussions involving all students are an important part of the learning process, but it is difficult for everyone to participate in these discussions when there are too many people present. Also, students in such classes have fewer opportunities to ask questions during lectures and discussions. Another disadvantage is that an overcrowded room is difficult to arrange so that learning can take place. The people in the back may not be able to see the board or hear what those in the front of the room are saying. There is more general distraction, and students are more likely to get involved in private conversations, missing out on important ideas presented in class. A final problem with overcrowded classes is that individual students are less well served. The teacher cannot devote as much time to each student, either working directly with the person on a one-to-one basis or offering feedback on the assignments prepared by the student. In this way, individual needs are less likely to be met. Learning is sacrificed in overcrowded classes, and at a time of keen international competition, cutting the budgets for our schools may well turn out to be false economy.

EXERCISE

Consider the following questions about the preceding paragraph, one at a time.

1. What is the topic of this paragraph?

2. What is the controlling idea?

3. What are the key supporting ideas?

4. What transitions highlight the main supporting sentences?

5. What kinds of explanations are given for each key idea?

6. What is the result of overcrowding classes as it appears in the concluding statement?

7. What opinion is given in the concluding statement?

8. Is there an implied suggestion in the concluding statement? If so, what is it?

The Essay

As you read the following essay, look for a controlling idea and some key supporting ideas.

Many traditional parents measure their success in bringing up their children in terms of how well they control them. These fathers and mothers feel that only with strong parental control is it possible to raise "good kids." As more and more people are coming to realize, however, such parent-oriented child raising actually has a number of long-lasting negative effects on children.

Young people raised by controlling parents, first of all, grow up with a distorted self-image. During childhood, emphasis has been placed on pleasing the parent, and any negative behavior has brought from the parent rejection not of the behavior but of the child as a person. This type of personal rejection over time seriously undermines the child's self-esteem. Also the traditional parent typically fails to give positive reinforcement for good behavior because the child is simply expected to be good and the parent perceives this normal behavior as not warranting comment. This lack of encouragement pushes the young person in one of two directions: some fall into a pattern of perfectionism, as they continue to seek the approval that never seems to come; and others fall into a pattern of negative behavior, which shows an attempt to gain the attention of the parent as a replacement for the missing approval. In either case, the young person develops low self-esteem, a problem that is very difficult to overcome later.

Authoritarian parents, with their focus on themselves rather than on the child, raise young people who also do not learn to communicate. The highly disciplined child is not encouraged to express feelings or opinions, but instead must constantly suppress both because of the need to please the parent. Consequently, the young person, for fear of disapproval or even punishment, must constantly override the truth. This need to hypocritically deny reality makes it very hard for the child to evaluate and deal with reality objectively and sensibly. In other words, the child, consistently having to calculate his or her actions according to the effect they produce on the parent—that is, thinking in other-oriented ways to avoid punishment—does not learn to talk openly about thoughts or feelings. Furthermore, since so much attention has been focused on avoiding negative consequences, the young person falls into the habit of negative thinking and regularly acts in order to prevent negative results rather than to bring about positive ones. This lack of focus on the positive continues into adulthood and severely limits the person's potential in life.

The lack of openness so characteristic of parent-oriented child raising makes it very difficult for the child to learn to trust anyone. The victim of such upbringing, unable to speak openly or express a desire with the confidence that someone else will want to see that desire fulfilled, finds it virtually impossible to develop positive relationships with other people. The young person who thus misses out on the trust that is necessary for closeness tends to grow up either behaving inappropriately in the presence of others or withdrawing from social interaction altogether.

Traditional parents, so certain they have done an excellent job of raising their children, are often perplexed in later years when their adult children do not show real caring. Furthermore, they still react with anger at the "misbehaving child," not only failing to see where they themselves went wrong, but not even suspecting that they, not the child, went wrong. Their children are the unfortunate victims of people who do not realize that parenting does not mean molding children but rather helping them develop as individuals who can use their greatest potential in dealing with their world as they find it.

E X E R C I S E

1-9

Consider the following questions about the preceding essay, one at a time.

1. What is the topic of the essay?

2. What is the statement being made about the topic?

3. What are the key ideas developed in the essay?

4. Where are the key ideas located?

5. In what way does the conclusion relate to the introduction?

THE THESIS STATEMENT: TOPIC + CONTROLLING IDEA

An essay, like a paragraph, is all about a particular topic. Similarly, the statement, or assertion, that is made about the topic is the controlling idea. The essay, like the paragraph, contains a sentence that formulates both the topic and the controlling idea. This is the essay's **thesis statement**. Like the topic sentence of the paragraph, the thesis statement is a general statement that provides the focal point for the entire essay.

ESSAY STRUCTURE

The structure of an essay is similar to the structure of a paragraph-length piece of writing. In both forms, a controlling idea is developed by some key supporting ideas. The essential difference between the two forms lies in the amount of information that needs to be included: if each key idea requires more than about five sentences of explanations, then there is too much material for a single paragraph, and each key idea with its supporting explanations should be broken down into a separate **body paragraph**. Thus the breakdown of the forms is as follows:

THE PARAGRAPH
Topic sentence

I. Key idea (in main supporting sentence)
  A. Explanations and illustrations

II. Key idea (in main supporting sentence)
  A. Explanations and illustrations

III. Key idea (in main supporting sentence)
  A. Explanations and illustrations

IV. (Concluding statement)

THE ESSAY
Thesis statement (in brief introductory paragraph)

I. Key idea (topic sentence of body paragraph)
  A. Structured main supporting sentences and explanations

II. Key idea (topic sentence of body paragraph)
  A. Structured main supporting sentences and explanations

III. Key idea (topic sentence of body paragraph)
  A. Structured main supporting sentences and explanations

IV. Conclusion (in brief paragraph)

These outlines show typical structures only. The actual number of key supporting ideas in a composition varies: there may be only two key ideas, or there may be several of them.

Notice that the entire essay, like the paragraph-length piece of writing, develops and explains the controlling idea.

Prewriting Assignment

EXERCISE

1-10

Find the topics and controlling ideas in the following statements. Then, working alone or with a group of your classmates, experiment with the development of each controlling idea. For example, for the first item, write down your thoughts on why the government should sponsor projects to plant more trees. Keep the ideas that you generate for this exercise. You will be able to use them for your writing assignments in Chapter 2.

1. The government should sponsor reforestation projects.
2. VCRs have changed many people's entertainment habits.
3. A greater awareness of eating disorders has developed in the last few years.
4. Shared custody is often detrimental to the child.
5. Legislation is being passed that gives greater opportunities to people who traditionally have lacked power in society.
6. Articles in some of the most popular news magazines contain misleading information.
7. A big city is a noisy place to live.
8. Those who prepare curriculum in the schools are finding it appropriate to include essay writing in nonacademic subjects as well as in academic ones.
9. Movements for women's rights and children's rights indicate a growing concern for the dignity of human beings.
10. A knowledge of history is valuable to students of journalism.
11. Children can be taught not to waste materials.
12. Children should be taught not to waste materials.
13. A shopping mall is more than a group of stores under one roof.
14. Slavery, officially abolished, still exists.
15. Adjustment to life in a foreign country is very difficult for most people.

Summing Up

You have discovered that a composition has certain basic elements, and you have experimented with several important ones:

Topic: A composition is about something.

Controlling idea: The writer is making a statement about the topic.

Development: Key supporting ideas develop the controlling idea; they bring up the main points that need to be made about the controlling idea.

Support: Explanations need to be given, providing answers to the readers' likely questions. We have seen supporting information that explains, for example, why writers panic, what the result of the panic is, and how a person can better approach the task of writing. We have also seen examples given to explain a point (the Latin grammar example). In the sample essay, we saw explanations of how the different negative effects come about and what their specific results are.

Focus: The entire composition develops the controlling idea.

Logic: Information in a composition should be put in an order that makes sense. We have seen, for example, that the approaches to writing described in the scrambled paragraph can be put in order from negative to positive.

Transitions: These help to connect our ideas logically. We have seen, for example, transitions that highlight a sequence of key ideas ("first of all"; "another/next"; "finally"); transitions that show a result ("as a result"; "therefore"; "thus"); and transitions that indicate a contrast ("however").

Conclusion: This wraps up and puts a finishing touch on the composition. We have seen several strategies used to conclude:

1. Restating the topic ("Latin"; "owning a car"). In the essay, "traditional parents" reminds the reader of the parents who orient child raising around themselves rather than the child.

2. Restating the controlling idea or in some way reminding the reader of it ("should have its place in the classroom" restates the idea that there are "reasons for bringing Latin back into the school"; "these shows" indicates the ones the writer "dislikes"; the word "knows" in "knows what is in the college catalog" restates the idea of "familiar"). In the essay, the reader is reminded of the negative effects, as the adult child who does not show real caring for the parent is still treated like a misbehaving child.

3. Using summarizing words (Latin is "very much alive in English"; "these inconveniences," summarizing the problems of owning a car; and "victims," renaming the adults who have acquired in childhood a low self-image and lack of ability to communicate or trust).

4. Indicating the result ("saving frustration later" is the result of knowing what is in the college catalog; the reasons for not owning a car show ownership as a "mixed blessing"; "learning . . . is sacrificed" is the result of overcrowding classrooms).

5. Making a suggestion (there is the implied suggestion in paragraph 6 that we should not cut the budget for education).

Compositions can be either of the following:

1. A single **paragraph**, which is a unit by itself, with a topic, a controlling idea, key ideas, supporting explanations, and a concluding statement.

2. An **essay**, which is a longer unit than the single paragraph. The essay contains more explanations. Like the single paragraph, it has a topic, a controlling idea, key ideas, and supporting explanations. The essential discussion comes in a series of body paragraphs, preceded by a short introductory paragraph and followed by a short concluding paragraph.

Both the single paragraph and the essay develop a controlling idea.

Well-written compositions do not just happen; they require a great deal of thinking and experimenting. There are certain basic steps in writing: prewriting, writing, and revising. However, writing is a circular process, which means that writers need to reconsider constantly, backtracking when appropriate and sometimes even starting all over again.

In Chapter 2 you will move farther into the process of writing.

BEGINNING TO WRITE: STARTING THE PROCESS

When we start to write, we do not simply put on paper what we hope to see as a finished product. Writing is a complex task, and we normally work through different stages of the writing process, keeping in mind that there are distinct purposes for what we do at each stage.

First of all, the thinking we do as we begin to write has two entirely different purposes: we do one kind of thinking in order to come up with potentially usable ideas for a composition, and we do another kind of thinking in order to make good use of our ideas.

The Creative and Critical Stages in Writing

When you are faced with the task of writing a composition within a 50-minute class period, you probably experience some panic. You may realize that the pressure created by the time limit can stifle the flow of thought. Furthermore, you may instinctively fear the compound task of generating ideas and making decisions about them all in a short time. Actually, your apprehension in this situation is entirely justifiable for one very good reason: our minds simply do not work creatively and critically at the same time. Thus, we need to give ourselves an opportunity to be creative while carefully postponing any critical judgment of what we produce. This means that, when we are writing a composition, we need to allow ourselves as much time as possible to generate thoughts before we start evaluating them.

When writing is done in class, there is very little time for the creative stage. Even so, if it is at all possible, it is desirable to devote a few minutes to writing down thoughts that are potentially useful for developing the controlling idea. If there is more time to complete the assignment, a longer session—or even several sessions—can and should be allotted to the creative, idea-gathering stage.

To get started writing, you can use a number of techniques that bring out your creativity.

Techniques for Generating Ideas

We constantly gather ideas that are potentially useful for writing. These ideas come from a wide variety of sources. We discuss things with other people, listening to their views and reacting with our own thoughts and opinions. We also come into contact with thought-provoking information through our constant exposure to the media. The information we gather from these and other sources can be of great value when we need to generate ideas for writing.

In addition to listening and discussing, keeping a personal journal is a way to collect ideas that are meaningful to you. By noting in your journal events, facts, statements, or thoughts that capture your interest in some way, you not only engage in a certain amount of critical thinking, but you also accumulate material that will be available to you for later reference.

When you have to come up with ideas for a specific college writing assignment, you need to use techniques that immediately enhance your creative powers. For this reason, you should carefully avoid the temptation to try to fill in an empty outline form when you need to generate ideas: outlining is a critical, not a creative activity. To gather thoughts for a paper, turn instead to one or more creative strategies. Some techniques that are especially useful for generating ideas are brainstorming, freewriting, and applying the journalistic questions.

BRAINSTORMING

Brainstorming is the process of listing on paper your ideas on a particular subject as they come to mind. Using free association, you write down your thoughts in the form of words or phrases, attempting to get as many ideas as possible recorded on paper.

This activity is an important part of the creative stage. As a result, when you brainstorm, you should avoid all critical evaluation of your ideas. You also should not let yourself get distracted by concerns over spelling or usage. You do not know at this stage which ideas you will actually use, so it is not really important whether they are expressed in correct English. Once you run out of ideas, you can reread the items on your list, considering them as possible sources of new trains of thought.

When there is time, more than one brainstorming session should be devoted to a composition.

FREEWRITING

Another technique that fosters creativity is **freewriting**. In freewriting, you record the thoughts that come to your mind on a particular subject, writing nonstop for several minutes without lifting the pen from the paper. Whereas brainstorming produces a list of ideas, in freewriting thoughts are recorded in the form of sentences, phrases, or even single words, in a rough paragraph form. Freewriting, like brainstorming, is strictly a creative activity; your purpose in freewriting is to get ideas on paper. Consequently, all reconsidering or correcting should be avoided.

Freewriting can be a useful technique for overcoming the problem of the blank page, since all critical activity is temporarily suspended. For this same reason, freewriting can be helpful later in the writing process, when the writer is trying to overcome problems with expressing ideas or explaining concepts.

You should avoid the temptation to try to use a freewritten paragraph or page as a first draft of a composition, since it rarely possesses a structure that is suitable for effective communication. Freewriting is a good technique for overcoming any writing block, however, and it is a good source of thoughts on a subject. These thoughts can then be singled out and itemized as the start of a brainstorm list.

JOURNALISTIC QUESTIONS

A third way to generate ideas is to apply the **journalistic questions** to the topic. Questions about *who, what, when, where, why,* and *how* help the writer discover additional information about items on a brainstorm list. A further advantage of this technique is that it helps provide supporting information and explanations that will be needed later—that is, material answering the questions *how, why,* and so forth, that the reader is likely to have about statements in the writing.

These creative strategies are extremely useful when you want to explore ideas early in the writing process. They are also helpful at other stages in the process, whenever you need to gather ideas creatively. Use them as you note down ideas from your various possible sources of information, such as your personal experiences and opinions; your interactions with those around you; your school, work, and community experiences; and your information drawn from the media and other sources.

E X E R C I S E

Working alone, try each of the three idea-generating techniques—brainstorming, freewriting, and applying the journalistic questions—on three of the items in Exercise 1-10. To get yourself started, consult the answers given for Exercise 1-10 in the answer key for suggestions about development, as well as the thoughts you created as you worked on Exercise 1-10. Once you have completed all three techniques for an item, add to your brainstorm list for that item any new ideas that you generated by freewriting and by asking journalistic questions. Also add to your brainstorm list any ideas you generated for the item as you did Exercise 1-10. Keep these lists of ideas; you will need them later in this chapter.

Organizing the Material Generated

Generating ideas is an important step in the prewriting process. Once you have put together a good list of ideas, the next step is to decide which ones you can use and how you can use them.

Working with ideas is a complex task. The following discovery exercises will help you understand what is involved in this task.

E X E R C I S E

Eliminate the nonrelevant item from each group, and identify what the remaining three have in common.

1. Madrid, Paris, London, Switzerland
2. Health insurance, wages, retirement plan, paid vacation
3. Baking pan, roaster, casserole dish, skillet
4. Goal, aim, effort, objective
5. Frustration, anger, fear, hope
6. Maintain, abuse, protect, keep up
7. Screwdriver, can opener, pliers, wrench
8. Honest, reliable, disadvantaged, open
9. Similarity, association, connection, relationship
10. Read, write, hear, speak

E X E R C I S E

Which item in each group is either more general or more specific than the other items? In which cases do the general items include everything else in the group?

1. Broil, fry, roast, cook
2. Painting, sculpture, art, drawing
3. Pollution, smog, acid rain, fumes
4. Rocket, missile, bullet, projectile
5. Salary, stipend, wages, pay
6. Assignment, work, task, job

7. Toys, books, musical instruments, video games

8. Furniture, appliances, curtains, plumbing fixtures

9. Tie, shirt, clothing, shoes

10. Education, schooling, training, instruction

The preceding exercises require you to think critically. In both sets, certain items do not fit in with the others. As you work with ideas, shaping them for a composition, you need to make many critical distinctions. For example, if you were writing about important centers of culture in Europe, you could use as support Madrid, Paris, and London—all cities—but you would not want to put Switzerland with them because a country is not comparable to a city. Similarly, a series of items used either as key ideas or as supporting information should not mix positives and negatives (Exercise 2-2, items 5, 6, and 8) or actives and passives (Exercise 2-2, item 10). A series of supporting items should not include both general and specific items, and it especially should not put on an equal level a specific item and a general one that includes the more specific one. For example, it does not make sense to write that the Louvre contains famous paintings, sculptures, drawings, and works of art because the first three are all particular varieties of works of art.

EXERCISE

2-4

Consider this short brainstorm list on the topic of the depletion of our forests. Divide the ideas into two groups for two separate compositions.

1. Restrict the cutting of trees

2. Impose penalties for illegal cutting

3. Protect animal habitat

4. Reduce greenhouse effect

5. Recycle paper

6. Employ more people to plant seedlings

7. Prevent erosion

EXERCISE

2-5

Which of the items in Exercise 2-4 develop the idea of why something should be done to stop the depletion of the forests? Which ones develop the idea of how we can protect our dwindling forests?

Notice that, if you were to write on the depletion of the forests, you would want to focus either on *why* we need to stop the damage or on *how* we can do so. A single controlling idea does not go in these two separate directions.

EXERCISE

2-6

Divide the following thoughts on housework into three groups:

> Why housework is tedious
>
> What about housework is tedious
>
> How a person can make housework less tedious

1. Take breaks
2. Reward self after completion of major task
3. Work itself is boring
4. Work is never finished
5. Looking for spots missed
6. Getting dirty
7. Listen to music while working
8. Takes long hours
9. Work is unappreciated
10. Cleaning for hours

These items lead in three different directions and thus would be usable for three separate compositions. Here are some possible topic sentences, together with the items that support each one:

> Housework is tedious for a number of reasons. [Items 3, 4, 8, and 9—why].
>
> What housework involves makes it tedious. [Items 5, 6, and 10—what].
>
> Housework can be made less tedious in a number of ways. [Items 1, 2, and 7—how].

EXERCISE

2-7

Divide the following thoughts on library distractions into three groups.

1. People talking
2. People walking by
3. Sit at the far end of the room
4. People passing by attract attention
5. Talking disrupts
6. Friends coming over
7. Face a corner
8. Friends interrupt
9. Occupy the next seat as well

Outline the following ideas on the advantages of Riverview Community College.

1. High academic standards
2. Wide variety of transferrable courses
3. Well-planned facilities
4. Large, well-stocked library
5. Small classes taught by highly motivated instructors
6. Convenient location
7. Ample, affordable cafeteria
8. Sufficiently large, well-lit parking lots
9. Near freeway exit
10. Near major shopping center

To outline the items in Exercise 2-8, you first had to group them. The key ideas are "high academic standards," "well-planned facilities," and "convenient location." The remaining items provide supporting information for the key ideas. Thus, the ten items can be put into three groups.

GROUPING IDEAS

To begin working with the ideas in a brainstorm list, try grouping them. Look for items that fit together, bearing in mind that a single item may fit in several different groups. At the same time, watch for general items that might include other, more specific items on the list.

If you are certain of your controlling idea at this stage of your writing, you should focus on whether each item actually supports the controlling idea and how those that do are related to one another.

If you have not settled on a controlling idea, try grouping your brainstorm ideas to determine the areas where you have more information. Your thoughts on paper may lead in a particular direction, thus helping you decide on your controlling idea.

As you work on grouping ideas, write down whatever additional thoughts come to mind, and consider how these relate to your original ideas.

Find some possible groups among the following ideas on hobbies.

1. Description of a particular hobby
2. Reasons for doing
3. Problems with doing
4. Entertaining
5. Relaxing
6. How to do a particular hobby
7. Affect life

8. Benefits of

9. Advantages of

10. Reasons for liking

11. Educational

12. Learn skills

13. Enjoy life

14. Motivation to improve skills

15. Comparison of different hobbies

16. Stimulate imagination

17. Bring out of bad mood

18. Discover interests

19. Different hobbies in different situations

20. Money-making potential

In Exercise 2-2, we saw that to be grouped together, ideas must have something in common. We observed sets of ideas—for example, European cities, fringe benefits, types of projectiles, and forms of art. The underlying idea tying each of these sets together could be used as the topic of a composition, and the individual items in the set could then serve as a series of key ideas in the composition. Similarly, a set of ideas can be used as a series of supporting points that form part of the explanations and illustrations of any other point in the writing.

Groups of related ideas can also lead us in the direction of a controlling idea. In Exercise 2-4, about the depletion of our forests, items 1, 2, 5, and 6 ("restrict the cutting of trees," "impose penalties for illegal cutting," "recycle paper," and "employ more people to plant seedlings") lead in the direction of *how* we can protect our dwindling forests; and items 3, 4, and 7 ("protect the animal habitat," "reduce the greenhouse effect," and "prevent erosion") explain *why* something should be done to stop the depletion of the forests. The first group might be used for a composition on the ways to protect our forests, with "can protect" as the controlling idea. The second would be useful for a different composition—one giving the reasons for taking action to protect our forests, with "should protect" as the controlling idea.

In other words, each group in Exercise 2-4 leads in a particular direction. This direction suggests both a controlling idea and the possible development of a composition.

EXERCISE

2-10

Develop some supporting information for each of the following topic sentences.

1. What Americans are eating now shows their growing preference for a healthful diet.

2. There is evidence around us that Americans are concerned with a healthful diet.

3. Americans are becoming more concerned about eating healthful foods for a number of reasons.

Notice that all three of these topic sentences have virtually the same topic—a healthful diet—but they lead in entirely different directions and would be developed in three separate compositions.

Consider the following classification of supermarket shoppers. Could these items be used as key ideas in a composition?

Those who are in a hurry
Those who shop carefully
Those who buy a lot of things

It would be difficult to write a good composition on the above categories of shoppers because three entirely different criteria are used to classify them: the first category focuses on how much time they spend shopping, the second deals with how much care they put into shopping, and the third classifies them by how much they buy.

In this classification of shoppers, the logic problem of the different criteria is further complicated by the fact that it is possible for one shopper to fit into all three categories. For example, someone who already knows what to buy can go to a store and quickly ("in a hurry") fill a shopping cart ("buy a lot of things") with high-quality ("shop carefully") products. Furthermore, a shopper in a hurry may pick out things either carefully or carelessly and may buy either a lot or a little. Similarly, those who shop carefully may do so either quickly or slowly, and so forth.

Thus, a more meaningful way of classifying shoppers would be according to one of the following:

The amount of time they spend at the market
The amount of care they put into their selection of products
The amount they buy
The amount they spend

This classification could then be developed. In the first category (those who spend little time at the market) we could put those who go around quickly because they already know what they want, those who have little time and therefore have to shop quickly, those who do not have the patience to spend time picking things out carefully, and so forth. Then shoppers who spend an average amount of time and those who spend a lot of time could be characterized similarly.

EXERCISE

 2-11

Develop several criteria for classifying each of the following.

1. College students

2. Automobiles

Notice that each separate classification leads in the direction of a separate composition. For example, if you classified college students according to their degree goals, you could discuss students who are working toward an academic degree, those who are going for a vocational certificate, and those who are attending classes but not seeking a degree.

DISTINGUISHING GENERALIZATIONS FROM DETAILS

In Exercise 2-3, some of the groups listed contain a general item plus three items that are included in the more general one. Exercise 2-8, on Riverview Community College, also has general and detailed items; and in order to outline the information in that exercise, you had to distinguish the level of generality of each item. In your own brainstorm lists, as you group your ideas to see how they fit together logically, watch for more general or more detailed items and also for items that may support others.

EXERCISE

2-12 Identify groups of ideas in the following class brainstorm list on the topic of *jobs*. Specify the generalizations and the details in your groups.

1. Search	**23.** Importance
2. Salary	**24.** Pressures
3. Hours	**25.** Fears
4. Enjoy/earn	**26.** "Jobs"
5. Boring	**27.** Creative ones
6. Don't use potential	**28.** First job
7. Survive	**29.** Why needed
8. Frustrations	**30.** Why people change
9. Motivation	**31.** Availability
10. Personal experience	**32.** Diversity
11. Good/bad	**33.** How to get
12. Challenge	**34.** Rewards
13. Dangerous ones	**35.** Opportunities
14. Meet people	**36.** School/work
15. Money	**37.** "Equal" opportunities
16. Independence	**38.** Goals/career
17. Self-esteem	**39.** Education/salary
18. Jobs that fit abilities	**40.** Qualifications
19. Coworkers	**41.** Conditions
20. Education	**42.** Part-time
21. Responsibilities	**43.** Bosses
22. Status	**44.** Sacrifices

The answer key lists ten possible groups for Exercise 2-12, and you probably came up with some different ones as well. Notice that each group of items leads in one or (in several cases) more than one possible direction, and that each group could therefore be used as the basis for a composition.

ELIMINATING NONRELEVANT MATERIAL

In Exercise 2-2, you sorted out items that were related to the remaining ones in the group but did not fit in with what the other three had in common. In Exercise 2-4, all of the ideas relate to the problem of our dwindling forests; but if you were writing a paragraph on that subject with a controlling idea of *why*, an item such as "restrict the cutting of trees" would be out of place as a key idea—in other words, as an emphasized idea—because this item explains *how* the problem can be solved, not *why* it needs to be solved. Likewise, if the purpose of your composition were to explain how we can solve the problem of our dwindling forests, you would need to focus on how to do it, rather than on why it needs to be done. In other words, for a composition about our dwindling forests, you would use as key ideas either items 1, 2, 5, and 6 ("restrict the cutting of trees," "impose penalties for illegal cutting," "recycle paper," and "employ more people to plant seedlings") or items 3, 4, and 7 ("protect the animal habitat," "reduce the greenhouse effect," and "prevent erosion"). If an item from the opposite group were used as a key idea, it would seem out of place.

This does not mean that every item on a brainstorm list that does not fall within a specified group should be rejected. Although the key supporting ideas need to lead in a particular direction (such as *why, how,* or *what*), the more detailed explanations and illustrations can include a variety of information leading in different directions. Consider, for example, the following paragraph on distractions in the library, which uses many (in fact, all but one) of the ideas in the list from Exercise 2-7.

Many distractions make the college library a difficult place to study. First, people walk by constantly. They attract attention, as any moving object tends to draw the eye. Also, they often make noise as they go by, or make attention-getting gestures to friends, or go back and forth several times before they finally settle down—or leave altogether. Second, people talk. Conversations nearby disrupt the focus of a person who is trying to concentrate on a textbook chapter or a difficult problem. If something interesting is said, the person trying to study is going to switch attention to the conversation and lose track of the lesson. Finally, friends often come over. They interrupt one's train of thought, and they often insist that it is time for a break, which frequently turns out to be an endless one. At times the only solution to the problem for the good student is to do what the bad student had to do in times past: sit in a far corner, facing the wall.

In this paragraph, the main supporting sentences state *what* the distractions are—the people who walk by (item 2), the people who talk (item 1), and the friends who come over (item 6). Then some of the brainstorm list items focusing on *why* (items 4, 5, and 8) are used to explain the distractions named. For example, the idea that people attract attention (item 4) helps explain why the people who walk by (item 2) are a problem. Notice that even some of the *how* items (3 and 7) are incorporated into the paragraph—in the conclusion, which suggests a solution to the problem.

EXERCISE

2-13

Brainstorm the following idea.

People are using too many disposable items.

The statement in Exercise 2-13 can lead in more than one direction. In brainstorming, you probably came up with items naming *what* people discard, as well as items showing *why* disposing of so many things is a problem. For example, your list may have included:

Landfills full
Disposable diapers

The fact that landfills are full shows why the use of too many disposable items is a problem; "disposable diapers" is a *what* item that names something people discard. Even if a statement is worded to lead in a particular direction, however, it is a good idea to list everything that comes to mind on the subject. Some of the items that are not directly relevant may still be useful later, either as supporting examples or as parts of necessary explanations. Furthermore, even if such items only remind you later of necessary explanations, they have served an important purpose. For example, "disposable diapers" would still be a useful item in a brainstorm list for writing on why the widespread use of disposable items is a problem. Obviously, the diapers themselves are not a reason why throw-away merchandise is a problem, but they help remind the writer of what some of the problems of throw-away articles really are: bulky diapers take up space, and they contain some materials that do not break down. Consequently, one can visualize growing mountains of such items as disposable diapers in populated areas. The idea of the diapers is useful, whether or not it is actually mentioned in the composition, because it reminds the writer of important disposal problems.

EXERCISE

2-14

Consider the topic sentence "Life is different for men in Vietnam." How can the following ideas be made to support the controlling idea of "different"?

1. Men have more freedom to go out.

2. Men are not expected to help at home.

3. A woman should serve first her father, then her husband, then her son.

First, the word *different* suggests a comparison and therefore requires clarification. A comparison of men in Vietnam could be made with women in Vietnam, with women and children in Vietnam, or with men in other countries.

Suppose for example, that the comparison is to be made between men in Vietnam and men in the United States; then items 1 and 2 support the idea of "different," but item 3 does not. What women *should* do is irrelevant to the idea of "different." Notice that item 1 is really an example of the more general idea that men have greater freedom to do what they want, while item 2 is an example of the more general idea that men have fewer responsibilities. Item 3 could be made to support the idea of "different" if it were used as an example supporting the more general idea that Vietnamese men have greater authority over women than do men in other countries. Everything in the original list could therefore be included in a comparison of men in Vietnam with men in other countries if the ideas were structured as follows:

Life is different for men in Vietnam.
  I. Greater freedom
     A. More freedom to go out
 II. Fewer responsibilities
     A. Not expected to help at home

III. Greater authority over women
    A. Women expected to serve father, then husband, then son

Consider the following three statements as possible key ideas on soccer as a beneficial sport:

1. Requires skill
2. Promotes health
3. Provides opportunities for socializing

Promoting health and providing opportunities for socializing are two benefits of soccer, but the fact that it requires skill is not a benefit. Still, the idea of skill is usable: physical skill developed for or by playing soccer is likely to be a benefit, and the physical exercise involved in using that skill may be another. There may also be some beneficial mental skill involved in the sport. Thus, "requires skill" is a potentially useful item on the brainstorm list.

Consider the following key ideas on the different attitudes that employees have toward their jobs:

1. Unskilled workers: negative
2. Trade workers: mixed
3. Professionals: positive

The preceding classification is not a good basis for organizing key ideas in main supporting sentences: categorizing should be based on the type of attitude (negative, mixed, and positive), not on the type of employee, because the two criteria do not go together consistently. For example, not all professionals—and perhaps not even most of them—have positive attitudes about their jobs. Still, information about the employees and their skill level might be used to explain and illustrate their attitudes. But the focus of the composition—and the key ideas—should be on the attitudes themselves.

Consider the following key ideas about problems new college students face:

1. Do not know campus
2. Must talk to a counselor
3. Make decisions about courses
4. Avoid problems in order to succeed

The first item names a problem, but the others do not. The second simply names something students must do. This idea, however, could be considered a problem if the emphasis were on the difficulties students face in talking to a counselor (for example, the problem of getting an appointment). The third item is similar; it would be usable if the emphasis were on the difficulties students face in making the right decisions about courses. The last idea implies that one problem, in itself, is to avoid problems. But the statement in item 4 indicates a condition (what one has to do to achieve success), not a problem.

The key ideas taken from a brainstorm list must be relevant to the controlling idea and must emphasize a particular direction in relation to the controlling idea.

The ideas that are used must also be relevant to the topic. For this reason, the topic itself must be clear. If more than one interpretation is inadvertently given to the topic, the focus of the writing will be lost. For example, a student who illustrates the topic "success" in terms of "happiness," "desired career," "wealth," "cheating," and "stealing" is using the term *success* to stand for two entirely different concepts: the attainment of goals (for the first three ideas) and the ability to get away with something (for the last two).

EXERCISE

Group the following ideas about how the effects of water pollution are dangerous. Then outline the 13 items.

1. Endangering health of humans and animals that drink it
2. Introduces dangerously toxic substances directly into body
3. Killing or harming life forms in the water itself
4. Causes genetic mutations
5. Adds to body's work in eliminating waste products
6. Evaporating, it pollutes atmosphere, creating vicious circle
7. Kills through direct toxic effects
8. Kills indirectly by destroying food sources
9. Contributes to buildup in body of substances that would be harmless in small quantities
10. Destroys resistance
11. Disrupts ecosystem
12. Rises during evaporation, contributing to air pollution problem
13. Combines with other pollutants in air, bringing them down with rain

---

PUTTING TOGETHER A PLAN

After you have generated and organized information for the composition, the next step is to set up a **plan**. The plan of a composition is the topic sentence (or thesis statement, if you are writing an essay) plus an outline of the ideas you intend to use.

The plan is an important part of the prewriting process for a number of reasons. First, it is easier to evaluate the content of the composition when the ideas are in outline form because the information is easy to visualize. Second, the outline shows at a glance the relationships between ideas. This makes an outline easier to work with than complete sentences in paragraph form. Finally, it is easier to make changes when the material is still in outline form, and changes made at this stage save a lot of time and frustration later, when attention has to be devoted to expressing ideas accurately in grammatically correct sentences.

Notice that the key supporting ideas in an outline for a composition are the items listed with Roman numerals (or at least aligned at the far left side of the page, next to the margin). These key ideas need to lead in a single direction—generally *what, why,* or *how.*

EXERCISE

2-16 Working alone or with your classmates, develop a plan for three of the statements in Exercise 1-10. Use material that you generated in Exercise 2-1, and brainstorm for additional new ideas. Then select and organize your material carefully to create a plan for each statement. In each of your final plans, make certain that your key ideas all support an answer to the same question—what, why, or how—according to the direction of your controlling idea.

Limiting the Topic

Suppose that you are assigned to write a paragraph on the topic of education. Obviously this topic is very broad—too vast to handle even in an entire book—so it is clearly out of the question to try to deal with it in a single paragraph. In fact, it needs to be narrowed down a great deal before a controlling idea can even be formulated. The following chart shows some of the many ways in which the topic of education can be limited.

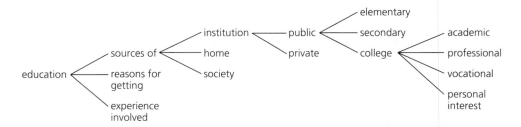

It is then possible to develop a controlling idea into a paragraph focusing on just one of the four types of college education.

EXERCISE

2-17 Practice limiting a topic: narrow down either "sports" or "animals" until you obtain a topic suitable for a paragraph-length composition. Compare your limited topic and how you arrived at it with the results achieved by some of your classmates.

Steps in Writing

As you have already seen, a writer needs to go back frequently and reconsider his or her thoughts on paper, make changes and improvements, and move forward as the thoughts take shape. The rethinking may lead to major or minor changes. Still, in the process of creating a composition, the writer works through three essential steps: prewriting, writing, and revising.

PREWRITING

Prewriting involves choosing a topic and limiting it, as well as working out the full, coherent development of the controlling idea. The writing at this point does not take the form of a draft; it consists of words and phrases, with few, if any, formulated sentences as yet. The goal here is to assemble information to support a statement and to put the information together in a logical way. The following outline illustrates the task of prewriting:

Prewriting
   I. Choosing and limiting a topic
  II. Gathering ideas
      A. Brainstorming
      B. Using other techniques
          1. Freewriting
          2. Asking journalistic questions
          3. Employing other strategies
 III. Organizing the material generated
      A. Grouping ideas
          1. Putting together related ideas
          2. Distinguishing generalizations from details
      B. Arranging the material logically
          1. Evaluating support
          2. Eliminating nonrelevant material
 IV. Preparing a plan (topic sentence + outline)

It is much easier to work with ideas in list or outline form than it is to work with the content of a draft because the list or outline enables the writer to see at a glance the essential ideas and how they may relate. This is extremely important because good writing requires that information be put together logically and coherently, with relationships between ideas clearly shown. Picking out individual ideas and seeing the connections between them is much more difficult in a draft because the additional words needed to complete the sentences have a cluttering effect and because the draft lacks the visual clarity that is so helpful in a logically developed outline. For this reason, the writer should spend as much time as is feasible prewriting.

Since ideas are easier to understand in outline form, the writer can usually anticipate problems in developing the composition if the ideas cannot be made to relate to each other logically in the outline. Minor changes are almost always necessary, and major changes may have to be made as well. In fact, when the writer encounters serious problems in developing a controlling idea, it is often best to change the topic or the controlling idea altogether, if that is possible, or to change the approach to the topic, if a particular topic has been assigned. Whenever major changes are necessary, the writer should return to the creative stage, gathering ideas and brainstorming all over again on the new topic or controlling idea. Thus, prewriting does not simply involve proceeding directly through the steps indicated by Roman numerals I through IV in the outline presented earlier; rather, it entails going back as necessary to change focus, add information, delete material, transpose ideas, and clarify ambiguities.

WRITING

The **writing** step involves composing a draft based on the plan. If the prewriting has been done carefully and the plan is logically coherent, the writer can pay some attention to wording and sentence structure even on the first draft.

REVISING

Any composition that is not done in class in the limited time allowed for such assignments should be reconsidered and rewritten before it is turned in. Effective **revising** is a rather lengthy process that goes from the general (the focus of the draft as a whole) to the particular (errors in individual sentences). In other words, revising is not simply a matter of looking for mistakes in grammar, spelling, and punctuation. Actually, such proofreading should come last.

When you revise a composition, your first concern should be for the coherence of the composition as a whole. This means that you are looking for the focused development of the controlling idea. Your attention should next go to the development and support of the key ideas. One or more additional readings should be devoted to the meaning of individual sentences and the precise use of vocabulary. Then, once all of the thought content has been revised, at least one final, slow, careful reading should be made for errors in grammar, spelling, and punctuation. Chapter 9 offers a more extensive discussion of revising.

E X E R C I S E

Conduct a peer conference on the three plans developed in Exercise 2-16. As your group goes over each plan, check the plan for a clear topic and controlling idea, for key ideas that develop the controlling idea in a specific direction, and for appropriate supporting information. Make improvements in each plan, as needed.

Writing Assignment

E X E R C I S E

Write a paragraph or short essay based on the plan from Exercise 2-18 that you feel has the best potential. After you have completed your draft, reconsider and revise your writing, examining it for focus (topic, controlling idea, and key supporting ideas that lead in a single direction) and support (appropriate and adequate explanations). Check your final draft carefully for errors in grammar, spelling, and punctuation.

Summing Up

You have seen that writing is a process that requires thinking and rethinking, and you have experimented on working with ideas, moving step by step through prewriting:

Creatively generating ideas

> *Brainstorming*
> Using other techniques such as freewriting or applying the journalistic questions

Critically working with ideas

> *Grouping* ideas
> Putting together items that have something in common
> Distinguishing generalizations from details
> Using detailed items to support more general ones
> Focusing on key ideas that lead in a single direction
> Giving information on *what, why,* or *how* in order to support the controlling idea
> Gathering additional support for each key idea
> Eliminating anything that is off the subject
> Putting together a plan (topic sentence + outline)

Moving back whenever necessary in this process
    To change or limit a topic
    To change the controlling idea
    To reconsider the use of ideas
    To generate new ideas creatively

Working with ideas is a fascinating task that requires a great deal of critical thinking.

In Chapter 3 you will learn more about working critically with ideas in order to support a statement.

SUPPORTING A STATEMENT

E X E R C I S E

Which of the following sentences support this statement?

Our government should take action to solve our environmental problems for several important reasons.

1. The damage to the ozone layer is extensive.
2. Many other nations are passing laws regarding the environment.
3. Industrial waste disposal should be controlled.
4. Scientific studies need to be conducted to determine the extent of current damage to the environment.
5. The loss of forests has contributed to atmosphere-related problems.
6. Limits can be placed on the amount of land to be developed.
7. The environmental damage is greater in some parts of the country than in others.

All of the preceding sentences are related to the environment, but only the first and fifth actually support the statement, by indicating reasons for which the government should take action to solve environmental problems. What is being done elsewhere (sentence 2), what exactly should be controlled (sentence 3), what studies need to be done about the problems (sentence 4), what can be done (sentence 6), and how damage compares in different areas (sentence 7) do not contribute to the idea that something should be done.

When we write, we make statements that need to be supported appropriately.

Identifying a Statement

E X E R C I S E

In each of the following groups of sentences, identify the statement that is supported by the rest of the information.

1. a. The television creates a constant distraction.
   b. The home can be a difficult place in which to study.
   c. There are reminders all around of work that needs to be done.
   d. Parents seem to think that the student's assignments are less important than their own concerns.
   e. Unexpected visits bring an end to many a study session.

2. a. Life seems fast paced.
   b. The number of mechanized devices commonly used may be surprising.
   c. The constant exposure to different kinds of product advertising may be annoying.
   d. An American language student's first few days in the United States are often bewildering.
   e. One may be treated as a friend by a total stranger.

3. a. Parenting means recognizing the child's reality.
   b. Acknowledging the child as a person means fulfilling one of the child's basic needs.
   c. Taking into consideration a child's problems that seem trivial to the parent is a good idea because these problems may be very important to the child.
   d. Listening to what the child says can be even more important than getting the child to listen to the parent.
   e. Using physical violence to get a child to obey teaches the child that the stronger person wins.

In college writing, the topic sentence of a paragraph or the thesis statement of an essay makes a statement, and the body of the composition provides the support necessary to convince the reader that the statement is valid.

EXERCISE

3-3

Examine each of the following groups of sentences for a statement.

1. As a child, I always hated unfairness. Whenever I saw a bigger child beating up on a smaller one, my first reaction was to try to stop the fight. At school, teachers who had pets made me feel outraged because I felt that at least adults should understand how to be fair. Where I worked during the summer, those of us who were still in elementary school made pennies, while the junior high school children made three or four times as much money; yet we worked as hard as they did and also produced as much.

2. As a child, I often dreamed of traveling to distant places. Monuments such as the Eiffel Tower or the Roman Colosseum held their fascination for me, as did scenic wonders like the mountains of Nepal. I also dreamed of being a performing musician. For this reason, I lost no opportunity to experiment with any musical instrument that I could lay hands on at school or in the homes of relatives. Another childhood dream of mine was to pilot an airplane. When, as a teenager, I learned to drive a car, somehow I even let my imagination convince me that I had taken the first step toward flying.

In the first group, a statement is being made about unfairness: the writer hated it. The remaining information supports that statement with relevant examples.

The second group contains several statements about the writer's various childhood dreams. In fact, the entire paragraph is about those dreams. However, no statement is made about the dreams as a whole; the writer simply wanders from one dream to the next. Thus, lacking a statement, or controlling idea, the composition in item 2 also lacks a clear purpose. This type of stream of consciousness writing can be useful for self-exploration and for creative purposes, but it is not appropriate for most college writing assignments, which require a controlling idea, not just a topic.

EXERCISE

3-4

Examine each of the following paragraphs for a clear purpose, indicated in the form of a statement.

1. We should teach our children to turn lights and television sets off when they go somewhere so that they do not use unnecessary electrical energy. Similarly, they should learn not to waste water by letting it run while they are washing the dishes or brushing their teeth. It is also essential that they learn to conserve on materials such as paper, wood, and plastics.

2. The freeways of California, unlike the toll roads of some other states and many foreign countries, are supported by a gasoline tax rather than by users' fees. The freeways also have frequent exits and entrances, making them very convenient even for local travel. Sometimes an accident will tie up the entire freeway, bringing traffic to a stop.

3. The tourists, as soon as they arrived in Paris, went straight to the Eiffel Tower. While they were there, they did not fail to enjoy the experience of a meal in one of the restaurants on the tower. Next, they went to see Notre Dame Cathedral. There, under the square in front of the cathedral, they discovered the remains of earlier structures, dating all the way back to Roman times. In the evening, they strolled along the Champs Elysées, taking in Paris illuminated at night.

4. Students who do not do reading assignments on time have problems when they go to class because they do not understand the lecture as well as they should. This means that note taking is then more difficult, and their notes will be neither complete nor coherent. Then, when they attempt to do later readings in the textbook, they will have difficulty understanding these because they have missed out on entire sections of the material. At the same time, they will perform poorly on tests, and this will bring the added disadvantage that the tests themselves cannot be part of the learning experience, since the students do not understand even when the correct test answers are later explained.

5. Seaside resorts around the world are running into the problem of promoting an unsalable product: the beach. Water pollution levels, already high, occasionally rise to a point that is dangerous even when exposure to the water is only brief or indirect. The growing world population is contributing at an alarming rate to the problem of contamination of our water. More people create more waste products. Some of these go directly into our waterways, and others go down into the ground and are then picked up by underground waterways.

EXERCISE

Which of the paragraphs in Exercise 3-4 provide appropriate support for a statement? For those paragraphs, what statement could be made, on the basis of the information given?

EXERCISE

What statement could be made for each of the following paragraphs?

1. Some teachers follow the traditional lecture method, speaking for the entire hour while the students take notes. These instructors attempt to provide students with all the necessary information, answering few, if any, questions, and answering them only at the end of the lecture. At the opposite end of the teaching spectrum are teachers who present very little information, but rather organize the students into groups and encourage the students to come up with ideas. The results of this method vary enormously: the students, working almost entirely on their own, may come up with a great deal of useful information, or they may accomplish virtually nothing. Other teachers introduce a limited amount of information, questioning the class in a way that enables the students to figure out on their own much of what they need to learn. These teachers emphasize the students' active understanding of the material. Consequently, the students find what they are learning highly meaningful.

2. People can now watch a great variety of video tapes at home on the VCR. Materials available include everything stocked at the local video store and movies or any other programs from the 24-hour selections on television, as well as tapes made at home or borrowed from friends. Such entertainment in the home is also more affordable than it is in public places. The greater convenience of watching tapes at any hour and pausing a tape or finishing it at a later time makes entertainment possible for people who have very limited opportunities to go to the movies or watch television. The VCR also enables family and friends to be together in a relaxed atmosphere, enjoying one another's company and also communicating in a way that is not possible in a movie theater.

3. There are always families picnicking in the park. Some bring old-fashioned picnic baskets, and others rely on modern plastics. Either way, the people seem to enjoy the food and the chance to be outdoors. Besides the picnickers, there are generally quite a few small children who have been brought to the park to spend time in the open. They play on whatever equipment the park has to offer. Some also enjoy traditional children's games such as hide-and-seek. In the quieter areas of the park, there are likely to be college students absorbed in their reading or asleep on the grass. On whatever pathways the park provides, the professionals and amateurs jog or ride bicycles, going around and around in silent determination. Last but not least are the dogs. Most of them have the air of owning the park, as they intensely enjoy the opportunity to run from one part of the green to another, checking on all the park visitors, present and past.

Functions of the Supporting Information

The supporting information serves two primary functions: it demonstrates the validity of the statement, and it provides information about the statement.

SHOWING THE VALIDITY OF THE STATEMENT

EXERCISE

3-7

Which of the following statements are convincingly supported by the information that follows?

1. The junction at the end of the Orange Grove Freeway is a potential danger point.

   I saw three different accidents there last month.

2. The junction at the end of the Orange Grove Freeway is a potential danger point.

   The traffic reporters on the radio constantly report accidents at that point.

3. Geese are good watch animals.

   My neighbor's geese attack everyone who comes close to the house.

4. Geese are good watch animals.

   Many books on keeping animals now routinely deal with geese as guard animals.

5. Cigarettes are not as harmful as many people would like the public to think.

   We all know people who have been heavy smokers for decades who have not had any ill effects from cigarettes.

6. Cigarettes are not as harmful as many people would like the public to think.

   One of the major cigarette companies has just released results of a new study showing fewer harmful effects than were claimed in the study done by the government.

Statements that are not self-evident fulfill their purpose only if they are convincingly supported. In other words, statements need to be clearly validated.

The common experience or belief of many is usually more convincing than a single or a few individual experiences or opinions. Therefore, when we write, we should constantly test our own experiences and beliefs to see how they compare with those of a broad range of people.

The fact that a belief is widespread, however, does not necessarily mean that it reflects reality. Even a common experience can be of questionable validity. For example, many people the world over believe in the principle of "Spare the rod and spoil the child." Yet we are finding out more and more about the negative results of hitting children to make them obey. The conviction that physical punishment is a necessary part of raising children is widespread, but not because many people have carefully considered different possible ways of treating children and found physical punishment best. They have instead been taught by their elders that the "rod" is the best way to keep control over their children, and they have more or less unquestioningly continued the practice. In other words, they have stayed with something that they assume is right. Such assumptions, obviously, do not provide good support for writers' statements; such support is to be found, rather, in common experiences that are based on real questioning and testing. Thus, we need to analyze very carefully what we use to show the validity of our statements.

EXERCISE

3-8

What problems can you find with the information given in support of each of the following statements?

1. The rising tuition costs in colleges are creating a hardship for many students.

Even with a part-time job, I am having problems keeping up with the cost of books and transportation, let alone the higher tuition.

2. Lifeguards have a strenuous job.

My younger brother, who works as a lifeguard on weekends, always comes home from work exhausted.

3. Many opportunities to use computers to advance current medical technology are not being utilized.

An April 1985 article in *Medical Science Today* explains that major corporations are not funding medical research utilizing computers because such studies bring uncertain returns.

4. Fish from rivers can be one of our most wholesome sources of nutrients.

The Idaho Department of Fisheries has published a report showing the high quality of fish as a food source.

Consider whether the following statement is convincingly supported:

Women are subject to limitations that define their role in society.

Their place is in the home.

They are less intelligent than men.

They do not know how to make decisions.

The preceding information, as it is presented, is not convincing. First, the statements do not serve to convince the reader who already holds those beliefs about women. Second, they offer no logical support to convince the reader who does not subscribe to those beliefs already. If, on the other hand, the writer's purpose in giving this information is not to convince the reader but rather to identify the beliefs that lead to discrimination against women, then this intent needs to be clearly indicated:

Women are subject to limitations that define their role in society. Barriers to women's progress are put up by people who believe that women's place is in the home, that they are less intelligent than men, and that they do not know how to make decisions.

PROVIDING INFORMATION ABOUT THE STATEMENT

EXERCISE

3-9

In the following sets of sentences, what question does each item of supporting information answer about the statement?

1. The laser is one of the major inventions of the twentieth century.
   a. It is a device that produces a very powerful beam of light.
   b. It was invented by Americans A. Schawlow and C. H. Townes and Russians N. G. Basov and A. M. Prokhorov.
   c. It was invented simultaneously in the United States and the Soviet Union.
   d. It was invented in 1958.
   e. It was invented to send light over long distances, among other purposes.
   f. It was invented through experimentation with light and crystals.

2. The flute is a musical instrument.
   a. It is a wind instrument.
   b. Some flutes are blown from the side, and others are blown from the end.
   c. Metal flutes have keys, whereas wood flutes may have either keys or holes.

3. The French Revolution had a great influence on European society.
   a. It was begun by nobles.
   b. A financial crisis led to the outbreak of the revolution.
   c. The French Revolution triggered revolution and counterrevolution in other European countries.

Consider the following statement:

Extraterrestrials have been on Earth.

Many questions are going to come to mind to people who read the statement. Here are some likely ones:

1. Who are the extraterrestrials?
2. Where are they from?
3. What do they look like?
4. What evidence is there that they have been on Earth?
5. Who on Earth has evidence of their having been here?
6. Where have they been on Earth?
7. When have they been here?
8. What have they done here?
9. How did they get here?
10. Why have they come here?
11. Are they here now?
12. Are they doing anything here now?
13. Are they watching us?
14. Are any "people" actually extraterrestrials?
15. Did they build some of the ancient monuments, such as the pyramids?

Obviously, to support the statement that extraterrestrials have been on Earth, we must provide answers to many questions. Most people would not be convinced that the statement is valid in the absence of solid explanations to dispel their doubts.

When we write, the statements we make normally raise questions in our readers' minds. To convince our readers of the reasonableness of our ideas, we need to provide answers to those questions. In other words, we need to support our statements by including in our writing the necessary information suggested by the statements themselves.

We have seen, in Exercise 3-9, supporting information that answers the journalistic questions (*who, what, where, when, why,* and *how*) and other questions, such as *what kind,* in addition to information explaining what caused something, what the effect was, and what differences exist between things (how they contrast). In answering our readers' probable questions about our statements, we can provide various types of information.

Illustration

Consider the information provided to support the following statement:

Computers make it possible for employees to assist customers much more efficiently.

1. Travel agents and airline company employees are able to determine instantly whether seats are available on any flight.
2. Bank personnel can access the current status of any account.
3. Utility company employees can assess the situation in an entire neighborhood in case of power failures or interruptions of service.

The information illustrates (that is, gives examples that support) the statement.

E X E R C I S E

 Give examples to support the following statement.

The effects of cutbacks in city budgets are evident.

Classification

Consider the following statement and supporting information:

The instruments in a symphony orchestra are grouped by type.

1. Wind instruments include those in which the sound is produced by a vibrating column of air.
2. Stringed instruments produce sound through the vibration of strings.
3. Percussion instruments have membranes that produce sound when they are struck.

The information explains the different categories, or classes, of musical instruments.

Classify possible approaches to a textbook chapter assignment.

_____

Cause

Consider the following statement and supporting information:

A number of key factors are contributing to the growing problem of homelessness.

1. High unemployment is making it impossible for many people to afford rent.
2. The closing of mental hospitals has left many people who have poor coping skills with no place to go.
3. Many people are not acquiring the basic skills necessary for most jobs.

The supporting information indicates some of the major causes of homelessness—that is, the reasons why the problem exists.

What caused the great popularity of the television series _Little House on the Prairie_ [or another series]?

_____

Effect or Result

Consider the following statement and supporting information:

Constructive activities can have a strong positive influence on disadvantaged young people.

1. Such activities can help these young people occupy their time in positive rather than negative ways.
2. They can make friends in positive settings.
3. They can develop a positive self-image.
4. They can discover skills and abilities, as well as interests.

The supporting ideas show the effects, or results, of constructive activities on disadvantaged young people.

What positive results can a child derive from extensive reading?

_____

Addition

Consider the following statement and supporting information:

A high school student who has a job learns responsibilities.

1. He or she also learns time management skills.
2. He or she also learns to establish priorities.
3. He or she also learns about the adult working world.
4. He or she also discovers abilities and aptitudes.

The information tells what the working high school student can learn in addition to responsibilities.

EXERCISE

What does routine maintenance on a car involve besides changing the oil?

Contrast

Consider the following statement and supporting information:

Some parents contribute to their child's development of low self-esteem.

1. They fail to acknowledge the child's feelings.
2. They fail to listen carefully to what the child says.
3. They fail to constantly be finding ways to be supportive.

The listed behaviors contrast with what more helpful parents do to build self-esteem in a child.

EXERCISE

3-15

What actions contrast with proper care of a forest area?

Comparison

Consider the following statement and supporting information:

Gangs and fraternities have a number of points in common.

1. Both are fraternal-based organizations.
2. Both have "respected" leaders.
3. Both motivate members to take action for the sake of action.
4. Both foster a "we and they" attitude in relation to outsiders.

The information shows how these two types of organizations are comparable in some ways.

Compare alcoholics and drug addicts.

Definition

Consider the following statement and supporting information:

> Many people who are active in clubs and organizations are hypocrites eager to be in the spotlight.
>   A hypocrite is a person who pretends to be different from what he or she is or pretends to believe differently from what he or she really believes.

The writer is stating that many socially active people are hypocrites, and a definition of the term helps the reader understand clearly what the writer is asserting.

Most households in America have at least one pet. Add a definition of *pet*.

Focus of the Supporting Information

Identify whether you would expect to find supporting information explaining *what, why,* or *how* for each of the following statements.

1. Most dogs can be trained.
2. We should be concerned about our environment for a number of reasons.
3. Some hands-on science museums include many displays that are intended to help the visitor understand scientific principles.

The first example raises the question *how* because the statement asserts that most dogs can be trained. In other words, if we are told that something can be done, our reaction is to ask how it can be done. Consequently, in a composition based on this statement, the writer needs to give key supporting ideas indicating how most dogs can be trained. The writer might, for example, use the following key supporting ideas to show how dogs can learn:

1. They can be rewarded with food when they perform the desired behavior.
2. They can be praised when they exhibit the behavior that is to be learned.
3. They can be shown another dog exhibiting the target behavior.

Similarly, a person reading that we should be concerned about our environment for a number of reasons will expect to be given supporting information indicating *why* this is so. Some key supporting ideas that the writer might use to show why are as follows:

1. Pollution is a growing problem.
2. Materials, especially nonrenewable ones, exist in limited amounts.
3. Waste disposal has become a serious problem.

And likewise, a reader of the third statement in Exercise 3-18 would expect to encounter key supporting ideas showing *what* displays are used to help visitors understand scientific principles.

The questions *what, why,* and *how* are usually open questions that require fairly lengthy explanations in order to be answered. Questions that are generally closed—*who, where,* and *when*—can often be answered in a single sentence or even in a single word.

Try answering the following questions:

1. Who was president of the United States during the Civil War?
2. Where was John F. Kennedy shot?
3. When did Albert Einstein live?
4. What were the causes of the Civil War?
5. Why was Kennedy shot?
6. How did Einstein arrive at his theory of relativity?

The first three questions have simple answers:

1. Abraham Lincoln [was president during the Civil War].
2. [He was shot] in Dallas.
3. [He lived] from 1879 to 1955.

The remaining three questions are far more complex. Long works have been written to try to explain what caused the Civil War, why Kennedy was shot, and how Einstein arrived at his theory of relativity.

EXERCISE

Determine the direction—*what, why,* or *how*—for each of the following statements, and develop some appropriate key supporting ideas.

1. In the past decade, several important films have focused on education.
2. Elementary school children should learn basic computer skills for a number of reasons.
3. People on a 1200-calorie-per-day diet can still eat well.

Notice how the direction of the key supporting ideas relates to the topic and to the controlling idea of the composition. In the first statement in Exercise 3-19, the topic is "films," and the controlling idea is that they have "focused on education." The reader of this statement will expect to be told *what* films have focused on education. A key supporting idea could be developed around *Stand and Deliver,* with explanations showing how the film focuses on education: the picture is the story of mathematics teacher and educator Jaime Escalante, whose teaching emphasizes real understanding of the material, utilizes practical applications of concepts, and maximizes the positive influence of people's passion for learning. Another key supporting idea could be developed around a film such as *Dead Poets' Society*. Additional key ideas could be based on other recent films that focus on education.

Similarly, the second statement in Exercise 3-19 can be supported with reasons explaining *why* children should learn computer skills; and the third statement can be made more convincing if the writer explains *how* to eat well on 1200 calories a day.

Determine which key ideas support each of the following statements, and find the logic problem in those that do not.

1. Los Angeles should have an efficient rapid transit system.
   a. There are too many cars for the existing freeways and roads.
   b. The present system does not meet the current demand for public transportation.
   c. Many people who could carpool do not.
   d. Buses should be kept in good running condition.
   e. Many car owners find it more practical to use public transportation.

2. New York City is a good place to go for a vacation.
   a. New York City offers unique places to visit, such as the United Nations headquarters.
   b. The tourist can go to a different theater every night.
   c. Reservations for the theater are usually necessary.

3. We should conserve our resources.
   a. Future generations will need them.
   b. The problem of waste disposal is becoming more and more critical.
   c. We need to save money.

4. Gang violence should be brought under control.
   a. Police protection should be increased.
   b. Police should be given more advanced weapons.
   c. Curfew should be established.
   d. Innocent people are victims of shoot-outs.

5. College is expensive.
   a. College tuition is high.
   b. Students have to buy expensive books.
   c. Transportation to and from school can be quite costly.
   d. It is cheaper to live at home.

Determine which key ideas do not support each of the following statements. Then see if you can change each ineffective idea into a relevant one.

1. The bus service in many large cities needs to be improved.
   a. People use the bus because it is their only means of transportation.
   b. Many people are poorer than they were a decade ago.

2. Efficiency is impeded when there are too many supervisors in a company.
   a. With too few lower-level employees, it is difficult to get work done on schedule.
   b. Conflicting instructions are sometimes given to employees.

3. The words in American English come from a variety of sources.
   a. Most of the words in British English have made their way over here.
   b. Words have come with the many immigrants from non-English-speaking countries.
   c. Many native American words are part of the standard language.
   d. Many words come and go as trends change.

4. Fireworks should be banned.
   a. They can cause fires.
   b. They can cause injuries.
   c. Children use them on the Fourth of July.
   d. Manufacturers state that fireworks are safe if used according to directions.

Supporting the Statement Logically: Criteria for Organizing Information

EXERCISE

Experiment with the order of the sentences in each of the following groups. Does it make a difference what order they are in? Does one particular order make the information easiest to follow?

1. a. As our airplane approached the coast, we had our first look at the Los Angeles Basin.
   b. In the distance, running around the city like a rim, were snow-capped mountains.
   c. Below us were broad beaches.
   d. In the middle ground was the enormous city of Los Angeles.

2. a. Using both hands, quickly close the dog's mouth.
   b. As you hold the dog's upper jaw open with one hand, place the pill at the very back of the dog's tongue with your other hand.
   c. Holding the animal's mouth closed with one hand, stroke the throat with a downward motion of your other hand until you are sure the dog has swallowed the pill.
   d. Praise your pet.
   e. There is a definite strategy to follow in giving a dog a pill.

3. a. They are used in many ways as a learning tool.
   b. They enable people to process quickly an incredible amount of information.
   c. Computers have various uses.
   d. Many games are computer based.

SPATIAL ORDER

In the first part of Exercise 3-22, it makes sense to describe the scene by moving from the beaches (closest to the plane), to the city (farther back), to the mountains (in the distance). In other words, the writer is moving through space, from the foreground to the middle ground to the background. The term **spatial order** is used for a systematic description that moves through space in an indoor or outdoor location.

CHRONOLOGICAL ORDER

The second part of Exercise 3-22 indicates steps in a process, and these are best put into **chronological order**, going from the first (or earliest) to the last (or latest).

This order is normally used for information explaining how to do something as well as for the narration of stories and historical events, in other words, whenever the writer finds it appropriate to move through time.

ORDER OF IMPORTANCE

The third part of Exercise 3-22 gives information that is best put into **order of importance**. Most readers are going to expect a discussion which begins with the most important use of the computer, that of processing information, and proceeds through other uses according to their importance. This systematic presentation enables the reader to follow more easily what the writer is presenting.

E X E R C I S E

Rearrange the following groups of sentences to achieve the most sensible results.

1. a. The beach is a popular destination for vacationers.
   b. It is a good place to relax.
   c. Beachcombers can collect seashells.
   d. Visitors can enjoy a number of water activities at the beach.

2. a. She will be treated as an intruder.
   b. She will be pressured into being the team servant and flunky.
   c. Hefty guys will gang up to hurt her so she will be sidelined.
   d. A girl who plays on a high school football team faces discrimination.

GENERAL TO PARTICULAR, AND VICE VERSA

The first group of ideas in Exercise 3-23 can be arranged from the general idea of "place to relax" to the somewhat more particular idea of "enjoy water activities at the beach" to the much more particular idea of "collect seashells."

CONCRETE TO ABSTRACT, AND VICE VERSA

In the second group of ideas in Exercise 3-23, it makes sense to proceed from the concrete idea of taking action to hurt the female player to the somewhat more abstract idea of pressuring her to be the team servant to the much more abstract idea of treating her as an intruder.

We thus communicate meaning more effectively by arranging the supporting information in some logical order. The order we choose depends on the information to be presented. Frequently, we use a combination of two or more patterns. Consider the following example:

A person may decide to trade in an old car for a number of reasons.

a. It has several mechanical problems.

b. The body needs expensive work.

c. It seems outdated.

These items go from what is usually the most important reason to the least important one and at the same time from the most concrete reason to the most abstract one.

Order of importance is often combined with either general–particular or concrete–abstract or both. These three patterns can also be reversed to create other effects, as in the following example:

Doctors often encourage their overweight patients to go on a diet.

 a. They are concerned about these patients' self-image.

 b. They want these people to be as active as people of normal weight.

 c. Above all, they feel that patients who are overweight have greatly increased chances of experiencing many different health problems.

In this case, the writer is going from the least important of the doctors' concerns—their patients' self-image—to the somewhat more important activity level and finally to the most important reason: avoiding the many weight-related health problems. This technique is valuable when you want to leave your strongest point fresh in your reader's mind.

We can also present our information in order from general to particular or vice versa. For example, if you wished to discuss the causes of the Persian Gulf War of 1991, you would probably want to describe the general factor of different countries' desire to control sources of oil before you discussed the much more particular issue of Iraq's invasion of Kuwait. The oil situation forms part of a background picture that a person must be familiar with in order to understand the invasion—the event that triggered the war.

On the other hand, if you wished to discuss the goals of a college student, you would probably get better results by starting with the particular and concrete idea of getting a degree, then working your way through less particular and less concrete ideas, such as networking for career purposes and socializing, and finally ending with the general and abstract idea of learning.

EXERCISE

Arrange each of the following groups of sentences in logical order, and indicate which order you have used: spatial, chronological, order of importance, general–particular, or concrete–abstract.

1. a. In Russia, local clubs have some very important functions.
  b. They offer teenagers a place where they can keep out of trouble.
  c. They sponsor concerts, lectures, and tournaments.
  d. They provide a locale for showing movies.

2. a. Replace the glass fixture.
  b. It is easy to change a light bulb in a chandelier.
  c. Take out the old bulb.
  d. Turn off the electricity.
  e. Put in a new bulb.
  f. Carefully remove the glass fixture.
  g. Turn on the current again.

3. a. He offers the class explanations that are easy to understand.
  b. He gives students help according to their individual needs.
  c. He often uses humor when he lectures.
  d. Dr. Martin is a fine instructor.

4. a. The stream right behind our campsite is glistening in the late afternoon sun.

b. On the other side of the tent, my little brothers are busy collecting pine cones.
c. My father looks triumphant, having just set up our tent.
d. One of my favorite pictures was taken during our camping trip last summer.
e. The forest in the background looks so peaceful.
f. My mother is in front of him, intent on cooking dinner over the fire.

5. a. The Eiffel Tower was the high point of our trip.
   b. Our trip to Paris was an unforgettable experience.
   c. We enjoyed touring three famous cathedrals.
   d. We visited a wide variety of museums.

E X E R C I S E

3-25

Which of the five orders identified in Exercise 3-24 would you use for each of the following?

1. A description of the interior of Westminster Abbey.
2. A description of the preparation of a Thanksgiving turkey.
3. The arrangement of items on an agenda.
4. The causes of a war.
5. The reasons why a college student chooses a particular class.

When we write an essay (or even a single paragraph), we often use more than one logical order in different parts of the composition. For example, one key supporting idea might best be explained by a series of items in order of importance, and another might best be illustrated by a series of examples in chronological order.

Supporting the Statement with a Purpose: The Rhetorical Modes

ILLUSTRATION

What is the writer's purpose in writing the following paragraph?

The person just learning to drive a car has several difficult tasks to master. First, the driver must learn to control the car. This means finding the correct pedal without looking, stepping neither too hard nor too lightly on the pedal, and steering down the road, all at the same time. In addition, the new motorist has to keep track of the situation on the road. This includes monitoring everything involved in normal driving conditions, as well as watching for any potential emergency situation. Finally, the learner must get used to following the rules of the road. This means learning the many pages of signs in the handbook, all of which somehow look a little different to the novice who is driving down the road for the first time, and mastering the established conventions for changing lanes, turning, and stopping. It is no wonder that some people give up on learning to drive before they ever get behind the wheel of a car.

The writer's purpose is to illustrate the tasks a person learning to drive has to master in order to show that they are difficult.

Consider the following questions:

1. What is the topic of the paragraph?
2. What is the controlling idea of the paragraph?
3. Is the direction of the paragraph *what, why,* or *how*?
4. How does the controlling idea relate to the illustration mode?

The topic of the paragraph is the "tasks" that the person learning to drive must master, and the controlling idea is "difficult." The key supporting ideas name the difficult tasks; in other words, the direction of the paragraph is *what*. As each key supporting idea brings up a task, the explanations illustrate why the task is difficult. In this way, the mode chosen—illustration—serves the writer's purpose of showing that the tasks are difficult.

WRITING ASSIGNMENT: ILLUSTRATION

EXERCISE

 Write a paragraph or short essay illustrating the difficulties involved in learning some skill, such as using a computer, playing a musical instrument, working as a disk jockey, repairing a car, or making something. In doing so, work through the following steps:

■ Prewrite carefully before you write a draft. Limit your topic and give yourself at least one uninterrupted opportunity to generate ideas creatively, brainstorming your topic. Discuss your topic with your classmates, with friends, with relatives, and with others. Think back to whatever you may have read about the topic or heard about it on television or the radio.
■ Organize your thoughts, going back to gather more ideas as your thoughts take shape.
■ Prepare a carefully focused and organized plan that clearly shows the development of your controlling idea.
■ Write your draft, concentrating on meaning and on expressing your ideas in effective sentences.
■ Reconsider and revise your draft, examining it for focus (topic, controlling idea, and key supporting ideas that lead in a single direction) and support (appropriate explanations). Go back in the process of writing whenever you must make major changes.
■ Check your final draft carefully for errors in grammar, spelling and punctuation.

Illustration Essay

The power struggle in Europe in the early 1700s involving absolute monarchies and Machiavellian politics was not destined to last indefinitely. A change in attitude was on the horizon, and a number of the leading thinkers of the time were beginning to find a new faith in science and reason. These thinkers, who believed that political and social problems could be solved through reason, wanted a rationally organized world in which enlightened progress would destroy the errors and prejudices of the past. The resulting movement, which came to be known as Illuminism, brought about a drastic rethinking of some important traditional institutions.

The first institution to find itself under fire was the church. Not only the Catholic but also the other established religions were targeted by philosophers, who preferred a sort of natural religion based on a belief in God, the immortality of the soul, and the traditional religious virtues. In this way, religion became more personal; and the concept of tolerance and religious freedom, already current in England, began to take hold in France and other countries as well.

Another system that came to be questioned was the state-directed economy. Leading thinkers in the field believed that certain natural laws regulated economics, just as others regulated science. They therefore advocated free trade and general economic freedom.

During this period, education was also drastically reconsidered as an institution. With the vigorous interest in the sciences and philosophy came the idea that public instruction—in other words, education for all—was highly desirable. The Illuminists therefore recommended that their governments find schools and hire teachers to instruct young people, with emphases on the history of civilization and on the sciences.

Finally, the institution of the absolute monarchy was brought into question. Montesquieu advocated the separation of powers, with the creation of executive, legislative, and judicial branches of government. Although this idea did not really pose a threat to the enlightened despotism of the time, it was nevertheless a revolutionary concept.

The new ideas of Illuminism took the form of thought rather than action, and they led not to revolution but to the rapid rise and fall of various reforms. These reforms were carried out by enlightened monarchs whose intention was to put their authority at the service of the people. They designed these reforms, however, according to their own beliefs rather than according to the people's real needs. There was still no question of democracy, with the continuing hatred of the common people on the part of even a Voltaire. Yet this extensive reconsidering of some key traditional beliefs was an important step forward in history and a crucial one for the later development of more democratic ideas.

QUESTIONS FOR CLASS OR GROUP DISCUSSION OR WRITING

1. Which issues raised during the period of Illuminism are still being debated?
2. Why is it difficult for people to agree on issues regarding religion, the economy, education, and leadership?
3. The new American nation was formed during the period of Illuminism. What direct influence did the movement have on our institutions?
4. In what ways is our society more democratic than the European and American societies of 200 years ago?

Additional Illustration Topics

1. What employers look for in prospective employees
2. Inventions that have been motivated by military needs
3. Difficulties of going to college

CLASSIFICATION

What is the writer's purpose in writing the following paragraph?

Teachers have different ways of conducting class. Traditional teachers use the class time to lecture to the students. They believe that they have the information the students need to learn and that students should listen and take notes in order to memorize as much of the information as possible. As these instructors equate learning primarily with rote memorizing, they measure students' progress by how much information the students can reproduce on tests. Other teachers use most of the class time for group discussions. They suggest ideas for groups to consider; and then, from time to time, they recapitulate and synthesize the information thus gathered. These teachers, who usually favor a student-oriented class, provide only a limited amount of information themselves and generally do relatively little testing to assess student learning. A final category includes teachers who structure class time so that the students will arrive at an understanding of certain concepts. Rather than lecture to the students, they guide them, through suitable materials and appropriate questions, to an understanding of the course content. They then test their students' active comprehension of the course concepts. As different as these types of classroom management are, they are all common in our schools today.

The writer's purpose is to classify teachers' ways of conducting class in order to show that they are different.

Consider the following questions:

1. What is the topic of the paragraph?
2. What is the controlling idea of the paragraph?
3. Is the direction of the paragraph *what, why,* or *how*?
4. How does the controlling idea relate to the classification mode?

The topic is teachers' "ways" of conducting class, and the controlling idea is that they are "different." The key supporting ideas show *how* teachers use class time differently. By classifying the ways of conducting class, the writer can readily show that they are different.

WRITING ASSIGNMENT: CLASSIFICATION

E X E R C I S E

3-27 Write a composition classifying students by goals, by age, by background, or by another criterion. Prewrite, write, and revise, as explained in Exercise 3-26.

Classification Essay

Department store employees who meet casually off the job tend to have as much to say about the store customers as they do about the products they sell. Some shoppers, they observe, try on a dozen garments but then buy nothing. Others leave the store with several purchases they will never use. Still others come in, buy something in a hurry, and then leave. Yet these behaviors, different as they are, all make sense for the simple reason that these customers have different purposes for coming to the store in the first place.

Some customers come to the store to buy something in particular. This may be something they need or want at the moment, or it may be something that is on sale. These shoppers usually go straight to where the item or items are located and make the purchase with a minimum of complication. Many people occasionally shop this way because they are in a hurry. Those who usually shop this way are generally people who for some reason do not really like to shop. Customers with a specific purpose are generally liked by the clerks because they buy and because they create little confusion.

Other customers come to the store just to buy. For many of these shoppers, money is no object. For others, with limited means, spending gives a sense of power. In either case, these customers go around the store accumulating packages, often with little real idea of what they are acquiring and generally no idea of how much they are spending. Like the shoppers who come in for something specific, these customers are highly valued by the store employees.

Many others come to department stores to bargain hunt. They typically spend hours at the store. Like the previous type of shopper, they are often motivated by a sense of power, but one of a very different kind. Theirs is the feeling of having "beat" the store out of something when they find a real bargain. Many take their sense of victory even further, showing their latest "deal" to their friends. These shoppers are not the employees' favorite customers because they may be fairly disruptive in their hunt for a bargain and because the employees' gain on an item with little markup may be very small.

Last are the customers who are not customers. These are the people who look, look, and look, but buy little or nothing. Some of these frequent visitors to the store have no money to spend and are spending time instead, looking, touching, and dreaming. Others are people who can spend money but have a chronic problem with making up their minds. Still others have the mysterious idea that the store owes them something for nothing, so they will do everything they can in the store short of actually buying something. These shoppers who do not buy are detested by the clerks, who must go around after them putting items back together again and figuring out where they were on display.

Some shoppers go to the department store with virtually the same purpose every time. Others come for different reasons on different occasions. Whatever the customer's purpose is, however, the experienced clerk can see it several counters away.

QUESTIONS FOR CLASS OR GROUP DISCUSSION OR WRITING

1. What may be the reasons underlying the different purposes of the customers described? Are you like any of the people described? Do you recognize friends or relatives in the descriptions?
2. Do the customers in a small family-run business have the same purposes as the department store customers?

Additional Classification Topics

1. Restaurants, by type of food, atmosphere, clientele, or another criterion
2. Hobbies, by the types of people they appeal to or another criterion
3. Parks, by their intended use or another criterion

CAUSE/EFFECT

What is the writer's purpose in writing the following paragraph?

Several factors have contributed to outbreaks of hostilities in Yugoslavia in recent years. The country, first of all, is composed of several ethnic groups. These groups are culturally diverse, with the Eastern-oriented Serbs using the Russian alphabet and the Western-oriented Croats writing in the Western alphabet. Another sizable part of the population is Moslem. Historical differences have also caused violence between the various groups. Different parts of Yugoslavia have belonged to a number of foreign powers over the past few centuries, so there is little feeling of loyalty toward a single country, but rather a tendency toward separatism. Thus, when the Nazis invaded the area during World War II, the different peoples of Yugoslavia fought against one another instead of joining forces to resist the invaders. Finally, the conflict in Yugoslavia has been aggravated by recent historical events. The breakup of the Soviet Union and the drive for self-determination on the part of countries in other areas of the world have served as reminders to the people of Yugoslavia that political autonomy can become a reality. The conflict in Yugoslavia is a tragedy. The various peoples there need to resolve their differences somehow and take their place in our new interdependent world.

The writer's purpose is to show what has caused the outbreaks of hostilities in Yugoslavia.

Consider the following questions:

1. What is the topic of the paragraph?
2. What is the controlling idea of the paragraph?
3. Is the direction of the paragraph *what, why,* or *how*?
4. How does the controlling idea relate to the cause mode?

The topic of the paragraph is the "factors," and the controlling idea is that they "have contributed" to the outbreaks of hostilities. The key supporting ideas show *what* factors have contributed to the problem. These factors are presented as the causes that have contributed to the conflict.

Notice that a cause/effect composition, in order to be focused, explains *either* the causes *or* the effects of something—not both.

WRITING ASSIGNMENT: CAUSE/EFFECT

EXERCISE

3-28 Write a composition showing the effects of a student's failing a class. Prewrite, write, and revise, as explained in Exercise 3-26.

Cause Essay

The growing number of homeless people is drawing more and more public attention. Many people assume that the homeless do not really want to take on the responsibilities that are part of a stable life. Another common belief is that those who have no home are nearly all substance abusers. However, these views, even though they are accurate in many cases, oversimplify a problem that in reality has a series of complex causes.

One cause may be found in our very system. Homeless people are proportionally more numerous in the United States than in industrialized countries that have more government involvement in the welfare of citizens. We traditionally want to keep government out of private citizens' business, and we take pride in being self-reliant. Thus, we believe that the needy can be helped by volunteer organizations and that temporary help is sufficient to tide people over until they can get back on track. Theoretically, this system sounds quite sensible. But when a changing situation has made it very difficult for so many people to lead a stable, financially secure life, the attitude that we can all take care of ourselves if we really want to becomes questionable. Nonetheless, both national and local policies have continued to reflect our assumption that people should be self-reliant. As a result, people who have lost their jobs and their homes have still had to rely primarily on their own resources. Many of these people, unable to find the personal drive or the opportunities to progress, have remained homeless.

The precarious economic situation of the country over the past two decades has aggravated the problem of the homeless. Not only are jobs harder to find now than they were twenty years ago, but the average paycheck buys much less now than it did then. In short, it is much more difficult to make a living wage now. With more people thus unable to afford housing, the number of homeless has grown.

Along with the difficult economy, we are also seeing growing problems in education. These difficulties stem in part from the precarious economic situation and in part from the constantly increasing number of people who should be in school. Dwindling school budgets are being stretched to serve more students. The resulting decrease in the quality of education, with overcrowded classrooms and inadequate teaching materials, leads to a higher number of dropouts and a greater percentage of people who get through school without receiving a solid basic education and usable skills. Many of these people, as a result, are finding it difficult to get a job that pays a living wage. Those who are unsuccessful in finding adequate employment and who have no one to rely on risk becoming part of the homeless population.

Both reduced government spending and the attitude, common here and abroad, that mental patients can get more personalized, loving care at home have brought about the closing of many state mental facilities. However, those who believe that the mentally ill are better off at home are overlooking the fact that many of their problems have only been aggravated in the home setting because of unresolved conflicts and problems there. Even when there are caring people at home, the financial and emotional burden of supervising the patient may be unbearable. Consequently, many released patients have ended up on the streets, where they make up a sizable part of the homeless population.

The problem is further complicated by the widespread use of drugs. People who cannot find adequate, stable jobs are discovering that money can be made in drugs. Many homeless people survive on a day-to-day basis in this way. This, of course, is a vicious circle, as the homeless person may both deal and use drugs. The resulting loss of any sense of reality makes it almost impossible for the homeless in this situation to return to a normal life.

Lacking normal nutrition and hygienic facilities, homeless people undergo changes once they are out on the street. Their deteriorated appearance and health make it even harder for them to find either employment or housing. In this way, they are for all practical purposes in a trap.

The problem of homelessness is growing, and solutions are not coming forth. Perhaps all of us need to take a closer look at this tragedy in our midst.

QUESTIONS FOR CLASS OR GROUP DISCUSSION OR WRITING

1. In what ways does a large homeless population reflect negatively on a country?

2. Some homeless people have a problem with substance abuse. In what ways does addiction make it difficult for people to hold down a job?

3. Many jobs that need to be done are not getting done. In addition to the recycling that many homeless people regularly do, what kinds of work could homeless people—as well as other jobless persons—be doing that would benefit society as a whole?

Additional Cause or Effect Topics

1. Causes that induce many people to leave their homelands to come to live in the United States
2. Effects of the large immigrant population on the United States
3. Effects of divorce on children

COMPARISON

What is the writer's purpose in writing the following paragraph?

A person who wants to lose weight can get better results from a slow weight-loss program than from a crash diet. The slow diet, first of all, is more effective nutritionally. The crash diet focuses on just a few foods, leaving the body nutritionally deprived after only a few days; in contrast, the slow diet involving a reduced number of calories and low fat content can leave the person, who is now thinking more clearly about the quality of the food, in better health than before. The slow diet is also a better choice physically. The crash dieter usually just diets, whereas the person with the slower, more carefully planned program is more likely to include the physical activity necessary for a body to be healthy. Finally, the slow diet is better psychologically. People who are overweight generally have both bad eating habits and psychological problems that aggravate their tendency to overeat. The crash diet does not address either of these areas, whereas the all-inclusive weight loss program takes into consideration the negative self-image as it helps the dieter gradually build better eating habits. For this reason, the weight lost in a gradual program is more likely to stay off. As far as dieting is concerned, it takes long-term methods to get long-term results.

The writer's purpose is to compare slow weight-loss programs with crash diets, in order to show that the slow programs get better results.

Consider the following questions:

1. What is the topic of the paragraph?
2. What is the controlling idea of the paragraph?
3. Is the direction of the paragraph *what, why,* or *how*?
4. How does the controlling idea relate to the comparison mode?

The topic of the paragraph is "diets," and the controlling idea is that a person "can get better results from a slow weight-loss program than from a crash diet." The key supporting ideas give the reasons *why* the slow diets are better. The mode chosen—comparison—serves the purpose of showing why the slow programs are better than the crash diets.

WRITING ASSIGNMENT: COMPARISON

EXERCISE

Write a composition comparing high school and college. Prewrite, write, and revise, as explained in Exercise 3-26.

Comparison Essay

Modern society, it is often said, has been desensitized to violence. Heavy criticism is aimed particularly at the media for unnecessarily exposing us to so much brutality. Nevertheless, while we may readily agree that both our news coverage and our entertainment contain too much violence, we should be cautious about assuming that we have actually come to accept brutality more readily in recent years than in the past. In reality, people's attitude toward violence is less tolerant now than it used to be.

It would be naive to think that violence itself is new. Life never has been for the fainthearted. Crimes of all kinds have been abundantly documented throughout the course of human history. The number of crimes has grown quickly over recent years, it is true, but so has the population. Moreover, as our means of communication have improved, information about violence in society is much more readily available to the public. Thus, it is difficult to make an accurate comparison of current levels of violence with the amount of violence in the past. Furthermore, from all that we can gather from history, the variety of forms of violence perpetrated on human beings is not new either. There are records of all kinds of mutilations. In addition, assassins—people who smoked or chewed hashish before they went out and murdered someone—have been known for hundreds of years. Moreover, ever since there have been cities, people have been fearful of sending their defenseless loved ones to these centers of crime. Sordid acts have always taken place in the countryside as well, but in the past these often went unnoticed because of the lack of communication and the greater tolerance for abuse. In fact, in past societies, slaves could be beaten and men could kill disobedient wives and children with no fear of legal consequences.

We should also remember that in the past, force was the most widely used—and accepted—means of resolving conflicts. People felt that the honorable way to settle their personal differences was with duels and shoot-outs. Moreover, human history is incredibly full of wars, whereas records of arbitration are comparatively scarce. It is unfortunately true that we still have wars; however, we usually attempt to settle our conflicts through some kind of arbitration, arriving at a compromise. In other words, we do not normally resort to force first, as was done in the past. And when war does break out, much discussion ensues as to how the violence might have been prevented. Even a former secretary of the navy, a career military person, publicly stated that the conflict in the Persian Gulf in 1991 could have been avoided because the parties involved could have negotiated a settlement. Furthermore, the very image of the career soldier has also changed over time. In the past, upper-class families encouraged their sons to become military men because they felt such a career brought honor to the family. Today most people would consider many other careers more prestigious than a military one.

Our frequent exposure to violence is not new either. We do all too often see scenes of brutality in films, television series, and news stories. But if we look into the past, we also find a great deal of public exposure to violence. In ancient Rome and elsewhere, gladiator fights and other spectacles of death were considered entertainment. In past centuries, executions were usually carried out in public; and the people, including the children, gathered to see them, getting what we now sarcastically call their cheap thrill for the day. We are justifiably horrified now at the tale of a teenager who did not know that a person who was shot suffered pain. But we must ask ourselves whether the child watching the public hanging understood the suffering of the victim or had any opportunity to talk to an adult about the event in more than a superficial way.

We are also critical now of animated cartoons in which the characters get mutilated and then miraculously rise and proceed to the next adventure. Yet the fairy tales children read in the past are full of the most horrendous—and senseless—violence. And to make the situation worse, the various violent acts in them are generally committed not against make-believe animals, but against people, giving children the impression that in real life the powerful enjoy some sort of inalienable right to torture others. This concept of survival of the strongest that children grew up on in the past, because it implies the use of force, is basically a doctrine of violence. Now, however, we at least recognize that children need exposure to positive models of behavior in their lives and that they also need to be able to express their feelings about violence or anything else they wish to an adult who truly listens.

At our present-day scenes of disaster, the looters are the spiritual descendants of the pillagers who scourged the cities of the past; and the looky-loos are the counterparts of earlier citizens who crowded forward to get a better look at the victim during a public execution. Certainly, we cannot condone the violence in our society today. But the preceding statement itself, set to the tune of "Beat It," is a sign of our times, not of past ones.

QUESTIONS FOR CLASS OR GROUP DISCUSSION OR WRITING

1. For what reasons do people use violence?
2. Is there any correlation between violence and deceit?
3. What can adults do to minimize children's exposure to senseless violence?

Additional Comparison Topics

1. Life in a large city and in a small town
2. Two sports (or other activities)
3. The roles of married women who primarily serve their husbands and those who are in a partnership situation with their husbands

ARGUMENT

What is the writer's purpose in writing the following paragraph?

Parents should not insist that their children go to college straight out of high school. First, the decision to go to college is a major one in life—one that needs to be made by the individual directly concerned rather than by the parent. The young person may not even want to continue with school. Also, it is very difficult for a student lacking positive motivation to be successful in higher education. Thus, the son or daughter who struggles with college primarily because of pressure from the parent accumulates frustration instead of knowledge. Another reason for the parent not to push the young person to go straight to college is that the decision may not be a suitable one. Often, the son or daughter who has just finished high school is not ready for college-level work. The recent graduate usually does not yet have clear ideas about a field of interest or a career goal. Furthermore, many teenagers are not mature enough to profit from college work. Once enrolled in class, they are faced with concepts they do not understand, and, unlike in high school, they must compete for grades with people in their twenties or older, who may understand those concepts very well because of their greater experience in life. As a result, the teenagers' immaturity becomes a real obstacle to success in their studies. A final problem is that recent graduates may have to leave good friends and favorite activities in order to go to college. In this way, their all-important social development is sacrificed. Parents may be doing a young person a real disservice by pressuring him or her to go to college.

The writer's purpose is to argue that there are valid reasons why parents should not pressure their children to go to college.

Consider the following questions:

1. What is the topic of the paragraph?
2. What is the controlling idea of the paragraph?
3. Is the direction of the paragraph *what, why,* or *how*?
4. How does the controlling idea relate to the argument mode?

The topic of the paragraph is parental "insistence" that children go to college, and the controlling idea is that they "should not" apply such pressure. The key supporting ideas bring up major reasons *why* this insistence is not good. In this way, the mode—argument—serves the writer's purpose of presenting the reasons why parents should not insist that their children go to college straight out of high school.

WRITING ASSIGNMENT: ARGUMENT

E X E R C I S E

3-30 Write a composition giving the arguments for allowing students to repeat a writing class. Prewrite, write, and revise, as explained in Exercise 3-26.

Argument Essay

Both Americans and people from other countries frequently say that families elsewhere are closer than American families. They feel that a family in which everyone is constantly out doing something different must necessarily be out of touch. Although this is often true, there are many American families that have a real closeness entirely uncommon elsewhere.

American family members, first of all, frequently have a very positive attitude toward one another. We now see in many homes a respect for the individual as a person rather than the "respect" for an authority figure that was common in the past. Perhaps our human rights movements of past decades, including the recent concern for children's rights, have helped us to find these new positive values. Whatever the reason, many Americans have come to realize that good human relationships are built on communication and understanding rather than on power. This realization, in turn, has led us to put much less emphasis on gender roles. For example, we now understand that when a woman takes on the responsibilities not only of running a household but also of providing for herself and others and of negotiating business in the world outside the home, she acquires a broader sense of what is real in a man's traditional environment. Similarly, when a man takes some responsibility for the household, including work that is not at all enjoyable, the home can become a more rewarding place for him. Furthermore, a child who sees the adult concerned and involved both in and out of the home can only feel a balance in the home that is lacking in one with sharply upheld gender roles.

Similarly, attitudes toward children have changed. In this country, many grownups have come to regard children as people, just as adults are, rather than as creatures to be seen but not heard. This new respect for children—part of a picture of greater equality and, therefore, respect in the home—has brought families much closer together.

American families often seem so busy that outsiders may assume that family members have no time for togetherness. However, the quality of the time is more important in the long run than the quantity. A stay-home mother who is physically present all the time still may not really be there for her child; physical presence does not guarantee communication or caring. In reality, when less time is available, more attention tends to be paid to the quality of the time. The needs of individual family members are more likely to be met because there is a concerted effort not to overlook them. Furthermore, individual family members who are involved outside the home in work, school, or personal activities, pursuing individual goals, have a greater chance to know and understand themselves as people. These self-fulfilled individuals then have more to offer to those around them. In this way, the busy family may actually be much closer than the family that spends more time together.

It is in America that we so frequently find family members and friends on outings treating each other not as father, grandmother, or child—superior or inferior—but as close friends and, more importantly, as people.

QUESTIONS FOR CLASS OR GROUP DISCUSSION OR WRITING

1. What opportunities are there in daily life around the home for family members to spend quality time together?
2. In what ways can the new respect for children as people make child raising a highly rewarding experience?

Additional Argument Topics

1. Why extracurricular activities in high school should be supported
2. Why all people should have health insurance
3. Why we should (or should not) replace individual automobile insurance with an added gasoline tax

NARRATION

What is the writer's purpose in writing the following paragraph?

The exhausting flight to Rome was finally over. So was the somehow even more exhausting ride from the airport to the air terminal, alongside the railway station in downtown Rome. But then, in front of the station, I discovered that the line of people curving around divider after divider stood between my tired body and a comfortable taxi ride to my hotel, near the Colosseum. So I decided that I would go for a new experience, and I descended a dark stairway into the subway station. The station itself was grimy and depressing, and the approaching train looked uninviting as well. However, the ride would be short since I was due to get off at the second stop, "Colosseo." As I entered the subway train, I was already visualizing what a hot shower would do for me, and I was still toying with such pleasant visions when my stop came. Anxious to get out of the underworld atmosphere of the subway, I quickly ascended the short stairway and opened the door to the blue sky outside. But I was entirely unprepared for the sight that appeared in front of me. The Colosseum, in all of its antique splendor, loomed immense, only a few feet away. I was stunned. The Colosseum, so close, had suddenly come alive for me, and the impression it made was one I will never forget. In this one brief instant I came to understand that travel, even with all of the fatigue it involves, can bring some truly incredible rewards.

The writer's purpose is to show, through the narration of the unforgettable experience of suddenly seeing the Colosseum at close range, that travel can bring some truly incredible rewards.

WRITING ASSIGNMENT: NARRATION

E X E R C I S E

Write a composition narrating an important experience in your life. Conclude it with a statement of what the experience meant in your life. Prewrite, write, and revise, as explained in Exercise 3-26.

Narration Essay

Sometimes it is difficult to say why we remember some events of our lives and forget others. My sheer audacity in chasing away the neighborhood bully, who was twice my age and size, would be reason enough to make the episode memorable; but as the years have gone by, I have come to realize that this story is meaningful in a much more important way.

I was five years old at the time, and I was the smallest child in the neighborhood and the only one not yet in school. So I was very eager to be in the group with my sister, who was nine, and her friends. One of these friends was Jodi.

I could not really understand my sister's friendship with Jodi because she did not treat any of the neighborhood kids well, and she was constantly pestering my sister about something. She did not actually present herself as an enemy or a rival. The two girls, sometimes with other kids and sometimes on their own, did things together. They often climbed trees or rode their bikes around the neighborhood. They frequently exchanged ghost stories. Moreover, Jodi occasionally shared something with my sister. But it was not a friendship based on equality. It was always Jodi who decided what they would do. It was always Jodi who dictated when they would start and stop anything. It was Jodi who took the liberty to get mad at my sister and say anything she wanted. My sister, however, would never have dared to say anything that Jodi would not like. In short, Jodi could always push my sister around and be confident about getting away with it.

There was nothing unusual about the day the situation changed. It was sunny and mild, the kind of day that can only bring out the best in a person. Best or not, in me it brought out something I had not experienced before. In our rather sleepy neighborhood, a residential area of older houses, each with a spacious yard and tall trees, school had just gotten out, and the children were on their way home. Jodi came by, as she often did. And as was often the case, she brought her other friends—three girls who, at eleven or twelve, seemed almost grown to me. On this occasion, it was apparent to me, small as I was, that Jodi was once again trying to prove something. She started bragging about something, clearly showing off in front of her friends, in a way that I sensed was very hurtful to my sister. I felt instantly angry. Then she started to bait my sister, evidently to show her friends that she could provoke other kids to anger, but no one would ever dare to strike back. Then she proceeded to pick a fight, one that she knew she would win. She pushed my sister down. I felt my anger mounting, as it had done so many times before. Then she pushed my sister down again. At that point, something in me snapped. I started to yell at Jodi. I told her how awful she was to my sister and everybody. I cried out that I wasn't going to let her do that any more. And I ran at her, fully intending to use some kind of superhuman force to show her she could not boss us around any more. At this point, to the surprise of all, Jodi turned and ran away, followed by her confused friends.

The first reaction of all the other kids present was amazement. Supercharged as I was from my uncontrollable anger, threatening as I must have seemed at that moment, I really stood no chance of physically dominating a kid who was so much bigger. But the amazement of everyone soon turned into a sense of elation. Some kind of weight had been lifted from our shoulders. And something very wrong had been made right.

After some time passed, Jodi came back to be our friend—and this time, more of a friend. Her attitude toward my sister changed for the better. She had no objections to my joining in some of their activities. Young as I was, I realized that she had in no way felt afraid of my beating her up; that was out of the question. Rather, she had felt shame at having a little kid point out to everyone just what she did not want people to realize: that she was a bully.

I felt better about myself after this incident. I had righted a wrong. I had helped someone to become a better person. I had made all the kids feel better about themselves and others. But more than that is evident to me now. I had cried out, for the first time, for equality.

QUESTIONS FOR CLASS OR GROUP DISCUSSION OR WRITING

1. Is the real meaning of the story indicated at the beginning?
2. What emotions are part of the story?
3. Why is it a problem if a preschool child has no one close in age for company?

Additional Narration Topics

1. Your first (or most interesting) long trip
2. Your first day at school (or at a particular school)
3. Your first day on a job

DESCRIPTION

What is the writer's purpose in writing the following paragraph?

The interior of a wide-bodied airplane is a world of its own. It easily reminds the first-time passenger of a movie theater, with row upon row of seats facing a large screen flanked on both sides by curtained doors. Then, after this first impression has taken hold, the traveler discovers that there are actually several of these "theaters," and that the one at the far end, two or three rooms away, is just barely visible. Another feature, however, soon reminds the passenger that this is not a series of projection halls, but an airplane: the small windows lining both sides of the room. These, as well as the large storage bins above them, full of pillows and blankets, speak of time to be spent and distance to be covered. The passenger, after taking in the picture of the whole room, is then ready to discover the smaller world around each individual seat. There are the standard airplane features: an individual air button and reading light above the seat and a tray table, magazine pouch, and telephone in front of the passenger. In the armrest of the seat itself, besides the seat belt and the button for reclining the seat, is a stereo system with channels for several kinds of music, for spoken radio, and for the soundtracks for the movies shown on board. The passenger, settling into a seat, may well be struck by the idea that this whole world, designed for people to continue their regular lives—eating, sleeping, working, and spending some time entertaining themselves—will actually lift off the ground and fly through the sky.

The writer's purpose is to describe the interior of a wide-bodied airplane, showing it to be a world of its own.

WRITING ASSIGNMENT: DESCRIPTION

EXERCISE

3-32 Write a composition describing a place that you have visited. Prewrite, write, and revise, as explained in Exercise 3-26.

Description Essay

The Getty Museum offers the Southern Californian a pleasantly different way to spend an idle summer afternoon. Located in Malibu, in the hills facing the Pacific Ocean, the museum has art and atmosphere that transport the visitor to other worlds and other times.

The museum is housed in a palace replicating an ancient Roman villa. Paths approaching the main building are flanked by porticos and a long, rectangular pool. Inside the villa are the courtyards and atrium typical of the wealthy Roman's home.

The art collection at the Getty Museum is superb. Priceless paintings of all periods from the late Middle Ages to the twentieth century fill room after room of the villa. The old masters are especially well represented, and there is a particularly valuable collection of Venetian and Flemish paintings.

There is also an important collection of antiquities. Greek and Roman statues and busts fill several of the lower rooms of the main building. In a nearby hall, Greek and Oriental vases are displayed.

Other exhibits are of special interest. An entire hall is filled with rare books, including illuminated manuscripts and some of the first volumes to come off the earliest printing presses. Next to this hall is a display of nineteenth-century photographs, many of which depict persons and places of historical importance.

The neoclassic halls on the upper floor also house collections of furniture of different periods, as well as individual pieces by famed cabinet makers. An unusually large number of ornate and ingeniously constructed clocks form an interesting part of the display.

The palace grounds alone would justify the visit. Nature dominates, as the trees and shrubs loom over the paths that wind among them. An occasional statue or alcove reminds the visitor that someone with exquisite taste created the entire effect. The outdoor tea room gives the guest an additional opportunity to extend a stay outside the museum itself. And the visitor has one last intensive look at nature during a walk through the herb garden, where the colors and aromas of the plants and the music of the birds blend to create one final special effect.

A visit to the Getty Museum is an experience that will not quickly be forgotten.

QUESTIONS FOR CLASS OR GROUP DISCUSSION OR WRITING

1. Why do we want—or need—to be transported occasionally to other worlds or other times?
2. If you had the fortune that it took to create the Getty Museum, what are some of the things you would do with your money?

Additional Description Topics

1. Your most (or least) inviting classroom
2. A scene in the country

DEFINITION

What is the writer's purpose in writing the following paragraph?

Quality time is time that is well spent. This term has become more and more frequently used in recent years as we crowd more and more things into our lives: family, friends, education, work, entertainment, and various obligations. However, the need to manage our busy lives has given us an opportunity to learn that the amount of time we spend with someone or something is often less important than the way we spend it. In other words, the quality of the time is more important than the quantity. For example, many children who grew up with stay-home mothers or a host of relatives around the home are now confused adults in therapy. In spite of all the physical time that was spent with them, their needs were still not met. In fact, instead of being children whose real welfare was their parents' primary concern, they may have been the easy targets of someone's frustration over matters not directly related to the child. These children are likely to be much worse off than those who spent far less time with the family. In fact, the adult who has little time to be with loved ones has a greater incentive to make positive use of whatever time they do have together. This means expressing thoughts and feelings and listening to and under-standing the thoughts and feelings of those around—in other words, establishing good communication and a strong basis for respect. People concerned with the quality of the time they spend together are also more likely to choose activities that will lead to rewarding experiences; they have no reason to "kill" time. Those who have not discovered the concept of quality time are missing out on something that really makes life worth living.

The writer's purpose is to define *quality time* and to give a more extended explanation of its meaning.

WRITING ASSIGNMENT: DEFINITION

EXERCISE

Write a composition defining *discrimination*. Prewrite, write, and revise, as explained in Exercise 3-26.

Definition Essay

Success, admittedly a hard word to define, essentially means the attainment of what a person desires to achieve in life. But people have extremely different goals in their lives. As a result, *success* is commonly defined in a number of different ways.

At the mention of *success*, many people think immediately of money. Attaining great wealth in the form of money or material possessions is the primary goal of many. They often feel that the person who has prospered materially is the one who has been successful. They also tend to associate knowing how to make money with knowing how to do other important things in life. A certain number of them even equate the ability to make money with intelligence. Some who think of success in terms of wealth emphasize the possession of money itself. For others, it is more a matter of the image of authority or importance that a wealthy person projects.

Other people, even though they are concerned with material well being, do not use money as a measure of success. To them, money brings a certain amount of basic security and provides some necessary conveniences in life so that they can focus their attention on what really matters. They may equate success with happiness of one kind or another. Rewarding relationships with other people may be the key to their success, or some significant accomplishment in a particular area of interest can bring a sense of personal fulfillment that they identify with success. In short, they feel that they have become successful when they have attained a goal or goals toward which they have been striving.

The "poor but happy" often claim to be successful in life. However, their disdain for the comfort that money can bring is often as real as the grapes were sour. Nevertheless, in spite of the hypocrisy so often used to hide envy or a lack of awareness of the world beyond, many poor people find things of value in life that are frequently overlooked by their wealthier counterparts. It does not, after all, take money to stop and smell the roses.

Just as what constitutes success is different for different people, how big an achievement it takes to make a person successful varies a great deal. But regardless of our interpretation, success, large or small, when it comes, should be recognized and appreciated.

QUESTIONS FOR CLASS OR GROUP DISCUSSION OR WRITING

1. What things of value in life can bring happiness to a poor person?

2. What frustrations can a person who is materially well off generally avoid?

Additional Definition Topics

1. responsibility
2. equality
3. punishment
4. a well-rounded person
5. a role model
6. a family
7. a pet
8. a parasite

PROCESS

What is the writer's purpose in writing the following paragraph?

Bath time for your dog is a time of close communication between you and your pet. First, however, you must postpone the communication and prepare everything for the bath ritual in the utmost secrecy. Next, you need to defy your dog's sixth sense and somehow catch your pet, bringing him or her to the scene of the outrage. Then lovingly lift your squirming animal into the tub. If you have an oversized dog, you are on your own as to how to accomplish that. Your next task is to get your animal wetter than yourself and to lather his or her entire body, beginning with the head and working your way down your angry animal, making sure no soap gets in the eyes or ears. Then rinse your pet thoroughly, using plenty of clean water to finish. At that point your dog will want to start the shaking process, which really does get more water off than you can take off with several towels. If the bath scene is not a suitable one for water flying in all directions, then once again you will need to lovingly carry your struggling pet to a better location. If that location is outdoors, you will need great strength as well as some of your dog's sixth sense to keep your pet from diving into the closest dirt hole. Once the bath is completed, you can take your dog to a place free of both water and dirt and affectionately blow-dry your pet. If you are good enough at this, you may begin to work your way back into your pet's good graces. Add your most lavish—and sincere—praise for your pet. This is also a strategically good time to pull out your doggy's favorite food treat. Finally, when you are all through with your dog, clean out your tub because now it is your turn.

The writer's purpose is to describe the process of bathing a dog.

WRITING ASSIGNMENT: PROCESS

EXERCISE

Write a composition explaining the process of making something. Prewrite, write, and revise, as explained in Exercise 3-26.

Process Essay

Many students go through school without learning to read critically. Faced with time constraints and the necessity of taking tests that are designed to show what percentage of the material they have learned, they acquire the habit of reading straight through textbook chapters, moving rapidly from sentence to sentence in search of material that needs to be memorized. This method of reading, however, is not a particularly effective one. A much more rewarding strategy is that of critical reading.

To read critically, first of all, you must prepare your mind for the task. Before you begin to read, be sure that you are ready to commit yourself to understanding rather than memorizing. Prepare yourself mentally to enter into dialogue with the writer. Be ready to move into the author's world and consider a view of reality that is different from your own.

As you approach the reading itself, you should give some thought to several questions. Before you actually do the reading, identify what you expect to be reading about, based on what you see in the title and any section headings, or if there are no headings, in the paragraph beginnings. Also, try to assess the author's credibility, taking into consideration how informed the author is likely to be, as well as how biased. Then, still during this prereading stage, you should give careful thought to what you already know about the subject and formulate questions, both open and closed, in connection with the subject. These strategies are helpful because it is easier to understand something new if we can relate it to something that is already familiar.

As you do the reading, continue to formulate questions and seek answers. Dialogue actively with the author, questioning the reasoning behind statements, interpreting meaning as you find it, and considering other possible interpretations. Examine the assumptions on which the information is based, as well as the resulting implications. Look for contradictions and insufficient or inadequate evidence. Determine the fundamental issue, and distinguish the author's main points from the more detailed supporting information. Evaluate the relevance of the support to the basic question. Decide whether the conclusions drawn by the author are appropriate.

After you have finished the reading, summarize it to yourself, actively reconstructing the author's meaning. Then, with different points of view in mind, evaluate the reading, recapitulating what was said and what it meant, accepting what makes sense and reconsidering what does not. Finally, incorporate your new understanding into your own framework of thought.

Admittedly, reading takes longer this way. However, these strategies help to make reading truly meaningful, since the reader both understands much more and remembers much longer. The extra time spent reading critically, consequently, is time well spent.

QUESTIONS FOR CLASS OR GROUP DISCUSSION OR WRITING

1. Why is some of the information in the daily newspaper inaccurate?
2. Has the college experience helped you find out what you know about life? What are some of the things you have discovered you knew?

Additional Process Topics

1. Taking a test
2. Preparing for a job interview
3. Changing a tire on a car
4. Detailing a car
5. Doing something in connection with a hobby

Summing Up

You have seen that a composition is the development of a specific statement.

Statement: Made in the *topic sentence* of a paragraph or the *thesis statement* of an essay. The *controlling idea* indicates the statement and gives the composition a definite *purpose*.

Supporting information: In the body of the composition, supporting information should show the validity of the statement and provide the necessary information about the statement. Support needs to be logically appropriate and arranged in a suitable order.

In Chapter 4 you will learn more about working critically with ideas.

WORKING WITH IDEAS

4

Identifying Main Ideas in Writing

What ideas are emphasized in the following paragraph?

Christmas has different meanings for different people. Some consider it primarily a religious holiday. These celebrants honor the birth of Christ by carefully setting up a creche where it can be admired by all who enter the home. The special church services held at Christmas are another important part of the holiday for them. Even the feasts of the season have a religious meaning for those who celebrate the birth of Christ. For other people, Christmas is primarily a time of togetherness for family and friends. They value the holiday because it provides an opportunity for close ones to gather and enjoy activities together. They also take advantage of the Christmas season, with its atmosphere of warmth and generosity, to call or write to those whom they care about but do not have a chance to contact more frequently. For yet other people, Christmas is not so much a time to celebrate a religious event or to contact people as it is a time to stop and appreciate a special beauty. For them, Christmas, with its feast of light and colors everywhere—from the decorated homes and streets to the delicately beautiful greeting cards—is a time of bright contrast that transforms winter from a season of bleakness to one of quiet splendor. The meaning of Christmas, thus, is truly an individual matter.

In this paragraph, the writer is clearly making the point that the meaning of Christmas is different for different people. This point is then reinforced by key supporting ideas that focus on different meanings: a religious celebration, a time of togetherness for family and friends, and a time of special beauty.

These main ideas—the topic ("the meaning of Christmas"), the controlling idea ("different"), and the key supporting ideas (religious celebration, time for togetherness, time of special beauty)—are emphasized, while the rest of the information in the paragraph consists of supporting explanations and illustrations.

When we read, we seldom take in everything. Therefore, as we read, it is important for us to identify both the point the writer is making (the writer's statement about the topic) and the key supporting ideas. If we clearly grasp these main ideas, we are more likely to remember some of the supporting details. In other words, if we understand the whole picture, we can get more meaning out of the details since we can see how they relate to the composition as a whole.

Consequently, when you read, you can get much more out of what you are reading if you make a point of identifying the author's main ideas—topic, controlling idea, and key supporting ideas (whether these appear in main supporting sentences of a single paragraph or in topic sentences of body paragraphs in an essay)—and distinguishing these main ideas from the supporting details. This is true not only of college readings, such as textbook chapters and outside reading assignments, but also of nonfiction and fiction in general. Reading becomes more meaningful and enjoyable when the author and reader communicate actively. The first step in this communication takes place when the reader identifies the writer's purpose by locating the writer's statement (controlling idea) about the topic and distinguishes the key supporting ideas from the more specific details.

Similarly, when you are writing, it is important to organize and word your ideas so that your purpose in writing and your emphasis are clear. Your readers can then follow your meaning much more easily.

EXERCISE

4-1

Identify the main ideas in the following compositions, distinguishing each one as a controlling idea, topic, or key supporting idea. Notice that not all writing begins with a formulation of the topic and controlling idea.

1. The plan is an important part of the prewriting process for a number of reasons. First, it is easier to evaluate the content of the composition when the ideas are in outline form because the information is easy to visualize. Second, the outline shows at a glance the relationships between ideas. This makes an outline easier to work with than complete sentences in paragraph form. Finally, it is easier to make changes when the material is still in outline form, and changes made at this stage save a lot of time and frustration later, when attention has to be devoted to expressing ideas accurately in grammatically correct sentences.

2. The federal budget deficit makes the news almost daily. But it is not only the country that is facing a financial crisis; most of the states are in a similar situation. The ax is currently falling heavily on all forms of state spending, including social programs, health care, and education. These cuts in spending for education are adversely affecting schools at all levels, and they are having a grave impact at the college level. In fact, these budget cuts are making the goal of a post-secondary education one that is very difficult to reach.

The most obvious effect of this decrease in state funding for colleges is that a growing number of students are not able to get the classes they need in order to pursue their educational goals. Fewer classes are being offered, and fewer sections of each class are available. The limited spaces are taken quickly. In many cases, virtually all new students and many continuing ones are able to enroll only in large or unpopular lecture or physical education classes. The students are more or less compelled to take these spots in order to put themselves in a position to register the following semester and take classes that fulfill requirements. Consequently, students need extra years to attain their degrees, with all of the personal inconvenience that the delays cause.

In addition to dealing with reduced availability of classes, students face a much greater financial burden if they wish to pursue a college education. Tuition is being raised by the institutions, as they attempt to balance their own budgets; and at the same time, financial aid is increasingly difficult to obtain. The extra years needed to complete a program also add enormously to the total cost of the education. The unfortunate result of the added expense is that fewer people can realistically hope to complete a college education.

The concept of lifelong learning has been a reality in the United States for several decades, as our people of all ages and backgrounds have pursued educational goals. Let us not undermine the strength of our society by regressing to a system in which only those who have time and money to throw away can get an education.

3. SLAVERY ENDS TODAY—ON PAPER

Jan. 1, 1863–President Lincoln today declared free all the slaves in the rebelling states in the South. The announcement, made in Washington, was enthusiastically received by large crowds of emancipated slaves.

The declaration will by no means affect all slaves. It is aimed at freeing the slaves in the Confederate states. However, the Union President's announcement will clearly not be heeded in the South. Also, it will have no effect on slaves in border states, not even on the many slaves now fighting on the Union side.

The President's order fulfills his campaign promise to end slavery.

4. Most people nowadays can look forward to a longer life than that of their forefathers. As they reach an advanced age, most continue to be active. It is not uncommon, for example, to see persons in their seventies gainfully employed. Furthermore, in addition to mental sharpness, many seniors also possess great physical strength and coordination. Two elderly Canadians, for example, were recently honored for having saved a woman from drowning in the fast-moving water above Niagara Falls. We should also recognize that, in addition to being longer, life now offers us much more than just the necessity of working, eating, and sleeping. For instance, many more people are now finding opportunities to get an education. Also, a much greater variety of facilities now serve both our needs and our interests. At the same time, recreational possibilities have grown enormously, since people's need to relieve their stress and to utilize their creative powers has become widely recognized. A final advantage to living in our times is that people communicate with one another a great deal more now than they did in the past. We are bombarded with ideas through our constant exposure to the media, and as a result, we have previously unknown opportunities for understanding how other people view the world. In this way, we have become more aware of others' attitudes and feelings and consequently more tolerant of other individuals. All in all, life truly has much more to offer us now than it did in the past.

Notice that the first passage was taken from Chapter 2 of this textbook. The purpose of the paragraph is to explain the importance of the plan in the prewriting process.

The purpose of selection 2, an essay, is to show that budget cuts are making it difficult for people to fulfill their goal of getting a college education. The two areas of difficulty developed are those of time and money.

The third selection is a newspaper article. The paragraphs are very short because newspaper articles are printed in narrow columns. Main ideas tend to be placed early in a newspaper or magazine article, especially if the article is long, because most readers focus on the beginnings of articles and may skim over or skip entirely the remainder of the passage.

In the fourth reading, the controlling idea, "has much more to offer now," is placed at the end rather than at the beginning. Although the topic and the controlling idea are usually identified early in a composition, you may sometimes find them in the middle or at the end of the writing. Occasionally, they are not stated at all.

To understand what an author intends to communicate, you should take the time to find or formulate (if it has not already been done) your author's controlling idea. Similarly, to make your own purpose clear when you write, it is advisable to state explicitly your topic and controlling idea. They usually function more effectively when placed near the beginning of your writing.

Outlining

E X E R C I S E

Read the following outlines and paragraphs one at a time. After you read each one a single time, write down what you remember about it on separate paper, reconstructing it as well as you can without looking back at the book. Make certain that you understand these directions clearly before you begin.

1. Hobbies
   I. How to do a particular hobby
      A. Description
      B. Comparison of different ones
      C. Discover interests
   II. Educational
      A. Motivation to improve skills
      B. Learn skills
      C. Money-making potential
   III. Enjoy life
      A. Relaxing

    B. Entertaining
    C. Stimulate imagination
  IV. Affect life
    A. Bring out of bad mood
    B. Problems with doing
    C. Reasons for doing

2. We are now seeing a trend toward a healthful diet. What we eat can make us either ill or strong. The combination of eating too much and exercising too little can be very hard on the body. What we eat can contribute to heart disease and other health problems. Maintaining a healthy, nutritious diet means understanding what to eat and the basic value of the four food groups: meats, dairy products, grains and cereals, and fruits and vegetables. All of the foods we eat contain some of these nutrients. On the other side of the dietary picture are the junk foods such as hot dogs, potato chips, and sodas. These foods raise cholesterol levels. To get out of the junk food habit, try to consume fresh fruits, raisins, and fruit juice or tap water, especially after exercising.

3. There is entirely too much violence on television. First, many of the regular programs are based on violence. Police dramas, for example, seem to include as much brutality as possible. This is in addition to the many movies full of crimes of all kinds. Television news also emphasizes violence. Disasters, accidents, and criminal acts are given prime coverage. Gruesome details are even reported live. Cartoons are another type of program in which too much of the action depends on violence, as characters are mutilated in different ways but somehow survive. Television producers should stop and consider how much violence they are showing to people.

4. Disadvantages to owning a car
  I. Expenses
    A. Price of car
    B. Insurance
    C. Maintenance
    D. Gas

  II. Need to taxi others
    A. Interrupts
    B. Takes time
    C. Takes money
    D. Some people take advantage of car owner
  III. Liabilities
    A. Legal ones
    B. Accidents

  When you have finished the exercise, check to see what you remembered from each of the four exercises:

    How much of the content of each one did you remember?
    Did you write what you remembered in the order in which it occurred in the original item?
    If it was not in the same order, was it at least in some logical order?
    Did you add any information that was not in what you read?

_____

    Most people can best reconstruct item 4, and they have the most difficulty with item 2. Results may vary, depending on the reader's previous knowledge of each topic.

You probably found the outline in item 4 easier to work with than the outline in item 1. This is because item 4 is coherent, focusing on *what* the disadvantages to owning a car are. In contrast, the outline in item 1 does not have a direction, and the various ideas concerning hobbies are not arranged logically. Similarly, the paragraph in item 3 was easier to work with than the one in item 2 because it is coherent, whereas item 2 is a freewritten collection of thoughts on "diet."

Although items 3 and 4 are both logically coherent, most people can reconstruct more of the outline than of the paragraph. This is because both the visual presentation of the outline and the use of words and phrases rather than sentences make the ideas in an outline easier to grasp.

This exercise illustrates some important principles in writing. First, ideas are generally easier to work with when they are in outline form. Second, material that is coherently organized communicates meaning more effectively. For these reasons, when you write, it is usually best to begin by listing your thoughts so that you can organize them in outline form before attempting to write a draft.

Effective outlining requires a great deal of critical thinking because it involves putting ideas together according to their logical relationships. Because a carefully constructed outline clarifies relationships between ideas, a draft can be written much more easily from a good outline.

Different lettering and numbering systems have been devised for outlining. The system of Roman numerals, capital letters, Arabic numerals, and lowercase letters used for the outlines in this text is the most common and, for that reason, the most universally understood outline form. It breaks down as follows:

(Heading)

I.

   A.

      1.

         a.

II.

and so forth

The positioning of the information on the page is particularly important—much more so than the lettering and numbering system used. The indentations should be done accurately to ensure that the relationships between ideas are correctly represented. This principle of visual presentation underlies the strategy most college students use when they take notes in class. They carefully indent the material, forming an outline in order to fit information together logically, but they generally omit the letters and numbers.

Whatever is placed below and to the right of an item in an outline gives further information about what is above and to the left of it. For this reason, material closer to the left-hand margin in an outline is usually both more general and more important. However, there are exceptions to this principle. Consider the following partial outline:

    I. Effects of European exploitation of islands in Indian Ocean

       A. Dodo bird became extinct

           1. Importance of protecting species not known until twentieth century

Here the more general observation at 1 explains the more specific fact at A.

When we prewrite, we normally use Roman numerals to precede our key supporting ideas, or we at least align these ideas carefully along the left-hand margin of the paper. The key supporting ideas provide the main support for the controlling idea, and they need to be logically comparable. Similarly, any set of ideas indicated with capital letters should consist of comparable items—that is, items that fit together logically. The same is true for any set of ideas with Arabic numerals or lower-case letters. This means, in other words, that any set of items aligned vertically should be comparable.

For additional examples of outlines, see the outline for sample paragraph 1 and both outlines for sample paragraph 3 of Chapter 1 in the answer key.

Formal outlines are those in which each item is expressed in a complete sentence. These are appropriate if completeness is necessary in the outline itself. When we prewrite, we do not usually need to produce a formal outline. What is important is to put together a highly functional and solidly logical structure of ideas before we begin a draft.

In formal outlining, there is traditionally no A without B, no 1 without 2, and no a without b. In outlines that you prepare as you prewrite a paragraph or essay, however, you may find it desirable to use a single subpoint for an example, definition, or further explanation.

Consider the following outline. Does it present an effective plan for a composition?

Substance abuse

  I. Effects

     A. Damages person physically

        1. Brain

        2. Liver

        3. Immune system

     B. Damages person socially

        1. Difficult relationships

           a. With family

           b. With friends

        2. Difficult to keep job

When we prewrite, we place our topic and controlling idea in the heading and our key supporting ideas at the Roman numerals. The outline above is not an effective plan for two reasons. First, no controlling idea is indicated; there is only the potential topic, "substance abuse." Second, all of the information explains "effects" of substance abuse. To transform this into a usable outline, we can change the topic to "effects of substance abuse" and add a controlling idea—for example, "are negative."

When you prewrite, make certain that your outlines contain a controlling idea and that the rest of your information supports that controlling idea.

E X E R C I S E

4-3

Outline the following paragraphs and the classification essay from Chapter 3.

1. The person just learning to drive a car has several difficult tasks to master. First, the driver must learn to control the car. This means finding the correct pedal without looking, stepping neither too hard nor too lightly on the pedal, and steering down the road, all at the same time. In addition, the new motorist has to keep track of the situation on the road. This includes monitoring everything involved in normal driving conditions, as well as watching for any potential emergency situation. Finally, the learner must get used to following the rules of the road. This means learning the many pages of signs in the handbook, all of which somehow look a little different to the novice who is driving down the road for the first time, and mastering the established conventions for changing lanes, turning, and stopping. It is no wonder that some people give up on learning to drive before they ever get behind the wheel of a car.

2. Teachers have different ways of conducting class. Traditional teachers use the class time to lecture to the students. They believe that they have the information the students need to learn and that students should listen and take notes in order to memorize as much of the information as possible. As these instructors equate learning primarily with rote memorizing, they measure students' progress by how much information the students can reproduce on tests. Other teachers use most of the class time for group discussions. They suggest ideas for groups to consider; and then, from time to time, they recapitulate and synthesize the information thus gathered. These teachers, who usually favor a student-oriented class, provide only a limited amount of information themselves and generally do relatively little testing to assess student learning. A final category includes teachers who structure class time so that the students will arrive at an understanding of certain concepts. Rather than lecture to the students, they guide them, through suitable materials and appropriate questions, to an understanding of the course content. They then test their students' active comprehension of the course concepts. As different as these types of classroom management are, they are all common in our schools today.

3. Several factors have contributed to outbreaks of hostilities in Yugoslavia in recent years. The country, first of all, is composed of several ethnic groups. These groups are culturally diverse, with the Eastern-oriented Serbs using the Russian alphabet and the Western-oriented Croats writing in the Western alphabet. Another sizable part of the population is Moslem. Historical differences have also caused violence between the various groups. Different parts of Yugoslavia have belonged to a number of foreign powers over the past few centuries, so there is little feeling of loyalty toward a single country, but rather a tendency toward separatism. Thus, when the Nazis invaded the area during World War II, the different peoples of Yugoslavia fought against one another instead of joining forces to resist the invaders. Finally, the conflict in Yugoslavia has been aggravated by recent historical events. The breakup of the Soviet Union and the drive for self-determination on the part of countries in other areas of the world have served as reminders to the people of Yugoslavia that political autonomy can become a reality. The conflict in Yugoslavia is a tragedy. The various peoples there need to resolve their differences somehow and take their place in our new interdependent world.

4. Classification essay (Chapter 3, page 51)

Summarizing

EXERCISE

Summarize the following article in one sentence.

The *Star Wars* film trilogy came out during the late 1970s and early 1980s. The three movies present different episodes in a space fantasy. The various characters include normal-looking people, such as Luke Skywalker, Princess Leia, Captain Han Solo, and Lando Calrissian. But important parts in the story are played by two-legged creatures from other worlds, such as Yoda and Chewbacca, other creatures in varying shapes, such as Jabba the Hut, and different robots, especially C3PO and R2D2. Many of these various creatures come together in the famous cantina scene in the first film. The episodes in the three movies take place in different imaginary locations in space. Viewers travel to the Dagobah planet, the moon of Endor, and the Death Star, an artificial satellite. The characters move from place to place at warp speed. The story contains some of the traditional themes of Earth literature: love, good versus evil, and the struggle for power.

After you have formulated your one-sentence summary, consider the following questions.

1. Is it important to name the characters in the summary?

2. Should the cantina scene be part of a short summary?

3. Do the different space locations need to be named?

4. Does it make any substantial difference whether the artificial satellite is called the "Death Star" or something else?

5. What are the really key ideas in the article (the ones that need to be included in a very brief summary)?

In answer to the first question, the names of the characters should not appear in a very short summary because what they are actually named does not make an essential difference.* The characters could have had other names and still represented the same beings. Similarly, the names of the space locations (question 3) and the name "Death Star" (question 4) are relatively minor details that should not be included in a brief summary. Regarding question 2, the fact that many of these extremely different creatures appear in the cantina is interesting rather than essential and therefore should not be included.

Going back over the reading, we can pick out the following main ideas:

Star Wars
film trilogy
space fantasy
characters—people, various other creatures, robots
various imaginary locations
traditional literary themes

These ideas can then be combined into a sentence:

The film trilogy *Star Wars* is a fantasy based on traditional literary themes, with people, a variety of nonhuman creatures, and robots acting out scenes set in various imaginary worlds.

---

*Some of the names of the characters in the trilogy are significant. For example, "Luke" comes from the Latin word for "light," and the concept of light is frequently associated with "good," the opposite of "dark" ("Darth" Vadar), indicating "evil." However, these considerations go beyond the scope of a brief summary.

As you can see from the preceding exercise, summary writing involves selecting the most important information so that the summary gives an accurate picture of the original writing. The one-sentence summary of the article about *Star Wars* would give a person who had not read the original article a good idea of what was in it.

A summary is intended to be a shorter version of a piece of writing. The summary must therefore report the most important ideas contained in the original. As a result, with the focus on essentials in summary writing, we generally leave out examples, definitions, and any explanations that are not absolutely essential to the basic meaning of the passage. And since a summary is a brief version of someone's writing, we report only ideas that are in that writing. Therefore, we carefully avoid bringing in our own ideas, opinions, and interpretations of the material. A summary should accurately reflect the author's ideas, regardless of whether we agree with those ideas.

Writing a summary does not mean copying key sentences from the original. Your summaries should be written in your own words. It is easier to avoid plagiarizing if you copy only key words and phrases from the original text and then write up your summary from the information you have gathered. Notice that this strategy was used to prepare the one-sentence summary of the article on *Star Wars*.

EXERCISE

4-5

Prepare a one-sentence summary of the first paragraph in Exercise 4-3.

Read the sample essay in Chapter 1, page 9, on the subject of "parenting." Which of the important ideas in that essay would you include in a one-sentence summary? What would you include in a summary of 100 to 125 words? After you have decided what each summary should contain, consider the following versions.

> Traditional parents who focus on themselves rather than on their children raise young people who do not develop a positive self-image, do not learn to communicate with themselves and others, and do not learn to trust anyone.

This sentence is based on the main ideas in the reading: topic, controlling idea, and key supporting ideas.

Traditional parents who focus on themselves rather than on their children raise young people who are not well prepared to deal with themselves or the world around them. These children develop a poor self-image because of the lack of positive reinforcement. Thus, they become either perfectionists or negative attention seekers. They do not learn to communicate what they really think or feel. Their negative opinions and feelings during childhood bring negative feedback, forcing them to deny rather than to express their own reality. This lack of openness also teaches them not to trust others. Consequently, they find it difficult to develop a positive relationship with another person. In this way, traditional parents who are self-centered actually bring children up to be victims.

This paragraph-length summary of the essay contains the topic and the controlling idea, formulated as the topic sentence of the summary. It also includes the key supporting ideas, which in this case indicate what the problems of parent-oriented child raising are. Then the major effects of those problems are reported.

The length of the summary depends on our purpose for writing it. One sentence gives an idea of what a reading is about, while the longer summary shows more of what the author actually discusses and reveals more of the author's position.

Compare carefully the following essay and summary.

The issue of whether we should have a gun control law has been debated extensively in the last few years. Opponents of gun control claim that private citizens at times need to be armed in order to defend themselves against a criminal who may be armed, since the police cannot always provide adequate protection. They also cite the Constitution, which guarantees the individual's right to bear arms. But the advocates of gun control have some particularly valid reasons for wanting to eliminate privately owned arms.

The cases of successful use of a gun by a private citizen are few if compared to the number of tragic accidents that have occurred as a result of guns being readily available. It is dangerous for people to keep guns when they are inexperienced in using them. In fact, most individuals who possess guns are neither trained properly in their use nor aware of the real legal implications of possessing a lethal weapon. Many law enforcement officers caution private citizens against attempting to defend themselves with a gun in an emergency situation.

The career criminal will probably always find a way of getting a gun. But most criminals, like law-abiding private citizens, would find it difficult to procure an arm if a realistic gun control law were passed and put into effect. Moreover, it would be far easier for the police to trace criminal activity and control it if possession of a firearm were illegal.

The freedom proclaimed in the Constitution should not be a principal issue in the matter. Certain freedoms, such as that of speech, should exist for all people at all times. But the need of private citizens to bear arms in this country 200 years ago, when the population was a small fraction of what it is now and when the forces of law and order were practically nonexistent, has no counterpart in the real needs of today's citizens.

The issue has been greatly distorted by the National Rifle Association and the gun manufacturers' lobby. Clearly, cases can be found in which a person has benefited from having a personal firearm. But we still need to reduce drastically the number of firearms carried by people who are not involved in the defense of the public and carefully trained for the purpose.

Here is a summary of the preceding essay:

Gun control is a hot issue. Most people feel they should be able to carry arms in order to protect themselves. They also believe it is their constitutional right to do so. Others think guns should be controlled. There are too many tragic accidents because people have guns available but do not necessarily know how to use them. The career criminal would find a gun anyway. The constitutional issue is not the main one because times have changed. The National Rifle Association and the gun manufacturers' lobby have distorted the issue. People should not just be able to carry guns around freely.

Does this summary accurately reflect the purpose and the content of the original essay? Go over it carefully to form your own opinion.

The summary essentially makes the same statements as the original essay, but it is rather vague and misleading because it does not take into account the purpose of the essay—which is to show that there are reasons for gun control—and it does not show how the various statements relate to one another.

Notice, first of all, that this summary begins with what appears to be a topic sentence, based on the opening sentence of the essay. However, the opening sentence of this essay has the purpose of introducing the topic, "gun control," and the idea that "there are reasons" for gun control is not expressed until the last sentence of the introductory paragraph. Therefore, since the topic sentence of a summary should formulate both the topic and the controlling idea of the original text, this summary is misleading from the very beginning.

The next two sentences in the summary state the chief arguments against gun control. These occur in the introductory paragraph of the original essay. However, without the transitions to show that the writer is acknowledging the other side of the issue rather than presenting the arguments as plain statements of fact, these sentences are misleading as well. The topic and controlling idea, "guns/should be controlled," are included in the following sentence of the summary, but they are not identifiable as the topic and controlling idea of the essay. Consequently, the focus of the original essay is not clarified in the summary.

The next three sentences in the summary reflect the ideas in the first sentence of each body paragraph of the essay. However, the writer of the summary has mistakenly assumed that body paragraphs in an essay always start with a topic sentence. One body paragraph begins not with the topic sentence but with an admission that the criminal will probably still find a way to get a gun (another argument on the opposite side), followed by the real point of the paragraph—that a realistic gun control law would make it more difficult for criminals to get guns. This latter idea, not the contradicting one, should have been included in the summary.

This summary, thus, is not effective because it does not give an accurate picture of the writer's arguments and supporting information.

Carefully examine the following outline, prepared for an essay. Are the ideas well structured to show their relationships and their relative importance? Could a good summary be structured from this outline?

Poverty predominates in some Latin American countries for a number of reasons.

I. Overpopulation
   A. Problem grows because based on traditions
      1. More children to provide more labor for farm or family business
      2. More children to help support elderly parents
      3. Attitude that extra mouth can always be fed
      4. Church influence
   B. Resources for individual limited
      1. Food

    2. Material goods

    3. Medical care

    4. Education

    5. Job opportunities

II. Corrupt government

    A. Dictators—own interests, not people's welfare

    B. Small wealthy class exploits large lower class

    C. Control society

        1. Legislation favors government

        2. Limited access to accurate information

            a. Media

            b. Schools

III. Exploitation by world powers

    A. Wealth exported

    B. Resources used for foreign benefit

    C. Large foreign corporations keep wages low

        1. Eliminate competition

        2. Control labor organization

    D. Unfavorable trade policies

IV. Only greater awareness of these problems will help bring a solution to the poverty cycle.

The information in the outline is well focused and structured. Consequently, the outline provides a good basis for a summary, such as the following one:

Several factors contribute to the poverty prevalent in some Latin American countries. Many people there are poor as a result, first of all, of overpopulation. Some traditions still strong in Latin America are conducive to a high birth rate. In addition to religious beliefs and the common idea that there will always be food on the table for an extra mouth, people continue to feel that many children can provide more help in the fields or family business as well as more support later for elderly parents. Overpopulation contributes to the poverty problem by limiting the individual's access to resources. These include not only food, material goods, and medical care, but also schooling and work opportunities. A second factor causing poverty in Latin America is governmental corruption. Many countries are run by dictators who act according to their own interests rather than the interests of the people. In addition, a small, wealthy class generally exploits the rest of the population. The few control the many by passing legislation in their own favor and by limiting the people's access to the truth both in the media and in educational institutions. Finally, poverty in Latin American countries is also the result of exploitation by various world powers. Much of the countries' wealth is exported, and their resources are carelessly used. Large foreign companies manage to keep the wage scale low by eliminating competition and by controlling any labor organizations. Trade policies that are unfavorable to the Latin American countries are often established, resulting in further impoverishment. Only a heightened awareness of the factors that contribute to the cycle of poverty will bring a change for the better.

Notice that the items in the outline need not appear in the summary in exactly the same order. Notice, too, that the ideas in the outline are reported carefully but the wording is not copied.

The next outline is followed by a summary based on it. Is the summary effective?

We should be making more use of solar energy.

I. Unlimited resource
   A. Can create electricity and replace gas
   B. Inexhaustible because it is not from earth
   C. No one controls or owns it
II. Environmentally efficient
   A. Not a pollutant
   B. No waste problem
III. Better alternative

Solar energy should be put to greater use. There is no limit to it. It can take the place of gas and electricity. It cannot be used up, because it comes from outer space. It does not belong to anyone. It has advantages for the environment. This form of energy does not cause pollution. There is no disposal problem. Solar energy is a better choice.

How much would you understand from the above summary if you had not seen the outline of the ideas?

The rewording has been done carefully to avoid any problems with plagiarism; but the summary does not communicate the information well because it lacks coherence. In other words, a reader cannot easily tell how all of the information fits together. The sentences are written as separate statements, without transitions to show how the ideas relate. The following version has these much-needed connections. Compare it with the first summary.

Solar energy should be put to greater use. In the first place, the energy from the sun is unlimited. This gives it an advantage over gas and electricity. It cannot be depleted because it comes from space; and we will always have it, furthermore, because it cannot belong to anyone. A second major reason for using solar rather than earth energy is that it does not harm the environment. This form of energy does not cause environmental pollution, nor does it present any waste disposal problems. Clearly, solar energy offers us a better choice.

Whenever you need to prepare a summary from a text, it is wise to pick out the information you need in the form of words and phrases. Then you can structure the ideas, thereby preparing an outline. This method also makes it easier to add, as you write, the necessary connections for a coherent summary.

EXERCISE

Prepare two summaries from the following outline: a short version in one sentence, and a long version containing all the information in the outline.

A proper diet is important for our health.

I. Body needs right foods
- A. Good ones for nutrition
    1. Complex carbohydrates
    2. Proteins
    3. Fiber
    4. Vitamins and minerals
- B. Wrong ones cause health problems
    1. Fat
        a. Overweight
        b. High cholesterol
        c. Cancer
    2. Sugar
        a. Overweight
    3. Salt
        a. High blood pressure

II. Additives harmful
- A. Those used to produce food
    1. Pesticides and herbicides
    2. Growth hormones
- B. Those used to treat and conserve food
    1. Preservatives
    2. Emulsifiers
    3. Coloring

EXERCISE

Write a summary of approximately 150 words of the cause essay in Chapter 3, on page 53.

EXERCISE

Write a summary of approximately 150 words of the argument essay in Chapter 3, on page 59.

Interpreting Meaning: Facts, Opinions, Reasoned Judgments

Do you believe that the following assertions are true?

1. There will be daylight outside at noon tomorrow.
2. Joe, who has A's on all of the quizzes so far, is in a position to do very well on the next quiz.
3. Carter was a better president than Reagan.
4. The *Mayflower* made numerous trips across the Atlantic Ocean.
5. There will be more riots in our large cities during the next few years.
6. The death penalty should be in force in every state.

For those statements in this list that you consider to be true, try to identify your reasons for believing them.

The first assertion is one that nearly everyone would readily agree with because what it states seems obvious. Even during a heavy storm or an eclipse of the sun, there is some daylight during the middle of the day.

The fourth assertion is also easy to accept as true. Various records indicate that the *Mayflower* brought the Pilgrims to what was later called Massachusetts and that the ship was afterward used to bring African slaves across the ocean.

These two assertions are statements of fact—in other words, statements of ideas that are indisputably true. A fact can be something obvious. For example, if the person sitting behind you says, "I am sitting behind you," this person is stating an obvious fact. Unquestionable evidence, such as thoroughly confirmed scientific or historical data, can also be the basis for a statement of fact.

The third assertion represents someone's opinion. There are several possible bases for this opinion. One basis might be a preference for a Democrat; another might be a simple preference for Carter as a person. An additional problem with this assertion is the choice of the word *better*. This term is vague and subjective: different things are better for different people. Even a detailed analysis of the country's situation under each president would not settle disputes over this statement of opinion because people do not easily agree on just what is good for the country.

The sixth assertion also expresses an opinion that is highly debatable rather than inherently convincing. Even people who favor the death penalty hotly dispute who should be put to death. Moreover, different individuals favor the death penalty for varying reasons. Some base their belief on the idea of "an eye for an eye"—a concept that is usually associated with religion. Some believe that capital punishment deters crime. Some argue that only with the death penalty does society get dangerous criminals off the streets permanently. Those who oppose the death penalty sometimes base their belief on a moral objection to taking anyone's life. Others believe that capital punishment encourages crime because it sends the message to the public that it is all right to take a life. Some believe, as part of their religion, that only God can take a life. Furthermore, many persons on both sides of the issue believe as they do primarily because a relative, friend, or other influential person voices a particular opinion. Finding objective, convincing support for the sixth assertion would be an extremely difficult task.

The second assertion involves a probability rather than an actual fact. Past successes tend to be fairly sound indicators of future successes. Furthermore, if the next quiz involves material and concepts covered on previous quizzes, Joe should be in a position to do well. However, we cannot simply accept the statement as unquestionably true. The quiz might cover something in which Joe is very weak.

Or he might not be prepared for the quiz—or even take it—for a variety of reasons. Our expectation that Joe is in a position to do well is an example of a reasoned judgment. But we cannot definitely state that he is in a position to do well.

The fifth assertion is similar. We can reasonably expect riots in certain cities because of serious problems not yet solved. But we cannot logically make a definite statement that there will be riots.

Beliefs or conclusions based on reasoned reflection from different perspectives, or points of view, are called reasoned judgments.

Are facts, opinions, and reasoned judgments all appropriate in college writing?

EXERCISE

To get a clearer answer to the above question, work through the next exercise. Decide whether each item in the exercise is a statement of fact, an opinion, or a reasoned judgment. Consider how you could support each item. Which ones could you support well enough to make them convincing to a reader?

1. Women who have an abortion deserve to be imprisoned.
2. The "force" in *Star Wars* is a supernatural power.
3. The "force" in *Star Wars* indicates the existence of God.
4. The Golden Gate Bridge crosses into San Francisco.
5. The French Revolution was inevitable.
6. Our political leaders in this country truly believe in democracy.
7. Americans generally believe in equality.
8. Many surgical techniques have been improved through the use of the laser.
9. Most telephones ring.
10. If someone shouts "Bomb!" and everyone starts running away, it is better to run away.
11. Hank Aaron broke the major league home run record.
12. Some races show more intelligence than others.

You could easily convince a reader of some of the above assertions. Others are too difficult to support for them to be usable as they are in college writing.

The statements of fact are easy to support. Geography books, tourist guides, and almanacs (just to mention printed material) all indicate that the Golden Gate Bridge runs between San Francisco and a county to the north. Almanacs and various sports publications, for example, show Hank Aaron's home run feats. We know from personal experience that telephones ring; most people would expect all telephones to ring unless it occurred to them that there is special equipment for some users with special needs. Although perhaps less obvious, support for item 8 is also available. Medical publications and surgeons on television programs, for example, document the advantages of using lasers in many kinds of surgery. They describe how lasers make many types of operations less invasive and cause much less bleeding, thus reducing the need for transfusions and permitting a much faster recovery time. Both medical sources and the personal experience of a large (and growing) number of people indicate that lasers enable doctors to perform new types of surgery that allow organs that formerly had to be removed or drastically altered to be returned to their normal state. Thus, it would be easy to convince readers that the use of the laser has improved many surgical techniques.

Items 4, 8, 9, and 11 could therefore be used to provide convincing support for an assertion.

Statements of opinion are of very limited use in college writing because they are very difficult to substantiate. A writer is unlikely to convince a reader who is not already of that same opinion simply by making a bold assertion of opinion. For example, to persuade readers that women who have an abortion should be put in prison, a writer would not only have to present a compelling argument establishing that abortion is a crime but would also have to demonstrate that it is a crime for which imprisonment is appropriate. Similarly, it would be extremely difficult to substantiate the idea that the "force" in *Star Wars* indicates the existence of God. Ascribing powers for which we have no scientific explanation to God is a matter of personal opinion, not a self-evident fact. The sixth statement would also be hard to support satisfactorily. It may be that many of our leaders' actions show their belief in democracy, but other actions do not. Moreover, not everyone agrees about just what constitutes democracy. The last assertion contains a term, *intelligence*, that has different meanings for different people. Whatever the interpretation of intelligence might be, the statement that some races show more intelligence than others would be very difficult to substantiate because scientific evidence seems to indicate the contrary.

One's individual opinions alone do not provide convincing support for a statement. When you write, avoid assuming that something is true just because you believe it. Look for independent evidence to substantiate your opinion. If you do not find objectively convincing explanations, reconsider your statement.

Compare the second and third statements. The idea that the "force" is a supernatural power is much easier to support. In the *Star Wars* trilogy, we see superhuman feats of strength, such as the raising of Luke's fighter plane from the swamp, attributed to the "force." This instance of telekinesis and other manifestations credited to the "force" go beyond the laws of nature as we know them. Analyzing specific examples of the "force" as it is presented in the films, we can make a good case for calling it a supernatural power.

In the second statement, we are dealing not with a cold and hard fact but rather with a reasoned judgment—a conclusion drawn on the basis of careful reasoning. Reasoned judgments can be appropriate in college writing when the reasoning behind them is made clear and when different possible perspectives on the matter are considered.

The fifth statement—that the French Revolution was inevitable—also represents a reasoned judgment. The political, economic, and social situation in France just before hostilities broke out made war difficult to avoid. An explanation of the prewar situation would make the statement credible.

The seventh statement does not assert that all Americans believe unreservedly in equality. Clearly, many do not. But much evidence could be offered in support of the idea that they generally believe in it. Evidence of a basic belief in equality includes the large number of laws and regulations on the books, such as those on equal employment opportunities and fair housing. Although these laws are often violated, their very existence shows that our society as a whole feels that equality is fundamental to a just society. Another fundamental belief based on equality is the idea that all people, not just certain ones, should have an education. In addition, those who do not personally believe in equality usually conceal their opinion on this point when talking to strangers because they feel that their views may expose them to disapproval and condemnation. Thus, statement 7 is a reasoned judgment.

The tenth item is also a reasoned judgment. Unless one has a good reason to do otherwise, it is a sound strategy to get as far away as possible from what may be a bomb.

Much college writing is based on reasoned judgments, supported by factual information and carefully considered reasoned judgments.

In your college writing assignments, avoid attempting to convince readers on the basis of nonfactual information that you have not deeply questioned and that you have not gathered sound evidence to support. Such information includes a great many of the beliefs and values that most of us are exposed to as children. These are sometimes based on faith (such as many religious beliefs) or on traditions (such as many of the values concerning people and how they live). Stereotyping is also logically weak because even though we have personally experienced many instances that seem to fit a pattern, we should not assume that a generalized statement based on that apparent pattern is valid.

E X E R C I S E

4-10

What might be the basis (underlying assumption) for each of the following statements?

1. You are supposed to eat the head of a fish.
2. You do not eat lemon and milk at the same meal (or two other foods together).
3. People should know their place and stay there.
4. Men should make more money than women because they are the breadwinners.
5. British English is really standard English.
6. The conservatives are trying to sell this country out to the rich.
7. Teachers are smart.
8. Abortion is wrong because it goes against God's laws.

An attempt to support an assertion like statement 8 is almost certainly doomed to failure. However, the idea is usable in other ways. For example, you could write about this as one of the reasons commonly given against abortion. Other possible angles to consider on the topic of abortion are those based on the reality of abortion, such as reasons people resort to it, statistics on back-alley abortions, methods of performing illegal abortions, psychological trauma associated with abortion and the alternatives, and so forth.

If you find that you are trying to develop an opinion that cannot really be substantiated, before you change your topic, you might want to consider another approach to the same topic.

Do you agree with the following statements? What is the basis for each?

1. Cupboards over kitchen counters are too high.
2. People work better when they are under pressure.
3. Writing a research paper is easy.

Your reaction to these statements may have been that it all depends. Actually, whether you agree or not depends on your point of view. If you are short, you are likely to agree with the first statement. If you work well under pressure, you may not be aware that many other people perform poorly under pressure. If you have enough successful experience writing research papers, you are likely to agree with the third statement. But people who have a different perspective may not agree with these statements.

When you write, you should be aware of your readers' divergent points of view, or frames of reference, and you should support your statements as objectively as possible. This does not mean that you have to make everybody happy with everything you say; that would not be possible. But if you try to substantiate your assertions with information that most people can relate to, your writing will be much more likely to convince your readers.

Most of your college assignments should be addressed to a college audience. At times, however, you may have a different audience for what you are writing. Whenever you write, you should give thought to your audience and the different points of view the individual readers may have.

E X E R C I S E

Imagine that you are trying to gather support from the members of your community for the construction of a shopping mall. Match each of the following specific appeals with the appropriate audience.

1. The proposed mall will bring the convenience of one-stop shopping to our community.

2. The proposed mall will bring many employment opportunities to our community.

3. The proposed mall will increase the value of commercial and residential properties in the area.

4. The proposed mall will have a movie complex and a large arcade.

5. The proposed mall will bring new customers to local businesses.

A. Local developers
B. Teenagers
C. Local college students
D. Working parents
E. Local restaurant owners

Creating Meaning

E X E R C I S E

Are the following statements convincing?

1. In 1992, most of Los Angeles was destroyed in one day of rioting.

2. Proper veterinary care helps eliminate pets that carry diseases.

3. Territory is often the cause of war.

4. The worst problem is the children who breathe second-hand smoke.

5. People who have positive minds are not affected by violence on television.

6. Fast foods are not as healthful as home-cooked meals.

7. Organized shoppers always bring a list to the store.

8. A used car costs around $3,000 or $4,000.

9. We can educate our children to be either open-minded or old-fashioned.
10. He may need surgery or a bypass.
11. A man who has two dependents and a house payment cannot manage on a minimum-wage job.
12. The lack of human compassion is at an all-time low.

All of these statements are illogical and therefore unconvincing.

Most of Los Angeles obviously was not destroyed in the 1992 riots. Even though there was extensive damage, most of the city did not suffer damage. This statement is an exaggeration.

The second assertion is also erroneous. Proper veterinary care is not supposed to eliminate pets, but rather their diseases. The statement should be worded accordingly:

Proper veterinary care helps eliminate the diseases that pets carry.

In the third, we have the statement that "territory is the cause" of war. But the territory itself does not cause war; rather, disputes over territory bring about conflict in some cases:

A dispute over territory is often the cause of war.

The problem in the fourth sentence is similar. The problem is not the children, but the fact that they breathe the smoke:

The worst problem is that children breathe the second-hand smoke.

The fifth statement is an inaccurate generalization. Many people with positive minds are still affected a great deal by the violence on television. The problem in item 6 is similar. Many home-cooked foods are unhealthful. Some much more specific statement needs to be made in both cases.

Organized shoppers, in the next assertion, always bring a list. In reality, they may not always do anything. Nor do used cars generally cost around $3,000 or $4,000, as the next sentence states; their prices actually vary tremendously.

The writer of statement 9 offers only two alternatives for raising children. Apart from the ambiguity of the terms, there are also other ways of raising children.

Statement 10 is faulty because *or* connects *surgery* and *bypass*, but the latter is a type of surgery, not an alternative to it.

The eleventh statement is inappropriate because the underlying assumption is that a woman does not have the same problem. The word *person* should be substituted for *man*.

The last assertion also uses faulty logic: the *lack* of something cannot be at an all-time *low*.

A statement must make sense. This implies that the words we put together as a sentence must fit together logically. You can follow several specific strategies to test the logic of your sentences.

First, whatever statement a verb makes about a subject must be logical.

E X E R C I S E

Find the logic problem in each of the following statements.

1. Looking more carefully at student loan requests will net millions of dollars for the state.
2. Some jobs are hiring students even before they get their degrees.
3. Television tries to emphasize the sensational side of events.
4. The warranty will fix the problem at no cost.
5. Any vehicle found without proper smog-control equipment should be fined.

Predicate nominatives and predicate adjectives must logically rename or modify the subject of the sentence.

E X E R C I S E

Find the faulty predication in the following sentences.

1. A family is a good reason to get an education.
2. The reason he chose that particular school is his major.
3. Fellow workers are another consideration when an employee is evaluating job satisfaction.
4. Bad grades are one of the conflicts in a student's reality.
5. Working on an assembly line is hard work.

Grammatically parallel ideas must also be logically parallel.

E X E R C I S E

Find the illogical parallels in the following sentences.

1. On adventure shows, children see murder and mischief.
2. College becomes more important and populated every year.
3. Toxic waste dumped into lakes kills fish and makes them sick.
4. The drug business has become very profitable and violent.
5. Many young people today have minimum-wage jobs, live on their own, and have children.

Parallel items are not logical if one includes another, if they are presented in the wrong order, or if they are incompatible in other ways.

E X E R C I S E

Find the illogical parallels in the following sentences.

1. A puzzle can teach a child colors, shapes, and patience.
2. Working with adults can help a teenager build and acquire communication skills.
3. Drug abuse can lead to AIDS, murder, and friction in the family.

4. Concerned journalists and independent publications are revealing much inaccurate information that we are being led to accept as true.

5. The implications of media manipulation are frightening and destructive.

6. Recycling conserves resources and makes sense.

7. At the community college, one finds many cultures and personalities.

8. Some police dramas have too many drugs and shootings.

9. On television, vulgarity, idolization, imagination, and violence become reality.

10. Many people lost their relatives and property in the disaster.

11. At the community college, one meets people of all ages, sexes, and backgrounds.

12. The government should not allow such pesticides to be used and purchased.

13. Smog can kill and restrict the growth of plants.

14. Agricultural dumping of unhealthful and carcinogenic substances is harmful to both plants and animals.

15. Many composers of music neither hope nor aim at mass popularity.

Absolute statements and statements that are so general that they imply an absolute situation should be used with great caution. Many absolutes are modifiers.

E X E R C I S E

Find the problematic absolutes and inaccurate generalizations in the following sentences.

1. People in the United States have equal educational opportunities.

2. It is a good idea to get a college education because college graduates are never easily tricked into believing false claims.

3. When both parents work outside the home, there is no quality time for the children.

4. You can do anything you put your mind to.

5. Dogs come in all sizes.

Inappropriate specific information, such as numbers and examples, can undermine the credibility of assertions.

E X E R C I S E

Find the inappropriate specific information in the following statements.

1. One of the reasons carpooling is advantageous is that it can save a person as much as $500 a year.

2. People find time to enjoy the holidays, like everybody else.

3. A major problem for a person who goes to live in another country is the language, such as the pronunciation.

4. The owner of a vehicle must deal with expenses, such as traffic tickets.

5. Community colleges provide a variety of services, from small children, with computer camp, to senior citizens, with special workshops.

EXERCISE

Find the logic problems in the following sentences.

1. Good writing skills can lead to careers.
2. Having good writing skills can be a good way to get a point across.
3. Poems and short stories are examples of being a good writer.
4. The way most Americans formulate pictures of the world in which they live is through television.
5. Television is a place where fantasy becomes reality.
6. Paintball is a quick-thinking game.
7. An example of the advantages of an education is the place where professionals work.
8. The streets are jammed with violence.
9. Most people have reasons for job satisfaction that are advantageous to them personally.
10. The dropping of the atomic bomb on Japan shocked the world and Japan.

EXERCISE

Find the logic problems in the following sentences.

1. We are cutting down too many trees to build homes and cities.
2. The benefits of a college education include enhanced career opportunities, responsibilities, and a better life.
3. Being prepared for class helps one be more organized.
4. An education tends to have people look up to one.
5. The car we drive and the clothes we wear lead our children to do the same.
6. A person who sets goals and reaches them could become the vice president or president of a company.
7. The program deducts 80% of the inmate's wages for work performed outside the prison.
8. During the lifetime of our older senior citizens, our nation went from volunteers to defend the country to the military defense we know today.
9. These parents are usually wealthy and put their business interests before the children. [two problems!]
10. Television is not bad; people are.

Writing Assignments

EXERCISE

Write a composition on one or more of the following topics. As part of the process, work your way through the following steps:

- In addition to brainstorming your topic, discuss it with your classmates and with others outside the class setting so that you become familiar with a variety of perspectives on the topic.
- Focus and organize your thoughts carefully, and write a draft.
- Revise your draft, moving from general considerations (topic, controlling idea, key supporting ideas) to more specific ones (supporting explanations and transitions) to sentence-level concerns (word choices, grammar, spelling, and punctuation) before you turn your composition in for a grade.

1. Many people object to keeping animals in zoos and animal parks. Give the arguments against keeping animals in captivity, and explain them.

2. Give the arguments for keeping animals in zoos and animal parks, and explain them.

3. Some people would like to revoke the right to drive of senior citizens past a certain age. Give and explain their arguments.

4. Give and explain the arguments for not revoking older seniors' right to drive.

5. Give and explain the reasons why some judges have allowed children to gain legal separation from their parents.

E X E R C I S E

 Working alone or with your classmates, examine your previous and current writing for meanings expressed in individual sentences. Watch especially for:

> An unsupported opinion
>
> An inadequately supported reasoned judgment
>
> An illogical statement made by a verb about a subject
>
> Faulty predication (illogical use of a linking verb)
>
> An illogical parallel
>
> An inappropriate absolute or inaccurate generalization
>
> Inaccurate specific information

Make any necessary changes.

Summing Up

You have seen that writing involves working very carefully with ideas so that you communicate appropriate meanings.

Main ideas (topic, controlling idea, and key supporting ideas) show the writer's purpose and emphasis. Make a point of identifying these when you read, and emphasize these when you write.

Supporting details offer the necessary explanations.

Outlines give a visual presentation that, when effective, clarifies main ideas and supporting details, showing how ideas relate.

Summaries are condensed versions of an original composition. They should:

1. Give an accurate idea of the original writing
   a. Contain the most important ideas from the original
   b. Reflect the original writer's purpose and emphasis
   c. Contain only the original author's thoughts
2. Paraphrase the original wording
3. Show connections between ideas

Different kinds of statements:

1. *Facts:* assertions that can be demonstrated as true
2. *Opinions:* conclusions that are highly debatable
3. *Reasoned judgments:* beliefs or conclusions based on careful reasoning

College writing consists primarily of reasoned judgments, supported by facts and by additional carefully considered reasoned judgments.

Individual statements in writing need to be logically coherent.

Some common logic problems in sentences:

The verb does not make a logical statement about the subject.

The subject complement is illogical.

There is an illogical parallel.

There is an inaccurate absolute or generalization.

There is inappropriate detail.

In Chapter 5 you will learn how to signal the relationships between ideas through the use of appropriate transitions.

TRANSITIONS

What do you understand from each of the following groups of sentences?

1. People who want to lose weight often exercise. They usually do not actually lose weight unless they reduce their intake of fat.
2. The children in the group were anxious to visit Disneyland. They were eager to see Universal Studios.
3. The children in the local elementary school district are currently doing several projects on different kinds of pollution. They are learning important facts about the environment.

Your impression may well be that you understood very little. Each individual sentence in the preceding set of examples makes a clear statement. But when statements follow one another, how they relate also needs to be clear. In the first example, the important idea of a contrast is missing. Compare:

> People who want to lose weight often exercise. *However*, they usually do not actually lose unless they reduce their intake of fat.

In the second example, another idea is added to the statement in front of it. Compare:

> The children in the group were anxious to visit Disneyland. They were *also* eager to see Universal Studios.

In the third sample group, the important idea of a result has been omitted. Compare:

> The children in the local elementary school district are currently doing several projects on different kinds of pollution. *As a result*, they are learning important facts about the environment.

The Purpose: To Show Relationships Between Ideas

When we write, we need to show how our ideas relate to one another unless the connection is obvious. In this way, our readers can follow our meaning more easily. Furthermore, logically structured writing that includes effective **transitions**—words, phrases, and sentences that make logical connections between ideas—has the added advantage of seeming to flow well. In contrast, writing that lacks necessary transitions seems disconnected and choppy.

E X E R C I S E

Identify words or phrases that can be added to make the following groups of sentences meaningful.

1. Mary wanted to drive from California to New York. She could not get enough time off to make the trip.
2. She had carefully prepared everything for her presentation. She was psychologically ready.
3. Joe forgot to bring his glasses. He was not able to follow what was happening in the movie.
4. College students should give careful thought to the choice of a major before they enter college. They may lose years by not taking prerequisite courses right away.
5. Speakers of one Romance language may be able to understand a great deal of what is said in another Romance language. Spanish speakers understand much of what they hear in Italian.

Your readers should not have to labor over your writing as much as you had to labor over the preceding sentences in order to figure out the intended meaning.

Types of Transitions

CONTRAST

Signals: *but, however, nevertheless, yet, on the other hand, still, in contrast, on the contrary, otherwise, although, even though, even so.*

Which of the preceding transitions would you use to connect the ideas in the following pairs of sentences?

1. They were already up to their limit on several credit cards. They bought a new stereo.
2. We need to conserve resources. Many public buildings have rooms with temperatures in the 60s due to faulty air conditioning.
3. Joe had hoped to go out to a movie. It was snowing too hard.
4. They needed to buy a new couch. They did not have enough money.

In the first two examples, the idea that logically connects the statements is *in spite of.* Some of the contrast signals—*yet, nevertheless, even though,* and *even so*—express this idea accurately. The word *but* is not as precise a choice. Some signals, such as *otherwise* and *on the contrary,* do not fit at all because they express other contrasting ideas. Thus, the sentences in the first example can be connected as follows:

They were already up to their limit on several credit cards, yet they bought a new stereo.

They were already up to their limit on several credit cards; nevertheless, they bought a new stereo.

Even though they were already up to their limit on several credit cards, they bought a new stereo.

They were already up to their limit on several credit cards. Even so, they bought a new stereo.

Notice the formation of main and subordinate clauses and the punctuation with the different types of conjunctions—coordinating, adverbial, and subordinating. These are described in Table 5-1 (page 103) and in the examples that follow, as well as in the discussion of sentence boundaries in Chapter 12.

The two sentences in the second example can be connected in the same ways as those in the first example.

The third and fourth pairs of sentences show a different type of contrast—that of simple contrary circumstances. Consequently, the words we used to connect the first two pairs of sentences would sound wrong here. We might write the following versions:

Joe had hoped to go out to a movie, but it was snowing too hard.

Joe had hoped to go out to a movie; however, it was snowing too hard.

The sentences in the fourth example can be connected in the same ways as those in the third example.

ADDITION/SEQUENCE

Signals: *in addition, moreover, too, furthermore, besides, also, again, and, then, next, another, first, second, in the first place, finally, last, last of all, above all.*

EXERCISE

5-2

Experiment with using transitions from the preceding list to connect the following ideas logically. Take care to use proper punctuation.

1. The professor explained and illustrated the principle involved. She gave the students some practice exercises.

2. At the end of the year, she had to pay $280 more in federal income tax. She had to pay almost the same amount in state taxes.

3. More and more people are carpooling. They want to save money. They recognize the need to save fuel. They are concerned about the environment.

4. VCRs have changed people's entertainment habits. People can entertain themselves much more economically. They have a much wider choice of films than what is available in the theaters and on television. They can socialize while they watch films.

Addition signals clarify our meaning when we are adding another point. **Sequence signals** help our readers to follow us through a series of points or items that need to stand out as a set. Any series of factors, reasons, or examples is potentially easier to understand if the items in the set are linked by carefully chosen transitions.

CAUSE

Signals: *because, since, as, for.*

EFFECT/RESULT

Signals: *therefore, thus, so, consequently, as a result, then.*

EXERCISE

5-3

Try different ways of connecting the following ideas in order to show either cause or effect. Watch your punctuation.

1. The vacationers left town without a map. They got lost.

2. Joe was careless about following directions. He failed the exam.

3. The child was playing very roughly with the dog. The animal bit the child.

Notice that we may show either cause or effect, but not both. Do not write, for example, "Because something happened, consequently, something else happened."

ILLUSTRATION

Signals: *for example, for instance, such as.*

EXERCISE

5-4

Use transitions in the following pairs of sentences to clarify that one statement is an example of the other.

1. To the visitor, Southern California appears to be a model of multicultural diversity. Many signs are only in a language other than English.

2. People who are no longer young often feel critical of parents today. They complain that children in stores are no longer supervised by their parents.

3. Some astronauts returning to Earth have not touched down in water. Those who have flown in the shuttles have not landed in the ocean.

Notice that we do not use *such as* to start a new sentence:

Many disabled people, such as some of those in wheelchairs, lead surprisingly active lives.

Do not put a comma after *such as,* and do not use *as* to mean *such as. For example* and *for instance* can be used in this same way:

Many disabled people, for example, some of those in wheelchairs, lead surprisingly active lives.

But unlike *such as,* they can also be used to start a new sentence:

Tortellini can be prepared in different ways. For example, they can be cooked and served in a tasty chicken broth.

COMPARISON

Signals: *likewise, similarly, in the same way.*

EXERCISE

5-5

Reword the following sentences so that a comparison is made. Watch your punctuation.

1. Students are required to take physical science classes to develop their general educational background. They have to take social sciences.

2. Far from the stabilizing influence of the Pacific Ocean, the deserts of the Southwest have temperatures that often rise to extreme heights during the day. These temperatures drop dramatically at night.

RESTATEMENT

Signals: *in other words, that is.*

EXERCISE

5-6

For each of the following pairs of sentences, add a transition so that the second sentence is clearly a restatement of the first (or of part of the first). Watch your punctuation.

1. Writers need to explain their key supporting ideas. They need to provide examples, illustrations, and definitions.

2. Many people avoid giving beggars money because they are afraid it will be used for the wrong purposes. The beggar may use it to buy alcohol or drugs.

TIME

Signals: *next, then, during that time, meanwhile, before, after, as soon as,* and many others.

EXERCISE

5-7

Add a time signal to connect each of the following pairs of ideas. Watch your punctuation.

1. We prepared the food. They got the sleeping equipment together.

2. They learned of their grandfather's death. They immediately made arrangements to attend the funeral.

3. Sue toured the United Nations buildings. She took a leisurely stroll around Greenwich Village.

Notice the variety of constructions that are possible with some time signals:

Joe checked his answers before he turned his paper in.   [*Before* is a subordinating conjunction followed by a subordinate clause.]

Joe checked his answers before turning his paper in.   [*Before* is a preposition, with the gerund *turning* as its object.]

Joe turned in his paper. Before that, he checked his answers.   [*Before that* is an adverbial conjunction, followed by a main clause.]

SPACE

Signals: *near, nearby, farther on, above, to the right, elsewhere,* and many others.

EXERCISE

5-8

Add a space signal to connect each of the following pairs of ideas. Watch your punctuation.

1. The new airport had every modern convenience. There was a heliport with direct flights to several city buildings.

2. The cliff dwelling was built in the depression in the rock. The cliff dropped off sharply.

EXERCISE

5-9

Add transitions to connect the following pairs of statements. Watch your punctuation.

1. Prisons are supposed to be places where criminals are rehabilitated. There is a great deal of criminal activity taking place inside them.

2. In Paris, the tourists saw the Eiffel Tower, the Arc de Triomphe, and Montmartre. They visited several museums.

3. People are finding it difficult to buy homes. They cannot qualify for loans.

4. Mary wanted her child to learn the responsibilities involved when one has an animal. She bought her a dog.

5. Many people want to get into the field of computers. They may not have the necessary math skills.

6. Some inconsiderate shoppers leave their carts next to display bins. It is difficult for other shoppers to get by.

7. Some supermarkets have lowered their prices on certain staples. One chain has cut the price of a pound of butter to $1.30.

8. We need to teach children to conserve. We must show them how to preserve the world they will inherit.

9. Sirens occasionally wake them. Nothing else disturbs their sleep.

10. The students in her class listen carefully. They learn a lot.

Punctuation with Transitional Words and Phrases

COORDINATING CONJUNCTIONS

Use a comma, a semicolon, or a period before a coordinating conjunction that begins a new main clause:

> She was unable to read music, *yet* she knew how to play several instruments.
>
> She was unable to read music; *yet* she knew how to play several instruments.
>
> She was unable to read music. *Yet* she knew how to play several instruments.

ADVERBIAL CONJUNCTIONS

Use a semicolon or a period before an adverbial conjunction that begins a new main clause:

> She was not able to read music at all; *however*, she knew how to play several instruments.
>
> She was not able to read music at all. *However*, she knew how to play several instruments.

A comma usually follows an adverbial conjunction.

SUBORDINATING CONJUNCTIONS

For ideas joined by a subordinating conjunction, keep both ideas in one sentence. Use a comma after a subordinate clause that comes before the main clause:

> Even though she was not able to read music at all, she knew how to play several instruments.

TABLE 5-1 *Transitional Words and Phrases*

TYPE OF TRANSITION	COORDINATING CONJUNCTIONS	ADVERBIAL CONJUNCTIONS	SUBORDINATING CONJUNCTIONS	OTHER FORMS
contrast	but yet	however nevertheless on the other hand still in contrast on the contrary otherwise even so	although even though whereas	in spite of
addition	and	in addition moreover too furthermore besides also again		in addition to besides another
sequence *all* addition, *plus:*		then next first second in the first place finally last last of all above all		
cause	for		because since as	because of due to
effect, result	so	therefore thus consequently as a result then		
illustration		for example for instance		such as
comparison		likewise similarly		like
restatement		in other words that is		

time		meanwhile
		*and many
		  others*
			while
			*and many
			  others*	

space				above *and many others*
alternative	or			
additional negation	nor			
condition			if whether unless	
purpose			so that	to in order to

If the main clause is placed first, use a comma after it only if the subordinate clause contains nonessential information:

> She knew how to play several instruments even though she was not able to read music at all.   [essential information]
>
> He knew how to play every single wind instrument, although he regularly played the clarinet in the local symphony.   [nonessential information]

OTHER FORMS

> Pronoun/adjective: *another*
> Part of infinitive showing purpose: *to, in order to*
> Prepositions and phrasal prepositions: all others

Other Transitional Devices

See if you can discover the technique that helps the following paragraph flow so coherently.

Dieters may at times seem ready to try almost anything to lose weight. However, certain strategies seem especially helpful to weight watchers. Most people who want to lose pounds get good results by carefully controlling their intake of calories and of fat. Also, many people on a diet have discovered that they can literally walk pounds off. Finally, those trying to lose weight get better results when they accept the fact that they are going to have to change their habits and regulate their lives accordingly.

If you did not find the four synonyms for *dieters,* go back through the paragraph and locate them. Then compare the same paragraph with the word *dieters* used in all five places:

Dieters may at times seem ready to try almost anything to lose weight. However, certain strategies seem especially helpful to dieters. Most dieters get good results by carefully controlling their intake of calories and of fat. Also, many dieters have discovered that they can literally walk pounds off. Finally, dieters get better results when they accept the fact that they are going to have to change their habits and regulate their lives accordingly.

SYNONYMS

The preceding example shows the value of synonyms in writing. With careful use of synonyms, we can avoid much annoying—and needless—repetition.

Synonyms are not words of absolutely equal value. Probably no two words in English are always interchangeable. Each word has associations that may make it uniquely appropriate in certain contexts. In the discovery exercise, all of the synonyms can have the meaning of "people who are trying to lose weight." But notice that the word *dieters* has other meanings besides this one. A dieter may be trying to gain or maintain weight. The individual may be controlling food intake for medical reasons, athletic objectives, or various cosmetic purposes, such as to improve the appearance of the skin. Similarly, the term *weight watchers* has its own set of meanings, including the idea of a person who is trying to lose weight.

In addition to using single-word synonyms, we can substitute other grammatical forms that express the same meaning. For *dieter,* we can use the following equivalents:

a person on a diet
a person dieting
a person who is dieting
a person who is on a diet
a person following a diet
someone on a diet
someone dieting
someone who is on a diet
someone following a diet
an individual on a diet   (etc.)
one on a diet   (etc.)

EXERCISE

What synonyms are used in the following passages?

1. The relationship between instructors and students is an important factor in student progress. When the association is based on open communication, more learning takes place.

2. Taking a car in for repairs can be a frustrating experience. The repair person first comes up with an estimate which the customer, who may know nothing about cars, must sign. The mechanic then promises to consult the customer in case other repairs are necessary, while the owner of the vehicle is too intimidated to ask the employee which repairs are considered "others." Finally, when the car is ready, the smiling garage worker presents the customer with two or three pages of a computer printout that would be hard to read even for people who know what the information is all about. The car owner, not smiling, makes out a check, all the while fantasizing about never needing to come back to the garage again.

EXERCISE

What synonyms are used in the following paragraphs?

1. The person just learning to drive a car has several difficult tasks to master. First, the driver must learn to control the car. This means finding the correct pedal without looking, stepping neither too hard nor too lightly on the pedal, and steering down the road, all at the same time. In addition, the new motorist has to keep track of the situation on the road. This includes monitoring everything involved in normal driving conditions, as well as watching for any potential emergency situation. Finally, the learner must get used to following the rules of the road. This means learning the many pages of signs in the handbook, all of which somehow look a little different to the novice who is driving down the road for the first time, and mastering the established conventions for changing lanes, turning, and stopping. It is no wonder that some people give up on learning to drive before they ever get behind the wheel of a car.

2. Parents should not insist that their children go to college straight out of high school. First, the decision to go to college is a major one in life—one that needs to be made by the individual directly concerned rather than by the parent. The young person may not even want to continue with school. Also, it is very difficult for a student lacking positive motivation to be successful in higher education. Thus, the son or daughter who struggles with college primarily because of pressure from the parent accumulates frustration instead of knowledge. Another reason for the parent not to push the young person to go straight to college is that the decision may not be a suitable one. Often, the son or daughter who has just finished high school is not ready for college-level work. The recent graduate usually does not yet have clear ideas about a field of interest or a career goal. Furthermore, many teenagers are not mature enough to profit from college work. Once enrolled in class, they are faced with concepts they do not understand, and, unlike in high school, they must compete for grades with people in their twenties or older, who may understand those concepts very well because of their greater experience in life. As a result, the teenagers' immaturity becomes a real obstacle to success in their studies. A final problem is that recent graduates may have to leave good friends and favorite activities in order to go to college. In this way, their all-important social development is sacrificed. Parents may be doing a young person a real disservice by pressuring him or her to go to college.

EXERCISE

What synonyms can you give for the following terms? Do not limit yourself to single-word synonyms.

1. photograph
2. tabloid
3. poverty
4. selfish
5. prove
6. shield (protect)

Whenever you foresee using the same term several times, spend a few minutes brainstorming or even freewriting in order to find other ways of wording the idea. By using these alternative wordings, you can avoid repetition but still make your writing easy for readers to follow.

See if you can discover the transitional device that gives coherence to the following passage:

> Undergraduates are generally expected to take classes in history, political science, sociology, and psychology. These social sciences are intended to give students a better understanding of how humans behave.

SUMMARIZING WORDS

The four fields of study mentioned in the preceding example are all social sciences. Thus, the phrase *these social sciences* summarizes the individual items brought up earlier. **Summarizing words**, like synonyms, are an extremely useful transitional device. They enable the writer to keep previously mentioned important ideas fresh in the reader's mind without resorting to annoying repetition.

Summarizing words may be used at any point in writing. Consider using them, for example, whenever you want to make a general statement that covers a set of individual items already mentioned or discussed.

An excellent strategy in writing is to use summarizing words for the key supporting ideas in the conclusion of a short composition. Carefully chosen summarizing words at the end of your compositions have the advantage of reminding the reader of your key ideas, which then do not need to be repeated.

EXERCISE

Find summarizing words in the concluding statements of the following paragraphs.

1. Many people who have access to good public transportation prefer not to own a car for a number of important reasons. First, it is expensive to have a car. The purchase price of even a basic transportation vehicle amounts to several months' wages for most people. Gas for the car is also a major expense, as are

routine maintenance and unforeseen repairs. In addition, there is the cost of insurance for the vehicle, which over the lifetime of the car may total more than the original purchase price. Another problem that vehicle ownership brings is legal liability. Anything that happens to the car or to anyone in it is ultimately the owner's responsibility. This liability can involve some real risks, too. For example, in an automobile accident, a person who was in no way at fault may still lose both money and a good driving record. Last, a person who has a car must put up with requests for rides from friends and relatives who do not have their own transportation. The problem is that others often expect favors at any hour of the day or night without seeming to understand that the driver also has a life to attend to. All of these inconveniences can make owning a car a mixed blessing indeed.

2. Teachers have different ways of conducting class. Traditional teachers use the class time to lecture to the students. They believe that they have the information the students need to learn and that students should listen and take notes in order to memorize as much of the information as possible. As these instructors equate learning primarily with rote memorizing, they measure students' progress by how much information the students can reproduce on tests. Other teachers use most of the class time for group discussions. They suggest ideas for groups to consider; and then, from time to time, they recapitulate and synthesize the information thus gathered. These teachers, who usually favor a student-oriented class, provide only a limited amount of information themselves and generally do relatively little testing to assess student learning. A final category includes teachers who structure class time so that the students will arrive at an understanding of certain concepts. Rather than lecture to the students, they guide them, through suitable materials and appropriate questions, to an understanding of the course content. They then test their students' active comprehension of the course concepts. As different as these types of classroom management are, they are all common in our schools today.

3. Christmas has different meanings for different people. Some consider it primarily a religious holiday. These celebrants honor the birth of Christ by carefully setting up a creche where it can be admired by all who enter the home. The special church services held at Christmas are another important part of the holiday for them. Even the feasts of the season have a religious meaning for those who celebrate the birth of Christ. For other people, Christmas is primarily a time of togetherness for family and friends. They value the holiday because it provides an opportunity for close ones to gather and enjoy activities together. They also take advantage of the Christmas season, with its atmosphere of warmth and generosity, to call or write to those whom they care about but do not have a chance to contact more frequently. For yet other people, Christmas is not so much a time to celebrate a religious event or to contact people as it is a time to stop and appreciate a special beauty. For them, Christmas, with its feast of light and colors everywhere— from the decorated homes and streets to the delicately beautiful greeting cards—is a time of bright contrast that transforms winter from a season of bleakness to one of quiet splendor. The meaning of Christmas, thus, is truly an individual matter.

E X E R C I S E

What summarizing words could be used for each of the following groups of ideas?

1. various containers, disposable diapers, unrecycled newspapers, old tires

2. hunger, environmental pollution, political unrest, discrimination

3. driving ease, low purchase price, low cost of insurance, good gas mileage

4. fear, anger, frustration, disgust

5. visiting monuments, going to theme parks, riding historic trains, exploring old urban centers

EXERCISE

5-15

Identify and explain the transitions and transitional devices in each of the following examples.

1. Electric mixers, knife sharpeners, and even can openers are expensive in comparison with manually operated tools. Moreover, these power utensils often break down.

2. Mental telepathy, clairvoyance, and precognition have been studied a great deal by psychologists. However, these manifestations of ESP are little understood as yet.

3. Children at the zoo can observe how tigers eat, how lions sleep, how hyenas move around watchfully, and how monkeys imitate other monkeys and humans. Young people visiting an animal park can thus learn a great deal about how animals behave.

4. Buying something in the former Soviet Union can be a frustrating experience. First, the shopper must elbow through crowds to get up to the counter in order to see how much the item costs—if it is available. Then the purchaser gets into the line at the cash register, waiting to pay for the item. Finally, receipt in hand, the buyer returns to the original counter and once again struggles to get the clerk's attention in order to turn over the receipt and take the article. It is no wonder that consumerism is a concept virtually unknown in Russia.

EXERCISE

5-16

What ideas do the following transitions from Exercise 5-15 connect?

1. *moreover* in the first example

2. *however* in the second example

3. *thus* in the third example

Writing Assignments

EXERCISE

5-17

Write a composition on one or more of the following topics. Prewrite carefully. Then, as you write and revise your draft, pay particular attention to the logical connections between your ideas, and add or change transitions where necessary. Check to see whether you have successfully used synonyms and summarizing words to avoid repetition, and make improvements where appropriate. Last of all, proofread your paper carefully for errors in grammar, spelling, and punctuation.

1. Effects of lack of education (on an individual or on a society)

2. Causes of lack of education

3. Arguments against experimentation on animals in high school science classes

4. Arguments for requiring high school students to take history (or another subject)

EXERCISE

5-18

Working alone or with your classmates, examine your previous or current writing for logical connections between ideas. Add transitions, synonyms, and summarizing words where appropriate.

Summing Up

You have seen that effective writing contains the necessary transitions to show connections between ideas.

Relationships that frequently need to be shown include the following:

Contrast

Addition

Sequence

Cause

Effect

Illustration

Comparison

Restatement

Time

Space

Other transitional devices can provide logical connections that help the reader follow meaning without the need for repetition.

Synonyms are useful when the same idea or term appears several times.

Summarizing words are useful when the writer needs to restate a set of previously mentioned ideas or terms.

In Chapter 6 you will learn how to combine ideas in order to express meaning effectively.

SENTENCE COMBINING

6

Why do the following sentences sound awkward? How would you improve them?

1. They called the television repair technician. The television repair technician fixed the problem.
2. He gave the sentence more specific meaning by adding some modifiers. Modifiers are words and groups of words that give additional information about another word or other words in the sentence.
3. The house number on the curb was hard to read. The house number needed painting.

In all three cases, repetition interferes with smooth communication of meaning. Combining each pair so that the repetition is eliminated improves the writing. Here are some possibilities:

They called the television repair technician, who fixed the problem.

or

The television repair technician they called fixed the problem.

Either version makes a more meaningful statement.

He gave the sentence more specific meaning by adding some modifiers, words or groups of words that give additional information about another word or other words in the sentence.

The house number on the curb, which needed painting, was hard to read.

or

The house number on the curb was hard to read because it needed painting.

Whenever your writing seems repetitious or unclear, consider using sentence combining to improve it. Effectively combined sentences focus the reader's attention on essential ideas; and additional details, though present, do not detract from basic meanings.

Notice that the different combined versions for the preceding examples 1 and 3 have different meanings. How you actually combine your sentences depends on the specific meaning you wish to communicate.

Placing the Main Idea

What point is the writer making in each of the following sentences? What is the difference in meaning?

Success, which has been defined in terms of money, prestige, or happiness, has been the subject of a number of recent books.

Success, which has been the subject of a number of recent books, has been defined in terms of money, prestige, or happiness.

In the first example, the writer is making the point that success has been the subject of a number of recent books. In the second, the writer is focusing on how success has been defined.

Meaning in an individual sentence centers on the subject and verb of the main clause. In other words, the essential message of the sentence derives from its subject and verb. This means that when we do sentence combining, our basic point is normally expressed in the main clause, with other essential and nonessential information added in the form of modifiers. In the first of the two preceding examples, the writer is stating that success has been the subject of a number of recent books; how success has been defined is interesting but nonessential information, added in the form of a subordinate clause. In the second example, the writer wishes to state that success has been defined in different terms, so this idea has been kept as the main clause. The interesting but nonessential idea that success has been the subject of recent books is put in a secondary position: in a subordinate clause.

In combining the following two statements, which would you put in the main clause?

Dog owners have their animals vaccinated against parvo. Parvo is a deadly canine disease.

When you are discussing something involving a term that needs to be defined, the definition of the term does not usually need to be emphasized. The reader may already know the meaning of the term and therefore may not be interested in seeing a definition. If the reader is not familiar with the word, the emphasis should still normally be on the ongoing discussion rather than on the definition. Consequently, the focus in the preceding example should probably be on the first statement:

Dog owners have their animals vaccinated against parvo, a deadly canine disease.

Thus, sentence combining can improve your writing in several important ways. You can eliminate wordiness, making your writing more agreeable to read. You can focus your reader's attention on your more important ideas, helping the reader identify what is essential to you. And you can avoid a great deal of needless repetition.

Combining Information

Statements can be combined in a number of different ways. The grammatical form you choose depends on the purpose of your statement.

COORDINATING TWO STATEMENTS

When you want to make two statements of equal value, you can combine them with the appropriate coordinating conjunction, as in the following examples:

On their trip to Paris, the professors visited the Louvre.
They took the elevator to the top of the Eiffel Tower.

On their trip to Paris, the professors visited the Louvre, *and* they took the elevator to the top of the Eiffel Tower.

They had been told that it rains a great deal in Europe.
They did not take umbrellas with them.

They had been told that it rains a great deal in Europe, *but* they did not take umbrellas with them.

They all spoke French.

They did not have a language problem.

They all spoke French, *so* they did not have a language problem.

SUBORDINATING A STATEMENT

When your statements are not of equal value, you can express the basic idea in a main clause and the additional information in a subordinate clause.

He refused the job offer.

He did not want to be alone all night in the store.

He refused the job offer *because* he did not want to be alone all night in the store.

Joe does not want to become a contestant on the game show.

Joe seems like a walking encyclopedia to his friends.

Joe does not want to become a contestant on the game show, *although* he seems like a walking encyclopedia to his friends.

In some instances, a subordinate clause with a relative pronoun may be the appropriate choice:

The students come to class regularly and listen carefully.

The students learn a great deal.

The students *who* come to class regularly and listen carefully learn a great deal.

People are afraid to use the Bay Area freeways.

The Bay Area freeways were damaged during the 1989 earthquake.

People are afraid to use the Bay Area freeways *which* were damaged during the 1989 earthquake.

A supervisor may have difficulty getting the job done.

Her workers do not communicate well in English.

A supervisor *whose* workers do not communicate well in English may have difficulty getting the job done.   [notice that the possessive "whose" replaces "her"]

Mary saw the professor walking along Fisherman's Wharf.

Mary had met the professor at a conference.

Mary saw the professor [*whom*] she had met at a conference walking along Fisherman's Wharf.

Joe thanked Mary.

Joe got help in math from Mary.

Joe thanked Mary, *from whom* he had gotten help in math.

London was still in many places like the city portrayed by Dickens and Conan Doyle.

Joe spent his summer vacation in London.

London, *where* Joe spent his summer vacation, was still in many places like the city portrayed by Dickens and Conan Doyle.

That was the moment.

Joe made his most difficult choice then.

That was the moment *when* Joe made his most difficult choice.

USING OTHER GRAMMAR FORMS TO ADD INFORMATION

Participles

> Joe was protesting.
>
> Joe still had to pay the rest of the bill.
>
> Joe, *protesting*, still had to pay the rest of the bill.

> Mary was worried.
>
> Mary was waiting for the results of her test.
>
> Mary, *worried*, was waiting for the results of her test.

> The parents were attentively watching their children.
>
> The children were wading across the rapidly moving stream.
>
> The parents were attentively watching their children *wading* across the rapidly moving stream.   [the present participle "wading" begins the participial phrase "wading across the rapidly moving stream"]

> The music was played by the local high school band.
>
> The music included both classical pieces and famous marches.
>
> The music *played* by the local high school band included both classical pieces and famous marches.   [the past participle "played" begins the participial phrase "played by the local high school band"]

Compare the two combined versions of the following statements. Which one do you prefer?

> The administrator was addressing the student body.
>
> The administrator explained the changes in course prerequisites.
>
> The administrator, who was addressing the student body, explained the changes in course prerequisites.
>
> The administrator, addressing the student body, explained the changes in course prerequisites.

The first combination has a subordinate clause beginning with the relative pronoun *who*; the second has a participial phrase beginning with the participle *addressing*. The second version expresses the same meaning but states it more concisely. This shorter version is the better choice in this case. Generally, the more concise version is the better alternative.

Many subordinate clauses can be reduced in this way to modifying phrases or other less wordy forms:

> The boys, who were trying to take a shortcut up to the lighthouse, were knocking rocks down into the trail below.

Reduced:

> The boys, trying to take a shortcut up to the lighthouse, were knocking rocks down into the trail below.

> Neil Armstrong, who was the first person to walk on the moon, has impressed people around the world with his great understanding of the human experience.

Reduced:

> Neil Armstrong, the first person to walk on the moon, has impressed people around the world with his great understanding of the human experience.

Prepositional Phrases

> The puppy was in the dog run.
>
> All of the guests wanted to see the puppy.
>
> All of the guests wanted to see the puppy *in the dog run*.

> The gifts were for the children.
>
> The gifts were put on two different credit cards.
>
> The gifts *for the children* were put on two different credit cards.

Infinitives

> Mary went to Paris last summer.
>
> Mary went to Paris to learn French.
>
> Mary went to Paris last summer *to learn French*.

Appositives

> Her desk was a storehouse for papers.
>
> Her desk gave everyone the impression that she worked hard.
>
> Her desk, *a storehouse for papers*, gave everyone the impression that she worked hard.

> The etymology is the origin of a word.
>
> The etymology is part of a dictionary entry.
>
> The etymology, *the origin of a word*, is part of a dictionary entry.

> His professor was Dr. Martin.
>
> His professor was a famous historian.
>
> His professor, *Dr. Martin*, was a famous historian.

E X E R C I S E

6-1

Combine the following sentences according to the specific instructions given.

Use coordination:

1. They bought a new lawn mower. They looked at various landscaping tools.
2. They looked at an edger. They did not buy the edger.
3. She was expecting an important phone call. She avoided tying down both phone lines.
4. They may use their vacation time to take a trip. They may stay home and do some remodeling.

Use subordination:

5. Many people do not recognize Columbus' discovery of America. It was a discovery only from the European point of view, and we are Americans, not Europeans.
6. We are not leaving now. We will leave when the others come.

7. Many people do not believe there is a problem with the ozone layer. Abundant evidence shows that a problem with the ozone layer exists.

Use a participle or participial phrase:

8. The band was leaving the field. The band was being honored with a standing ovation.

9. The cord was tied in a tight knot. The cord needed to be undone in order to be usable.

10. The students bring their lunches from home. The students save money and eat better food.

Use prepositional phrases:

11. She needed the paper. The paper was on the bottom of the pile.

12. There was an awards ceremony before the game. Many students took part in the awards ceremony.

Use infinitives:

13. She gave her daughter a picture book of animals. She gave her the book to help her learn about nature.

14. He bought a sturdier backpack. He bought the backpack to carry several heavy books.

Use appositives:

15. His dog is a Siberian husky. His dog likes to eat the plants in people's gardens.

16. Some parents seem to be unaware that discipline is supposed to be a learning experience rather than merely punishment. *Discipline* is a Latin word that means instruction.

17. The banana is a tropical fruit. The banana is a good source of potassium.

18. Nathaniel Hawthorne was an unconventional thinker and writer. Some of our country's most famous novels and short stories were written by Nathaniel Hawthorne.

In sentence combining, as in other areas of writing, we use commas to set off nonessential information. Thus, if we combine

The seeds had been sown a week before.

and

The seeds were beginning to germinate.

we may obtain

The seeds that had been sown a week before were beginning to germinate.

Alternatively, we may express the same idea with the subordinate clause reduced to a participial phrase:

The seeds sown a week before were beginning to germinate.

In both cases, only the seeds sown a week before were germinating; the sentence implies that other seeds existed, but they were not germinating.

If we write

> The seeds, which had been sown a week before, were beginning to germinate.

or with reduction to a participial phrase,

> The seeds, sown a week before, were beginning to germinate.

we imply that no other seeds existed.

EXERCISE

The following sentences are already combined. Reduce the subordinate clauses to appositives, participial phrases, prepositional phrases, or infinitive phrases. Use commas accurately, placing them around non-essential information.

1. There is ferry service from La Paz, which is at the southern end of Baja California, to Mazatlan.
2. Mazatlan, which is an Indian name for deer, has the world's highest lighthouse.
3. The player who was named rookie of the year comes from her home town.
4. The lady who is working the cash register is bilingual.
5. They will spend their vacation in Egypt because they want to see the pyramids.
6. She bought several pieces of matching furniture, which were to be placed in her living room.
7. When we recycle paper, we save trees, which are a valuable resource.
8. The deposits which are collected on recyclable materials provide an incentive for people to conserve.
9. Their broom closet, which is located in the kitchen, is a convenient place to store a number of items.
10. The people who were sitting around the table were watching the children eat strange new foods.

Combining to Achieve Meaning

We can combine

> They took the stairs to the first level of the Eiffel Tower.
> They rode the elevator from there to the top of the tower.

in different ways:

> They took the stairs to the first level of the Eiffel Tower, *and* they rode the elevator from there to the top of the tower.
> They took the stairs to the first level of the Eiffel Tower, *but* they rode the elevator from there to the top of the tower.
> *After* they took the stairs to the first level of the Eiffel Tower, they rode the elevator from there to the top of the tower.

The first version simply indicates that they did two things. The second contrasts the two ways of going up the tower:

> . . . *took* the stairs . . . but *rode* . . .

The third version indicates a time sequence. All three sentences are correct. But the proper one to use is the one that is appropriate in its context—that is, the one that expresses the writer's intended meaning.

The following subsections present examples of ideas combined to achieve meaning in a single sentence.

ADDITION

We can use *and* to combine two ideas of equal value:

> She purchased a queen sleeper in order to accommodate guests, *and* she bought some extra bedding to use on it.

Alternatively, we can emphasize one idea by putting it in a main clause and adding the other idea to it:

> *In addition to* Italian I, she enrolled in an Italian conversation course.

CONTRAST

We can use *but* to contrast two ideas of equal value:

> She spent a day at Disneyland, *but* she did not go to Knott's Berry Farm.

Alternatively, we can emphasize one idea by putting it in a main clause and adding the other idea to it:

> *Although* she spent a day at Disneyland, she did not go to Knott's Berry Farm.

We can express unexpected contrast with several combinations:

> She had a college degree, *yet* she became a stay-at-home mother.
> *Even though* she had a college degree, she became a stay-at-home mother.
> *In spite of* having a college degree, she became a stay-at-home mother.

CAUSE

We can combine ideas in different ways to show cause:

> She did not go out to work, *for* it was a family tradition for women to stay home.
> She did not go out to work *because* it was a family tradition for women to stay home.
> She did not go out to work *because of* a family tradition for women to stay home.

Sometimes a present participle shows cause:

> He went to Los Angeles, *wanting* to get on a television quiz show.   [= because he wanted to get on a television quiz show]

EFFECT

> He could tell how the movie would end, *so* he changed channels.

ILLUSTRATION

> Many spices, *such as* sweet basil and allspice, enhance a basic tomato sauce.
> Many spices, *for example*, sweet basil and allspice, enhance a basic tomato sauce.

COMPARISON

Major sports figures, *like* film stars, are besieged by autograph seekers.

RESTATEMENT

Home improvement stores, *that is*, stores that sell all kinds of materials for repairing and remodeling, often do well even in difficult economic times.

Home improvement stores, *in other words*, stores that sell all kinds of materials for repairing and remodeling, often do well even in difficult economic times.

PURPOSE

He came to this school *to get* a degree.

He came to this school *in order to get* a degree.

He came to this school *so that he could get* a degree.

Notice that most of the preceding eight meanings—addition, contrast, cause, effect, illustration, comparison, restatement, and purpose—can be expressed with an adverbial conjunction, but more than one sentence (or one sentence with a semicolon) is needed. In this chapter, we are focusing on the possibilities of combining more than one idea into a single sentence.

E X E R C I S E

6-3

Combine each pair of ideas into a single sentence, according to the specific instructions. Watch your punctuation.

1. Express addition in two different ways.

> She bought the plane ticket.
> She made a reservation for a hotel room.

2. Express contrast in two different ways.

> He consulted an expert on his problem.
> He still could not find a solution to his problem.

3. Express cause in at least three ways.

> She bought a new umbrella.
> The rain had been predicted to last at least a week.

4. Express cause in two ways: with a subordinate clause and with a present participle.

> Joe needed a new camera.
> Joe was saving money.

5. Express effect.

> The weather was finally starting to warm up.
> Joe opened all the windows.

6. Combine the example with the main idea.

> Small appliances are often given to newlyweds.
> Coffee makers and juicers are small appliances.

7. Combine to show comparison.

> Mustangs are still popular cars.
> Volkswagens are still popular cars.

8. Combine, restating the explanation.

> The less expensive means of transportation in Europe tend to be crowded.
> The less expensive means of transportation in Europe are the bus and the train.

9. Express purpose in three ways.

> He bought a repair manual for his truck.
> His intention was to learn how to repair his own vehicle.

E X E R C I S E

Combine each pair of sentences in different ways to achieve the meanings indicated. Watch punctuation.

1. Express first addition, then time.

> The girls got their tennis rackets.
> They went to the park.

2. Express addition, then contrast, then time, then cause.

> They were going to play in a tournament.
> They were going to watch the national championships on television in the recreation room to learn something from the professionals.

E X E R C I S E

Combine each pair of sentences into a single sentence. Watch your punctuation.

1. Marie had never worked with the public before. Marie got a job as a receptionist.

2. Joe did not have time to study for the final. Joe did well on the final, to his great surprise.

3. Julie did not understand restaurant menus in most European countries. Julie usually ended up ordering spaghetti.

4. It had stopped raining. Joe did not take his umbrella with him.

5. Sue could tell that there was a garage sale going on down the street. Cars were going by one after another.

6. Many people do not know it. The tax changes of the 1980s hurt the lower and middle classes.

7. The tourists drove across the Golden Gate Bridge. The tourists took the elevator to the top of Coit Tower.

8. The explorer was covered with snow. The explorer crawled into the tent.

9. The candidate has an excellent record of public service. The candidate does not necessarily win the election.

10. Shakespeare is the author of some of the best plays ever written. Shakespeare would have won many literary prizes had he lived in our century.

11. I knew I would need my watch during the test. I forgot to bring my watch with me to the test.

12. She read the important letters carefully. She dumped the junk mail into the recycle bin.

13. City parks provide much-needed space for urban dwellers. Green belts are city parks.

14. Joe was standing at a call box. Joe's car had broken down on the freeway.

15. The man went on an archeological expedition to Yucatan last year. The professor spoke about the man.

16. We visited San Francisco in the summer of 1989. We bought some sourdough bread there.

17. They have been enjoying cooking dinners together. They like eating what they prepare.

18. They spent the whole day looking in vain for just the right tool. They decided to try a different model.

19. She bought the red one. She was not happy with it after she got it home.

20. The bulletin board was a constant eyesore. It was always messy.

E X E R C I S E

6-6

Combine each group of sentences into one sentence. Watch your punctuation.

1. She resisted the temptation to add color to her handouts. She had all of her printing done on white paper. She wanted to avoid contributing to environmental pollution.

2. Joe was eager to get as much as possible out of the class. He attended regularly. He made friends with other highly motivated students. He discussed the class work with the students.

3. People were unhappy with the new mayor. He allowed taxes to be raised on low-income housing. He did nothing to stop businesses from moving to areas where labor was cheaper.

4. Some environmentalists may actually be hurting what they stand for. The environmentalists do things. The environmentalists tie themselves to trees. The environmentalists seem to be more concerned with participating in a cause than in helping the environment.

When we combine several sentences, we still need to focus the information on a main point. Which of the following ideas seems the most important?

The secretary was new on the job.

The secretary made several serious mistakes.

Someone else had to correct the mistakes.

The second statement expresses the idea that probably motivated the writer to put the situation on paper. Therefore, in combining the sentences, we should focus on that statement. We can write, for example,

Because the secretary was new on the job, she made several serious mistakes that someone else had to correct.

EXERCISE

Combine each group of sentences into one sentence. Watch your punctuation.

1. Some people flock to college writing classes. Some people want to improve their writing skills. Some people realize something. It is up to writers to clarify meaning. It is not up to readers to clarify meaning.

2. People in Los Angeles are working to rebuild a city. The city will be a better one. There were riots in Los Angeles in 1992.

3. There were only two promising programs on television that evening. She did not finish watching either one. One was unnecessarily violent. One was a rerun. The rerun was something she had already seen.

4. Hawthorne was born in Salem, Massachusetts. Salem was the scene of witch hunts in the 1600s. Hawthorne uses the supernatural extensively. Hawthorne uses the supernatural in his short stories and novels.

5. Students who major in a foreign language have to take courses. They have to take linguistics. Linguistics is the study of the structure of the language. They have to take philology. Philology is the study of the historical development of the language.

EXERCISE

Combine the following sixteen sentences into four sentences. Begin by grouping the sentences logically. Then combine each group. As you rephrase the ideas, make sure that the focus in each sentence is on the ideas that need to be stressed, with the remaining information presented in the form of modifiers or appositives.

1. The term is *critical thinking*.

2. The term goes far back.

3. The term goes at least to the early part of the century.

4. One of the early critical thinking scholars was Edward Glaser.

5. Glaser published *An Experiment in the Development of Critical Thinking*.

6. He published it in 1941.

7. He had already developed the *Watson-Glaser Critical Thinking Appraisal*.

8. He developed the *Watson-Glaser Critical Thinking Appraisal* in collaboration with Watson.

9. The *Watson-Glaser Critical Thinking Appraisal* is a test of students' ability to reason.

10. Critical thinkers endeavor to figure things out.

11. As they endeavor to figure things out, they back their assertions.

12. They back their assertions with strong evidence.

13. They back their assertions with carefully considered reasoned judgments.

14. Some teachers follow the principles of critical thinking.

15. The teachers associate knowledge with real understanding.

16. They do not associate knowledge with the rote memorization of facts.

Writing Assignments

Write a composition on one or more of the following topics. Prewrite carefully. Then as you write and revise your draft, pay particular attention to sentence combining. Use coordination and subordination, and add information in the form of appositives, participles, and infinitives, as well as prepositional and other phrases. Reduce clauses to phrases when appropriate. Word your sentences so that the focus is on the essential information. Use appropriate transitions. Last of all, proofread your paper carefully for errors in grammar, spelling, and punctuation.

1. Marriage is more satisfying when the husband and wife see themselves as a team rather than as two people with separate roles.
2. The civil rights movements of the last four decades have helped women to improve their status in society.
3. Military service should not be compulsory in any country.
4. Examinations in school serve some important purposes.

Working alone or with your classmates, examine your previous or current compositions to determine how effectively you have used sentence-combining strategies. Consider combining ideas if any of the following problems are present:

- Your writing seems wordy.
- Your writing seems choppy.
- You note what may be unnecessary repetition of a word, phrase, or clause.
- You have not used a variety of grammatical forms in expressing your ideas.
- The focus is not clearly on your more important ideas.

Summing Up

You have learned that effective sentence combining improves your writing in several important ways.

Better focus: Details can be added, but the main focus is still clear.

Less repetition: Fewer statements are necessary because additional information can be attached to the essential main clauses.

Less wordiness: Fewer words are needed because not everything needs to be expressed in separate statements.

COMBINING TECHNIQUES

Coordinate two or more main clauses for ideas of equal value.

Subordinate one or more clauses containing additional information.

Put additional information in the form of a

     participle or participial phrase

     prepositional phrase

     infinitive or infinitive phrase

     appositive

Commas are used to set off nonessential information.

Subordinate clauses can sometimes be reduced to phrases.

We can achieve different meanings that depend on the transitions we use in combining ideas.

In Chapter 7 you will learn strategies for writing introductions.

INTRODUCTIONS

Consider the following introductory paragraphs to short essays. Are they effective introductions?

Television came into existence around half a century ago. Since then, it has been a part of everyday life. The difference between then and now is that television was a luxury. Television provides an escape from the real world.

Every day in the newspapers we read about crimes committed by juvenile offenders. These crimes range from minor incidents of vandalism to felony offenses, including murder.

Try to imagine what you would be reading about in each essay according to the preceding introductions. Can you tell what the writer's point is in either case?

What, in your opinion, is the purpose of an introduction at the beginning of a piece of writing? Why do we need one at all?

The first sample introduction obviously brings up a topic, "television." But the central point the writer is planning to make about television in the essay is not clear at all. Statements are made about when television was first invented and what role it played in those days, sandwiched around a statement about its current importance. A comment about what television does follows. The introduction has no direction, however, and for this reason we really do not know what the essay will discuss.

The second introduction, unlike the first, seems to start off in a particular direction. However, no controlling idea is indicated, so this introductory paragraph also fails to accomplish the purpose of beginning a composition.

An introduction should, first of all, introduce. This means that what is in the introduction should reflect what is in the essay. Since the composition is centered on a *topic* and is written with the purpose of developing the writer's point about that topic, in other words, the *controlling idea*, the topic and the controlling idea need to appear in the introduction. The two sample opening paragraphs are ineffective because they do not indicate one of these essential elements: a controlling idea.

Consider the following introduction:

Capital punishment needs to become a reality for all perpetrators of major crimes. We should get behind our legislators to push for widespread use of the death penalty. We should all get involved personally to make this punishment a reality for all hardened criminals.

Would most people read the essay?

The introduction does not clarify whether the essay will discuss *why* we should work to see the death penalty enforced ("needs to become a reality") or *how* we can work for capital punishment ("should get behind our legislators to push"). The resulting ambiguity renders the introduction ineffective. But this opening paragraph also has two other serious faults. First, it takes a side on a debatable issue, without any indication that the writer is aware of the one-sided presentation of ideas. Moreover, the writer evidently intends to use an opinion as the basis of the essay. The writer is therefore likely to lose the serious consideration of readers who do not agree with that opinion. The second problem is that, in spite of the emotionally charged topic, the writer's assertions generate little real interest, and the reader who does not get involved while reading the opening paragraph is likely to read no further.

Consider the following introduction:

Modern society, it is often said, has been desensitized to violence. Heavy criticism is aimed particularly at the media for unnecessarily exposing us to so much brutality. Nevertheless, while we may readily agree that both our news coverage and our entertainment contain too much violence, we should be cautious about assuming that we have actually come to accept brutality more readily in recent years than in the past. In reality, people's attitude toward violence is less tolerant now than it used to be.

Can you identify the purpose and direction of the essay from this opening paragraph?

The first sentence brings up the question of society's desensitization to violence. The second indicates the media's heavy involvement in our exposure to violence. The next sentence makes the point that our frequent exposure to brutality does not necessarily indicate our acceptance of it. The introduction ends with the thesis statement: our attitude toward violence is actually less tolerant now than it was in the past.

This opening paragraph effectively prepares the reader for an essay explaining *how* our attitude toward violence is less tolerant now than it was in the past. In other words, both the *direction* and the *purpose* of the essay to follow are clear.

The Purpose of the Introduction

It is in the body of an essay that we systematically bring up our key supporting ideas and detailed explanations. Since the essential contents of the essay are presented in the body paragraphs, the purpose of the introductory paragraph is to prepare the reader for the body of the essay.

Clarifying the topic and the controlling idea in the introduction serves both the reader and the writer. A reader who is misled in the introduction is likely to be annoyed and therefore uninclined to read the essay. The writer's purpose is thus defeated. To get the reader sufficiently involved to continue reading the essay, the writer should carefully establish in the introduction what topic will be discussed and what statement about that topic will be supported.

Compare the next two opening paragraphs. Try to predict something about the essay each introduces. Which one do you think works better?

Many elementary school districts are beginning to offer elective classes for their pupils after the close of the regular school day. Such a program is proving to be advantageous in a number of ways. It provides a place to go for the many children who do not have anyone at home during the late afternoon and who are therefore in need of supervision. It also enables students to take additional classes and thus learn new information, possibly discovering new aptitudes as well. Furthermore, it gives the children an opportunity to spend time with friends in a setting which is more relaxed than that of the traditional classroom, an advantage often overlooked by both teachers and parents.

Many elementary school districts are beginning to offer classes for their pupils after the close of the regular school day. Such a program is proving to be advantageous as it gives children the opportunity to stay in a supervised setting in the company of their friends, learning new information and perhaps also discovering new aptitudes.

Both paragraphs contain a clear topic and controlling idea, and both are potentially involving to readers, since they deal with important concerns regarding children: education, social skills, and problems with responsible supervision. But if you try to map out the essay to follow each one, you will find that only the second version is an easily usable introduction. Notice that in both versions, the key supporting ideas are brought up, but the first version also includes some explanations. This supporting detail in the introduction, however, creates a problem. In fact, explanations should be given in the body, and the introduction should do no more than indicate the key ideas to be covered in the essay, even simply pointing out the direction of the key ideas rather than spelling them out.

To understand this concept better, try to imagine a body paragraph developing the idea that after-school classes can provide a place for children to go. The first sample explains *why* children need somewhere to go: there is no one at home, and the children therefore need supervision. Thus, the reader does not need to go on to the body of the essay in order to find a discussion of the point. Moreover, it would be difficult to launch a more detailed discussion of this particular issue involving latchkey children without repeating the same ideas at the beginning of the body paragraph that specifically addresses it. The same problem would arise with regard to developing the other two key supporting ideas: so much has already been said in the introduction that it would be difficult to initiate a discussion of each idea. And it would be especially challenging to bring up each point once again without repeating some of the wording that was used in the introduction.

Thus, key supporting ideas usually do not need to be stated in the introduction of a short essay. Notice, for example, that the key supporting ideas in the sample classification essay are not given in the introduction:

Department store employees who meet casually off the job tend to have as much to say about the store customers as they do about the products they sell. Some shoppers, they observe, try on a dozen garments but then buy nothing. Others leave the store with several purchases they will never use. Still others come in, buy something in a hurry, and then leave. Yet these behaviors, different as they are, all make sense for the simple reason that these customers have different purposes for coming to the store in the first place.

The key ideas are the purposes that draw customers to the store:

> to buy something in particular
> just to buy
> to bargain hunt
> to look only

The point is made that the customers have different purposes for coming to department stores. Then each body paragraph deals with one purpose, identifying it and explaining it.

Notice that the sample illustration and cause essays in Chapter 3 follow this same strategy. Instead of the key ideas, other relevant information is given. To introduce the essay on Illuminism, the writer offers a brief but necessary historical panorama. The introduction to the essay on the problem of homelessness appropriately includes a reference to widespread beliefs about homeless persons. In most college writing, you can use such strategies to your advantage, as long as you make your key ideas in the body paragraphs easy to find and to follow.

Length of the Introduction

Would you write a half-page introduction to a two-page essay? If that sounds out of balance to you, you are right. Since the body of the essay contains the major points and the explanations, most of the words in the essay need to be in the body. Often, a short essay (as most college essays are) needs only a three- or four-sentence opening paragraph—just enough to permit the writer to establish the direction of the essay.

The Controlling Idea and the Introduction

Consider the following introduction. What point do you expect the essay to make?

Over the past few years, there has been a dramatic increase in crime in our major cities. We hear on a daily basis about all kinds of robberies. All too often we also hear about acts of violence, including murder. More people are committing crimes because they believe they will gain more that way than by working a low-paying job. People are also joining gangs in order to attain a form of recognition in society. We need to control our crime problem not only by keeping hardened criminals in prison but also by breaking the poverty cycle in our cities.

The topic of the essay—crime in our major cities—is clear. But the controlling idea is not. In this opening paragraph, the writer indicates *what* kinds of crimes there are, *why* these crimes are taking place, and *how* we can deal with the problem. In other words, the introduction lacks a specific, unifying direction. As we have seen in Chapter 2, a college composition usually develops a statement that leads in the direction of *what, why,* or *how.* The specific direction should be made clear in the introduction.

In summary, an opening paragraph serves to introduce an essay. For this reason, it should identify the topic, the controlling idea, and the direction of the controlling idea: *what, why,* or *how.*

E X E R C I S E

7-1

Write an introduction to an essay for each of the following plans.

1. Topic: A college education
   Controlling idea: Prepares a person for life
   I. Teaches concepts
      A. Knowledge in various fields
         1. For general purposes
         2. For career purposes
         3. For personal growth
      B. Concepts from outside the classroom
         1. Other activities

    II. Teaches student to deal with others
        A. Contacts with instructor and school personnel
        B. Contacts with other students
            1. Communication
            2. Collaboration
            3. Form and test friendships
   III. Gives opportunities for networking
        A. Contacts in field of study
        B. Other contacts

2. Topic: Shared custody
   Controlling idea: Creates serious problems for child
   I. Develops no real sense of home
        A. Does not "belong" in either home
        B. Constantly feels uprooted
        C. Difficult to develop proper sense of boundaries
   II. Has normal contacts interrupted
        A. Friends
        B. Social environment
            1. School
            2. Community
   III. Is raised in two different ways
        A. Confusion from different role models
        B. Learns different principles
        C. Consequences of behaviors inconsistent

Strategies for Introductions

Consider the following introduction to an essay on illiteracy.

[handwritten: Good for Research Paper]

Since the beginning of the century, governments the world over have assumed the very heavy burden of educating their people. Yet in spite of these efforts, illiteracy in the world has actually increased. For a number of reasons, too many people are still not acquiring even basic reading and writing skills.

The startling statement that illiteracy has actually increased is very likely to draw the reader's attention and interest.

THE ELEMENT OF SURPRISE

Since the purpose of writing an introduction, beyond clarifying the point and the direction of the essay, is to involve the reader and to motivate him or her to read the whole composition, an element of surprise in the opening paragraph can be valuable.

Consider the following introduction to an essay on shared custody:

When parents divorce, the adults involved usually voice their great concern over the fate of any children born in the marriage. However, while pursuing what they feel is in the best interests of the child, they often settle on what may be in the parents' best interests but is ironically very damaging to the child. In fact, few things in life can tear apart a child as much as shared custody.

The irony of a solution that is supposed to help the child but that really ignores the child's true interests is again likely to draw the reader's attention.

IRONY

Like the element of surprise, irony is a useful attention-drawing device that skilled writers often use.

Irony, real or apparent, is all around us. For example, the homeless do not qualify for certain government aid programs because they do not have an address. Also, people who have a regular job can deduct many of their expenses for an additional temporary job; but people who cannot get regular work are not allowed to deduct expenses they incur in working from time to time for an employer. In other words, those who need the tax break are not the ones who get it. Thus, the existing system only makes it harder for people on welfare to find the motivation to work a temporary job. Ironic situations like these will engage readers.

CONTRADICTION

Both surprise and irony draw a reader's attention because they contain an element that contradicts what we would normally expect. Other kinds of contradictions can serve the same purpose. Notice the one in the following introduction:

Cars are undoubtedly an important part of our daily existence. We talk about them constantly, we patiently allow ourselves to be bombarded by commercials about them, and we even enjoy the reruns of a television series about a futuristic talking car. Admittedly, part of our occupation with the car is pure preoccupation—with the dangers, the costs, and the plain frustrations. Yet even with the obvious worries that our cars bring on, for most of us, the advantages of owning a car far outweigh the disadvantages.

This sample illustrates the advantages of bringing up the other side in the introduction. First, it creates interest because of the idea of a contradiction, which tends to activate the reader's thoughts on both sides of the question. Thus, the reader becomes involved. In addition, the other side may constitute an important part of the content of a paper. As we saw earlier in this chapter (in the introduction on capital punishment), writing that presents only one side, with no acknowledgement that another opinion exists, tends to be unconvincing. This principle is important especially but not only in argument writing. Often, an efficient way to handle this contradictory information is to place it in the introduction. Notice how this is done in the opening paragraph of the essay on gun control from Chapter 4:

The issue of whether we should have a gun control law has been debated extensively in the last few years. Opponents of gun control claim that private citizens at times need to be armed in order to defend themselves against a criminal who may be armed, as the police cannot always provide adequate protection. They also cite the Constitution, which guarantees the individuals right to bear arms. But the advocates of gun control have some particularly valid reasons for wanting to eliminate privately owned arms.

The second and third sentences, clearly presented as the opposing point of view, state three key arguments against gun control.

The preceding introduction follows a typical pattern for an opening paragraph. The first sentence brings up the topic, indicating it as a current issue. After that, the other side is very concisely presented. A contrast signal then helps the reader make the transition to the writer's thesis statement, which contains the controlling idea. This statement concludes the introduction, and the reader can move easily from the thesis statement at the end of the introduction to the key ideas in the body paragraphs.

Notice the similar structure in this introduction from Chapter 3:

The growing number of homeless people is drawing more and more public attention. Many people assume that the homeless do not really want to take on the responsibilities that are part of a stable life. Another common belief is that those who have no home are nearly all substance abusers. However, these views, even though they are accurate in many cases, oversimplify a problem that in reality has a series of complex causes.

The topic, but not the controlling idea, is introduced in the first sentence. Then comes the other side, in the form of common but questionable views about the causes of homelessness. The introduction ends with the thesis statement, clarifying the controlling idea—"has a series of complex causes"—and the direction of the essay—*what* those complex causes are.

The following introduction to an essay on the language problem most foreigners face has a similar structure:

Life in a foreign country is unquestionably difficult. Customs are different. Daily living involves a great deal of adjustment. Problems come up that require new types of solutions. But the greatest single problem for most foreigners is the language barrier.

After beginning with the statement that life in a foreign country is difficult, the writer names some important difficulties that are not going to be discussed in the essay. This strategy serves both to acknowledge the existence of these major problems and to put in perspective the difficulty that the language barrier presents. Once again, the thesis statement is the final sentence of the introduction, and it leads the reader in the direction of the impending discussion showing *how* the language barrier is frequently the greatest single problem.

A variation of this structure is used in the introduction to the essay on department store shoppers:

Department store employees who meet casually off the job tend to have as much to say about the store customers as they do about the products they sell. Some shoppers, they observe, try on a dozen garments but then buy nothing. Others leave the store with several purchases they will never use. Still others come in, buy something in a hurry, and then leave. Yet these behaviors, different as they are, all make sense for the simple reason that these customers have different purposes for coming to the store in the first place.

The reader can actually visualize some of these behaviors. We can thus summarize the basic strategies for introductions:

Purpose
    To clarify the point and direction of the essay
    To involve the reader
Elements
    Topic
    Controlling idea

Direction of essay (usually *what, why,* or *how*)
Other appropriate information
  Relevant background information
  Other important points (such as other key reasons) that will not be discussed
  Common misconceptions or highly questionable arguments
  A contradiction (opposing arguments or other conflicting ideas)

OTHER STRATEGIES

The introduction about department store customers, like the four preceding ones, contains a reference to the topic in the first sentence but clarifies the controlling idea only in the last sentence. The three sentences in between show some of the "different" (the controlling idea) behaviors of the customers. This visual introduction to the different behaviors, which are then systematically named and explained in the body of the essay, is another effective strategy for drawing and holding the reader's attention.

The following introduction to a definition essay on "mass hysteria" makes extensive use of visual imagery:

People who have seem films of World War II can visualize scenes of Hitler or Mussolini in front of enormous crowds cheering or chanting. In the 1960s, the Beatles, whenever they appeared in public, were surrounded by bodyguards to hold back the screaming hordes of fans who attempted to push forward to touch their heroes. And several times in recent years, masses of spectators at soccer games have poured onto the field, causing serious injuries and even death. All of these behaviors are irrational. This suspension of judgment under the influence of the crowd has come to be termed *mass hysteria.*

Most people can picture these scenes, so the crowd behaviors described in the essay have intense meaning for readers.

Just as descriptive, narrative, definition, and other types of essays may contain visual imagery in the introduction and just as an argument essay typically presents the main contradictory arguments in the opening paragraph, essays that clarify the effects of something frequently include concise references to the causes in the introduction. Pinpointing the causes of an event or situation is a good way to introduce the topic and to involve the reader in the essay. Notice the causal factors in the introduction to the essay on parenting from Chapter 1:

Many traditional parents measure their success in bringing up their children in terms of how well they control them. These fathers and mothers feel that only with strong parental control is it possible to raise "good kids." As more and more people are coming to realize, however, such parent-oriented child raising actually has a number of long-lasting negative effects on children.

Several causes of the long-lasting negative effects are included in this introductory paragraph. First, the term "traditional parents" implies those who raise their children according to traditions rather than question methods of child raising to see what really works best. Another cause of the negative effects is the parental goal of having strong control. A third is the parent-oriented concept of child raising. These thought-provoking causes of a problem will make most readers interested in and prepared for the text that follows.

EXERCISE

7-2

At what point in each of the following introductions is the topic introduced? Where does the controlling idea appear? Is there some kind of contradiction (other side)? What, in the content, is likely to draw the reader's attention?

1. Television has recently been targeted as the cause of serious problems in society. Violence, lack of education, and even low intelligence have been blamed on television. However, as necessary as it is to understand the potential harm of television broadcasting, we must also realize that in a number of important ways television has had a strong positive influence on society.

2. Television has recently been targeted as the cause of serious problems in society. Violence, lack of education, and even low intelligence have been blamed on television. However, this type of argument makes about as much sense as blaming single mothers for the high crime rate. People who exaggerate in this way the importance of one possible factor in a complex problem are only trying to avoid the responsibility of dealing with the actual causes of problems.

When you are working on an essay, do not feel obligated to put together a good introduction as soon as you have finished prewriting. If you encounter problems with the opening paragraph, try coming back to it after you have written the body of the essay; the process of working through the information in the body of the essay may help you identify exactly the ideas that you want to incorporate into the introduction. Another reason to postpone the introduction when it does not come easily is that if you decide to change the focus of the paper while you are working on the body, you have not wasted valuable time struggling with an introduction that was destined not to be used.

Introductions in student papers are often ineffective because they lack a clear topic, an explicit controlling idea, and an unmistakable direction for the essay. Several other problems frequently occur in opening paragraphs as well.

EXERCISE

7-3

Identify the weakness in each of the following introductions.

1. There is much to be said about capital punishment. I will discuss the key arguments.

2. What is the value of television? Is society affected by it? Can we learn from it? These are some of the questions that come to mind when we think about television.

3. It has often been said that television is to blame for the decline in education among our children. But television alone is not to blame. If a child watches television continuously from the end of the school day until bedtime, there is definitely a problem. But the child out playing all those hours is not doing homework either.

4. Television is good for society because of the variety of the programs. People can watch the news, documentaries, sitcoms, talk shows, and films. Those who have cable can watch an even greater variety of programs.

5. Television plays an important part in society today. When people have nothing to do, they sit in front of the television. They spend long hours watching. Television has many good effects and many bad ones on people.

6. Television, in addition to entertaining people, is also part of their education. There are many programs on television that are educationally challenging. Some of the documentaries and even some talk shows and game shows provide learning experiences. Viewers can learn about academic subjects such as science and history as well as current issues on the news.

7. There is a growing trend in the United States today. People are eating foods that are healthful.

The preceding examples illustrate some problems that you should take care to avoid.

First, do not announce what you will be discussing in your essay. Simply make sure that your thesis statement in the introduction clearly indicates both the topic and the controlling idea.

The second example involves the use of questions. In the introduction, as well as elsewhere in an essay, it is almost always preferable to make statements rather than to ask questions: the writer is supposed to be presenting a convincing argument, not interrogating the reader. Thought-provoking questions can be worded as thought-provoking statements. Instead of writing

How did the state go so quickly from apparent prosperity to serious deficit?

use a statement:

We may well wonder how the state went so quickly from apparent prosperity to serious deficit.

The third introduction in Exercise 7-3 illustrates another important principle about opening paragraphs: detailed information is out of place. The explanations given there belong in the body of the essay. In the sample, the third and fourth sentences discuss ways some children spend their time between the end of the school day and bedtime. But these are specific examples of activities that can interfere with homework; the writer should have stated instead that any nonscholastic after-school activity—not just television watching—can contribute to the decline in education. The introduction should bring up general principles, and the specific details should be systematically covered in the body of the essay.

Anything that is off the subject should be avoided in the introduction as well as anywhere else in the essay. In the fourth example, the fact that people who have cable television can watch a greater variety of programs than those who do not have cable does not directly relate to the idea that television offers a variety of programs.

The fifth introduction has a split personality. We do not know whether the controlling idea is *good* or *bad*. Even a comparison essay that describes strong contrasts needs to have a controlling idea.

The sixth opening paragraph also goes in two separate directions. It is unclear whether the essay will discuss what educational programs television offers or what people can learn from educational programs.

Did you know that "there is a growing trend in the United States today"? There are countless growing trends in this country. It is not helpful at all to make a statement like the one in example 7. Even though individual statements in a composition should be interpreted in context, you should avoid making assertions that taken alone are pointless. Here is a similar example:

There are many problems in the world today. One is the increase in the number of homeless people.

In both introductions, sentence combining can be used to make the writing meaningful.

There is a growing trend in the United States today toward the consumption of foods that are healthful.

One of the many problems in the world today is the increase in the number of homeless people.

Writing Assignments

E X E R C I S E

Write a composition on one or more of the following topics. Prewrite carefully. Then, as you write and revise your draft, pay particular attention to your introduction. It should clearly indicate the topic, the controlling idea, and the direction of the composition. It should not contain irrelevant information or inappropriate details. If you are writing an essay, consider whether your introduction contains an idea that will interest readers; identify the components of your introduction that are likely to encourage readers to read the entire essay.

1. A problem that large cities are facing
2. The long-range disadvantages of a voucher system in the schools
3. The uses of a particular invention
4. A wise way for the government to spend some imaginary additional tax money

E X E R C I S E

Working alone or with your classmates, examine your previous or current compositions to determine how effectively you have introduced the body of your writing.

- Are the topic, the controlling idea, and the direction clear?
- Have you included appropriate statements of opposing arguments, background information, key ideas that will not be discussed, causes, or other relevant information?
- Have you included something that will get the reader involved?
- Have you avoided the following undesirable elements?
  An announcement of what you will discuss
  Questions that could be in the form of statements
  Information that is off the subject
  Anything else that is not helpful

Summing Up

You have discovered that an effective introduction really leads the reader into the essay.

Purposes:
   To clarify the writer's statement to be developed
   To involve the reader in what the writer has to say

An introduction should include:

The topic of the essay

The controlling idea of the essay

The direction—usually *what, why,* or *how*—of the essay

An introduction may also include:

A contradictory element:

An element of surprise

Irony

The other side

Another element that gets the reader involved:

Visual imagery

An appropriate element such as an indication of causes in an effect essay

An introduction should not include:

An announcement of what the writer will do

Questions in place of statements

Details and explanations that should be placed in the body (introductions are general)

Information off the subject

A split controlling idea, such as advantages and disadvantages or two different sets of *what* items

A vague opening statement

In Chapter 8 you will learn some strategies to use when you write conclusions.

CONCLUSIONS

8

Compare the main ideas in the paragraph on the reasons for not owning a car, from Chapter 1. Does the concluding statement simply reword the topic sentence?

Topic sentence: *Thesis*

Many people who have access to good public transportation prefer not to own a car for a number of important reasons.

Key supporting ideas: *Claims*

First, it is expensive to have a car.

Another problem that vehicle ownership brings is legal liability.

Last, a person who has a car must put up with requests for rides from friends and relatives who do not have their own transportation.

Concluding statement: *= Concluding ...*

All of these inconveniences can make owning a car a mixed blessing indeed.

Good

Written in 3rd Person

The topic sentence and the concluding statement are actually quite different, but they do contain some of the same elements. The topic, "owning a car," is in both. The controlling idea, "reasons not to own one," is reflected in the negative ideas of "inconveniences" and "mixed blessing"; these words remind us of the controlling idea, so there is no real need to repeat it.

The Purpose of the Conclusion

Just as an introduction serves the purpose of introducing the body—the substance—of the essay, the conclusion is what we use to bring the essay to a close. Accordingly, what we put in our conclusion should reflect the content of the essay and should sound final. The topic and the controlling idea, consequently, are usually reflected in a concluding statement. Furthermore, the final sentence or paragraph is often related to the rest of the composition in other ways as well. As we saw in Chapter 1, the words "these inconveniences" summarize the problems with car ownership that were brought up in the key supporting sentences. The summarizing words logically connect the content of the paragraph very nicely, with the added benefit that they eliminate any need for repetition.

Another strategy in this conclusion is the indication of a result: the inconveniences spelled out in the paragraph lead to the result that owning a car is a "mixed blessing." Showing a result at the end of a composition offers two distinct advantages: that of reminding the reader of the content of the composition, and that of indicating the bottom line—something that sounds final. In other words, indicating a result, when appropriate, fulfills the two basic purposes of a conclusion: to reflect the content of the essay and to sound final.

Strategies for Conclusions

Compare the topic, controlling idea, and result as indicated in the concluding statement for the paragraph on the overcrowding of classes, from Chapter 1.

Topic sentence:

> The overcrowding of classes due to budget cuts in education is having some negative effects on student learning.

Key supporting ideas:

> Overcrowded classes, first of all, are more difficult to teach.
>
> Another disadvantage is that an overcrowded room is difficult to arrange so that learning can take place.
>
> A final problem with overcrowded classes is that individual students are less well served.

Concluding statement:

> Learning is sacrificed in overcrowded classes, and at a time of keen international competition, cutting the budgets for our schools may well turn out to be false economy.

The topic, "overcrowding," reappears in the concluding statement in the form of "overcrowded." The controlling idea, that it has "negative effects," is reflected in the negative idea of "sacrificed." The word "sacrificed" also shows the result of overcrowding.

Notice that the preceding conclusion has some additional meaning appropriate to the paragraph: "false economy" implies that sacrificing education because of budget problems is a bad strategy. In this way, a suggestion not to cut education budgets is implied.

FIVE BASIC ELEMENTS

Concluding statements for paragraphs and concluding paragraphs for essays usually include some of the following five elements:

CONCLUSION
- topic
- controlling idea
- summarizing words
- result
- suggestion/advice

EXERCISE

8-1 Which of the five elements just listed are present in the conclusion of each of the following examples (three paragraphs and one essay)?

1. Teachers have different ways of conducting class. Traditional teachers use the class time to lecture to the students. They believe that they have the information the students need to learn and that students should listen and take notes in order to memorize as much of the information as possible. As these instructors equate learning primarily with rote memorizing, they measure students' progress by how much information the students can reproduce on tests. Other teachers use most of the class time for group discussions. They suggest ideas for groups to consider; and then, from time to time, they recapitulate and synthesize the information thus gathered. These teachers, who usually favor a student-oriented class, provide only a limited amount of information themselves and generally do relatively little testing to assess student learning. A final category includes teachers who structure class time so that the students will arrive at an understanding of certain concepts. Rather than lecture to the students, they guide them, through suitable materials and appropriate questions, to an understanding of the course content. They then test their students' active comprehension of the course concepts. As different as these types of classroom management are, they are all common in our schools today.

2. A person who wants to lose weight can get better results from a slow weight-loss program than from a crash diet. The slow diet, first of all, is more effective nutritionally. The crash diet focuses on just a few foods, leaving the body nutritionally deprived after only a few days; in contrast, the slow diet involving a reduced number of calories and low fat content can leave the person, who is now thinking more clearly about the quality of the food, in better health than before. The slow diet is also a better choice physically. The crash dieter usually just diets, whereas the person with the slower, more carefully planned program is more likely to include the physical activity necessary for a body to be healthy. Finally, the slow diet is better psychologically. People who are overweight generally have both bad eating habits and psychological problems that aggravate their tendency to overeat. The crash diet does not address either of these areas, whereas the all-inclusive weight loss program takes into consideration the negative self-image as it helps the dieter gradually build better eating habits. For this reason, the weight lost in a gradual program is more likely to stay off. As far as dieting is concerned, it takes long-term methods to get long-term results.

3. Parents should not insist that their children go to college straight out of high school. First, the decision to go to college is a major one in life—one that needs to be made by the individual directly concerned rather than by the parent. The young person may not even want to continue with school. Also, it is very difficult for a student lacking positive motivation to be successful in higher education. Thus, the son or daughter who struggles with college primarily because of pressure from the parent accumulates frustration instead of knowledge. Another reason for the parent not to push the young person to go straight to college is that the decision may not be a suitable one. Often, the son or daughter who has just finished high school is not ready for college-level work. The recent graduate usually does not yet have clear ideas about a field of interest or a career goal. Furthermore, many teenagers are not mature enough to profit from college work. Once enrolled in class, they are faced with concepts they do not understand, and, unlike in high school, they must compete for grades with people in their twenties or older, who may understand those concepts very well because of their greater experience in life. As a result, the teenagers' immaturity becomes a real obstacle to success in their studies. A final problem is that recent graduates may have to leave good friends and favorite activities in order to go to college. In this way, their all-important social development is sacrificed. Parents may be doing a young person a real disservice by pressuring him or her to go to college.

4. Topic: Problem of the homeless

    Controlling idea: Has complex causes

    Key supporting ideas:
        Our type of system
        Precarious economic situation of country
        Problems in education
        Attitude toward mental patients
        Use of drugs
        Deteriorated physical state of homeless

    Conclusion: The problem of homelessness is growing, and solutions are not coming forth. Perhaps all of us need to take a closer look at this tragedy in our midst.

E X E R C I S E

8-2

Which of the preceding five elements are present or reflected in each of the following concluding statements?

1. Topic sentence: Community colleges perform important functions in their communities.
    Key ideas:

They give people who may not be able to go to college elsewhere the opportunity to take college-level classes.

They offer a variety of academic, vocational, and personal interest courses not generally available at other institutions.

They sponsor different cultural activities for the community.

They provide a forum for ideas.

Concluding statement: The community college is a useful institution that is here to stay.

2. [Same topic sentence and key ideas]

Concluding statement: The community college is a place where one can make life happen.

3. [Same topic sentence and key ideas]

Concluding statement: The community college gives virtually everyone a chance to improve as a person and advance in society.

4. [Same topic sentence and key ideas]

Concluding statement: Those who do not give it a try are depriving themselves of something worthwhile.

5. Topic sentence: Convenience stores could well be called inconvenience stores instead.

Key ideas:

The items are often hard to find.

The store is frequently out of what the customer wants.

The customer usually has to wait in line to pay for something.

The prices for the items are high.

Concluding statement: A visit to a convenience store can be a frustrating experience.

6. Topic sentence: A major earthquake can bring ruin to a populated area.

Key supporting ideas:

Causes medical emergency

Destroys homes

Damages infrastructure

Concluding statement: People in earthquake areas should prepare for a major one in order to reduce the disastrous effects.

7. [Same topic sentence and key ideas]

Concluding statement: After an earthquake, it takes a great deal of human energy and money to bring life back to a semblance of normality.

Consider the following thesis statement, key supporting ideas, and conclusion. Is the concluding paragraph effective?

Thesis statement:

The United Nations should have more authority in the affairs of individual nations.

Key ideas:

Many wars could be avoided.

World economy could be improved.

Sensible control over the environment could be established.

International communication and cooperation would increase.

Conclusion:

> In the twentieth century, countries are still constantly at war. Relatives are shooting at each other in Central America. People are fleeing from Vietnam. The different peoples in Yugoslavia are engaging in hostilities. When will it all stop? When will good people get in control?

This conclusion has several major problems. First of all, it contains too much detailed information. Conclusions, like introductions, usually contain general rather than specific information. The general statement that countries are still constantly at war provides a sufficient reminder of the details that were probably given in the first body paragraph. In addition, the detailed information in the conclusion focuses exclusively on the problems of wars, with no mention of anything that relates to other global areas—the economy, environment, and communication—that are in need of improvement. The misleading emphasis in the conclusion thus ruins the balance of the essay.

Another problem in this closing paragraph involves its use of questions. The final two questions do not enhance the meaning of the essay. Here, as elsewhere in an essay, it is usually better to make pointed statements than to ask questions.

A final problem is that the conclusion contains an idea that wanders off the subject. The concept of "good people" seems irrelevant in a discussion of the authority of a worldwide institution. The writer in this case may have been equating "good people" with the existing leadership of the United Nations and wishing that the UN had more practical authority to end senseless and bloody conflicts; but this connection is not made explicitly, and the words lend themselves to other interpretations less relevant to the thesis. You should be especially careful to avoid leading your reader astray in a conclusion.

We frequently use certain types of conclusions for certain types of compositions. We have already seen that the causes of an event or situation can appropriately be noted in the opening paragraph of an essay that discusses effects. Similarly, the effects of an event or situation, concisely stated, are meaningful in the conclusion of an essay describing its causes because these effects are the results of what has been explained.

In the same way, an argument essay can conclude with a suggestion. For example, a composition asserting that the government should not cut funding for education could be concluded with any one of a number of suggestions.

Possible concluding statements:

> The government should tune in to the needs of the people.

> Those in government would do well to realize that educational funding is indispensable but politicians are not.

Possible concluding paragraphs:

> There are still too many people today who lack an education. The government should try to reduce that number, not add to it.

> Even though some budget cuts are clearly necessary, it is wiser to trim elsewhere. Only in this way can the important area of education continue to function.

The concluding paragraph of a narrative essay often indicates the result of the experience—the attainment of a goal, perhaps, or the outcome of a learning experience, such as a greater understanding of something, a personal triumph of some kind, or another idea that represents the essential meaning of the experience to the writer. Several results are stated at the end of the narrative essay in Chapter 3:

> I felt better about myself after this incident. I had righted a wrong. I had helped someone to become a better person. I had made all the kids feel better about themselves and others. But more than that is evident to me now. I had cried out, for the first time, for equality.

Notice that both immediate and long-term results are emphasized in this conclusion.

OTHER ELEMENTS

[handwritten: KICKERS = ENDING STATEMENT THATS FUNNY.]

Other elements can also contribute to a meaningful conclusion.

Contrary Results
[Housework is still drudgery in spite of modern appliances]

> Perhaps that is why so many homemakers do as much of their work as possible in front of the ultimate appliance—the television set.

[Importance of attending class]

> If one misses class, one misses out.

[Advantages of getting a college education]

> Those who do not get a college education are left behind to do the dirty work.

[Problems students entering college face]

> The new student cannot afford to become overwhelmed by problems. One who does so risks losing sight of some truly important goals in life.

[Government should not cut educational funding]

> Less money for education means that many people who currently expect to go to school will lose that opportunity. In this way, we may see the massive growth of a category of people that Voltaire and even some of our own founding fathers feared: the uneducated rabble. Perhaps we should make a concerted effort not to let history repeat itself.

or

> Our government has enough problems without that of a proportionally large uneducated population.

or

> Our government is facing an important decision: whether to create a society that is educated or to create one that is not.

or

> During the 1980s, the government gambled with public education. We can see where that has left us in the international scene. We are in the position of contestants on a quiz show: we are running out of time.

[Factors motivating nations to go to war]

> No motivational factor can be unquestioningly accepted as just.

or

> Whatever motivates a country to go to war, the result is death. War is humanity's greatest flaw.

A Desired Result
[Advantages to getting a college education]

> Perhaps some day almost all Americans will get a college education as they now get a high school one.

An Observation or Analysis
[Supermarket shoppers can be classified by how organized they are]

> These shoppers have only one thing in common: they go to the supermarket for food.

or

> The organized shoppers are those that reap the greatest benefits.

[Husband and wife should share the responsibilities around the home]

> The family is not only his or hers. It is theirs.

Writing Assignments

E X E R C I S E

Write a composition on one or more of the following topics. Prewrite carefully. Then, as you write and revise your draft, pay particular attention to your conclusion. The reader, while going through your conclusion, should remain aware of your topic and controlling idea. Your concluding remark or remarks should also sound final. Include summarizing words, if possible.

1. Effects of overpopulation on a local or worldwide level
2. Something irresponsible that an organization (social, political, religious, etc.) is advocating
3. Negative results of an educational system that emphasizes rote memorization
4. Arguments for or against censorship

EXERCISE

8-4   Working alone or with your classmates, examine your previous or current writing to determine how effective your conclusions are.

- Does the conclusion reflect the content of the composition through the rewording of the topic and the controlling idea and through the use of summarizing words for your key ideas, whenever these strategies are appropriate?
- Does your conclusion sound final?
- Have you avoided details, irrelevant information, and ideas that lead in a different direction?

Summing Up

You have discovered that an effective conclusion enables the reader to come to final terms with the composition.

Purposes of a conclusion:
>   To reflect the content of the composition
>   To add something that sounds final

Elements that can reflect the content of the composition:
>   Topic
>   Controlling idea
>   Summarizing words
>   Result

Elements that can sound final:
>   Summarizing words
>   Result
>   Suggestion

Some other possibilities:
>   A contrary result
>   A desired result
>   An observation or analysis

Certain types of compositions can logically lead to certain types of conclusions:
>   Cause to a result
>   Argument to a suggestion
>   Narrative to the result of the experience

A conclusion should not contain:
>   Detailed information (because conclusions, like introductions, are general)
>   Information requiring further explanation
>   Information off the subject
>   Information leading in a new direction
>   Questions that would be better expressed as statements

IMPORTANT

In Chapter 9 you will take another critical look at your writing as you learn specific strategies for revising your work.

- *Every* thing in Conclusion, must also be in Thesis.
- So no new information in conclusion.

REVISING

9

Would you turn in the following paragraph to an English instructor for a grade?

Movies today are only geared toward one thing. Todays movies seem to only lean toward one idea, that idea is violence. No matter where one turns violence can be seen in any movie. Films, like "Indiana Jones and the Temple of Doom," "Gremlins," are blockbuster presentations, the whole plot is based around violence. A person can not critisize the producer's for creating these films because this is what the public is demanding, especially the younger generations. The teenagers of today are definetely the bread and butter of the film industry. Todays theater's have become hangouts, and there are a very large volume of teenagers seeing these films. I just wish there was a different trend in films.

You probably would not expect to receive a passing grade for the preceding paragraph. Look it over carefully to identify the changes that need to be made. Then compare the following version. What changes have been made? Is the paragraph effective in this form?

Movies today are geared toward only one thing. Today's movies seem to lean toward only one idea; that idea is violence. No matter where one turns, violence can be seen in any movie. Films like *Indiana Jones and the Temple of Doom* and *Gremlins* are blockbuster presentations. The whole plot is based around violence. A person cannot criticize the producers for creating these films because this type of production is what people, especially the younger generations, are demanding. The teenagers of today are definitely the bread and butter of the film industry. Today's theaters have become hangouts, and a very large number of teenagers are seeing these films. I just wish there were a different trend in films.

Did you notice that the only changes made were corrections of the errors in grammar, spelling, and punctuation? Did these corrections turn the paragraph into a satisfactory one?

There are still major problems with the paragraph. First and foremost, it does not have a controlling idea. Instead of developing a point, the writer rambles on about the lamentable trend toward violence in movies. Compare the previous paragraph with the one that follows.

The emphasis on violence in movies has grown out of proportion because so many people are contributing to this violent trend in films. The producers themselves bear much of the responsibility for the trend. After all, they create the movies—and the violence in them. Claiming that they are only making what the public wants, the producers, both in the films themselves and in the advertising for them, emphasize and even glorify the violence. The teenagers who seem to live for these films should also take part of the blame. They are old enough to understand the senseless cruelty and outrageous disregard for human life in these films, yet they patronize them as if it were a sacred duty. The parents of these young people and the adult generation as a whole should also assume responsibility for the trend. Mature people are in a position to be healthy role models for the children, but when the adults choose these films over more positive ones, they are sending the wrong message to the younger generation. People need to become aware of what they are doing to themselves and to society by supporting this industry of violence.

Besides the lack of a controlling idea, what other problems can you find with the original paragraph? In searching for the weaknesses, ask yourself, as you go through the writing, what specifically is being communicated to you. Compare the original paragraph with the second revised version, targeting the people who make the trend toward violence in films a reality.

You may have noticed that the first half of the original paragraph revolves around the idea that there is violence in most films. Then in the middle, there is a sharp change in direction: the writer remarks that a person cannot criticize the producers for creating these films. However, the question of responsibility is one for a separate composition. At this point, the original paper jumps again, from the responsibility issue to the subject of the movie theater as a hangout for teenagers. The final statement returns to the idea of violence in films. With this lack of focus, it is unclear what the writer intends to communicate in the composition as a whole. In other words, individual sentences or small groups of sentences may have meaning, but the paragraph taken as a whole does not.

It is difficult to assess the effectiveness of the supporting information when it is unclear what this information is supposed to support. In any case, however, the paragraph contains very little explanation. Only the titles of the two films clearly constitute supporting information.

The sentences present other problems besides the errors in grammar, spelling, and punctuation. Both ideas and individual words are repeated excessively. Moreover, the relationships between individual ideas are not shown. For example, we see that the theaters are a hangout for teenagers and that a large number of teenagers see violent movies. However, the actual connection does not involve *addition* but rather *cause and effect:* because teenagers tend to congregate in the area of movie theaters, many of them go to many movies, and vice versa.

Word choices are weak, too. "Hangout" is slang, and "bread and butter" is a cliché. Both need to be replaced with specific, meaningful, college-level terms.

Notice that the first revised version of the paragraph still contains all of the same problems because only errors in grammar, spelling, and punctuation were corrected. In other words, the proofread version is still an ineffective piece of writing.

The Purpose of Revising

The basic reason for revising a composition is to improve it. This involves carefully considering everything in the paragraph or essay to be revised.

We saw in the sample paragraphs about violence in the movies that simply correcting the mistakes in grammar, spelling, and punctuation did not produce good writing. Examining writing for errors of these kinds can be a very valuable exercise if you are trying to sharpen your sentence skills. But if your purpose is to revise a composition, not to practice your sentence-level writing, you need to follow a very different procedure.

Consider what you would do to revise the following paragraph:

Setting a goal for a career may require precise planning in college. The first step is making a decision regarding a career. Once the decision is made, the person can work toward that goal. Suppose someone chose marketing as a field. He or she would then need to find out what product is best to sell and what techniques are needed to sell it. Marketing also requires good communication skills as a way of selling a product. College helps a person speak effectively and confidently. These things are included in college training, depending on what one studies. Therefore, learning techniques is a way of gaining knowledge.

Can the preceding paragraph be revised without a great deal of change? It, like the first sample in this chapter, rambles. In fact, both paragraphs appear to be specimens of freewriting. In each case, the writer has noted down thoughts as they came to mind. But the results are exactly that: a series of random thoughts.

Like most freewriting, the preceding sample paragraph cannot be revised without a great deal of change because it lacks one of the essential elements of a good college composition: a controlling idea. In fact, before doing anything else to revise it, the writer must decide what statement he or she wants to make. In other words, to produce a usable paragraph, the writer needs to start all over again. The information in the original paragraph may be useful as a source of ideas, but the ideas destined for inclusion in the final composition must be restructured and refocused. Take another look at the revised version (not the proofread one) of the paragraph on violence in the movies. Some of the information in the original addressed the issue of who is responsible for the trend. The revised version makes this issue its central focus, identifying the role teenagers play (an idea from the original paragraph) and citing producers as also being responsible (in the original, they were described as not being responsible). The adult public, the other major category of people blamed for the trend in the revised version, did not appear in the original paragraph at all.

Thus, if no controlling idea emerges in the composition that is to be revised, there may be little or nothing to save from it. When you revise, your options are severely limited until you settle on a controlling idea—that is, decide what point you want to make about something.

The following paragraph has a serious structural problem. See if you can identify it.

Parents can be role models who help children learn several positive behaviors. First, children need to learn to communicate openly. Those whose parents are open and honest with them have an easier time learning to speak the truth. Second, by making sure they spend quality time with their children, parents have a positive influence on their young people. This means making some sacrifices. For example, the parent who would like to watch a favorite television program after a hard day's work may have to forego this privilege in order to watch the child participate in an event or help the youngster make a sound decision. Parenting is a difficult job, but seeing a child grow into a well-adjusted adult is an invaluable reward for a job conscientiously done.

You may have discovered that the key supporting ideas in the preceding paragraph above do not lead in the same direction. The first focuses on something children need to learn. In other words, it goes in the direction of *what*. The other key supporting idea brings up *how* parents can influence their children positively. As we saw in Chapter 2, the function of the key ideas is to support the controlling idea; and in order to do so, they must be logically consistent. The problem in this sample paragraph on parenting actually begins in the topic sentence itself: it is unclear whether the point is that parents can be role models or that there are several behaviors children learn according to what the parents model. Thus, the topic sentence itself does not clearly indicate either *how* or *what*. The unclear direction of the paragraph is the first problem to resolve in a revision of this particular composition. In revising it, the writer would also have to make other major changes.

What is the major problem in the following paragraph?

It is important to get a college education. First, people need to learn a great deal to get along in today's world. They are better off if they have specialized in some field. In addition, college gives people an opportunity to learn about themselves. This helps them to become productive citizens. Furthermore, people can develop socially in college. They meet many different types of people there and can make useful contacts. College truly unlocks the doors to the future. It is almost a must to have a college education if one is to survive.

Did this paragraph heighten your awareness of anything? How much did it really communicate to you? Does it resemble something other than a composition?

From the topic sentence, we get the impression that the writer is going to provide insight into *why* it is important to get a college education. But the rest of the paragraph consists of unsupported generalizations that read more like a list of ideas than like a composition. Lacking the detailed explanations, the composition communicates very little.

In your writing, be alert for statements that need to be supported with meaningful detail.

What problem in the following paragraph particularly needs to be addressed?

People thinking of going to college are concerned with the cost of tuition. However, a student entering college actually faces several major expenses. The first of these is, of course, the tuition. This costs hundreds of dollars a year even at a state school; and at a private school, it may exceed a person's income from a full-time job. The student can get a loan to help cover this expense. In addition to the tuition, other fees add to the cost of going to college. These include health service, library, and lab fees, besides the usual charge for a student body card. Some classes also have a materials fee. A third major cost is that of books and supplies. Several books may be required for a single class, and special materials are often needed for classes. Expenditures for writing paper and other basic supplies also add up quickly. Transportation to class is another major financial drain. Whether the student takes a bus or drives a car, paying for parking as well, this regular cost is not small. The student who has a car will also want to use the vehicle for purposes unrelated to school. If the student has to pay for room and board, too, the cost of going to college can be even more staggering. All of these expenses should make one think twice before deciding to enroll in college.

When you revise, watch out for anything that is off the subject. In the preceding paragraph, two ideas are irrelevant. The student's option of getting a loan does not add anything useful to the discussion of the different major expenses; *how* the student can come up with money does not explain *what* the expenses are. Similarly, in the explanation of transportation expenses, the idea of using a car for purposes unrelated to school is irrelevant.

What is the most serious problem with the following paragraph?

Many people prefer not to buy a home because of the extra responsibilities ownership involves. A renter generally writes one check each month. The homeowner makes several monthly payments. There are mortgage, water, trash, street-sweeping, gas, and electricity payments. The person who owns the home has to take care of maintenance and any repairs that are needed. Repairs can be extremely costly. The yard has to be kept up. The owner may not know how to take care of plants. The owner may not have time to do yard work. Sweeping dirt and fallen leaves off porches, driveways, and walkways takes time. Various serious legal liabilities are part of home ownership. Some people who rent would not have it any other way.

The overall structure and focus of the paragraph are adequate, but meaning is sacrificed because each idea is expressed as a separate entity instead of as an important part of a larger whole. In other words, the transitions that would enable us to understand how the ideas relate are missing. Notice how much more meaningful a version with logical connectors is:

Many people prefer not to buy a home because of the extra responsibilities ownership involves. First of all, whereas a renter generally writes only one check each month, the homeowner must make several monthly payments. In addition to the mortgage payment, there are water, trash, and street-sweeping charges, besides the regular gas and electricity bills. The person who owns the home also has to take care of maintenance and any repairs that are needed. This upkeep is a major responsibility because repairs can be extremely costly. Another task requiring the homeowner's attention is the upkeep of the yard. This is especially burdensome if the owner does not know how to take care of plants or does not have time to do yard work. Jobs such as sweeping dirt and fallen leaves from porches, driveways, and walkways can be quite time consuming. Last but not least, serious legal liabilities are part of home ownership. With all of the responsibilities that are tied to owning a home, some people who rent would not have it any other way.

What would you change in the following paragraph?

The movie theaters of yesteryear are long gone. The coziness, first of all, of the old theaters has almost entirely disappeared. Now there are only modern plastic theaters, with their nylon curtains, rayon seats, and synthetic armrests. The single movie theater is also extinct. Nowadays some theater complexes have upward of ten theaters, each sucking in viewers with commercial indifference. The affordable cost of the movie is also a thing of the past. Two tickets for a double feature could be had for an hour's pay at minimum wage, whereas one ticket for a single feature now soaks the viewer as much as two hours' pay at minimum wage. Going to the theater is certainly not what it used to be.

This paragraph loses some of its effectiveness because of poor word choices. The language is repetitious, and individual words do not fit well because their level is inappropriate or their specific meaning does not match what is needed in the context. Compare the following version, noting the changes that have been made:

The movie houses of old are long gone. The coziness, first of all, of the old theaters has almost entirely disappeared. Now there are only modern plastic theaters with their nylon curtains, rayon seats, and synthetic armrests. The single movie house has also nearly gone out of existence. Nowadays some movie complexes have as many as ten theaters, each drawing in viewers with commercial indifference. The affordable cost of the movie is also only a memory. Two tickets for a double feature could be purchased for an hour's pay at minimum wage, whereas one ticket for a single feature now costs as much as two hours of minimum pay. Going to the movies is certainly not what it used to be.

What is the major problem in the following paragraph?

A college education is a necessity for a person who wants to get a job that brings some kind of satisfaction in life. First, a degree can get a person a better paying job than without one. An example of this is a high school job like working at a fast-food place compare to a job with a college education like becoming a executive, doctor, and even a professor. Compare the fast-food wages to a doctor. Also, a degree can get a person a more pleasant job. Like one that is not stressful. When you get home at the end of a work day, you still feel like doing something, you still have some energy left. College is a must if one is to get a desent job.

Mistakes in grammar, spelling, and punctuation mar every sentence but the first one in this paragraph.

EXERCISE

Go through the preceding paragraph and identify the various errors in grammar, spelling, and punctuation. Then compare your findings with those of several classmates.

EXERCISE

The following paragraphs contain various problems that have been discussed in this chapter. Identify as many individual problems as possible. After you complete each paragraph, compare your findings with those given in the answer key.

1. If you want to enjoy your evening to the fullest; the movies are a nice place to go. After a long day of school or work, the movies are a great place to go and enjoy yourself. If you like you could also take a friend or the family. Its very economical for one thing. You don't have to worry about spending to much money. There's popcorn, candy, and all kinds of snacks and food there at your convience. Let's not forget what we went their for, the movie. You can get all of this in one full-action packed evening for a little of nothing. When your searching for something to do one evening remember, there's always the movies.

2. One of the best ways to look for a movie to see is through a newspaper instead of just going to the theater. Going to the theater without knowing what is being shown is a hard way to distinguish what movie to see because it's a waste of time and one might not like what's being shown once he gets there. The easiest way to look for a movie to see is thru a newspaper. In every newspaper there is a calendar section, for example, the Los Angeles Times. In each section the listings are specified where to see the movie, what time the movie starts, what is being shown, and who are the leading actors and actresses. Therefore, it is always best to look in the newspaper first.

3. The movies is a good place to go when you are bored. It doesn't cost very much and it is a good source of entertainment. Sometimes a movie can be very enlightening and educational. The movies give you something to do when you have no other plans. And for alot of young kids the movies is the thing that keeps them from getting into trouble. Meeting new people always happens when going to the movies, and because of this you might not get another chance to become bored again. So whenever you have no other plans for the day or evening, try going to the movies, it is a very good source of entertainment and company.

A Guide to Revising

In the exercises at the end of the preceding section, you looked for different kinds of problems in the writing samples. If you are revising your own writing, however, the procedure is quite different.

If you are given a revision to do as an assignment, your first concern should be whether you correctly followed instructions in doing the original work. You should also make sure that you understand any new instructions given in connection with the revision.

Except as amended by any special directions from your instructor, your method for revising a composition already graded should be the same as your method for revising a first draft that you want to develop into a polished composition.

As you saw from the samples throughout the previous section on the purpose of revising, there are many ways in which writing may need to be improved. You saw that proofreading (that is, correcting errors in grammar, spelling, and punctuation) is neither the primary task in revising nor the first one to undertake. In fact, when we revise, we work from the general to the particular. This means beginning with the composition as a whole, focusing on the topic and the controlling idea, then working our way through the supporting information, and finally examining the individual words and how they fit together in sentences. Thus, although you may backtrack frequently when you revise, the following series of steps should be taken basically in the order in which they are presented.

TOPIC AND CONTROLLING IDEA

If the topic and the controlling idea are not clear, your work needs major changes. Begin revising a composition by reading it straight through to ascertain whether you have any problem identifying your topic and controlling idea. If these two essential elements are not clear, begin your reconsideration here.

Remember that your reader must understand what specific statement you are making about your topic. As you begin revising, make a decision about that controlling idea.

Keep it:
If you still agree with it
If it can be supported
Change it:
If, after having explored it in writing, you find that you cannot support it
If you are not sure whether you can support it
If you decide to adopt something easier, more familiar, or simply different

If you change your topic and/or your controlling idea, you will need to brainstorm your new idea, in other words, go back to the creative stage and repeat the idea-gathering and organizational work that is part of prewriting.

KEY SUPPORTING IDEAS

If your topic and controlling idea seem strong, your next step is to read your composition again in order to analyze the key supporting ideas. As you read, try to answer the following questions:

> Do the key supporting ideas all support your controlling idea (are they all relevant)?
> Are they the strongest points you can find to support your controlling idea?
> Have you left out any strong point of support?
> Do your key ideas all go in the same direction (*what, why,* or *how*)?
> Is this direction consistent with your purpose in writing the composition?
> Are the key ideas arranged in logical order?
> Are they all expressed consistently? Have you avoided mixing affirmatives and negatives, actives and passives, general and particular items, and items that include other key ideas (for example, dogs, cats, and animals)?

If your key ideas need to be revised, you should return to the prewriting step in order to reconsider them and to add supporting information to your formulated key ideas.

ADDITIONAL SUPPORTING INFORMATION

Once you have supported your controlling idea with effective key ideas, you are ready to analyze your explanation of each key idea. Examine your key ideas and their support, one at a time. This information should:

> Validate the key idea, by showing how it supports the controlling idea
> Clarify the key idea, by answering questions readers are likely to ask about it (this involves taking different readers' perspectives into account)
> Be clearly relevant
> Be in logical order
> Be accurate
> If reasoned judgments, be based on factual information and carefully considered reasoned judgments
> If taken from sources, be from credible sources
> Take into account the implications and the logical consequences of the statements made
> Be free of irrelevant ideas, contradictions, oversimplifications, and unsupported general statements

When we revise, we often have to find new ways of explaining concepts. This means going back to the prewriting step and gathering more information for each key idea that needs better support. Brainstorming the individual idea is a good strategy at this stage because thinking creatively and generating new information may be essential, and this necessitates postponing critical analysis. Similarly, if you are having a problem with the wording of individual explanations, it can be a good idea to freewrite on whatever idea seems difficult to express clearly. To follow this strategy, try writing the same idea in different ways. Imagine that you are explaining the individual point to different people, such as a college instructor, another student, an adult with little formal education, and an adolescent, one at a time, writing down the words you would use in each case. In this way, you will develop different wordings for the idea; then you can review these alternatives and more easily construct a version that expresses the concept effectively.

TRANSITIONS

Once you have devised effective explanations for each key supporting idea, give careful thought to the relationships between ideas. As you move from clause to clause (statement to statement) and from key idea to key idea, add or change transitions as necessary to make the connections clear.

WORD CHOICES

The next step in revising is to consider word choices. Reread your composition slowly, focusing on individual words as they are used in context. Try to answer the following questions:

> Do the words you have chosen accurately express your ideas?
> Are all of your word choices appropriate for college writing?
> Have you avoided unwarranted repetition by using synonyms and alternative
>   ways of expressing ideas?

ERRORS IN GRAMMAR, SPELLING, AND PUNCTUATION

You will need one or more slow, very careful readings in order to find and eliminate errors in your sentences. Watch out for the following mistakes:

Run-together sentences	Problems with pronoun form
Fragments	Problems with reference
Problems with modifiers	Faulty predication
Agreement errors	Punctuation errors
Shifts in person or verb tense	Capitalization errors
Problems with parallelism	Spelling errors

In addition to these problems, all of which are common in college writing, be vigilant for the types of mistakes you have made on papers previously submitted. The following types of errors are frequent in student writing.

Faulty Word Combinations

Avoid writing, for instance, that people "discriminate others" or that something "results to" something. We say and write, for example:

> discriminate *against* somebody
> result *in* something
> discuss something   [not "*about* something"]
> affect something or someone   [*no* preposition]
> *used* to
> *supposed* to
> *such* as   [not just "as"]   (before examples)

Extra Prepositions in Subordinate Clauses
Example:

> In that class, the students learn skills useful on jobs *in which* they are striving
>   *for*   [should be: "jobs *for which* they are striving"]

Grammar Problems

Missing endings on verb forms. Examples:

> Perjury is *punish* by law.   [should be: "*punished*"]
>
> The officer *dismiss* us.   [should be: "*dismissed*"]
>
> Class is *dismiss*.   [should be: "*dismissed*"]
>
> Those people have little education *compare* to the average person.   [should be: "*compared*"]

Missing article before a singular count noun.

Noun or pronoun instead of a possessive adjective before a gerund. Example:

> When communication between the parent and the child is good, there is less likelihood of the *child* getting into trouble.   [should be:"*child's*"]

Missing relative pronoun. Example:

> Everyone *lives* in this society *has* to work.   [should be: "Everyone *who* lives . . ."]

Faulty subject. Example:

> *By having* celebrities promote a cause influences people to be in favor of the cause.   [subject does not make sense with verb, *influences*; a better statement: "Celebrities who promote a cause influence people to be in favor of the cause."]

Faulty conditional. Example:

> Next is the slow driver, who *would drive* fifteen miles an hour below the posted speed limit.   [should be: "who *drives*" or "who *tends to drive*"]

Logic Problems

Examples:

> People with only a high school diploma do not make the *best* money.   ["People with only a high school diploma do not usually make high salaries."]
>
> Daytime television brightens the *dead lives* of stay-at-home parents.   ["the *dull* lives"]
>
> Air pollution may even *help* cause skin cancer.   ["may contribute to the development of skin cancer"]
>
> Feeling lonely, he decided to call *friends and pizza*.   ["to call friends and to order a pizza"]
>
> The prospective employee may need skills that are different from those needed for *his* previous employment.   [applies to men only]
>
> > Possible solutions:
> > Use the plural   (". . . employees . . . their . . .").
> > Use a specific word   (". . . for the job seeker's previous . . .").
> > Use "*his* or *her*."

Mistaken Words

Examples:

He drives an *arrow*-dynamic car.

The ball joint enables the part to move any *witch* way.

Budget cuts in the 1980s seriously under*mind* education.

The decisions of short*sided* politicians can have disastrous effects on any country.

If teenagers can be paid a subminimum wage, employers will *higher* them to replace adult minimum wage earners.

Many students are *hopping* to pass their classes.

In her paper on fashion design, she described the *cloths* students wore on campus.

Clichés

Find specific words to replace them. Examples:

Many others are *in the same boat.*   ["in the same situation"]

Knowledge is the *key to opportunity.*   ["Through knowledge, a person acquires greater opportunities."]

College gives us *new avenues* to explore.   [opens "new possibilities"]

It is better to be a *well-rounded* person.   ["versatile," "flexible," or whatever the writer means specifically]

A SAMPLE REVISION

The following revision of a short essay shows the step-by-step process the writer used in order to produce a better version of the writing.

Original Essay

Students sometimes blame other people when they fail a course. They may say that the class was just too difficult or that the college expects too much. Or they may find fault with the teacher. Much more often, however, the reasons for failing grades center around the students themselves.

Bad study habits, first of all, can cause students to fail. This happens when they do not study enough to pass their tests. Students who procrastinate when they have something that needs to be done will see their school work suffer. Also, students who go out with friends or get involved in other activities, thinking they will find the time to study later, are typically heading for trouble. Inefficient study habits can also contribute to students' failure. The common belief that a person can watch television or talk to people while studying often destroys test scores. Students who are disorganized or have poor study skills also frequently fail classes.

Another important cause of student failure is attendance. Students may be very tired or they just may not want to get up in the morning and go to school. This sometimes happens because they have been out partying or because they are lazy. Either way, when they miss class, it lowers there grade. Then they don't understand what is going on when they do go back to class.

Their attitude about the course can also make them fail. If they are not interested in the subject, it will be difficult for them to accomplish much. An unfavorable attitude about school in general will do the same thing. When the teacher is not a likable person or does not explain what they need to know makes another serious problem even if the students want to learn.

People that have to work are usually at risk in school. A job takes away alot of a student's time and may even interfere with attendance in class. If a person works 25 hours a week and attends class 15 hours a week, it is hard to find enough time and energy to study.

Personal problems make it difficult to concentrate on school work. This is the case when someone in the family dies or when there is a divorce under way. If parents don't encourage their kid to go to school puts an extra burden on someone. A constantly running television set can be hard to study by.

Finally, low test scores can make students fail their classes. Many teachers give homework for a grade. Some teachers even allow students to do extra credit to help their grade.

These aspects are familiar to most students. It is up to them to find the solutions and succeed in school.

Ideas for Revising

1. Topic and controlling idea
   Topic ("reasons for failing") and controlling idea ("center around students") are workable. Essay contains a great deal of information to support this controlling idea.
2. Key supporting ideas
   "Bad study habits": good, but find a synonym for *bad*
   "Attendance": good, but needs to be worded to indicate *poor* attendance
   "Attitude": good, but word as a *negative* attitude
   "People that have to work" and "personal problems" are good ideas but are part of the more general idea of a student's difficult situation outside the school setting. Combine these.
   "Low test scores" does not fit as a key idea. It is a possible result of problems brought up in other key ideas.
   Word all key ideas as reasons why students fail classes.
3. Additional supporting information
   First body paragraph:
   "Going out with friends" is really an example of "other activities." Use it as an example, and add another example or two.
   Develop with explanations "disorganized" and "poor study skills."
   Second body paragraph:
   Explain less about why attendance is poor and more about why poor attendance contributes to failure.
   Third body paragraph:
   Add further explanations: lack of interest leads to lack of involvement; unfavorable attitude about school indicates that a student does not fully appreciate the purpose of going to school and will therefore not profit from the education; the problems with the teacher are part of the teacher's lack of a solid understanding of the students' real needs.
   Fourth and fifth body paragraphs:
   Combine as forms of difficult situation outside the school setting.
   Explain more about interference of work with study: scheduling problems, physical and mental effects, priorities.
   Eliminate inappropriate specific information about hours.

On personal problems, divide into groups and include examples:
Stressful events:
    death
    divorce
Lack of consideration for student:
    lack of encouragement for what student is doing
    continual interference
        disruptive environment (television, etc.)
        frequent interruptions
Sixth body paragraph:
    Supporting information indicates how students can improve grades, not why they get bad ones. Eliminate, along with key idea.
4. Introduction
    Restate "college expects too much."
5. Conclusion
    Clarify meaning, and reword.
6. Transitions
    These are needed in many places. Reconsider after ideas are in place.
7. Word choices
        bad [negative, poor, ineffective]
        heading for trouble
        either way
        do the same thing
        hard to study by [is a distraction that makes studying difficult]
        aspects [reasons for failure]
    Reconsider wording after ideas are in place.
8. Sentence problems
    Reconsider after ideas are in place.

Revised Essay

Students who fail a course sometimes blame other people for their lack of success. These students may say that the class was simply too difficult or that the expectations for student performance in the course were too high. They may also find fault with the teacher. Much more often, however, the reasons for failing grades center on the students themselves.

Poor study habits, first of all, can cause students to fail. People risk not passing their tests if they do not, for whatever reason, study enough. Those who typically procrastinate, counting on having enough time to study later, or get involved in other activities such as watching television or going out with friends, losing track of how much time is really left to prepare, are likely to perform poorly on upcoming tests. Besides not studying enough, many people enrolled in classes have inefficient study habits. They may have difficulty identifying what is important to learn and using their time well in order to master the essentials. Chronic problems with concentration also interfere with work that requires a person to be focused. People who are typically disorganized are bound to have problems preparing for exams because they waste both time and energy.

Irregular attendance in class also puts students at risk of failure. People who miss class are taking chances, since they can lose credit for a quiz—announced or not—or another in-class graded assignment. When they skip class, they also miss the teacher's explanations of the course material as well as the opportunity to talk to other students about the work and to ask the teacher questions. Students who do not attend regularly then have difficulty understanding work in progress when they return to class.

A negative attitude can put a student's success in jeopardy. Those who are not interested in a subject often are insufficiently involved in the work to pass the class. Similarly, students who lack a positive attitude about attending school frequently perform poorly; until they come to appreciate the purposes of going to school, they are unlikely to profit from what they are supposed to be learning. Students can also be at risk when they have a negative attitude toward a teacher who does not relate well to them or does not explain the course material in a way that they can readily understand. Those who are overly distracted by such negative feelings tend to get poor results in class.

The inability to cope with a difficult situation outside the school setting is a further source of problems affecting a student's grades. People who work at a paying job more than just a few hours a week find themselves in the situation of juggling two major occupations. In addition to scheduling problems, they must deal with the mental and physical strain involved. Personal problems can also aggravate the burden. Stressful circumstances such as those of the death or divorce of a close one can put a student's success in jeopardy. Other types of problems involving the people around the student can unduly interfere with his or her studies. Inconsiderate family members not only fail to provide the psychological support the student needs but also tend to interfere directly with the student's work by interrupting constantly and by creating a generally disruptive environment. The student who does not find a way to deal with these added difficulties will usually not succeed in classes.

These problems are familiar to most students. It is up to the individuals concerned to find workable solutions so that they can be successful in their scholastic careers.

E X E R C I S E

The following paragraphs contain problems discussed in this chapter. Identify the problems. After you have worked alone finding problems, compare your notes with those of some of your classmates. As usual, once you have finished one piece of writing, go over the material in the answer key before you begin the next one.

1. Today nearly every home has a television set. For some, watching television is a waste of time. For others, television is a source of information. For yet others, watching television is a favorite pastime. Some people depend on television as a source of news. Watching can be addictive. Some watch hour after hour, they may even get angry if someone comes along and interrupts. The people who feel that television is a waste of time. They may prefer to read newspapers to fined out what is happening and go out to be entertained. Thus, television can be useful, but people need to control themselves.

2. Some physical activity is part of good health. There are many kinds of recreation that people can enjoy after school or work. They can get involve in active sports such as soccer or tennis. Swimming and brisk walking which provide both physical and mental benefits. Even an activity such as gardening requires some fairly strenuous movements. It is very important that people who sit for long hours during the day at work or school get real physical exercise. They need it not only to stimulate the circulation and digestion, exercise also helps a person maintain a normal energy level. Furthermore, it gives the person a fit image that promotes a healthy, positive self-image. The wise exercise.

EXERCISE

9-4

The following compositions contain various problems discussed in this chapter. First, identify the problems. Then, working from the general to the particular, decide how you would revise each composition. After you have had a chance to work alone, compare your ideas with those of some of your classmates. Check to see whether you and your peers found the same problems and whether your ideas on revision are similar. You may have made different decisions about revising, depending on what you want to clarify as the topic and the controlling idea. As usual, once you have finished your revision of one piece of writing, go over the material in the answer key before you begin revising the next composition.

1. It is really necessary for a person to choose the right career. Why is it so important? Because we will be sorry for the rest of our lives if we choose the wrong major. Two factors should be considered. To avoid this problem. The first is picking something interesting for a career. There are some jobs a person can enjoy doing. When you like your job, your whole life seems nicer. Being realistic is the second factor. A person should try to get into a field in which he will be needed. He also needs to pick something that he will actually be able to complete. It also depends on luck.

2. Teen suicide is the third leading cause of death for people between the ages of 15 and 24. In the United States, the two leading causes are: accidents and homicides. There are two types of resources, professional and nonprofessional, available to the troubled teenager. Professional resources include: social workers, private therapists, and psychiatric hospitals. Social workers are agencies that can help when family conflicts is at the root of the problem. Another type of aid is private therapists. Private therapists are for people who are looking for psychiatric treatment. The last type of aid in this category is the Psychiatric hospital. Referrals to such a resource are made when it is thought that the patient might harm himself or other's. The second type of resource is nonprofessional. The family is one of the most valuable resources. The family must be involved in accepting responsibility and helping the troubled teenager. Another type of aid is friends. Friends can be used in the same way as family members. As you can see there are a number of ways to get help for a teenager who is contemplating suicide.

3. There are many pros and cons about election campaigns for public offices. Several of the good things are that it lets the public know everything about the candidate. This is helpful because the public votes for the best candidate. Campaigns can also bring out scandals or affairs that a candidate has been involved in. There are a few bad things about campaign advertising. A candidates advertising doesn't always discuss anything about that particular candidate. It is usually used to discredit and put down the other candidates. Other negative aspects are that sometimes a candidates personal and family life are brought into the campaign because of scandals and other things. This has the possibility of ruining not only the candidates life and career but also ruining his families life and reputation. I believe that campaigning is necessary and helpful, but I wish it wasn't used as a weapon or as a game, as it is sometimes misused.

4. Computers have benefited our modern world. Paper work gets done faster on a computer. Communication has been greatly improved through the use of computers. Companies that use computers have been able to cut back drastically on their work force.

The amount of time it takes an employee to do a report is much less than it was before computers began to be used. It is fast to make changes in a manuscript on the computer since the entire text does not need to be retyped. The computer will also do your dictionary work for you at the flick of a switch. The person typing also does not need to worry about neatness because the computer will take care of everything.

The ability of computers to network with other computers is also a great advantage. Businesses connect all their computers together so people can transfer information from machine to machine. In this way, one person can prepare a report and immediately transfer it to someone else, anywhere in the world. People doing research can get information from someone else's computer instead of having to go somewhere to get it. Other people are enjoying the benefits of being able to work out of their homes.

Companies are now starting to cut back a lot on their employees because computers can do so much of the work. In fact, one machine can do the work of several people. Some jobs have been entirely replaced by computers.

Computers are one of the world's most important inventions. Society has been completely changed by them. If you want to succeed in the world today, you have to be good on the computer. If you are not, you may get left out in the cold.

EXERCISE

9-5

Working alone or in groups, revise previous writing assignments of your own. Follow the guide to revising given in this chapter.

Suggestions for Writing and Revising in Class

When you write in class, you usually have little or no time for revising. If you must write a paragraph in no more than a 50-minute class period or an essay in 1 hour and 50 minutes, you do not have enough time to prepare a rough draft and revise it properly. Therefore, it is generally preferable to prewrite very carefully, planning your topic sentence or thesis statement, your key ideas with their direction, and your supporting explanations. Then you can slowly write your draft, concentrating on expressing your meaning accurately. The last few minutes should be spent making any necessary changes in wording and in grammar, spelling, and punctuation.

If you have 2½ or 3 hours to write, you can generally revise and recopy a draft. You should still spend 20 to 30 minutes prewriting, making a good plan before you begin a draft. Take care to leave yourself a few minutes to check your recopied paper for errors.

Whenever you write paragraphs and essays in any class, leave space around your writing for changes you want to make, as well as for appropriate annotations by your instructor. Leave proper margins along both sides of the paper. If your writing is large, skip lines. Use ink when you write a draft to turn in; bring correction fluid, and be neat in using it.

You may be assigned a specific number of words for a composition. If you are supposed to write 500 words, for example, make sure that you actually write between about 450 and 550 words. So that you do not have to waste time counting words during timed writings, figure out in advance how many words you write on a line, on the average, and how many lines of writing you get on each page. In this way, you can quickly estimate the number of words you have written.

Summing Up

Revising, like prewriting, is an important step in writing that, whenever possible, should be included in the process of developing a composition.

When to revise a composition:

After you have completed a first draft, but before you turn your composition in for a grade

When you are assigned revision or rewriting

Revise a composition to make it communicate meaning more effectively.

Revise a composition by moving from general to particular concerns. Look for:

    Clear topic and controlling idea

    Effective key ideas and single direction

    Adequate and appropriate support

    Transitions where appropriate

    Precise word choices

    Correct, logical sentences

    Correct spelling

Part Two

SENTENCES

THE SENTENCE

The sentence is the shortest grammatical unit in which a complete thought can be expressed. The student writer should be concerned with the expression of meaning in this short form, as well as in longer compositions.

As with the paragraph or longer composition, an effective way to see how sentences are constructed is to experiment with actually putting them together.

EXERCISE

10-1

Unscramble the following three groups of words to make sentences.

1. is best honesty the policy

2. cane and street a crossed the with went a into store man a

3. from hill fallen many the at barn the of top tree beyond had the apples the

The Subject

As you looked at the scrambled sentences, you probably asked yourself, perhaps without realizing it, what each group of words could be about. In the first example, the sentence could have been about "honesty" or about "policy," the only words that name something. The second group of words could have been about a "cane," a "street," a "store," or a "man." The third sentence could have been about a "hill," a "barn," a "tree," "apples," or a "top." One more possibility is "many," which could be used as a pronoun indicating many of something already mentioned.

In the process of instinctively going over the words in each sentence to identify what the sentence was about, you were actually looking for one of the fundamental parts of the group of words we call a sentence: you were looking for the subject. The **subject** is what a sentence is about. It names what the writer is talking about.

The Verb

Your second step in analyzing the scrambled sentences in Exercise 10-1 was probably to look for what happened or what was being said about the subject. In the first example, because the sentence is so short, it is easy to see that "is," although it does not show action, links "honesty" and "policy." In the second sentence, two words denote actions: "crossed" and "went." Of the four possible subjects, only the "man" would be likely to "cross" something or "go" somewhere. Thus, you were probably able to add the other fundamental part of the sentence, the verb, to the subject. The verb in the third sentence is "had fallen," and the potential subject that most obviously makes sense with it is "apples."

In each sentence, you tried to figure out what was being said about the subject—in other words, what statement was being made about the subject. In the first example, the writer is saying that "honesty is" something. In the second one, we are being told that the "man crossed" something and "went" somewhere. In the third sentence, what is being said about the "apples" is that they "had fallen."

The second fundamental part of a sentence is the **verb**—the statement the writer is making about the subject.

The Four Basic Elements in the Sentence

After identifying the subjects and verbs in the preceding sentences, you probably found that you could group some of the other words together. You may have combined "with a cane" and "into a store" in the second sentence. In the sentence about apples, if you experimented enough, you may have found "from the tree," "at the top," and "beyond the barn." These phrases could then be added to the subjects and verbs, to provide additional information about them.

Compare the following sentences. What is each sentence about? What statement is made in each sentence?

1. Dogs bark.
2. The enormous guard dogs in the neighbors' backyard bark furiously during the night at every car that passes the house.

In spite of the difference in length, in both sentences the writer is talking about "dogs," and in both sentences the statement being made about dogs is that they "bark."

ESSENTIAL ELEMENTS: SUBJECT AND VERB

The first sentence contains only a subject and a verb. Yet it is a complete sentence because it also has meaning: it identifies what noise dogs make. The subject and verb—the only elements in this sentence— are essential elements in any sentence.

ADDITIONAL ELEMENTS: MODIFIERS AND CONNECTORS

The second sentence gives additional information about both the subject and the verb. Two adjectives, "enormous" and "guard," tell us more about the dogs, as does the prepositional phrase "in the neighbors' backyard." The adverb "furiously" gives us more information about "bark," as do the prepositional phrases "during the night" and "at every car."

These words and phrases that add further information are called **modifiers**. The added details provided by modifiers answer questions such as *which, when, where, why,* and *how.*

Here is the second sentence, with arrows indicating what each added element modifies:

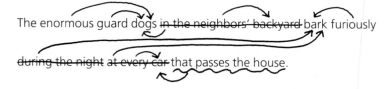

The enormous guard dogs in the neighbors' backyard bark furiously during the night at every car that passes the house.

The word "in," a preposition, links the word "backyard" to "dogs." "Backyard" is the **object** of "in." "Neighbors'" modifies "backyard." The entire prepositional phrase "in the neighbors' backyard" tells *where* the dogs are. Similarly, the preposition "during" links its object, "night," to the verb "bark"; and the entire phrase "during the night" tells *when* the dogs bark. The other prepositional phrase, "at every car" ("at," the preposition; its object, "car"; plus the modifier, "every"), also gives more information about "bark." The subordinate clause, "that passes the house," provides an explanation about "car."

Modifiers are the third basic element in the sentence. They provide information that may be necessary or simply helpful about other words in the sentence. Modifiers can be single words, phrases, or subordinate clauses.

Connectors are the fourth basic element. They link parts of the sentence together. They include prepositions ("in," "during," and "at," in the preceding example) and conjunctions:

Joe *and* Tom heard the news of the merger *and* of the changes that would take place in the company, *but* they preferred not to sell their shares.

The first "and" joins two words ("Joe *and* Tom"), and the second one joins two phrases ("of the merger *and* of the changes"). "But" joins two clauses ("Joe and Tom heard the news . . . *but* they preferred not to sell their shares").

Thus, the logic of the sentence and the logic of the longer composition are basically the same:

1. The writer has to be talking about something. This is the subject of the sentence and the topic of the paragraph or essay.
2. The writer has to be saying something about that subject or topic. This is the verb of the sentence and the controlling idea of the paragraph or essay.
3. The writer usually gives additional necessary or helpful information. This is provided in the form of modifiers in the sentence and in the form of additional sentences in the paragraph or essay.

We can show the logical correlation between the sentence and the longer piece of writing as follows:

LOGICAL ELEMENT	SENTENCE	COMPOSITION
What the writing is about	subject	topic
What the writer is stating	verb	controlling idea
Additional information	modifiers	additional sentences

PRACTICE WITH THE FOUR BASIC ELEMENTS

Subjects, Verbs, Modifiers

Examples: 1. Big dogs bark loudly.

2. Children on vacation usually play in the morning.

EXERCISE

10-2

Mark the subjects, verbs, and modifiers in the following sentences. Use a single line under the simple subject, a double line under the verb, and a single line through each prepositional phrase. Draw an arrow from the modifier to the word it modifies.

1. New cars run efficiently.

2. Many people read widely.

3. Most teenagers often go to the movies.

4. Large airplanes can fly to distant places.

5. Restaurant owners often work in the evening.

Notice that modifiers answer questions about other words in the sentence. In the examples in Exercise 10-2, for example, "loudly" tells *how*; "usually" tells *how often*; "in the morning" tells *when*; "to the movies" tells *where*; and so forth.

Subjects, Verbs, Modifiers, Direct Objects

Examples: 1. The English drink tea.

2. He returned the history book to the library.

E X E R C I S E

Mark the subjects, verbs, and modifiers as in the preceding examples. Mark each direct object D.O.

1. Television talk shows frequently present important topics.

2. The children were watching the men on the roof.

3. Local architects have drawn a new set of plans for the project.

4. Instant replays provide valuable information during athletic events.

5. Most city dwellers dread heavy morning traffic.

The **direct object** is the object of the verb. It answers the questions *whom* or *what* about the verb:

Whom were the children watching?   the men
What do instant replays provide?   information

Subjects, Verbs, Modifiers, Direct Objects, Subordinate Clauses

Examples: 1. The book that you took belongs to my roommate.

2. We go to the beach when the weather is hot.

E X E R C I S E

10-4

Mark the subjects, verbs, modifiers, and direct objects as in the preceding examples. Draw a wavy line under each subordinate clause.

1. We stayed home because it was raining.

2. They will go to the game if they get tickets.

3. They will wait until they hear the news.

4. The movie that we saw on television yesterday has caused considerable controversy

about the idea of life after death.

5. The lady who came in at 7 P.M. presents workshops on writing.

Notice that "when the weather is hot" (example 2 preceding Exercise 10-4) does not constitute a sentence because it does not have meaning all by itself. But it does have its own subject ("weather") and its own verb ("is"). It is a subordinate clause, and it modifies "go," explaining *when* we go.

There are two kinds of clauses: one that has meaning by itself, and one that does not. "They will go to the game" expresses a complete thought, so it has meaning; but "if they get tickets" does not.

A **main clause** (also called an **independent clause**) has a subject and a verb, *and* it has meaning. A main clause can be a sentence:

The book belongs to my roommate.

A **subordinate clause** (also called a **dependent clause**) has a subject and a verb, but it does not have meaning. A subordinate clause cannot be a sentence:

that you took

Subjects, Linking Verbs, Predicate Nominatives or Predicate Adjectives

Examples:

1. Mr. Smith is an engineer. (N, PRED. NOM)

2. Mr. Smith is wealthy. (N, PRED. ADJ)

EXERCISE

Mark the subjects, linking verbs, and predicate nominatives (P.N.) or predicate adjectives (P.A.) in the following sentences.

1. Their neighbor is a doctor.

2. Their neighbor is intelligent.

3. He is an interesting person.

4. He was a good student.

5. He was studious.

Linking verbs (*is, are, was, were,* and others) connect the subject with something that renames the subject (predicate nominative) or with something that modifies the subject (predicate adjective). "Doctor" renames "neighbor"; that is, the writer can call that particular person either a "neighbor" or a "doctor." In the second sentence, the predicate adjective "intelligent" modifies "neighbor."

Compound Sentences

Examples: 1. Dogs bark, but cats meow.

2. The older children were playing soccer, and the younger ones were going on the swings and bars.

EXERCISE

Mark the subjects and verbs in the following sentences.

1. Birds fly, but chickens only flutter.

2. He is a doctor, and he is also a golfer.

3. The students may enroll in classes in Paris during the summer, or they may just travel

    around France.

4. He ate all of the pasta, and he had a big serving of dessert.

5. He knew his neighbors, but he almost never talked to them.

The Concept of Function in the Sentence

Grammar is complex even in a language such as English that has relatively few forms. A single word in a sentence may be classified in different ways, and some of the classifications may overlap. The college writer generally does not need to know all possible grammatical labels; however, an understanding of basic grammar is important for students doing college writing assignments.

The concept of **function** in grammar is an especially important one. Words have different forms and different uses, depending on their function in the sentence.

Compare the functions of the word *light* in the following sentences:

1. The *light* in the yard repels insects.
2. The custodians *light* the stadium for night games.
3. The *light* fixture needs repairs.

In the first sentence, "light" is a noun naming an electrical device. In the second, it is a verb making a statement about what the custodians do. In the third, it is an adjective describing the kind of fixture.

Compare the functions of the word *actor* in the following sentences:

1. The *actor* played a major role in the film.
2. The director praised the *actor*.
3. The director gave the *actor* the new script.
4. We read an article about the *actor*.

"Actor" is the subject of the first sentence, and it is the direct object of the second (that is, the object of the verb "praised"). In the third sentence, "actor" is the indirect object ("script" is the direct object, and "actor" explains *to whom* the director gave the script); and in the fourth, it is the object of the preposition "about."

Notice that a single word may have more than one function. "Actor" in all four sentences is a noun because it is naming a person who performs. At the same time, it can be a subject or an object, depending on what it names: what the writer is talking about (the subject of the sentence) or the object of another word in the sentence.

Compare:

1. The *sun* warms our planet.
2. We see the *sun* during the day.
3. The people on the beach were lying in the *sun*.

"Sun" is a noun in all three sentences. It is also the subject in the first one, the direct object in the second one, and the object of the preposition "in" in the third one. Consequently, when we analyze sentences, we may put more than one label on a single word. For example:

$$\begin{array}{c} \text{PRON} \qquad \overset{\text{D.O.}}{\underset{\text{N}}{}} \quad \text{PREP} \qquad \text{N} \\ \underline{\text{We see the sun}} \;\; \text{during the day.} \end{array}$$

Here, the word "sun" is marked as a noun because it is naming something, and it is also marked as a direct object because it is the object of the verb, "see."

Parts of Speech

Refer to Table 10-1 on the following page for a description of the parts of speech.

Putting the Sentence Together

EXERCISE

10-7

Identify the following elements in the sentences given next.

1. simple subjects
2. verbs
3. modifiers

TABLE 10-1   *Parts of Speech*

PART OF SPEECH	FUNCTION	EXAMPLES
Words that name		
nouns	name persons, places, things, and ideas	The **hat** is on the **table**. Joe visited **Hawaii**.
pronouns	take the place of nouns	**I** took **it**. **That** tells **me everything**.
Words that make a statement		
verbs	make statements	Her car **runs** well. It **is** new. It **has** power steering.
Words that modify		
adjectives	modify nouns, pronouns, or gerunds	**Her new** house **is big**. It is **expensive**. **Her** buying it was an achievement.
adverbs	modify verbs and adjectives, adverbs, or other modifiers	He answered **quickly**. **Too** many trees were cut. They **hardly ever** come.
Connectors		
prepositions	relate their objects to other words in the sentence	The pen **on** the desk was used **for** important documents.
conjunctions	join words, phrases, or clauses	She can rent the movie in English **or** Spanish. The boy ran through the yard **and** down the alley. Dogs bark, **but** cats meow.

Note: Interjections (Wow! Ouch!) are seldom used in college writing.

EXERCISE 10-7 *continued*

4. phrases

5. parts of speech (N, PRON, ADJ, ADV, PREP, and CONJ)

Example: The young boys in our town often swim in the lake beyond the farms on warm nights.

1. The big dog under the tree watched the cat in the window of the mansion.

2. The inexperienced travelers unwisely took several suitcases on their trip to Europe.

3. The crafty elderly lady and the clever young man quietly hid the microchip in the cigarette case and left through the back door.

4. The smaller children in the school playground were running toward the swings near the cafeteria.

5. The tall tree on the hillside was swaying wildly in the wind.

Notice that once we have drawn the arrows connecting the modifiers to what they modify, we have divided the sentence into two parts—the **complete subject** (the simple subject plus its modifiers) and the **predicate** (the verb plus its modifiers and its object, if there is one). In other words, the complete subject is what the writer is talking about, with its added information; and the predicate is the writer's statement, with its added information. The added information in the complete subject and predicate may be necessary to the basic meaning of the sentence, or it may simply be helpful.

We can use a slash mark to divide each sentence into its components, the complete subject and the predicate. In the example, the slash mark between the complete subject and the predicate would go between "town" and "often."

EXERCISE

Divide the five sentences in Exercise 10-7 into two parts by putting a slash mark between the complete subject and the predicate. The object of the verb (direct object) is part of the predicate.

As we have seen, clauses, unlike phrases, have a subject and a verb. Consider the clauses in the following sentence.

He stayed home because he wanted to see a movie he had rented.

The essential statement here is "he stayed home," and the rest of the sentence is additional information. We can analyze the sentence as follows:

Two subordinate clauses modify other words in the sentence: "because he wanted to see a movie" tells *why* he stayed home, and "[that] he had rented" modifies "movie," telling *which* movie. We can mark the subjects and verbs of subordinate clauses in parentheses, to distinguish them from the subjects and verbs which make sentences complete—those of main clauses.

EXERCISE

10-9

Identify the simple subjects, verbs, modifiers, phrases, parts of speech, complete subjects and predicates, and subordinate clauses in the following sentences.

1. The English of all social classes drink tea when they need consolation.

2. The girls who have finished school sometimes work for the local storekeepers

   as clerks or bookkeepers.

3. Retired people in the country gladly spend their spare time in their vegetable gardens

   because they want produce that has not been sprayed with insecticides.

Compare:

He likes *to travel* abroad.

He travels abroad *to learn* about other cultures.

In the first sentence, the infinitive "to travel" names *what* he likes; it is the direct object. In the second, "to learn" explains *why* he travels; it modifies the verb *travels*. **Infinitives** are the basic form of the verb plus *to: to go, to study, to drive*, and so forth. Infinitives have one of two functions in a sentence: they either name something or modify something.

Notice the modifiers in the following sentences:

1. The boy telling the lie was punished.
2. The secretary typing the letter works fast.
3. The letter written by the secretary was a request.
4. The decorations prepared for the celebration were a work of art.

In sentence 1, we learn that the "boy was punished." "Telling" identifies *which* boy: the one telling the lie. Sentence 2 states that the "secretary works" fast, and "typing" tells us *which* secretary: the one typing the letter. "Telling" and "typing" are **present participles**: the basic form of the verb + *-ing*. They are modifiers, not verbs: "telling," all by itself, cannot make a statement, whereas "tells" or "is telling" can.

The third sentence states that the "letter was a request." "Written [by the secretary]" tells us *which* letter: the one written by the secretary. In sentence 4, the "decorations were a work [of art]." "Prepared [for the celebration]" tells us *which* ones. "Written" and "prepared" are **past participles**. Like present participles, they are modifiers, not verbs.

E X E R C I S E

10-10

Find the infinitives and the participles in the following sentences.

1. They prefer to go to school at night.
2. The children especially wanted to visit the theme parks in the area.
3. Mary took a writing class to improve her composition skills.
4. The new company ran an advertisement in the local paper to get more business.

5. The person driving the car is responsible for the passengers.

6. Tom's boss, trying to get all the work done, was driving everyone crazy.

7. The tree, struck by lightning, was burning.

8. The paintings stored in the basement are worth more than those on display.

9. Tom, working from dawn until dusk, wanted to finish the harvest.

Infinitives and participles are called **verbals** because they come from verbs but they are not verbs themselves. A third kind of verbal is the **gerund**. The gerund has the same form as the present participle (the basic form of the verb + -*ing*), but it has an entirely different function: it names, whereas the present participle modifies. Compare the function of the word *revising* in the following sentences:

Revising takes time.

The lady revising the essay teaches English.

In the first sentence, the gerund "revising" names an activity. In fact, it is the subject of the sentence because it names what the writer is talking about. We can analyze the sentence as follows:

GER   D.O.
              N
Revising takes time.

In the second sentence, we learn that "the lady teaches English." Here "revising" is a present participle telling *which* lady the writer means.

E X E R C I S E

Identify the present participles and gerunds in the following sentences.

1. Decorating a cake requires a steady hand.

2. The boy decorating the cake won a prize.

3. He likes decorating cakes.

4. They enjoy composing music and playing it.

5. They always talk about composing and performing.

6. The children playing in the yard found some old tools.

7. He knows the man trying to set a new record for a solo flight.

8. She told us about the thief's opening the door right under the guard's nose.

Notice that in sentence 8 "thief" becomes the possessive adjective "thief's" before the gerund. Similarly:

I heard about his winning.

The correct form before the gerund "winning" is the possessive form "his," not the object form "him."

E X E R C I S E

10-12 Mark the subjects, verbs, and prepositional phrases in the following sentences. Refer to the list of common prepositions in Appendix B, as needed.

1. We drove home yesterday.

2. People and their pets have things in common.

3. Joe reads and writes Spanish.

4. We are in the twentieth century.

5. There are many museums in Los Angeles.

6. There is a vase on the shelf.

7. One of the supervisors comes to class.

8. She will have been typing for five hours by the time she finishes her research paper.

9. Your book must have been taken by your roommate.

10. Walking toward the dugout, the injured pitcher was cheered by everyone.

11. I will go out to shop when it stops raining.

12. He read the book that had been recommended by his instructor.

In the first sentence in Exercise 10-12, "home" is an adverb telling *where* we drove; it is not a direct object.

Compare:

They drove their new motor home.

In this case, "home" is the direct object; it is *what* they drove.

In sentence 2, two subjects "have" something. In sentence 3, two statements are being made about Joe. In sentences 5 and 6, the verb agrees with the postponed subject. The seventh sentence illustrates the principle that a subject is never in a prepositional phrase; the real statement is about "one" person. In the eighth sentence, there are four words in the verb. There is also a subordinate clause ("she . . . paper"), with *that* not expressed. Again in sentence 9 there is a four-word passive verb. (The roommate probably took the book.) In sentence 10, "walking" is a present participle modifying "pitcher"; the real statement here is that the pitcher "was cheered."

E X E R C I S E

10-13

Identify the subjects, verbs, and prepositional phrases in the following sentences.

1. Children and young animals play.

2. Horses can carry riders and pull carts.

3. Bicycles and scooters are used for transportation.

4. There was an interesting movie at the local theater last night.

5. I like to swim when I go to the beach.

6. There are too many bosses in most companies.

7. The employees wanted to leave early to see the holiday parade.

8. Their relatives would have liked to visit Disneyland.

9. All of the apples were eaten.

10. There should have been more people in the history class.

E X E R C I S E

10-14

Identify the subjects, verbs, and prepositional phrases in ten sentences of your own writing and in ten sentences of published writing (taken from a textbook, newspaper, or magazine).

Summing Up

You have discovered that a sentence—a group of words with a subject and a verb and with a complete and independent meaning—has certain basic elements, and you have experimented with several of these.

ESSENTIAL ELEMENTS

Subject: what the sentence is about

Verb: the statement made about the subject

ADDITIONAL ELEMENTS

Modifiers: words, phrases, and clauses that give more information about something else in the sentence. They answer questions such as *why, how, when, how much,* and so forth, about something else in the sentence.

Connectors: prepositions and conjunctions that serve to connect other words

Logical relationship between the sentence and the longer composition:

SENTENCE	PARAGRAPH OR ESSAY
subject	topic
verb	controlling idea
modifiers	additional sentences

Function: This is an important concept in sentences. The same word in the same form can be more than one part of speech, depending on its function among the other words in the sentence. For example, "down" can be a noun, an adjective, an adverb, a preposition, or a verb, depending on whether it is

Naming something, such as a play in football   [noun]
Making a statement, such as *swallow*   [verb]
Modifying, as in a *down* payment   [adjective]
            or as in he looked *down*   [adverb telling where]
Connecting, as in *down* the hall   [preposition]

Moreover, the same word, as the same part of speech, can have different functions in different sentences. For example, "child" can be

The subject of the sentence, if the writer is talking about the child
The direct object, if "child" answers the question *whom* about the verb
The indirect object, if "child" answers the question *to whom* about the verb
The object of a preposition or other form

Parts of speech: These are labels that help us classify words by their functions:

Nouns and **pronouns** name.
Verbs make a statement.
Adjectives and **adverbs** modify.
Prepositions and **conjunctions** connect other words.

Clauses and *phrases:* These are groups of words:

Phrases do not have subjects and verbs.
Clauses have subjects and verbs.
    Main clauses have meaning by themselves.
    Subordinate clauses do not have meaning by themselves.

Infinitives: These elements of speech consist of *to* + verb. They can name or modify.

Participles: **present** (for example, *taking*) and **past** (for example, *taken*) **participles** are formed from verbs, but they do not make a statement; they modify.

Gerunds: These are also formed from verbs. They name.

In Chapter 11 you will learn more about developing sentences.

DEVELOPING THE SENTENCE

Patterns of Sentences

Find the subjects and verbs in the following sentences. Notice what else, if anything, is needed to complete the meaning.

1. He passed.   [= He did not take his turn.]

2. He passed the salt.

3. He passed her the salt.

4. She named her pet alligator Nosey.

5. Her other pet is a tortoise.

Compare your answers with those in the answer key.

The preceding examples show the five basic patterns through which we express meaning in sentences. In the first of these patterns, meaning can be expressed through a subject and a verb alone:

He passed.

Birds fly.

Modifiers can be used to add information to the subject and verb:

Some birds fly high.

Some birds in cages never fly.

Birds migrating to other continents must fly very far.

Birds that migrate fly to the south.

Birds that migrate fly to the south when fall comes.

E X E R C I S E

11-2

Mark the subjects, verbs, and modifiers in the following sentences.

1. People speak.

2. Many people speak fast.

3. Many people in a hurry speak fast.

4. Many people who are in a hurry speak fast.

5. Many people speak fast when they are in a hurry.

6. Students in large lecture halls must listen carefully.

7. During the winter, dusk comes in the afternoon.

8. It is raining.

9. It is raining hard.

10. It rains often in tropical zones.

The second pattern has a subject, a verb, and a direct object:

He passed the salt. *D.O.*

The travelers watched the sunset. *D.O.*

Modifiers can add information to the subject, verb, and direct object:

The tired travelers lazily watched the colorful sunset. *D.O.*

The travelers in the cafe watched the sunset in the western sky. *D.O.*

The travelers who were sitting by the window watched the colorful sunset until it disappeared. *D.O.*

Mark the subjects, verbs, direct objects, and modifiers in the following sentences.

1. The puppy dug a hole.

2. The older puppy furiously dug an impressively deep hole.

3. The puppy in the neighbors' backyard quickly dug a big hole behind a tree.

4. The puppy that the neighbors had just bought dug a hole because he smelled something in the ground.

5. The neighbors take the puppy on a walk whenever they can.

6. Joe took the silverware from the drawer.

7. Some people eat too many sweets.

8. Mary should have filled the gas tank before she entered the freeway.

9. The mother of the nine neighbor children is taking karate lessons.

10. More people are now getting regular exercise because they are thinking more about their health.

The third pattern has a subject, a verb, an indirect object, and a direct object:

I.O. *D.o.*
He passed her the salt.

I.O. *D.o.*
The company offered Joe the job.

In the first example, *what* he actually passed (that is, what he picked up and handed across the table) was the "salt," not "her." Thus, "salt" is the direct object. "Her" is the indirect object. An indirect object answers the question *to whom* or *to what* about the verb. "Her" explains *to whom* he passed the salt.

In the second example, "Joe" explains to whom they offered the job.

Compare "me" and "the children" in the following examples:

             I.O.   *D.O.*
He offered me money.

               I.O.   *D.O.*
He told the children a story.

Modifiers can add information to the subject, the verb, the indirect object, and the direct object:

                                           I.O.   *D.O.*
The busy father still told the young children an animal story.

                                              I.O.   *D.O.*
The uninvited guest unwillingly passed the family members the main dish.

EXERCISE

11-4

Mark the subjects, verbs, indirect objects, direct objects, and modifiers in the following sentences.

1. Mary showed Joe the photographs.

2. She also showed him the souvenirs that she had bought.

3. She did not tell him the reason for her trip to Florida.

4. She had already shown her neighbors everything.

5. Joe gave Mary some advice.

6. She brought him a gift that she had bought in Florida.

7. He gave her flowers for the first time.

8. She passed him the plate of cookies.

9. The president of the school gave the graduating students their awards.

10. Extracurricular activities in high school can teach students of all backgrounds many valuable

    lessons.

In Exercise 10-5 and its explanations, we saw that linking verbs (verbs such as *be, become, appear, seem, look, feel,* and *taste*) connect the subject with an element that either renames the subject (predicate nominative) or modifies it (predicate adjective).

EXERCISE

Determine whether the word in italic type in each of the following sentences renames the subject or modifies it.

1. Joe is an *instructor*.
2. Joe is *rich*.
3. His neighbor is a *vegetarian*.
4. Mary was *busy* with her new job.
5. Mary later became an *executive*.
6. The food looked *good*.

Words that rename or modify the subject of a sentence are sometimes called **subject complements**.

We can also rename or modify the direct object of a sentence:

D.O.   O.C.

She <u>called</u> Joe a hero.

D.O.   O.C.

She <u>called</u> Mary intelligent.

"Hero" renames the direct object, "Joe." "Intelligent" modifies the direct object, "Mary." Words that rename or modify the direct object of a sentence are sometimes called **object complements**.

Sentence 4 in Exercise 11-1 follows this pattern:

D.O.   O.C.

She <u>named</u> her pet alligator Nosey.

The object complement "Nosey" renames the direct object, "alligator."

EXERCISE

Mark the subjects, verbs, direct objects, object complements, and modifiers in the following sentences.

1. The salesman called the car a bargain.

2. The customer later called the car a lemon.

3. The club elected Joe treasurer.

4. The instructor found the class well prepared for the test.

5. The students found the discussion stimulating.

6. She finds him sensitive and shy.

7. The sportswriters named the player rookie of the year.

8. The government declared the earthquake a natural disaster.

9. The committee nominated Mary chairperson.

10. From her position of power, Mary called everyone lazy and incompetent.

Sentence 5 in Exercise 11-1 has a subject, a linking verb, and a subject complement.

S.C.
Her other pet is a tortoise.

The subject complement (predicate nominative) "tortoise" renames the subject "pet."

E X E R C I S E

11-7 Mark the subjects, verbs, subject complements (the predicate nominative or predicate adjective), and modifiers in the following sentences.

1. Her father is a doctor.

2. He is extremely busy.

3. Her mother is a chemist.

4. She is very creative.

5. Mary was an honor student.

6. She looked intelligent.

7. She was very talented in music.

8. Dan became a computer expert in his spare time.

9. He became quite adept at programming.

10. All of them often felt tired.

Thus, the five basic sentence patterns are as follows:

1. Subject + verb
2. Subject + verb + direct object
3. Subject + verb + indirect object + direct object
4. Subject + verb + direct object + object complement [something that either renames or modifies the direct object]
5. Subject + verb + subject complement [a predicate nominative (which renames the subject) or a predicate adjective (which modifies the subject)]

E X E R C I S E

Mark the subjects, verbs, direct objects, indirect objects, object complements, subject complements, and modifiers in the following sentences.

1. Horses can sleep while they are standing.

2. Mary's cat used to walk the three dogs in the morning.

3. Cows give their calves milk.

4. Everybody considered the proposal outrageous.

5. The sunset was an enormous splash of rich colors.

6. Everyone called the sunset spectacular.

7. The car salesman sold the customer a lemon.

8. Elephants work hard for people in India.

9. Elephants, because they are so strong, can lift very heavy objects.

10. Animals can be extremely useful to people in many ways.

Types of Sentences

CLASSIFICATION BY CLAUSES

EXERCISE

11-9

Find the main clauses and subordinate clauses in the following sentences.

1. Birds fly.

2. Birds fly, but fish swim.

3. Birds search for food while they fly.

4. When the cat appeared, the birds flew away, and the dogs started barking.

In the first sentence, the statement, "fly," is being made about the subject, "birds." This is a **simple sentence**.
Compare:

Children and puppies run and play.

This is a simple sentence because the two statements, "run" and "play," are both being made about the two subjects, "children" and "puppies." In a simple sentence, one or more statements are made about one or more subjects. A simple sentence contains only one main clause and no subordinate clauses.
Compare:

Earthquakes, tidal waves, floods, and fires often cause extensive damage to property,

complicate already existing environmental problems, and create great fear.

Here, all three verbs, "cause," "complicate," and "create," make statements about all four subjects, "earthquakes," "waves," "floods," and "fires." Consequently, although the sentence is long, it remains a simple sentence, consisting of a single main clause.
In the second sentence in Exercise 11-9, the verb "fly" makes a statement about the subject "birds," and the verb "swim" makes a statement about the subject "fish," so there are two main clauses. Consequently, this is a **compound sentence**—a sentence containing two or more main clauses and no subordinate clauses.
The third sentence has a main clause:

birds search for food

and a subordinate clause:

while they fly

This is a **complex sentence**. A complex sentence contains a main clause and at least one subordinate clause.
The fourth sentence has two main clauses:

the birds flew away

and

the dogs started barking

plus a subordinate clause:

when the cat appeared

This is a **compound-complex sentence**. A compound-complex sentence has two or more main clauses plus at least one subordinate clause.

E X E R C I S E

Identify the clauses in the following sentences. Then classify each sentence as simple, compound, complex, or compound-complex.

1. The beginnings of some movies are confusing.
2. The VCR has made it possible to watch both recent and older films at home, so fewer people are going out to the movies.
3. Teenagers and young adults often prefer to go out to the movie theater, while people in other age groups tend to watch more movies at home.
4. When the public shows an interest in a particular kind of film, movie producers are quick to notice, and similar films soon appear.
5. The clouds above the mountains resemble the head of a dog.
6. The students and their parents enjoyed the trip to the park.
7. One of the students took pictures, and another wrote an article about the trip for the school newspaper.
8. Fruits and vegetables should not be sold to the public if they have been sprayed with dangerous chemicals.
9. Growers need to be especially careful about using pesticides because people nowadays are exposed to so many other environmental pollutants.
10. As soon as the sun came up, a layer of mist seemed to hug the ground, and a faint chill pervaded the air.

CLASSIFICATION BY VOICE

In addition to categorizing sentences according to their clauses, we can classify them according to whether the subject is acting or being acted upon.

E X E R C I S E

11-11   In the following sentences, determine whether the subject is performing an action or whether someone or something else is performing an action on the subject.

1. The mechanic is fixing the car.
2. The car is being fixed by the mechanic.
3. The mayor threw the first ball of the season.
4. The first ball of the season was thrown by the mayor.
5. The child took the keys.
6. The keys were taken by the child.

In the first two sentences, the mechanic is performing the action, and the meaning of the two sentences is close. However, there is a difference in emphasis: since the subject of a sentence is what we are talking about, it is the subject that we emphasize. This means that in sentence 1, we are focusing on the idea that the mechanic is fixing something; and in sentence 2, we are focusing on the idea that the car is being fixed—that is, that the repairs are being done.

A sentence worded so that the subject performs the action is said to be in the **active voice**. A sentence in which the subject does not act but is instead acted upon is said to be in the **passive voice**.

Consider:

Gas is burned to produce energy.

In this sentence, which uses the passive voice, the people who burn the gas are not even mentioned because the emphasis is on the gas and what happens to it, not on who is using it. Thus, the person(s) or thing(s) performing the action reported in the sentence are frequently not mentioned.

Consider:

English and French are spoken in Canada.

It is not important here to indicate who speaks these languages; obviously, people do. The emphasis is on which languages are spoken. In a passive sentence, it is better to omit the performer—expressed in the prepositional phrase *by someone/something*—when this information does not really contribute to the meaning of the sentence. Similarly, it is usually better to write in the active voice unless the emphasis really needs to be on the receiver rather than the performer of the action.

Compare:

The relevant textbook chapters should usually be read before students go to lecture classes.

Students should usually read the relevant textbook chapters before they go to lecture classes.

The second version is stronger because what students should do needs to be emphasized rather than what should happen to textbook chapters.

EXERCISE

11-12

In each of the following sentences, identify the performer and classify the sentence as active or passive.

1. In elementary school, one teacher teaches all subjects.
2. In elementary school, all subjects are taught by one teacher.
3. The host sent invitations to everyone.
4. Invitations were sent to everyone by the host.
5. The conference was attended by over a thousand people.
6. The people attended the conference to learn more about teaching.
7. Hurricanes have caused extensive damage during the past few years.
8. Extensive damage has also been caused by recent earthquakes.
9. The coastal village was raided by the Vikings.
10. Detailed astronomical observations were made by some ancient peoples.

EXERCISE

11-13

Rewrite the following sentences, changing the weak passive to a more effective active form.

1. Omelettes were ordered by the couple.
2. In high school, math is taken by most students.
3. The play was canceled by the producers.
4. The medicine was well tolerated by the patient.
5. Thunderbolts were launched by the gods at the invaders.
6. More legislation should be passed by the government to control environmental pollution.
7. Negative feelings are experienced by a highly qualified person who is turned down for a job.
8. A new record for home runs was set by Hank Aaron.
9. The leaves had been blown by the wind all over the lawn.
10. The opening night of *The Phantom of the Opera* was eagerly awaited by those lucky enough to get tickets.

CLASSIFICATION BY PURPOSE

A third way of categorizing sentences is according to their purpose. Compare purpose in the following sentences:

1. We need to do the dishes.
2. Do the dishes more carefully!
3. If the dishes were done, we could go out walking.

The first sentence is a simple declarative statement. We use the **indicative mood** of verbs to make such statements. The second sentence is a command; it is in the **imperative mood**. The third expresses a hypothetical (contrary to fact) situation; the verb "were" is in the **subjunctive mood**.

Sentences in the indicative can be affirmative, negative, or interrogative:

He brought his camera.   [affirmative]

He did not bring his camera.   [negative]

Did he bring his camera?   [interrogative]

We use the imperative when we express commands and when we give directions or describe a process:

To correct an error from a previous line, *return* to the line and *position* the carriage on the wrong letter. *Press* the CODE key and the CORRECT key, and *type* the incorrect letter to erase it. Then *type* the correct letter in the space, and *proceed* with your work.

The subjunctive is used relatively little in modern English. It expresses hypothetical situations:

If he *were* rich, he would buy the house on the hill.   [not *was*]
She acted as if she *were* the boss.

We also use the subjunctive after certain verbs that call for a specific kind of action, such as *ask, require, order, demand, insist, urge, suggest,* and *recommend*:

1. He *suggested* that she *get* tutorial help.   [not *gets*]
2. The supervisor *required* that everybody *arrive* on time.   [not *arrives*]
3. The instructor *insisted* that the student *revise* the composition.   [not *revises*]
4. He *asked* that we *be* there on time.   [not *are*]

E X E R C I S E

Complete each sentence with the correct form of the verb in brackets, and identify the mood of the verb.

1. Everyone demanded that he _____ the job.   [finish]

2. He usually _____ his work on time.   [finish]

3. Put in the coins and then _____ the button.   [push]

4. He always _____ the wrong button.   [push]

5. He insisted that she _____ his book.   [return]

6. A person who wants to avoid problems _____ materials on time.   [return]

7. _____ the book by Friday or you will have to pay a fine.   [return]

8. He _____ not _____ the last book he borrowed on time.   [return]

9. _____ he _____ to New York next week?   [go]

10. I will suggest that he _____ to New York.   [go]

Summing Up

You have discovered that meaning is expressed through various sentence constructions.

SENTENCE PATTERNS

Subject + verb:

Airplanes fly.

Subject + verb + direct object:

D.O.
Airplanes carry people.

Subject + verb + indirect object + direct object:

I.O.   D.O.
The company gave her an award.

Subject + verb + direct object + object complement:

D.O.   O.C.
The club elected Mary president.

Subject + verb + subject complement:

S.C.
Mary is industrious.

Object complements either rename or modify the direct object:

She called Commitmentman her hero.   [hero renames Commitmentman]

She called Commitmentman wonderful.   [wonderful modifies Commitmentman]

Subject complements either rename or modify the subject of the sentence:

Commitmentman is the hero of the 90's.   [hero renames Commitmentman; it is

a predicate nominative]

Commitmentman is loyal.   [loyal modifies Commitmentman; it is a predicate

adjective]

TYPES OF SENTENCES

By **clauses**
Simple: one main clause:

The girl went out.

Compound: two or more main clauses; no subordinate clause:

The girl went out, but the boy stayed in.

Complex: one main clause and one or more subordinate clauses:

The girl went out because the weather was nice.

Compound-complex: two or more main clauses and one or more subordinate clauses:

The girl went out because the weather was nice, but the boy stayed in.

By **voice**

Active: The subject is performing the action

Mel took the books.

Passive: Someone or something else is performing the action

The books were taken by Mel.

By **purpose**

Indicative: makes a statement:
In the *affirmative:*

Dan left.

In the *negative:*

Dan did not leave.

In the *interrogative:*

Did Dan leave?

Imperative: gives an order:

Leave!

Subjunctive: indicates a hypothetical situation or a call for action:

He wishes he were rich.
We insisted that he be on time.

In Chapter 12 you will learn how to handle problems in sentences.

WRITING CORRECT SENTENCES

Do any of the following "sentences" communicate meaning effectively?

1. The English drink tea the Germans drink beer.
2. Even though the contestant knew the answer.
3. By the way they went out.
4. Hanging from the tree limb, we saw a bat.
5. There is some apples in the fruit basket.
6. If a person seems unprepared for an interview, you do not get the job.
7. He likes camping, hunting, and to fish.
8. People blame television for everything that is wrong in society and come to believe it.

All of the preceding "sentences," as you probably noticed, are confusing. Actually, each one contains an error that interferes with the communication of meaning. In the first example, one statement is made about the English, and another statement, about the Germans, follows immediately, with no connection shown between the two ideas. The second example, by itself, does not make any statement, nor does the third, simply because it is not correctly punctuated.

Example 4 communicates the wrong meaning because the words are not arranged properly. Examples 5, 6, and 7 contain inconsistencies that interfere with understanding. The last example has an error in function that makes the meaning unclear.

Compare each of the original sentences with the corresponding corrected version. Notice how the revised version communicates a specific meaning:

1. The English drink tea, but the Germans drink beer.
2. Even though the contestant knew the answer, he did not manage to respond in time.
3. By the way, they went out.
4. We saw a bat hanging from the tree limb.
5. There are some apples in the fruit basket.
6. A person who seems unprepared for an interview does not get the job.
7. He likes camping, hunting, and fishing.
8. People who blame television for everything that is wrong in society may come to believe that television really is the cause of most of society's problems.

Effective writing depends on the accurate expression of meaning at the level of individual sentences. For this reason, you need to be able to recognize and correct problems in sentences.

Problems with Sentence Boundaries

Is either of the following sentences correct?

Dogs bark cats meow.

Dogs bark, cats meow.

The first presents the same problem as the earlier sentence about the English and the Germans: one statement immediately follows another with no connection between the two indicated. The second example, even though it is punctuated differently, illustrates a similar problem.

RUN-TOGETHER SENTENCES

We can analyze the type of error in the first example as follows, with MC to indicate a main clause:

Dogs bark cats meow. = MCMC

The problem is that the writer has run together two main clauses without indicating how they relate logically. We can use the term **run-together sentence** to indicate this type of sentence error.

The second version of the sentence in question presents the same problem even though it has a comma between the two main clauses:

Dogs bark, cats meow. = MC,MC

A comma is not a strong enough punctuation mark to signify that the statements are completely separate and independent of each other. Thus the second sentence still has two main clauses run together without any indication of how they relate logically.

You can correct a run-together sentence in various ways. The one you should choose depends on the meaning you wish to express.

Independent Statements

Two entirely independent statements (set off by a period) can be made. These indicate no particular relationship between the ideas:

Dogs bark. Cats meow.

If the ideas have a definite logical relationship even though they are separate statements, we can use a **semicolon** between them:

Dogs bark; cats meow.

Consider the following separate but related statements, punctuated with semicolons:

She felt ecstatic; she had just won first prize.

In some colleges, academics are given great emphasis; in others, sports count more.

In the first statement, the logical relationship is cause/effect: her ecstatic feeling resulted from her having won first prize. In the second, a comparison is made.

EXERCISE

Separate the following statements by punctuating them correctly. Notice that the commas separating the main clauses are incorrect. Replace them with periods or semicolons.

1. Bookstores sell books libraries loan them.

2. It had rained heavily the night before the grass looked fresh and green the next day.

3. Books take time to publish, magazines may have more up-to-date information.

4. He did not understand accounting he sometimes fell asleep in class.

5. People who are busy with their jobs all week sometimes enjoy cooking on the weekends, cooking is a creative occupation.

6. The contestants all arrived at the finish line the first three were awarded prizes.

7. Smog is a combination of fog and atmospheric pollutants, it now covers much more than our cities.

8. The car came to a stop, it had run out of gas.

9. People tend to raise their children the way they were raised they feel more comfortable with what is familiar to them.

10. Successful students have often learned good study skills, unsuccessful students typically waste much of their time.

We actually use few semicolons in writing because we usually indicate the specific relationships between ideas by means of appropriate wording. The next three subsections on run-together sentences explain various possible relationships and some words you can use to make them clear.

Coordinated Statements

Two coordinated statements can be used to correct a run-together sentence:

Dogs bark, but cats meow.

The relationship in this example is that of contrast between two statements of equal value: the conjunction "but" contrasts the noise cats make with the noise dogs make.

The conjunctions we use to make coordinated statements are called **coordinating conjunctions**. They connect statements of equal value. These conjunctions are:

and–indicates addition:

A Hovercraft goes on water, and it can also go on land.

but–indicates contrast:

Tom likes the car very much, but he is not going to buy it.

or–indicates alternative:

Alice has read the article, or at least she is quite familiar with what is in it.

for–indicates cause:

Yolanda knew the answer, for she had seen it in a book.

nor–indicates additional negation:

Peter did not leave on schedule, nor did he arrive on time.

so–indicates effect or result:

The students had not read the chapters assigned, so they failed the test.

yet–indicates something contrary to what would normally be expected:

The bill was long overdue, yet he had not paid it.

When two main clauses are joined by a coordinating conjunction, a comma is usually placed before the conjunction:

All of the tourists had studied Spanish, but most of them were hesitant about using it.

Occasionally, however, we use a semicolon or a period before the conjunction. These marks may facilitate communication if the new main clause follows a series because the subject of the new main clause can be misread as an object in the preceding main clause:

The club president will call the vice president, the treasurer, and the activities director; and the secretary will notify all of the members of the board.

They are also useful in instances in which the main clauses are long and grammatically complicated, especially if they already contain commas:

The travel organizer was supposed to have made all the necessary arrangements, including booking hotel rooms for the members of the group, getting their train tickets, and arranging classes for them. But on their arrival, they discovered that no arrangements whatsoever had been made.

A third situation in which a semicolon or period is appropriate arises when the greater focus is on the statements themselves rather than on how they relate:

He was amazed at how well the weight loss program had worked. And he was extremely pleased about his success.

EXERCISE

Correct the following run-together sentences by adding a coordinating conjunction. Add punctuation if necessary.

1. The first airplanes flew, they went slowly compared to today's jets.
2. On their trip to Los Angeles, they visited several museums, they went to the theater every evening.
3. The children fell asleep in the car after leaving Disneyland they were tired.
4. The student needed to review the material carefully, she would fail the course.
5. She studied hard she passed.
6. Joe did not care for the food at the reception he liked the champagne.
7. Joe knew he had drunk too much at the reception, he got behind the wheel of his car.
8. Joe stopped the car, he showed the officer his license.

Statements Connected with Adverbial Conjunctions

Two statements can be related logically through the use of an **adverbial conjunction**, also called a *conjunctive adverb:*

Dogs bark; however, cats meow.

The adverbial conjunction *however* shows a contrast between the two main clauses.

Many words and phrases can function as adverbial conjunctions and can therefore indicate the logical relationship between main clauses. Some of these are:

accordingly	in fact
also	likewise
as a result	meanwhile
besides	moreover
consequently	nevertheless
finally	on the other hand
furthermore	otherwise
however	then
in addition	therefore
indeed	thus

When two main clauses are connected with an adverbial conjunction, the conjunction is preceded by either a semicolon or a period:

Major advances in medicine have been made through laser technology; consequently, the quality of life has been greatly improved for many people.

The actors concluded their performance; then they went to the cafe to relax over a pizza.

Newscasters are showing dogs from the pound to the public during their programs. As a result, many dogs have found homes.

A comma usually follows an adverbial conjunction.

All of the ski equipment had been rented out; consequently, Joe and his friends were unable to ski.

E X E R C I S E

12-3

Correct the following run-together sentences by adding an adverbial conjunction and suitable punctuation.

1. They painted the entire house, they redid the roof.
2. The student wrote the essay very carefully it came out well.
3. The tape broke the audience missed the rest of the song.
4. The boxes were empty, they were easy to carry.
5. The ticket prices had gone up, the travelers could not afford to fly.
6. The converter box was not working properly, they managed to get a picture by bypassing it.
7. The tourists brought back an entire suitcase of souvenirs, they had problems getting through customs.
8. A recent study has shown coffee to be no more harmful to the health than tea or caffeinated sodas, many avid coffee drinkers are happier now.

Two main clauses connected logically with an adverbial conjunction need either a period or a semicolon:

Dogs bark; however, cats meow.

or

Dogs bark. However, cats meow.

The writer who places a comma (or nothing at all) between the two main clauses creates a run-together sentence:

INCORRECT: Dogs bark, however, cats meow.

INCORRECT: We finished everything, then we left.

INCORRECT: The students had prepared their work conscientiously, thus they knew all the answers.

All three of the preceding sentences are run together. They require a period or a semicolon in place of the comma.

Since a semicolon is normally used only between main clauses, you should be careful to follow this pattern:

MC;MC

An exception to this pattern is discussed on page 216, in the section on punctuation.

EXERCISE

12-4

Correct the following run-together sentences by adding suitable punctuation.

1. All of the books Joe needed for his research paper were checked out consequently he had to change his topic.

2. Dan wanted to hear the group's latest tape therefore he bought it.

3. Mary stopped to buy some take-out food then she went home.

4. Some of the first-year students spent their money without thinking thus they ran out.

5. The rental movie lasted four hours however everyone watched it twice.

6. We set up the camp meanwhile they prepared dinner.

7. The team played extremely well last season nevertheless they did not win the pennant.

8. At first, the new director was afraid he could not handle everything then he found he could manage very well.

9. She is a really careful driver therefore she has never gotten a ticket.

10. Some college instructors travel a great deal as a result they have many interesting experiences.

A Statement with Subordinated Information

A final way to correct a run-together sentence is to subordinate one statement to the other. This involves keeping one point as the main clause and expressing the other in a **subordinate clause**, with the relationship between the two shown by the subordinator:

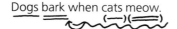

Dogs bark when cats meow.

The subordinate clause "when cats meow" now modifies "bark," the verb of the main clause.

Subordination is a useful strategy for eliminating a run-together sentence when one idea is more important than the other:

INCORRECT: Everyone stayed home, it was snowing.

CORRECT: Everyone stayed home because it was snowing.

Subordinating conjunctions, such as *when, because,* and *if,* and **relative pronouns,** such as *which* and *that,* start subordinate clauses. Here is a list of common subordinators:

after	even if
although	even though
as	ever since
as if	how
because	if
before	in order that

since	where
so that	whereas
than	wherever
that	whether
though	which
unless	whichever
until	while
what	who
whatever	whom
when	whose
whenever	why

If the subordinator is a conjunction, we can place either clause first. We put a comma after the subordinate clause if it comes first:

When cats meow, dogs bark.
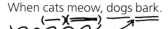

If the main clause comes first, we do not put a comma after it unless the subordinate clause gives information that does not really make a substantial difference in the sentence:

They will arrive on time, unless the sun and the moon collide.
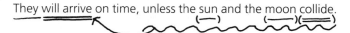

The subordinate clause in the preceding sentence contains nonessential information, so it is separated from the rest of the sentence by a comma. The same principle applies to subordinate clauses that start with relative pronouns: we use the comma only when the subordinate clause gives nonessential information. Compare:

We saw some paintings by Leonardo da Vinci, who worked during the Renaissance.

and

That is the lady who won the trip to London on *Wheel of Fortune*.

In the first example, the essential information is all in the main clause. In the second example, the subordinate clause adds essential information identifying which lady the writer means.

E X E R C I S E

12-5

Add punctuation to the following sentences as needed.

1. Whenever it rains the streets get flooded.

2. Few people can afford to buy it if it costs too much.

3. All of us got home late because our plane came in late at the airport.

4. Although the contestant accumulated several thousand dollars she did not win the game.

5. The man at the entrance began admitting people after everything had been set up.

6. He sent his aunt a telegram before he phoned her.

7. They have been using English ever since they came to live in the United States.

8. I do not know who wrote that story.

9. I knew her history professor who was an extremely knowledgeable person.

10. Since the rain would spot his recently detailed car Dan decided to postpone his trip to the store.

EXERCISE

Reverse the items in Exercise 12-5 in which the main clause comes first and a subordinating conjunction starts the dependent clause, making any other changes that are appropriate. Punctuate your new sentences carefully.

EXERCISE

Correct the following run-together sentences in one of the four ways discussed earlier.

1. To those in the areas severely damaged, it was not just another earthquake, it was a major disaster.

2. Six members of the team were coaches from the local schools, most of the others were athletes who competed locally.

3. The only people who will register guns are law-abiding citizens, criminals will not register theirs.

4. Registering guns would not eliminate the danger, accidents would still happen.

5. Those against gun control claim a Constitution-based right, those for control emphasize the danger factor.

6. Is it not enough for some to own a house, their house must be nicer than their neighbors' homes.

7. The team ran the length of the field then they scored a goal.

8. The game was long however we stayed until the end.

9. The team travels out of town several times during the season, therefore they have high operating costs.

10. They have won all their games so far this season, thus they have a good chance to win the championship.

EXERCISE

Correct the run-together sentences in the following set. Do not make changes in any sentences that are already correct.

1. Peter may not graduate, his grades are not good.

2. He has also been having trouble getting the classes he needs, he has to fit them around his work schedule.

3. Many advanced classes are now offered only every fourth semester this scheduling makes it more difficult for some people to graduate.

4. Some people can study with the stereo on, others cannot do two things at the same time.

5. Mary was not interested in a career when she got out of high school, then she changed her mind.

6. Tom failed the class even though he studied hard.

7. He took the class from an instructor who routinely fails half of the students.

8. He did all of the assignments nevertheless he did not get credit for the ones not done correctly.

9. He was also taking a Russian class he found it especially difficult.

10. He goes to the beach to relax he is under so much stress.

E X E R C I S E

12-9

Correct the following run-together sentences.

1. They are going on vacation, then they are enrolling in some classes.

2. Mary is taking a British literature class she finds it highly challenging.

3. Joe likes physics Mary prefers English.

4. Mary was interested in the cliff dwellings of Mesa Verde she went there during spring break.

5. She had read up on the culture of the Indians who built them, thus she was able to appreciate what she was seeing.

6. They had built their dwellings right in the depressions in the cliffs, as a result, their enemies could not destroy their homes.

7. Mary is thinking about changing her major to archeology, she is also considering a double major.

8. She is fascinated with ancient civilizations, in fact, she hopes to go to Yucatan before the end of the year.

9. She cannot afford to fly there, however, she may go by bus.

10. She is looking for a traveling companion, otherwise, she will have to pay the full expense for lodging.

Consider:

> When cats meow.

This, by itself, does not make a statement: the word *when* makes the clause depend on something else for its meaning. In other words, it expresses an incomplete thought. This is the same problem that we encountered in the second example at the beginning of this chapter:

> Even though the contestant knew the answer.

FRAGMENTS

The **fragment**, or incomplete sentence, is another type of error involving sentence boundaries. In a fragment, too little—less than one main clause—has been put together as though it were a sentence, whereas with the run-together sentence, too much—more than one main clause—has been put together and punctuated as though it were just one sentence.

We use fragments constantly when we speak because, in conversation, expressing everything in complete sentences would involve much unnecessary repetition. We also use fragments in certain kinds of writing, such as informal messages to people we know. But in college composition, it is the writer who must clarify and explain concepts accurately, and this is best done in complete sentences.

A fragment lacks one or more essential sentence elements. The subject, the verb, part of the verb, or both the subject and the verb may be missing.

Missing Subject

The following group of words does not communicate meaning:

> Thought he knew everything there was to know about repairing a car.

A statement is being made, but the subject about whom it is being made is not identified in the sentence. The writer could have in mind any one of a number of possibilities:

> He thought he knew everything there was to know about repairing a car.
>
> The mechanic thought . . . .
>
> Joe thought . . . .
>
> Joe's girlfriend thought . . . .
>
> Nobody thought . . . .

and so forth.

EXERCISE

Supply each of the following fragments with a subject.

1. Will pay off the national debt.
2. Got effective environmental protection laws enacted.
3. Invented a truly safe passenger automobile.
4. Will create a new *Star Wars* series.
5. Ordered ham on rye.

Missing-subject fragments frequently occur in student compositions.

EXERCISE

Find the fragments in the following passage, and correct them by supplying a subject or joining them to another sentence.

The most enjoyable trip can become a nightmare when something goes wrong with the car. While driving across the state last year, my friend and I unexpectedly found ourselves negotiating curves along a mountain road. Traveled through one dense grove of trees after another for a long time, with no sign of civilization. The sun had gone down, and our lights were on. Finally, the road began to straighten out somewhat. Also became less hilly. Then, suddenly, the car began to slow down—on its own. Then stopped altogether. We had run out of gas! And were most likely stranded, as no cars had gone by in either direction for miles. We sat for some time in silent frustration over our predicament. Finally, I, being the more athletic of the two, decided to start off in search of help, going in the direction in which we had been headed. Half walked, half ran down the road until I came to a place, a mile or so from the car, where the road dropped down into a valley. There, to my relief, I saw what I had been hoping to see: lights. I did not know what was there. Certainly hoped it was a gas station. I ran back to the car. And told my friend that there was salvation after all. Since it was downhill, we were able to push the car to where the lights were visible. Then coasted the rest of the way down. At that point discovered, to our delight, that we had come upon not only a gas station, at which we were able to fill the tank, but also a cafe, where we wound down over a hot drink, and a convenience store, where we bought a road map in the hope of never making the same mistake again.

Missing Verb

What do you understand from the following:

Dogs that are trained for police use.

The writer appears to be talking about dogs, but no statement is made about them, and thus we do not have a sentence. Like the subject, the verb is an essential part of a sentence—the part that expresses the writer's point. Without the verb, we have only a fragment.

Using the words in the preceding example, we could make any one of a number of statements about dogs:

Dogs that are trained for police use are public servants.

. . . are on a controlled diet.

. . . appear to be serious professionals.

. . . do not usually make good pets for children.

E X E R C I S E

Supply each of the following fragments with a verb.

1. People who borrow things but never return them.
2. The astronauts who were the first to see the other side of the moon.
3. The airplane that just landed on the runway.
4. Formulating a clear topic sentence with several key supporting ideas.
5. The last person to leave the room.
6. The tourists in the first car behind the engine.
7. The benefits, most of which are very important to those who choose such a career.
8. Depression, so common that it is considered to be one of the major health problems in this country today.
9. The steps to follow in order to bake potatoes, which are in any beginner's cookbook.
10. His truck, since it would stall even though he had just had the carburetor worked on.

Partially Missing Verb

Consider:

She drunk all of the wine left in the bottle.

This is also a fragment. The word *drunk* is not a verb, by itself, but only the past participle of the verb *drink* (past tense, *drank*; past participle, *drunk*). Since it is not a complete verb, it does not make a statement. We can add a helping verb, *has* or *had*, to correct the fragment.

She has drunk all of the wine left in the bottle.

She had drunk all of the wine left in the bottle.

Similarly,

The game taking a long time to end.

is a fragment. We can write a meaningful sentence by adding the rest of the verb:

The game is taking a long time to end.
The game was taking a long time to end.

EXERCISE

Complete the verb in order to correct each of the following fragments.

1. The game taken over three hours already.
2. The student writing research papers for several classes.
3. He done everything that he was supposed to do.
4. They always striven to succeed.
5. Those tourists flown to Mazatlan nearly every year since 1977.
6. The race begun before we got to the track.
7. Their neighbors come to see what all the noise was about.
8. People coming from everywhere just to see what the police were doing about the incident.
9. They grown up in a small town in Colorado.
10. They riding in the Calgary Stampede next year.

Missing Subject and Verb: Entire Main Clause Missing

What meaning is there in the following?

Because the band had taken sweepstakes several times the previous year.

This subordinate clause gives the cause of something, but there is no indication as to what this caused; consequently, no complete thought is expressed here. To make a complete sentence out of this fragment, we need to add an entire main clause. We can say, for example:

Because the band had taken sweepstakes several times the previous year, they were looking forward to another successful year.

A subordinate clause alone does not make a sentence because the subordinating word in it makes it depend on a main clause for its meaning.

For subordinators, refer to the list on page 203, in the section on run-together sentences.

EXERCISE

Add a main clause that will give meaning to each of the following subordinate clauses.

1. Since it had been raining for days.
2. After she bought the new curtains.
3. While they were at their friends' house for dinner.
4. As if he knew where he was going.

5. Even though it was a hot day.

6. Unless the government implements a realistic solution to the state's financial problems.

7. Where all of the trash will go in the next century.

8. That he has been talking about all along.

9. Whichever solution they adopt.

10. Whose needs are being overlooked.

College writers frequently create fragments rather than sentences when they attempt to give additional information:

1. Joe stayed up all night studying. To do well on his test.
2. Joe slept soundly the next night. Being tired from the night before.
3. Joe hated staying up all night. Especially for a test.

In the first example, the infinitive phrase "to do well" was meant to explain *why* he "stayed up all night." It needs to be joined to the main clause:

Joe stayed up all night studying to do well on his test.

In the second sentence, the participial phrase "being tired" was intended to describe "Joe" in order to explain why he slept soundly. It therefore needs to be placed so that it can modify "Joe":

Joe, being tired from the night before, slept soundly the next night.

or

Being tired from the night before, Joe slept soundly the next night.

In the third example, the prepositional phrase "for a test" logically modifies "staying up" and needs to be placed in the same sentence:

Joe hated staying up all night, especially for a test.

EXERCISE

Join each of the following added-information fragments to the corresponding main clause in order to produce correct sentences.

1. Joe was saving money. Wanting to make a large down payment on a car.

2. Alice did all of the problems in the chapters assigned. Including the extra-credit ones.

3. She called early for an appointment. To get a convenient time.

4. She packed all of her things carefully the night before. To be ready for an early morning departure.

5. We enjoy walking in the evening. All around the town.

6. Many people have voiced complaints about the practice of keeping animals in captivity. In zoos and other kinds of animal parks.

7. He forgot to buy some of the ingredients he needed for the pizza. Even the mozzarella.

8. He is always extremely well prepared for his speeches. And carefully dressed.

9. Erin and Pete enjoy training dogs. Particularly those belonging to movie stars.

10. They like to spend time in the movie stars' homes. To have the run of dream houses.

EXERCISE

The following sentences contain different kinds of fragments. Correct the fragments, using different strategies for making complete sentences.

1. They ate out often on Friday nights. Especially when there was nothing at home that could be prepared quickly and easily.

2. Whenever they go to their friends' house for dinner and invite us as well.

3. If it costs too much and nobody can afford to pay for it.

4. They made a point of leaving before the traffic got too heavy. So that they would not risk being late for their plane.

5. The members of the band often meet on their own. To practice the music.

6. Most teenage girls give up dieting sooner or later; either when they have reached their desired weight or when they come to realize that they need food.

7. If there are too many negative ions in the air we breathe will cause health problems.

8. How one can learn a foreign language without going to the country where the language is spoken.

9. Since they had all agreed to meet at Pete's house and then they all got there late.

10. Because if the leader does not know what is going on at all times, some confusion may arise in the organization.

EXERCISE

Correct each of the following fragments.

1. Erin and Pete checked out more than a dozen books from the library. In hopes of having all of the information they needed for their new job as dog trainers.

2. Joe's supervisor needs to learn to deal with people in positive ways. Instead of being sarcastic so much of the time.

3. Decontrol means that oil producers can charge a higher price per barrel of oil; thus increasing profits.

4. There were no special requirements for joining the Penitentes; although novices usually came from Penitente families.

5. Computers often limit verbal communication among people in places such as offices and banks; in this way contributing to the communication gap.

6. Steinbeck's *The Pearl* shows that people in small towns are not necessarily more warm and caring than their city counterparts; envious, in fact, of the good fortune of another villager.

7. The people of the small town follow the family to the doctor, staring with brazen curiosity that does not come from human compassion; as do many of the people on our big-city freeways who slow down to stare at an accident scene.

8. People in small towns also combat boredom by gossiping a great deal; often saying disrespectful things about their neighbors.

9. The benefits of that job are the good pay, the convenient location, and the daytime hours. All of these factors being important to most people.

10. Convenience stores sell many highly processed foods that are not good for people. Not to mention the fact that these foods are overpriced.

Correct the fragments in the following paragraph.

Many students graduating from high school find it worthwhile to continue their education at the local community college. A two-year college, first of all, can offer them a start in higher education. Preparing the students until they feel ready for a four-year university. Also, going to the local college is financially advantageous. They can normally continue to live with their families. Without needing to pay rent for an apartment. Also taking public transportation to school. This usually makes it unnecessary to buy a car. Unless the student needs the car to go to work. The experience of going to the community college also gives the recent high school graduate an opportunity to become more independent. And mature as well. For example, it is entirely up to the student to attend class. Students in college are more likely than those in high school to take this responsibility seriously. Partly because they are usually the ones paying for their classes. A final advantage to attending the local community college is that students have an opportunity to make friends at school with people of different ages and backgrounds. In this way, further enriching their learning experience. For many, it is thus a wise decision to include in their lives some time at the community college.

Identify and correct each of the following run-together sentences and fragments.

1. You do not have to pay for it now, all you need is a deposit.

2. He turned in his exam without looking it over carefully, thus he made some mistakes.

3. The students finished the group project for their history class, those who were better in English checked it over.

4. We need to finish painting the house this weekend, otherwise, it will not be ready in time for our coming guests.

5. There are three important advantages to attending Riverview Community College. First, the wide variety of courses. Second, the convenient class times. Third, the excellent instructors.

6. Joe plays baseball, he also enjoys soccer.

7. They put up a fence, however, the neighbors' dogs get in under it.

8. Joe finished writing the letter then he sent it.

9. I like Italian food Mel does too.

10. He wanted to learn to play the organ; although he did not know how to read music.

Identify and correct each of the following run-together sentences and fragments.

1. He likes physics; even though it is difficult.

2. The grass was green the day of the field show tournament. Because it had rained intermittently for several days preceding the event.

3. The local band performed well in the event, they won several sweepstakes awards.

4. Although they did well in all categories and won awards in several.

5. They prepared carefully thus they did well.

6. They performed in the field show tournament then they left for the Hollywood Christmas Parade.

7. Many of them are serious musicians, therefore, their music sounds good.

8. While everybody was busy trying to find out what had happened.

9. Mary was wearing gloves; in spite of the fact that it was quite warm.

10. Whereas in reality everything had been prepared well in advance.

E X E R C I S E

Not all of the following are run-together sentences or fragments. Identify the faulty sentences and correct them.

1. They usually stayed up late, yet they always got up early.

2. Mel will change the oil on his truck, then he will check the air filter.

3. He does not have to pay for the ticket right away all he needs is a deposit.

4. Borodin was a famous musician; who was also a chemist.

5. Since it had been raining all morning; the traffic was moving slowly.

6. She did not have confidence in the dentist, he was keen on astrology.

7. It is hard to get up Monday mornings; especially if one has gone away for the weekend.

8. Joe tried to fix his own car; the result being that it would not even start.

9. They will clean up everything in their backyard, then they will do the front.

10. Some people can do two things at the same time, others are not so lucky.

E X E R C I S E

Not all of the following are run-together sentences or fragments. Identify the faulty sentences and correct them.

1. First you brainstorm a topic until you run out of ideas, then you organize your thoughts.

2. He likes to travel, however, it is expensive.

3. He always reads for an hour after dinner he watches television later.

4. The children go swimming whenever the weather is nice.

5. Her relatives went to Balboa Park yesterday they will go to Sea World tomorrow.

6. If you go to Europe; you should take an umbrella with you.

7. They enjoyed Paris the most, we liked Rome better.

8. To the people in the areas hardest hit, it was not just another hurricane, it was the worst nightmare of their lives.

9. But if we do not finish, we will not get paid.

10. In his time, there was not the air pollution that exists today; not to mention the technological advances that have played a major role in creating that pollution.

E X E R C I S E

Identify and correct the run-together sentences and fragments in the following passage.

Many of life's dreams go unfulfilled. Yet we continue to let them occupy an important part of our lives. One of my great but as yet unfulfilled desires is a simple one. To live close to the sea. I have always felt I have missed something important. Never having had the experience of waking up to the sound of the waves. I had another childhood dream, it came to me often. The chance to fly in a glider. I was curious to know what it would be like, I also could imagine how beautiful the ground below might be. Although I was always afraid of heights. And I was also bothered by the idea that visibility is poor, at times even reduced to nothing, when the sky is cloudy. Clouds which are beautiful to look at but frightening to fly through. They hide the land, they block out the sun. My final dream was to travel. To see the Taj Mahal, the Swiss Alps, and Tierra del Fuego. All of these dreams are as yet unfulfilled. Perhaps it is our continuing desires that keep us motivated in life. That give us a reason to go on. In spite of all of the difficulties. Giving life a meaning it would not otherwise have.

E X E R C I S E

Working alone or with a group of your classmates, check your current and previous writing for run-together sentences and fragments. As you go through your writing, look for a subject and a verb in each sentence. Watch for sentences in which more than one main clause is combined in a single sentence but not related logically by means of an appropriate connector or by proper punctuation. Make any necessary changes in your sentences, taking care to express your precise meaning.

Punctuation and Capitalization

We have seen that correct sentence boundaries depend on correct punctuation: the misuse of a period, a semicolon, or a comma can create a run-together sentence or a fragment.

THE FUNCTION OF PUNCTUATION

Incorrect punctuation, as we have seen, can interfere with the communication of meaning. The third example at the beginning of this chapter

By the way they went out.

is actually a fragment because we sense the word *that* before "they," making "they went out" a subordinate clause modifying "way":

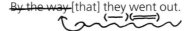

Lacking the main clause, the words do not express a complete thought. We can add a main clause to these words to give them meaning:

By the way they went out, I think they are very angry with us.

Or we can add punctuation to show that "by the way" is not an essential part of the sentence:

By the way, they went out.

In other words, how we punctuate a sentence can make a difference in meaning.

Keep in mind that how we correct the preceding example—or any other sentence—depends on what meaning we wish to express.

PUNCTUATION MARKS

End Punctuation

A period marks the end of a sentence. It is used after a statement:

Dogs bark.

after an indirect question:

My neighbor, who does not know English well, asked me *what noise dogs make*.

and after a mild command:

Please buy some stamps when you go to the store.

A period is also used after most abbreviations:

Mr. Sulu	54 B.C.
Ms. Addams	A.D. 25
Dr. Who	5 P.M. (or p.m.)
Mary Jones, Ph.D.	p. 46
St. Louis	pp. 46–48
Washington, D.C.	dogs, cats, etc.
U.S.A.	

If an abbreviation ends the sentence, no additional period is used:

The meeting was adjourned at 9 P.M.

A question mark comes at the end of a direct question:

What noise do dogs make?

An exclamation point shows emphasis. It does not always follow a complete statement:

He thought that Lincoln was the first president of the United States!
Hurry up!
Wow!

EXERCISE

Add periods, question marks, and exclamation points where necessary in the following sentences.

1. Who invented the laser

2. Do you know who invented the laser

3. The instructor did not know who invented the laser

   4. The eruption of Vesuvius in A D 79 destroyed the cities of Pompeii and Herculaneum

   5. Ms Belmont was born in St Cloud on May 1, 1950, at 4 P M

   6. Don't touch that wire

   7. Cows, horses, sheep, etc , are common farm animals

   8. Julius Caesar was born in 100 B C

   9. Our flight will leave for Washington, D C , at 10 A M

   10. Dr Martin Luther King, Jr , is an important figure in the history of human rights

---

Semicolons

Semicolons are used to separate main clauses. The writer may choose the semicolon instead of the period in order to keep the clauses together in one sentence when their statements are closely connected:

> It rains often in England; many of the English regularly carry an umbrella.

> He loves desserts; however, he is not currently eating them because he is trying to lose weight.

> Ms. Jones strongly feels that all animal parks should be shut down because it is cruel to keep animals in captivity; yet she keeps her pet dog in her fenced backyard.

Semicolons are also used to separate the items in a series that contains internal commas as well:

> Her favorite films are *Return of the Jedi*, starring Mark Hamill, Carrie Fisher, Billy Dee Williams, and Harrison Ford; *Indiana Jones: Temple of Doom*, starring Kate Capshaw and Harrison Ford; and *Witness*, starring Kelly McGillis and Harrison Ford.

This use of the semicolon is the exception, mentioned on page 202, to the pattern of main clauses both before and after any semicolon.

EXERCISE

12-26

Add semicolons where they are needed in the following sentences.

1. Most printing is done on white paper the colors used to color paper add to environmental pollution.

2. We like the old-fashioned theaters they prefer the modern cinema complexes.

3. Mary had found everything she needed for her sociology paper however, she had not yet checked out any materials.

4. Ann briefly visited London, Paris, and Rome then she went on to Moscow.

5. Manny brought the speakers, the amplifier, the turntables, the mixer, and several crates of records but he forgot to bring some country music even though it was sure to be requested.

6. One of the players hurt his hand another sprained her ankle.

7. The recipe calls for lamb, chicken, and beef, which are best if they are rubbed with spices and cooked in the oven vegetables, especially carrots, onions, green beans, and garbanzos, cooked in a spicy tomato sauce and a special pasta, over which the meat and vegetables are served.

8. People continue to be interested in new frontiers the popularity of science fiction shows this fascination with the unknown.

9. Animals tend to draw people's attention therefore, television advertisers are using them more and more in commercials.

10. People are dumping waste in storm drains it is then turning up on the beach.

Commas

Consider the meaning of the following sentences:

> I told Ann and Alice informing the others enabled them to prepare for a possible emergency situation.
>
> If you do not put enough oil in the engine will overheat.
>
> We gave holiday gifts to Mary Lou Nina and Carlos.

These sentences are confusing because we need to indicate separations between some of the words. The third sentence without commas does not even have meaning because we do not know whether three or four people received gifts. Notice how the commas facilitate understanding:

> I told Ann, and Alice, informing the others, enabled them to prepare for a possible emergency situation.
>
> If you do not put enough oil in, the engine will overheat.
>
> We gave holiday gifts to Mary Lou, Nina, and Carlos.

Commas are used in certain situations in which misunderstandings are likely to occur. In other words, we follow several conventions on the use of commas in order to avoid potential problems.

After Introductory Elements

We have already seen that

> If you do not put enough oil in the engine will overheat.

is unclear on a first and even a second reading. We have also seen that

> By the way they went out.

leaves us guessing at the writer's intended meaning.

Words in English tend to occur in a particular order. The subject generally comes first, followed by the verb, followed by any direct object or subject complement (predicate nominative or adjective):

> *D. O.*
> The president made the announcement during the meeting.

> *PRED. ADJ*
> The vice president is responsible when the president is away.

If we change this order, so that our sentence begins with a phrase or a subordinate clause, adding a comma to separate the introductory element from the rest of the sentence can be helpful:

> If you do not put enough oil in, the engine will overheat.

or even necessary:

> By the way, they went out.

Identify the subject and the verb in each of the following sentences, and add a comma after the introductory phrase or clause.

1. For the marathoners running is a career.

2. In the army dogs are trained to attack the enemy.

3. In the past conglomerate mergers were subject to antitrust laws.

4. Until all of the people had exited the doors were kept unlocked.

5. After Mary had calculated everything she figured her tax.

6. By the way the mayor is coming to dinner.

7. If you know Latin you can understand many more words in English.

8. Although he killed the insect he failed to destroy its nest.

9. When we go to San Francisco in December we will visit the Golden Gate Park museums and

   Alcatraz Island.

10. On her way to Texas Mary flew over the Colorado River.

Between Main Clauses

Try to figure out the following sentence:

> He hit Tom and Bill and Joe joined the fight.

We do not know whether he hit both Tom and Bill or whether Bill, together with Joe, joined the fight. When a comma is left out, the reader may not be able to determine whether a noun is another object in the first main clause or the subject of a new main clause. The preceding example could mean either

> He hit Tom, and Bill and Joe joined the fight.

or

> He hit Tom and Bill, and Joe joined the fight.

This degree of confusion is unusual, but to avoid possible misinterpretation, we customarily add a comma (or occasionally a semicolon or period, as described on page 200, in the section on run-together sentences) before a coordinating conjunction that connects two main clauses.

EXERCISE

12-28

Identify the subjects and verbs in each sentence, and put a comma before the coordinating conjunction that connects the main clauses.

1. We carefully prepared everything for the experiment and the results came out as we had expected.

2. The animal control officer caught the stray dog but then she could not find the owner.

3. Joe especially liked the movie *Gandhi* so he saw it a second time.

4. There would be less concern over the scarcity of natural resources if solar energy were more widely used and oil could be put to other uses.

5. He will do the dishes or she will be very angry.

6. They will not paint their house this year nor will they replace the missing boards in the fence.

7. The new candidate promised to give the economy top priority and he said he had a plan that had met with the approval of many economists.

8. Mary had run out of money by the end of November yet she managed to finish the school year.

9. She took extra units each semester and went to summer school so she finished college in three years.

10. It was a frightening event but he made it a learning experience.

In a Series

Consider the following example:

The Los Angeles riots of 1992 left behind entire buildings destroyed by fire partially damaged structures in need of extensive repairs and rubble blocking streets everywhere.

The reader has to work hard to figure out what goes with what. Commas, however, make the sentence instantly clear:

> The Los Angeles riots of 1992 left behind entire buildings destroyed by fire, partially damaged structures in need of extensive repairs, and rubble blocking streets everywhere.

The writer is naming what the riots left; and in order to be clear, each element in this series needs to be separated by commas.

Some writers systematically omit the comma before the *and* in a series when the meaning is clear and the individual items are short. This punctuation style is all right if there is no possibility of confusion:

> The basic elements of words are roots, prefixes and suffixes.

However, the comma before the *and* is always acceptable.

> The basic elements of words are roots, prefixes, and suffixes.

For the sake of consistency, it is a good idea always to use a comma before the conjunction in a series.

E X E R C I S E

12-29

For the following sentences, add commas to separate the items in each series.

1. Doctors recommend a low-fat diet the elimination of smoking and stress management.
2. The people who took the all-day tour saw Runnymede Stonehenge and Bath.
3. Hawthorne's novels are *The Scarlet Letter The House of the Seven Gables The Blithedale Romance* and *The Marble Faun*.
4. On the mountain pass, driving is dangerous when rain pours down gusty winds blow and dense fog covers the roadway.
5. They had tea coffee cake and sandwiches at tea time.
6. They had orange juice bacon and eggs toast and coffee for breakfast.
7. The telephone book contains a calendar of events local points of interest and zip codes.
8. Mary has not taken chemistry physics or biology.
9. The tool set on sale contained screw drivers of different sizes pliers and wrenches.
10. Sentence errors include run-together sentences and fragments dangling and misplaced modifiers agreement errors shifts and faulty parallelism.

To Separate Nonessential or Extraneous Elements

According to the following sentence, how many sisters does Joe have?

> Joe's sister who lives in Denver teaches music.

Can "Joe" in the following sentence be the same person as "Joe" in the preceding sentence?

> Joe's sister, who lives in Denver, teaches music.

In the first example, Joe has more than one sister, and the subordinate clause, "who lives in Denver," is identifying which sister teaches music; in other words, it enables us to understand that the sister who teaches music is the one who lives in Denver, not some other sister. This subordinate clause gives essential information because without it, we do not know which person the writer is talking about. In the second example, Joe is a different person—someone who has just one sister. The subordinate clause, separated from the rest of the sentence by commas, could be taken out of the sentence without a change in meaning. This is because in the second example the writer is basically saying

Joe's sister teaches music.

We can recapitulate this information as follows:

Joe's sister who lives in Denver teaches music.   [= the one that lives in Denver teaches music.]

Joe's sister, who lives in Denver, teaches music.   [= his sister teaches music.]

Reasoning in this way, we always put commas around information that is not essential to the basic meaning of the sentence.

E X E R C I S E

Set off with commas any nonessential information in the following sentences. (Not all of them contain nonessential information.)

1. Yellowstone National Park her favorite vacation place was struck by a major earthquake in 1959.
2. Her father's father who was a storekeeper lived in several different states.
3. Hawthorne wrote *The Blithedale Romance* which shows life in a socialistic community.
4. Hawthorne's first novel *The Scarlet Letter* is an interesting study in human nature.
5. Hawthorne's novel *The Marble Faun* is set in Italy.
6. Some of the principles of the French Revolution had already been tested during the American Revolution which had been fought several years earlier.
7. Senior citizens can greatly improve their physical condition if they follow a regular exercise program.
8. Christopher Columbus who traveled to America could communicate with sailors from different countries.
9. The book that he did not return to the library contains useful information on plant care.
10. Addressing our serious environmental problems which are getting more public attention now than they did a few years ago has become an important part of every politician's agenda.

In sentence 9 of Exercise 12-30, the word *that* introduces essential information, so the clause it introduces should not be set off with commas. Notice that clauses beginning with *who, whom, whose,* or *which* may contain either essential or nonessential information, but those starting with *that* invariably add essential information:

1. Abraham Lincoln, who was president during the Civil War, signed the emancipation Proclamation.   [nonessential]
2. The boy who lives across the street speaks Spanish fluently.   [essential]
3. Her best friend, whom she met through relatives, is a realtor.   [nonessential]

4. The man whom she presented to all the guests is the one she plans to marry.   [essential]

5. Mary, whose sister works at a day-care center, is a full-time student.   [nonessential]

6. The girl whose purse was stolen had to make out the report herself.   [essential]

7. An electric lawn mower, which makes mowing a lawn much less strenuous, is expensive.   [nonessential]

8. A car which needs a paint job can be difficult to sell.   [essential]

The word *that* can be used only in sentences 2, 4, and 8, replacing *who, whom,* and *which*.

Notice that the words *such as* can introduce either essential or nonessential examples, and commas are omitted or added accordingly:

Jobs such as computer programming require a person to sit for long hours.   [essential]

Some of the famous Western outlaws, such as Billy the Kid and Jesse James, have been both heroes and villains in movies.   [nonessential]

Like nonessential information, an **interrupter** is separated from the rest of the sentence:

She knows, of course, that we are right.

She will, however, do what we are recommending.

The folk instruments of the Andes, for example, are used in some of the background music for commercials.

The pan pipe, an Andean instrument, produces hauntingly beautiful tones.

The name, title, or term indicating a person being directly addressed is set off by commas:

I hope, Mary, that you will go with us.

The voters, Mr. President, want to know where their tax money is going.

Hurry up, children, or you will miss the bus.

I told you, you fool, that it was not going to work!

If the nonessential or extraneous words come at the beginning or end of the sentence, only one comma is needed:

She knows, of course, that we are right.

Of course, she knows that we are right.

She knows that we are right, of course.

He refused to sign the document, however, because it might jeopardize his position.

However, he refused to sign the document because it might jeopardize his position.

The above example with "however" does not take a semicolon because it has only one main clause.

EXERCISE

12-31

Add commas where necessary in the following sentences to separate nonessential or extraneous elements.

1. You know Joe that you really need to study more.

2. That means among other things spending more time reading the textbook and thinking about the information it gives.

3. The textbook that we are using is very helpful.

4. Mary's father whom I met by chance at a luncheon is one of the trustees.

5. Joe found out moreover that there would be a long delay.

6. Tom you should try to get your work finished before we have to close.

7. Our current idea of benefiting from the taxes we pay to the government goes back to the American Revolution which started in 1776.

8. *Moby Dick* a novel by Herman Melville is thought by some critics to be America's finest novel.

9. He knew however that the design would not turn out well.

10. Mary Kelly whose sister lives in San Francisco travels a great deal around the country.

EXERCISE

12-32

Add commas where necessary in the following sentences to separate nonessential or extraneous elements.

1. The guest list that the secretary prepared for the reception includes some local business people.

2. The ones who are coming are to let the secretary know in advance.

3. The local librarian who was the first person to be invited is the guest speaker.

4. The chairperson whose speech is always prepared by someone else puts everyone to sleep.

5. The member whose speech was the best liked last year discussed strategies for improving communication in a global environment.

6. She did not tell the audience however exactly which countries she had visited.

7. Her own field of study psycholinguistics is one she feels will become extremely important in the near future.

8. She believes furthermore that worldwide television broadcasting will revolutionize many cultures.

9. Airplanes which are about as old as automobiles became feasible after the invention of the internal combustion engine.

10. Take the books back people or you will have to pay a fine.

In Dates and Addresses

Notice the use of commas in the following sentences:

> Mary knew that Hawthorne was born in July 1804 in Salem, Massachusetts, although she did not know that he was born on July 4, 1804, or that his birth took place in a house on Union Street.
>
> Joe lives at 13600 Santa Monica Boulevard, Los Angeles, California 90025.

In dates, no comma goes between the month–day combination, but a comma separates the month–day combination from the year, and another follows the year if the sentence continues. The month and year alone, however, do not require commas.

Street addresses, cities, and states (or state plus zip code) are separated by commas. A comma also follows the state (or zip code) if the sentence continues.

E X E R C I S E

12-33

Add commas where necessary in the following sentences.

1. Mary's grandmother moved to Chicago Illinois on March 10 1948.

2. She lived there until April 1973 or April 1974 I am not certain which.

3. She then moved to 426 Chapman Avenue Santa Ana California 99802.

4. She lived there until August 1 1977 when she moved to Rancho Cucamonga California.

5. Mary has lived in Tucson Arizona Las Vegas Nevada and Orange California.

In Direct Quotations

The elements in a direct quotation are separated by commas:

He said, "I would rather be back in time for the game."

"I would rather," he said, "be back in time for the game."

"I would rather be back in time for the game," he said.

Notice that both commas and periods go inside quotation marks.

E X E R C I S E

12-34

Add commas where necessary in the following sentences.

1. Joe asked "When will they get here?"

2. Mary answered "They still have not let me know."

3. Barbara replied "They will let us know when they are ready."

4. She said "If you really want to go on the expedition, you will have to take the class first."

5. "If you really want to go on the expedition" she said "you will have to take the class first."

6. "If you really want to go on the expedition, you will have to take the class first" she said.

Avoid using a single comma between the subject and the verb or between the verb and its direct object, regardless of the length of the sentence. You may, however, need to use a pair of commas to set off words between the subject and the verb or between the verb and the direct object.

Colons, Dashes, and Parentheses

What is the function of the **colon** in the following sentences?

1. We purchased all the equipment for our trip: a tent, sleeping bags, air mattresses, and cooking equipment.

2. You can make a delicious spaghetti sauce with the following: onions, garlic, olive oil, crushed tomatoes, tomato puree, basil, thyme, allspice, salt, pepper, vinegar, and brown sugar.

3. American political leaders operated for decades according to one principle: fight communism.

In the first example, a list explaining "equipment" follows the colon. In the second example, the list of ingredients explains "the following"—that is, with *what* you can make the sauce. In the last example, "fight communism" explains "one principle."

In this way, colons are used to link explanatory material introduced in the statement before the colon.

A main clause comes before the colon. What comes after the colon, however, is grammatically separate. It may be a single word, a group of words, or a main clause. Compare:

Last semester, Ann took English, history, astronomy, French, and swimming.

Last semester, Ann took the following classes: English, history, astronomy, French, and swimming.

In the first example, the list of classes names *what* Ann took: it is the direct object of the sentence—an essential part of the sentence itself—and thus it is not introduced with a colon. In the second example, there is a complete statement before the colon. The list after the colon then explains "classes."

Dashes or **parentheses** can be used to separate an element from the rest of the sentence:

The reason he gave—and it was the only reason he could possibly have found—was that he had been delayed by car trouble.

Her long residence in Paris (1978–1982) gave her ample opportunity to learn French.

The elements set off may be grammatically independent from the rest of the sentence.

Dashes tend to call attention to what they set off, while parentheses downplay the words enclosed.

Both dashes and parentheses should be used sparingly; commas are a better choice as long as the meaning of the sentence is clear.

E X E R C I S E

Add colons, dashes, and parentheses where appropriate in the following sentences.

1. Friendship is a two-way relationship each person must give to the other a little of himself or herself.

2. You need several ingredients to make bread flour, shortening, milk, salt, sugar, and yeast.

3. Joe has already passed his exams in the following subjects English, art, geology, anthropology, and Italian.

4. Napoleon made one disastrous error in judgment he decided to invade Russia.

5. Television he had grown up on the adventure programs and documentaries offered by cable had been his real link with the world outside his own community.

6. Most sections of the required classes at community colleges English and math fill very quickly.

7. The Civil War 1861–1865 was fought over both economic and human rights issues.

8. The frequently performed various stage versions and films story of the phantom of the opera touches some of our deepest feelings.

Quotation Marks

Compare the following sentences. Is there a difference in meaning?

> Joe said he is going to night school.
>
> Joe said, "He is going to night school."

Even though the words in these two sentences are the same, two entirely different people may be going to night school. The first example is an **indirect quotation**, in which Joe is talking about someone. In this sentence, "he" could refer either to Joe or to another person; the meaning would have to be made clear by the context. The second example is a **direct quotation**, reporting Joe's actual words. In this sentence, Joe is definitely referring to another person; if he had been speaking about himself, the sentence would have been written as follows:

> Joe said, "I am going to night school."

Thus, quotation marks enable us to express a speaker's exact words, with the difference in meaning that that may make.

Notice the punctuation with direct quotations:

1. The instructor explained, "If you have completed Anthropology 101, you qualify to participate in the expedition."

2. "If you have completed Anthropology 101, you qualify to participate in the expedition," the instructor explained.

3. "If you have completed Anthropology 101," the instructor explained, "you qualify to participate in the expedition."

As you can see in the preceding examples, commas separate the *who said* statement from the quoted words, whether the tag comes at the beginning, at the end, or in the middle of the quoted words.

If a question mark or exclamation point comes at a place in the sentence where a comma or period would normally go, the comma or period is omitted.

> "Go away!" she screamed.   [The exclamation point replaces a comma.]
>
> She screamed, "Go away!"   [The exclamation point replaces a period.]
>
> "Have they arrived yet?" she asked.   [The question mark replaces a comma.]
>
> She asked, "Have they arrived yet?"   [The question mark replaces a period.]

In all of these examples, the quoted words are the direct objects of the verbs ("said," "explained," "screamed," and "asked"). This is an exception to the principle mentioned in the section on commas (page 224) about not placing a single comma between a verb and its direct object.

Commas are not usually used around quoted words that are not the direct object:

The mayor described the situation as "disastrous."

"Disastrous" was the term the mayor used to describe the situation.

In the first example, "situation" is the direct object; and in the second, there is no direct object.

If the quoted words make up more than one sentence, one or more periods and multiple capital letters are necessary:

1. Joe said, "We've already seen the zoo. We want to go somewhere else this time."
2. "We've already seen the zoo. We want to go somewhere else this time," Joe said.
3. "We've already seen the zoo," Joe said. "We want to go somewhere else this time."

Commas and periods always go inside quotation marks:

"I'm finished now," he said.

He said, "I'm finished now."

Semicolons and colons always go outside quotation marks:

He said, "I don't want any of that"; therefore, we kept it all for ourselves.

Joe called her comment "appropriate": she had truly understood the entire situation.

Question marks and exclamation points go inside or outside quotation marks, depending on whether the quotation alone or the whole sentence expresses the question or exclamation:

1. He asked, "Really?"
2. He shouted, "Run!"
3. Did she say, "I want to buy a house"?
4. He is going to get out of doing all the "unimportant work"!
5. Did he shout, "Run!"?

In example 1, the question involves only the quoted word, "Really," so the question mark goes inside the quotation marks. In example 2, the exclamation point goes with the quotation only and is therefore placed inside the quotation marks. In example 3, the entire sentence is a question, so the question mark comes last, outside the quotation marks, as does the exclamation point in the fourth sentence. In the fifth example, the quoted word is an exclamation, with the exclamation point inside; and the entire sentence is a question, with the question mark coming last.

EXERCISE

Add quotation marks to the following sentences. Place them carefully, keeping in mind where they belong in relation to other punctuation marks.

1. Mary said, I really like that dress!

2. I really like that dress! Mary said.

3. Mary asked, Do you like it too?

4. Do you like it too? Mary asked.

5. Joe commented after the election, The president really has his work cut out for him!

6. Mary said, My mother will be arriving at six o'clock.

7. My mother will be arriving at six o'clock, Mary said.

8. Did she shout, Stop!?

9. I know, he said, that you were a big help.

10. I also know, he continued, that we can count on your help in the future. We have a lot of faith in you.

Quotation marks are also used to identify titles of short works and portions of longer works. These include short stories, poems, songs, chapters of books, and articles in magazines or newspapers:

Langston Hughes writes about children in his short story "Thank You, Ma'm" and in his poem "Kid in the Park."

The local newspaper recently carried an article entitled "The Gang: A New Family?"

The song "Simple Gifts" was performed by the school band.

The book's last chapter is entitled "A New Beginning."

Underlining is used to indicate the titles of longer works—books, magazines, newspapers, journals, films, television shows, and stage productions (plays, operas, and musicals). These titles are printed in italics when they occur in books and magazines:

An interesting review of *The Phantom of the Opera* appeared in yesterday's *Los Angeles Times*.

Most high school students read Dickens' *A Tale of Two Cities*.

There was a long article about the movie *Tron* in *Popular Science*.

Underlining (in print, italics) is also used for a word that is being discussed as a word and for a term that is considered foreign:

The word *success* has different meanings for different people.

Both dogs and wolves belong to the genus *Canis*.

CAPITALIZATION

Compare

when something happens to certain people, it always makes news. for example, at christmas 1991, mother teresa, a macedonian nun famous for her work in india, was hospitalized at the scripps facility in san diego after a visit to tijuana, mexico.

and

When something happens to certain people, it always makes news. For example, at Christmas 1991, Mother Teresa, a Macedonian nun famous for her work in India, was hospitalized at the Scripps facility in San Diego after a visit to Tijuana, Mexico.

The second version communicates meaning more effectively during a first reading because the capital letters identifying the beginnings of sentences and the various proper nouns are visual devices that make it easier to follow the writer's meaning.

We capitalize titles of persons when they are used in front of a name or in place of the name:

> We sent a birthday gift to Dr. Stine because to us she is Aunt Rebecca.

Notice that the recipient's given name, *Rebecca,* could be substituted for either "Dr. Stine" or "Aunt Rebecca." In the following sentences, however, a proper name could not be substituted for "aunt," "uncle," or "senator":

> Mary gave her aunt and uncle a gift.
>
> She interviewed the senator before the meeting began.

Thus, capitals are not used for these titles.

The names of particular places and things are capitalized:

> The Empire State Building is in New York City.
>
> The Rotary Club meets in the Turner Complex, on Twelfth Street.
>
> The students from Serrano Hills High School went to the Colorado River and Lake Mead during the week before Easter and again on Labor Day.
>
> For Easterners, the West begins on the western side of the Appalachians; but for Californians, anything east of the Rocky Mountains is the East.

In the final example, "western" and "east" indicate directions only, while "West" and "East" indicate geographical areas. Notice also that words such as *city, club, street, school, river, mountains,* and *day* are capitalized when they are part of the name.

The days of the week and the months are capitalized, but the seasons are not:

> Last spring, there were five Wednesdays in May.

Words indicating languages, nationalities, ethnic groups, and religious groups are capitalized:

> Mr. Raimondi, an Italian Catholic, is studying Spanish at the local college.

Names of specific courses are capitalized, but areas of study are not, unless they come from proper nouns (such as "Spanish," in the preceding example):

> The Smiths were interested in child psychology, so they enrolled in Psychology 254 at Riverview Community College.

You should also capitalize the first word of a direct quotation, the first word of a title, and all other words in a title except *a, an, the,* and short connecting words (*and, but, in, at,* and so forth). Capitalize the title of a document.

EXERCISE

Add capital letters to the following sentences where appropriate.

1. i read the novel *pride and prejudice.*

2. he was studying the following: psychology, american history, and german.

3. robert louis stevenson, a famous scottish poet and novelist, lived in monterey, california, before he moved to the samoan islands.

4. she was born on the first wednesday in june in o'connors hospital, on san carlos avenue, san jose, california.

5. the mojave river flows north from the san bernardino mountains.

EXERCISE

Add the appropriate punctuation marks and capital letters to the following sentences.

1. william faulkner who wrote the sound and the fury won the nobel prize in 1949

2. did the contestant yell i won

3. i read the last chapter of balzac's novel eugenie grandet it is entitled so goes the world

4. the last chapter of balzac's novel eugenie grandet is entitled so goes the world

5. the song old man river is from the musical show boat

6. she was born on july 10 1950 in portland oregon and now lives in idaho

7. the teacher shouted hurry up children or you will be late

8. ann spent all morning visiting the tower of london then she went on to greenwich in the afternoon

9. ann voted for the incumbent for one reason he was strong on environmental issues

10. the emancipation proclamation was written during the civil war

EXERCISE

Add the appropriate punctuation marks and capital letters to the following sentences.

1. her grandfather moved to 860 stevens creek road san jose california on june 20 1964

2. the poem autumn leaves is in the book collected poems

3. we will see the statue of liberty the world trade center and the hudson river when we fly over new york city

4. she asked what time are you leaving

5. chicken fish meat and eggs are good sources of protein

6. my aunt's doctor died last summer

7. what sort of person would hurt an animal her son asked

8. i am due to leave from san francisco at 9 a m and will arrive in chicago at 2 p m at o'hare international airport

9. we enjoyed the play moreover we saw it a second time

10. we were convinced moreover that they were right

E X E R C I S E

Add the appropriate punctuation marks and capital letters to the following sentences.

1. we used tomatoes onions garlic and spices to make the sauce
2. you know barbara that you need to do well in that class he reminded her
3. the appointment on wednesday july 10 is theirs
4. shakespeare who was born in 1564 was a famous english playwright and poet
5. she bought the house for one simple reason it was a bargain
6. they stayed i believe to see the entire movie therefore they got home late
7. george washington who led the colonial forces during the american revolution did not write the declaration of independence
8. i sent the package to professor john smith 348 north union street salem massachusetts
9. working all night and attending classes all morning joe usually felt tired
10. the last chapter of agatha christie's novel passenger to frankfurt is entitled journey to scotland

E X E R C I S E

Add the appropriate punctuation marks and capital letters to the following sentences.

1. he asked why did you do that
2. why did you do that he asked
3. why he asked did you do that
4. gogol's story the nose is in the book petersburg tales
5. we read the book star trek before we saw the movie
6. my neighbor professor smith teaches art at riverview community college
7. they have already decided he said to postpone the job until summer
8. he said that they had already decided to postpone the job until summer
9. more and more people are becoming aware of environmental problems he noted they are also starting to take action on them
10. unless you take latin you will have a difficult time with scientific terminology the instructor told joe

E X E R C I S E

Working alone or with a group of your classmates, check your current and previous writing for errors in punctuation and capitalization.

Modifier Errors

What do the following sentences really state?

Lying under the coffee table, the instructor found her missing red pen.
At the age of five, my mother was already teaching me to play chess.

As they are written—and how we communicate depends on how we write our sentences—the sentences state that the instructor is lying under the coffee table and that the mother is only five years old.

We should not expect our readers to guess or figure out on their own what we mean; we should express our meaning accurately:

The instructor found her missing red pen lying under the coffee table.

When I was five, my mother was already teaching me to play chess.

In both cases, the original version of the sentence had a problem with a **modifier**:

Lying under the coffee table, the instructor found her missing red pen.

At the age of five, my mother was already teaching me to play chess.

In the revised version of each sentence, this problem has been corrected:

The instructor found her missing red pen lying under the coffee table.

When I was five, my mother was already teaching me to play chess.

We can place "lying under the coffee table" after "pen" so that it modifies "pen." And we can change "at the age of five" to "when I was five" to explain accurately who was five.

A number of different grammatical forms can be used to add information to the fundamental parts of the sentence—the subject and the verb—or to other elements in the sentence. Each modifier answers a question such as *which, when, how,* or *how much* about one or more other words in the sentence.

Modifiers include adjectives, adverbs, present and past participles, some infinitives, most prepositional phrases, and most subordinate clauses.

Adjectives modify forms that name (nouns, pronouns, and gerunds):

They purchased the bigger house even though it was expensive.

Her studying Spanish was a good idea.

Adverbs modify forms that make statements (verbs):

He withdrew his hand quickly.

They also modify forms that themselves modify (adjectives, adverbs, participles, infinitives, prepositional phrases, and subordinate clauses):

In the future, almost every car will have air bags.

He opened the package very carefully.

He has traveled all over the world.

Present and past participles modify forms that name:

The lady writing letters is a tourist.

The letters, written on hotel stationary, are going to her various friends at home.

The ones receiving the letters will be happy.

Some infinitives act as modifiers, in one of three ways. First, they may modify forms that name:

He is not one to avoid responsibility.

Second, they may modify forms that make a statement:

She is walking several miles a day to lose weight.

Third, they may modify forms that modify:

They go to the market early to avoid the crowds.

Most prepositional phrases can act as modifiers in the same three ways. They can modify forms that name:

The puppy in the window drew the attention of many people passing by.

They can modify forms that make a statement:

The logs were floating down the river.

And they can modify forms that modify:

The logs floating down the river had been cut the previous day.

Most subordinate clauses are modifiers. These modify forms that name:

No one knew what was in the box that was lying on the table.

Or they modify forms that make a statement:

After they read the document carefully, they signed it.

Identify the modifiers in each of the following sentences. What does each one modify?

1. The large tiger in the cage paced impatiently while the keeper fed the other animals.

2. The keeper opened a panel and threw a chunk of meat in.

3. Lying on a ledge, the hungry animal quickly ate the food.

4. The paper used for newspapers is often recycled.

5. He needed the class to fulfill a requirement.

MISPLACED MODIFIERS

A modifier that is misplaced creates confusion:

She made pizza for the men with pepperoni.

We can correct the problem by moving the modifier to a place where it makes sense:

She made pizza with pepperoni for the men.

Prepositional phrases and subordinate clauses modifying nouns, pronouns, and gerunds usually come immediately after the word they modify:

The cows in the field are grazing.

The programs that have been tested will soon be put into operation.

Participles, too, can directly follow what they modify:

The people working on the project are staying late.

Participles placed at the beginning of a sentence normally modify the subject:

Staring into the evening sky, the boy thought about space ships and satellites.

Prepositional phrases placed at the beginning of a sentence usually modify the verb:

In the backyard, the dogs were digging furiously.

Analyze and correct the misplaced modifiers in the following sentences.

1. Sitting on the chimney, we saw a rare bird.
2. He went out in the freezing wind and picked the vegetables in a bad mood.
3. The students heard the stories of how the new elements were discovered in their chemistry class.
4. Rolling under the stone, the hiker saw the bottle cap.
5. Their new neighbors saw some squirrels on the way to the mall.
6. Joe noticed a large power mower leaving the store.
7. Sue bought a washing machine from her new neighbor lady that did not agitate very well.
8. Badly burnt, the guests did not enjoy the roast.
9. The new faculty members received a copy of the school's statement on cheating on Thursday night.
10. Powerful countries waste money on nuclear weapons such as the United States.

Analyze and correct the misplaced modifiers in the following sentences.

1. During the Los Angeles riots of 1992, many people suffered enormous losses such as store owners and local employees.
2. *Dead Souls* is a novel about a tax fraud by Gogol.
3. Gogol uses humorous names for his characters like Dickens.
4. We donated an artifact to the museum that was very valuable.
5. Many athletes are accepted into universities that do not have a good academic preparation.
6. The tourists almost visited all of the museums in Paris.
7. Annoyed by their lack of action, many legislators received letters from constituents.
8. Radio was the main source of information about what was going on in the world aside from the newspaper.
9. Young people are influenced by other youths who drive around in luxury cars in expensive clothing.
10. Parents should make clear to their children the dangers of drugs in the home.

DANGLING MODIFIERS

Consider the following sentence:

After running ten miles in the park, our shoes were hurting our feet.

Obviously, shoes do not run. The people who did the running need to be identified in the sentence:

After we had run ten miles in the park, our shoes were hurting our feet.

A modifier that logically should modify something not in the sentence is said to be **dangling**. Many dangling modifiers are participles:

Reading the newspaper, violence seems to be everywhere.   [The participle, "reading," is modifying the subject, "violence."]

Others are prepositional phrases, especially those in which the object is a gerund:

By following the directions, the toy is easy to assemble.   ["By following" is modifying "toy."]

These sentences can be rewritten as follows:

To a person reading the newspaper, violence seems to be everywhere.

If the buyer follows the directions, the toy is easy to assemble.

E X E R C I S E

Analyze and correct the dangling modifiers in the following sentences.

1. Watching television for long hours, reading enough becomes difficult.
2. Frustrated by the situation, our next move was to leave.
3. When getting someone's help, learning to play the piano can be a rewarding experience.
4. The information given in class may be invaluable when studying for a test.
5. Before discovering the hole in the pan, a puddle of oil had already formed on the garage floor.
6. Many medical clinics charge a fee to be treated.
7. When comparing CDs to tapes, there are several important differences.
8. Safety windows are a desirable feature in a car in which small children ride: they cannot fall out while driving.
9. Many stress-related complaints develop from hours spent stalled in traffic.
10. Capitalizing on the convenient location, mini-markets are generally built near gas stations or large housing tracts.

An especially frequent problem is a dangling participle, usually at the beginning of the sentence, that inadvertently modifies the word *it*, the subject of the sentence:

Looking at the statistics, it is clear that inflation remained high in the 1980s.

We can correct the error in this case by giving the participle, "looking," something logical to modify:

Looking at the statistics, we can clearly see that inflation remained high in the 1980s.

Or we can replace the dangling participial phrase with a subordinate clause:

If we look at the statistics, we can see clearly that inflation remained high in the 1980s.

However, the idea "if we look" does not contribute to the meaning. A better way to express the essential point of the sentence is to say

The statistics clearly show that inflation remained high in the 1980s.

Analyze and correct the dangling modifiers in the following sentences. As in the preceding example, consider any better way to express meaning.

1. Looking back twenty years, it can be seen that there was a need for environmental regulation.
2. Watching television for long hours, it is not possible for children to read enough.
3. Having lost everything in the fire, it was difficult for them to face the future.
4. Sailing along the coast, it was possible to see clearly the mountains beyond the coastal lowlands.
5. Considering the evidence, it is obvious that these are the right conclusions.
6. Coming from a family of doctors, it was natural for her to go into medicine.
7. Examining the characteristics of the disease, it is evident that there is risk of contagion.
8. Listening to the forecast, it is easier to figure out what to wear.
9. Stirring the boiling hot coffee, it was not too hot to drink.
10. Weighing the two sides, it should be easy to arrive at a sensible decision.

If the modifier is dangling, rearranging the sentence does not correct the error:

It was all right for us to leave, having finished everything.

Here, "having" still modifies "it."
Furthermore, adding a word such as *by* or *while* does not correct the problem.

By taking precautions, many potentially dangerous situations can be avoided.
While taking precautions, many potentially dangerous situations can be avoided.

Both are incorrect. There are several different ways of expressing this idea correctly:

A person who takes precautions can avoid many potentially dangerous situations.
By taking precautions, a person can avoid many potentially dangerous situations.
Many potentially dangerous situations can be avoided if a person takes precautions.

OTHER PROBLEMS WITH MODIFIERS

Consider the following sentences:

The small children on the farm had to be carefully watched around the large horses and cows.
The children quickly ran and hid.

In the first sentence, the word "large" modifies both "horses" and "cows." In the second example, the word "quickly" modifies both "ran" and "hid." The meaning of these sentences is clear. However, the same modifier cannot add information to words that are not grammatically parallel or that occur in different parts of a sentence. Notice the confusing modifier in this sentence:

> When he moved to a crowded apartment in the city, he had to leave some of his belongings that he had been attached to at home.

Here "at home" seems to tell both where he had to "leave" his belongings and where he had been "attached" to them. This sentence needs separate modifiers for the two ideas. Instead of repeating "at home," we can use the word *behind* to explain "leave":

> When he moved to a crowded apartment in the city, he had to leave behind some of his belongings that he had been attached to at home.

> Find the problem modifier in this sentence:

> The driver that everyone thought would win the race without a doubt disappointed the spectators by coming in third.

It is unclear whether the prepositional phrase "without a doubt" modifies "win" or whether it goes with "disappointed." If we choose to have it modify "win," we can rephrase the sentence as follows:

> The driver that everyone thought would undoubtedly win the race disappointed the spectators by coming in third.

If "without a doubt" is supposed to modify "disappointed," we can revise the sentence as follows:

> The spectators were without a doubt disappointed when the driver everyone thought would win the race came in third.

A modifier must be expressed in the proper grammatical form. There is a modifier problem in the following sentence:

> He was sent to jail for writing something libel.

The word libel is intended to explain "something," but it cannot be used as an adjective in its present form. The correct form of the word is the adjective *libelous*:

> He was sent to jail for writing something libelous.

An inappropriate modifier can also interfere with the logic of the sentence. Consider the following statement:

> He is such an egoist when people talk to him.

This sentence gives the impression that as long as no one is talking to him, he is not an egoist. But egoism is a trait that does not come and go, so the subordinate clause with "when" is illogical. The writer probably intended to say the following:

> When people talk to him, they realize that he is quite an egoist.

The following sentence offers a similar example of the illogical use of a modifier:

The island was the ideal getaway for the busy lives of city people.

The prepositional phrase "for the busy lives" modifies the noun "getaway." But lives do not need a getaway; people do. The intended meaning can be expressed more accurately as follows:

The island was the ideal getaway for city people with busy lives.

Another common problem with modifiers involves the use of an absolute form such as *all* or *always* when the real situation does not warrant it:

People who live in large cities always have problems sleeping because of noise.

In reality, some residential areas in large cities are very quiet, and some people seldom have problems sleeping even in noisy environments. The following statement makes a more reasonable claim:

Many people who live in large cities have problems sleeping because of noise.

The following example contains another untrue assertion:

People are having trouble finding work because there are no jobs available.

"No jobs" means none whatsoever, and this is inaccurate. We can say

People are having trouble finding work because very few jobs are available.

or

People are having trouble finding work because it seems as if there are no jobs available.

Notice that this second version describes the impression that job seekers have, not the actual situation regarding jobs.

E X E R C I S E

Correct the modifier problems in the following sentences.

1. The 1992 Los Angeles riots had nothing to do with the verdict in the Rodney King case.
2. Riots historically have never brought change.
3. Homeless people always turn to addictive substances to escape from their desperate reality.
4. All college students have to juggle classes and part-time jobs.
5. A student should always write legible when taking lecture notes.
6. Most students have financially problems.
7. He is a humorist person.
8. The verdict was an example of unfair justice.
9. The play was real well choreographed.
10. On hearing the news, we acted quick.

E X E R C I S E

Correct the modifier problems in the following sentences.

12-49

1. Burbling along, the hikers found the stream inviting.

2. Going camping every year, the park's best-known bear became the favorite subject of our pictures.

3. Dragging his feet, the child's car came to a stop.

4. Having finished all the sauce, the spaghetti could not be served to the guests.

5. Having smoked several cigarettes, the hike left Joe out of breath.

6. Upon arrival, my original impression changed.

7. After running hard for most of a long block, the bus pulled away just as Mary was reaching it.

8. Feeling sleepy during the long lecture, it was difficult to follow the speaker.

9. Taken at face value, we were shocked by his statement.

10. She promised to treat all of her friends to dinner on the telephone.

E X E R C I S E

12-50

Working alone or with a group of your classmates, check your current and previous writing for problems with modifiers. Watch for any that are misplaced or dangling. If you have started sentences with participles, make sure that you intended for these to modify the subjects of the sentences. Also check for inaccurate or inappropriate modifiers. Make any necessary changes.

Inconsistencies

FAULTY AGREEMENT

Would you write sentences like these?

> One of the little league umpires are constantly shouting at the crowd.
>
> All of the people at that table are well-known nuclear scientist.

Would you write these?

> One are shouting.
>
> All of the people are scientist.

All four sentences have incorrectly matched singular and plural forms. The singular subject "one" in the first and third examples does not **agree** with the plural verb "are shouting." In the second and fourth examples, the predicate nominative "scientist" does not agree with the plural "all are." These sentences should be worded consistently.

> One of the little league umpires is constantly shouting at the crowd.
>
> All of the people at that table are well-known nuclear scientists.

Subject/Verb Agreement

A singular subject requires a singular verb, and a plural subject needs a plural verb:

A dog barks.

Dogs bark.

Notice in the preceding examples that adding an *s* to a noun makes the noun plural, but adding one to a verb makes the verb singular.

It runs.

They run.

Some common pronouns are singular even though they are used in situations that involve a plural concept:

Everybody in both classes plays some musical instrument.

The pronouns *everyone, somebody, someone, anybody, anyone, nobody,* and *no one* are also singular:

Everyone in her class plays two or more instruments.
Somebody among so many contestants was sure to know the answer.

The words *each, either,* and *neither* are also singular:

Each of the trains has a dining car.

Either of those ties goes with that suit.

Neither of the puppies sleeps in the house.

These pronouns are singular because they focus on each individual member of a group. We can also use them as adjectives to modify the pronoun *one*:

Each one has a dining car.

Either one goes with that suit.

Neither one sleeps in the house.

Agreement of the verb with the subject in *either . . . or, neither . . . nor,* and *not only . . . but also* constructions follows a different principle:

Either the puppy or the kitten makes a good gift.

Not only the horse but also the cows stay in the barn when it rains.

Neither the clarinets nor the oboe is working.

In each case, the verb agrees with the closer subject. Thus, in the third example, the singular verb "is working" agrees with "oboe." This is logically awkward, however, because the other subject, "clarinets," is in the plural. A better version of this sentence is

Neither the oboe nor the clarinets are working.

In other words, we can place the plural subject second so that the verb will be in the plural.

Other multiple subjects require a plural verb:

His brother and he were both musicians.

Both the puppy and the kitten are playful.

The following are not considered multiple subjects.

Bacon and eggs is a popular breakfast dish. [The dish is considered a single unit.]

Two dollars is too much to pay for a dessert. [Two dollars is treated as a total

amount, not as two separate dollars.]

Three miles is a long distance for a student carrying a load of books to walk. [Three

miles is a total distance, not three separate units of length.]

The Brothers Karamazov is one of the masterpieces of Russian literature. [A title

constitutes a single unit.]

The terms *a lot, some, any, none, all, more,* and *most* are either singular or plural, depending on whether they represent **count nouns** or simply a quantity of something:

A lot of the apples are ripe.

A lot of the fruit is ripe.

Some of the dollars were in the box.

Some of the money was in the box.

There are separate words for some singular/plural ideas:

Many of the sandwiches were eaten.
Much of the coffee was drunk.
A *few* of the sandwiches were left.
A *little* of the coffee was left.
Fewer of the regular participants attended this time.
Less than the usual amount was spent.
A small *number* of sandwiches were left.
A small *amount* of coffee was left.

Notice that "a number" is plural, expressing the idea of "several" or "quite a few," whereas "the number" is singular, indicating the total number:

A number of people were present at the event, but the number of participants was

not divulged.

The word *there* never acts as the subject of the sentence. The verb must agree with the real subject:

There were a hammer and a box of nails on the shelf.

Just as subjects and verbs of main clauses must agree, so must subjects and verbs of subordinate clauses:

Everybody knew that he and his brother were musicians.

Relative pronouns—*who, which,* and *that*—are singular or plural depending on whether they replace a singular noun or a plural noun.

She invited only people who do not smoke.

In the preceding example, "who" is plural because it is taking the place of "people." Similarly, we would write

He took the papers that were lying on the table.

He took the document that was lying on the table.

Just as subjects and verbs must agree, a predicate nominative, since it renames the subject, must also agree with the subject (and therefore with the verb, too):

Many of the presenters *were* research *chemists*.

E X E R C I S E

12-51

Choose the verb that agrees with the subject in each of the following sentences.

1. Each of the girls go/goes to a different school.
2. She and her sister was/were interested in the discussion.
3. One of the local law enforcement officers come/comes to our English class.
4. A large amount/number of countries was/were represented at the meeting.
5. There was/were a lot of very influential people present.
6. Neither the girls nor their mother speak/speaks fluent English.
7. There was/were only a turkey and a pie in the freezer.
8. Neither of the brothers are/is able to fix the car.
9. Frequent headaches are/is a problem for many people.
10. It is the ecologist who often predict/predicts serious environmental problems.

E X E R C I S E

12-52

Choose the verb that agrees with the subject in each of the following sentences.

1. He and I was/were there.
2. There are/is two empty places at the table.
3. One of the puppies go/goes to obedience class.
4. Some of the fruit are/is falling from the tree.
5. Some of the apples are/is falling from the tree.
6. A large number/amount of components was/were rejected.
7. Not only the students but also the instructor learn/learns in a well-run class.
8. There was/were a coach and a trainer in the locker room.
9. There are/is few books in this library that contains/contain the information we need.
10. Either of those perfumes make/makes a good gift.

Pronoun/Antecedent Agreement

In the following sentence, who runs the risk of being prosecuted?

If a person commits perjury, they run the risk of being prosecuted.

The pronoun "they" is probably meant to refer to the "person" who commits perjury, but the plural "they" does not agree with the singular "person." Substituting "he or she" for "they" corrects the problem:

If a person commits perjury, he or she runs the risk of being prosecuted.

The preceding solution can seem wordy, however, especially if the double form occurs more than once in the same passage. Notice, for instance, how awkward the following sentences are:

> If a person commits perjury, he or she runs the risk of being prosecuted. He or she may be arrested, and his or her reputation is consequently ruined.

Several other versions of the sample sentence are better:

> A person who commits perjury runs the risk of being prosecuted.
>
> A person that commits perjury runs the risk of being prosecuted.
>
> A person committing perjury runs the risk of being prosecuted.
>
> If people commit perjury, they run the risk of being prosecuted.

Notice that the last version repeats the original sentence, but with the subject and verb made plural. Often a sentence containing "he or she," "him or her," "his or her," or "himself or herself" is better if changed to the plural because the one-word forms "them," "their," and "themselves" are then appropriate.

EXERCISE

The following sentences have faulty pronoun/antecedent agreement. Identify the error; then rewrite each sentence in more than one correct version.

1. If anyone wants a ticket, they have to go to the box office to get it.

2. One can enroll in the local college and take as many classes as they want.

3. A person graduating from high school often does not know what career they want to pursue.

4. If anybody crosses the line, they are out!

Agreement of Possessive with Possessor

Do you consider the following sentence correct?

> Everybody told their own story.

This usage is common in conversation, but in college writing we avoid such grammatical inconsistencies. Since "everybody" is singular, a possessive that refers to it must also be singular. We can correct this error by replacing "their" with "his or her":

> Everybody told his or her own story.

Once again, the plural form is preferable:

> *All* of the *people* told *their* own *stories.*

Similarly, the grammatically incorrect

> Everyone brought their camera on the trip.

can be expressed in plural form as

All of the tourists brought their cameras on the trip.

Or, in this case, we can omit the possessive:

Everyone brought a camera on the trip.

E X E R C I S E

Rewrite the following sentences so that possessives and possessors agree.

1. Everybody passed their finals.
2. Each of the students brought their own book to class.
3. Everyone in the office uses good English in their letters.
4. Each of the boys has their own room.
5. Each of the children has their own room.
6. Nobody remembered to bring their key.
7. Has anyone picked up their ticket yet?
8. Neither of the players turned in their uniform.
9. One of the members of the orchestra brought their own music stand from home.
10. Somebody left their notebook here.

Agreement of Adjective/Noun Combinations

Consider the meaning of this sentence:

Japan has little import products.

As the sentence is written, it might be interpreted as a reference to *bonsai*, although Japan is much more likely to export miniature plants than to import them. More likely, the writer meant to say that Japan has "few" import products. But the singular "little" communicates an entirely different meaning.

Several adjectives, like *little* and *few*, have separate forms for the singular and plural.

Many sandwiches were eaten.

Much coffee was drunk.

Few sandwiches were left.

Little coffee was left.

Fewer papers were completed this time.

Less paper was thrown out this time.

The *fewest* people were present at the Sunday afternoon performance.

The *least* advice was given by her own boyfriend.

Compare agreement in these sentences with agreement in the sentences on page 243 involving nouns and pronouns that have separate forms (*many, much,* and so on).

Notice the differences in meaning in the following examples:

A few sandwiches were eaten.   [some, several]

Few were eaten.   [not many]

Few sandwiches were eaten.   [not many]

A little coffee was drunk.   [some, a certain quantity]

Little coffee was drunk.   [not much]

Little was drunk.   [not much]

EXERCISE

Choose the correct form of the adjective to use in each of the following sentences.

1. There are fewer/less cars on the roads on Sunday mornings than on other mornings.
2. Fewer/Less traffic means fewer/less pollution.
3. Too few/little trees are left in many parts of the world.
4. Too few/little timberland is left in Europe, for example.
5. Far too few/little people signed up for the project, so it had to be canceled.
6. Not many/much furniture was sold at the auction.
7. Does your father give you many/much advice?
8. Poor spellers usually read fewer/less books than good spellers.
9. Who ate the fewest/least desserts?
10. Who ate the fewest/least fruit?

EXERCISE

Identify which words in each of the following sentences should agree but do not. Then write at least one correct version of each sentence.

1. One of her most important goals for the next few years have always been to get a degree.
2. The repair shop's estimate for some of the repairs seem high.
3. He said that Jim and he was absent that day.
4. Scientist make mistakes too.
5. The amount of notices sent to customers was larger last month.
6. Neither the cows nor the horse mind the rain.
7. Neither of those jobs are easy.
8. There is a number of problems to solve.
9. Neither their collie nor their neighbors' terrier are going to win the prize.
10. Try to share thoughts with your child by sitting down with them and talking about school activities.

EXERCISE

Identify which words in each of the following sentences should agree but do not. Then write at least one correct version of each sentence.

1. Ansel Adams found Yosemite to have a vast amount of excellent locations for photographs.
2. One of his most famous pictures show the play of light and shadow on Half Dome.

3. Neither the puppies nor the child know how to sit still.

4. The book was written by ecologist who are concerned about the Amazon Basin.

5. Either of those videos are worth renting.

6. Many feel that we need a national health care system to reduce the amount of uninsured people.

7. Neither of her sisters were present.

8. There is less accidents when people avoid drinking and driving.

9. When anyone wants to drop a course, they have to process a drop.

10. A working teenager learns to understand how important responsibility to themselves and others are. (there are two agreement errors in this sentence)

SHIFTS

Each of the following sentences has a logic problem.

> When a person goes to the store, you should count your change.
>
> The thief raced downstairs in his attempt to escape and runs right into the detective.
>
> When tourists go to San Francisco, public transportation is frequently used by them.

In the first example, the same individual is referred to as "a person" and as "you." In the second example, the time is established as past by the verb "raced"; then the time is changed, without reason, to the present ("runs"). In the third example, the focus needlessly shifts from "tourists" to "public transportation." We can express each of these thoughts consistently, as follows:

> People who go to the store should count their change.
>
> The thief raced downstairs in his attempt to escape and ran right into the detective.
>
> When tourists go to San Francisco, they frequently use public transportation.

Shifts in Person

We have three possible **points of view** when we write or speak

First person: *I, we* = the speaker or speakers
Second person: *you* (singular and plural) = the person or persons addressed
Third person: *he, she, it, they* = the person, thing, persons, or things spoken about

When we write, we choose a basic point of view, and we stay with it unless there is a reason to change.

The first person, *I* or *we*, is used primarily in the narration of personal experiences. Occasionally it is appropriate in other writing, such as a report or research paper for which an instructor has assigned a statement of personal opinion.

The second person, *you* (singular or plural), is the point of view we use to give directions or to describe a process. In writing, the word *you* refers to the reader; avoid using *you* in writing to indicate people in general even though this usage is acceptable in conversation. For example, do not write

> When you go on a long trip, you should take part of your money in traveler's checks.

Instead, adopt the third person:

> When people go on a long trip, they should take part of their money in traveler's checks.

Write from the third person point of view in college compositions unless you have a specific reason for doing otherwise, and use the third person consistently.

How would you correct the following shift? See if you can work out several ways to express the idea.

> If a person works hard, you can accomplish a great deal.

If we change "you" to make the subject consistent with "person," we have

> If a person works hard, he or she can accomplish a great deal.

To avoid the wordy double form, we can usually express the idea in the plural.

> If people work hard, they can accomplish a great deal.

The idea can also be expressed in other ways:

> A person who works hard can accomplish a great deal.
> A person that works hard can accomplish a great deal.
> People who work hard can accomplish a great deal.
> People that work hard can accomplish a great deal.
> A person working hard can accomplish a great deal.
> A hard-working person can accomplish a great deal.

EXERCISE

Correct the shifts in person in the following sentences. Experiment with different versions. Compare your answers to those of several classmates.

1. If one wants to go abroad, you need to save money.
2. If a student misses too many classes, you may fail a course.
3. First, one reads an essay over; then you go back and rewrite it.
4. They always watch television programs that keep you from sleeping.
5. When a person wants to go to a very popular restaurant, you make reservations.
6. In elementary school, the teacher would punish you if you did not have your homework.
7. I like working with someone you can talk to openly.
8. After one completes an application, you should check it over carefully.
9. When you go to your first job interview, you feel nervous.
10. Before electricity came into use, you had to carry candles from room to room.

Shifts in Verb Tense

What is the time reference here?

> We were sound asleep when the whole house starts shaking violently.

The writer starts with "were," establishing a time in the past, but then shifts to "starts," indicating the present. However, for meaning to be clear, the time element in the sentence must remain consistent:

We were sound asleep when the whole house started shaking violently.

When we write, we choose the appropriate time reference, and we stay with it. This means selecting a basic verb tense and making the verbs in the composition—whether it is a single sentence, a paragraph, or an essay—correspond to that basic tense.

In the corrected version of the preceding example, both verbs are in the past tense because the time reference is the same for both. Frequently, however, the time element changes; and when this happens, the additional verbs must show time related to the basic tense:

He said he had taken a psychology class.

In this example, he took the class *before* he said that he had, so the idea of "took" is expressed in the past perfect ("had taken") to clarify this time relationship.

Compare the following pairs of sentences:

He said, "I will call."
He said that he would call.

She said, "I have already finished."
She said that she had already finished.

When we talk about what someone said, we often need to make changes in verb tenses to show the different time relationships.

Consider meaning in the following examples:

If he wants, he could eat the rest of the pie.
A person studying history can see that a dictator would fight for wealth and power.
A tourist in London would have an opportunity to see Queen Elizabeth.

In the first example, the hypothetical "could eat" is inconsistent with "wants," a verb indicating a real situation. This is how the verbs should be coordinated:

If he *wants*, he *can eat* the rest of the pie.   [There is some pie left, and he may eat it.]

If he *wanted*, he *could eat* the rest of the pie.   [There is some pie left, but he probably will not eat it.]

If he *had wanted*, he *could have eaten* the rest of the pie.   [The pie is gone now, and he did not take advantage of his opportunity to finish it.]

In the second example, the hypothetical "would fight" again does not accurately express meaning. Dictators currently fight for wealth and power, as they have done in the past and will probably continue to do in the future. Consequently, the present tense, not the unreal conditional, is appropriate:

A person studying history can see that a dictator fights for wealth and power.

The third example is inconsistent, too. The opportunity to see Queen Elizabeth is real, even though most tourists do not actually see her; therefore, the hypothetical "would have" is incorrect. We can use "may" to show this possible but unlikely present situation:

A tourist in London may have an opportunity to see Queen Elizabeth.

EXERCISE

Correct the shifts in tense in the following sentences.

1. Soon after they left on their hike, they come to a river that they cannot cross.
2. Mary worked in the store all summer, but then she finds out, to her disappointment, that she cannot stay on the job part-time during the school year.
3. The shoplifter was moving toward the door when suddenly the clerk shouts.
4. They said they will come home early.
5. If she goes to New York for her vacation, she could visit the United Nations buildings.
6. If he goes to Mexico City for two years, he would become fluent in Spanish.
7. Her uncle always liked to discuss the changes that have taken place in his line of work.
8. The teacher said she would not be able to help the students a great deal unless they help themselves.
9. They could use the interlibrary loan if they want.
10. Shakespeare included ghosts in several of his plays, such as *Hamlet*, in which Hamlet's father appears in the form of a specter.

EXERCISE

Identify and correct the shifts in the following sentences.

1. Joe was hoping to go to the game, but then it starts raining.
2. Mary gave us the materials and then forgets to tell us how to use them.
3. With a 1.5% blood alcohol level, people could do things they would not normally do.
4. If a student wants to succeed, you have to work hard.
5. When a person speaks to an audience, you have to make sure they can hear you.
6. We were watching a murder mystery on television when all of a sudden the lights go out.
7. Many people make money from a war by selling arms; others would gain by selling results of research to develop new weapons.
8. Cagliostro put her in a trance and then has her jewels removed.
9. When traveling abroad, tourists need to know the value of money, or people will cheat you.
10. If she likes, she could ride with us.

EXERCISE

Identify and correct the shifts in the following sentences.

1. In high school, students have to take the classes the counselor gives you.
2. The local college is convenient because students would not have to drive far.
3. The death penalty is a reminder of what would happen if a person kills someone.
4. In *Animal Farm*, the animals took over the farm, but they have many problems as they try to run it.
5. Mary did not realize that Joe has changed jobs.
6. Mary was leading the race when Barbara catches up.
7. If a person likes working with the public, you should not become a laboratory technician.

8. After the workers completed the construction project, they reopen the freeway.

9. If they want, they could study French during the summer.

10. Her friend called her and says he will see her later.

FAULTY PARALLELISM

Consider the following example:

She likes coffee and dogs.

Why does it seem illogical?

Your reaction to this sentence may have been that coffee and dogs do not go together. As nouns, the two words fit together grammatically, but there is still a logic problem: ideas that we link with *and* need to be comparable, going together both grammatically and logically. In other words, they need to be **parallel**.

How would you express the following idea?

They like golfing, sailing, and to hike.

The three items in the series name *what* "they like"; thus, all three are direct objects. But the series of direct objects is not grammatically parallel. Unlike the sentence with "coffee and dogs," however, this sentence can be corrected:

They like golfing, sailing, and hiking.

They like to golf, sail, and hike.

They like to golf, to sail, and to hike.

We use *and* and the other coordinating conjunctions to join only comparable elements:

Joe attends college, and he also works.   ["and" joins two main clauses]

Mary will take notes or photocopy some of the information.   ["or" joins the two verbs]

You can usually correct faulty parallelism by putting the elements in question in grammatically (and logically) parallel form. Occasionally, you may find it worthwhile to change the wording so that what needs to be parallel also changes. Consider the following statement:

Women get irritated with men who always assume that the woman will cook dinner, serve it, and that she will also clean up everything afterward.

We can reword this sentence so that the three elements are parallel:

Women get irritated with men who always assume that the woman will *cook* dinner, *serve* it, and *clean* up everything afterward.

Alternatively, we can change what needs to be parallel:

Women get irritated with men who always assume *that the woman will cook and serve dinner* and *that she will also clean up everything afterward*.

In this last version, the first "and" joins two verbs, "cook" and "serve." The second "and" joins the two subordinate clauses beginning with "that."

EXERCISE

Correct the errors in parallelism in the following sentences.

1. In Florida, people can go to theme parks, visit Cape Canaveral, and they can enjoy the beaches.
2. They are scholars, educators, and they write books.
3. They hope to move soon and that they will enjoy their new home.
4. Her name regularly appears in magazines, newspapers, and she is often mentioned in trade journals.
5. He is a young pianist of great talent and who hopes some day to perform professionally.
6. The problem with those cars is their noise and that they run hot.
7. They enjoy talking, listening, and even to criticize.
8. She was intelligent but an impractical person.
9. The student decided to schedule her study time, avoid parties, or she would be unhappy once again with her final grades.
10. Fast-food restaurants are creating an overweight and lazier population.

Articles, possessives, and other modifiers, as well as prepositions and infinitives, do not normally need to be repeated before each item in a series. If one is repeated, however, they must all be repeated:

He looked for the tool *in the* closet, store room, and garage.

or

He looked for the tool *in the* closet, *the* store room, and *the* garage.

or

He looked for the tool *in the* closet, *in the* store room, and *in the* garage.

EXERCISE

Correct the errors in parallelism in the following sentences.

1. He refused to read, discuss, or to sign the document.
2. She is interested in anthropology, archeology, and in history.
3. He borrowed all the books, magazines, and the newspapers that gave information on the subject.
4. He is a poet, gourmet, and a world traveler.
5. She has worked in education, the travel business, and with a major food producer.
6. She sold her stereo, bookcases, and her lawn mower.
7. She did not eat many apples, oranges, or much pineapple.
8. He is an architect, engineer, and an athlete.
9. When they went on vacation, they took their tent, camp stove, and their canoe.
10. They like to go boating, fish, and to look for seashells.

Consider this statement:

Joe is rich, has a new Lamborghini, and travels all the time.

The "and" connects a series of verbs, but the sentence is weak because different types of statements are joined: he *is* something, *has* something, and *does* something. The following statement is better:

Because Joe is wealthy, he *drives* a new Lamborghini and *travels* all the time.

EXERCISE

Make each of the following statements logical.

1. He is an excellent artist and sells many paintings.
2. Mary works in an office and is also a notary public.
3. They were intelligent children and they appeared frequently on quiz shows.
4. Joe has a tractor and he rents it out.
5. Basketball is a game that encourages social interaction, develops in the player a sense of responsibility, and is a way of releasing emotions.

Any other elements in sentences that are coordinated or compared must be grammatically and logically parallel:

Joe told his son *either to wash* the dishes *or to clean* the house.
Mary wants *neither landfills nor prisons* in her town.
Joe *not only creates* his own products *but also markets* them.
Mary *both draws and paints*.
Mary wanted the book signed by *the named author, not the ghost writer*.
Mary wanted *to find* a job *rather than to get* welfare checks.

EXERCISE

Word the coordinated or compared elements in each of the following sentences in parallel form.

1. Off-road vehicles not only disturb the peacefulness of the desert, but also they harm nature's balance.
2. He wanted either to study French or, better yet, go to Paris.
3. He wanted to get the job by qualifying for it rather than use someone's influence.
4. Recycling both conserves resources and it helps solve our trash disposal problem.
5. They neither smoke nor do they drink.
6. He prefers to work out at a health club, not spending all the money it would take to buy his own equipment.

The following examples also have elements that are not parallel:

A problem the working high school student faces involves maintaining an acceptable level of performance in both school and work.

An employee given a job may not have a clear understanding or reason for doing the job.

Because of the holes in the ozone layer, the sun is more damaging than years ago.

Compare these corrected versions:

A problem the working high school student faces involves maintaining an acceptable level of performance *both in* school *and at* work.

An employee given a job may not have a clear *understanding of* or *reason for* doing the job.

Because of the holes in the ozone layer, the sun is more damaging *now* than it was *years ago*.

E X E R C I S E

Correct the errors in parallelism in the following sentences.

1. Tim wants to become a lawyer, an inventor, or go into business.

2. He either reads the materials he wants right in the library or he photocopies them and takes the photocopies home.

3. She not only swims well, but also she dives like an expert.

4. They sell neither books nor are there any instruction manuals in that electronics store.

5. He went to Europe both to see famous places and eat the various national dishes.

6. To lose weight, eat less food, consume fewer calories, and you should walk a lot.

7. The advantages of a warm climate are that people's heating bills are lower, they need less clothing, and that they can enjoy more outdoor activities.

8. She got good grades by always attending class, taking notes carefully, and by reviewing her notes as soon as possible after class.

9. He likes to swim first, hike next, and eating after the other activities.

10. We are destroying our planet by wasting materials, polluting our air and water, and we pretend that everything is all right.

E X E R C I S E

12-67

Correct the errors in parallelism in the following sentences.

1. Basketball is good for those who appreciate and play the game.

2. Five people who have never played together and without knowing each other can immediately become a team.

3. They do so by relying on signals, quick decisions, and by establishing order with one another.

4. Joe speaks French, Spanish, and he understands Italian.

5. The author is comparing living conditions in the United States to other countries.

6. When we conserve materials, we help the situation on our planet by not exhausting our resources and giving them time to replenish themselves.

7. A busy person can have something to eat more quickly at a fast-food restaurant than cooking at home.

8. Public transportation is inexpensive, convenient, and a safe way to travel.

9. If more people used public transportation, there would be fewer cars on the road, less time wasted in transit, and people would also save money.

10. The proposed program would be not only helpful to the people, but it would also be economical for the government.

E X E R C I S E

12-68

Correct the errors in parallelism in the following sentences.

1. Athletes who smoke are slower, have less stamina, and suffer from shortness of breath.

2. Until another source is developed that will provide energy at a price comparable to petroleum, all industrialized nations will continue to depend on oil.

3. Employers tend to hire people with better educational backgrounds than those who do not.

4. The alcoholic's situation gets worse until either the drinker goes bankrupt or gets help.

5. Leonardo da Vinci was an engineer, painted pictures, and would invent things too.

6. My neighbor is addicted to not only drinking but also to gambling.

7. An increase in global temperature will melt the polar ice caps, the water from which will flood many valleys and thus disturbing nature's balance.

8. The public sometimes forgets that people want to find adequate employment rather than staying on welfare.

9. The cost of a community college education is reasonable compared to a private university.

10. The difference in cost is important for those unable to pay the higher amount but want the education.

E X E R C I S E

12-69

Working alone or with a group of your classmates, check your previous or current writing for inconsistencies in your sentences. Correct any errors in agreement, shifts, and faulty parallelism.

Errors in Function

Do any of the following sentences communicate meaning effectively?

> Mary invited Joe and I to go with her.
>
> Some people are enthusiastic about designer labels, and designers profit from them.
>
> Working conditions can be a factor in job satisfaction. It is the case when the work area is neat.
>
> Poor writing and a lack of advertisers were the end of the local newspaper.

All of these examples contain words that do not perform their intended functions. In the first, "I," the subject form of the pronoun, is used in place of the object form, "me." In the second example, the reader cannot tell whether "them" replaces "people" or "labels." In the third example, "it" does not refer to anything in particular. In the fourth example, the statement is essentially that "writing" and "a lack of advertisers" were the "end" of the newspaper. Functional errors like the preceding four can make writing difficult or even impossible to understand.

FAULTY PRONOUN FORM

The personal pronouns in English have different forms for their use as subjects, objects, or possessives.

The **subject** forms are *I, you, he, she, it, we, you* (plural), and *they*. We use these forms for four different elements:

The **subject** of a sentence:

They arrived early.

The **predicate nominative**:

The wealthiest person present was *he*.

The **subject** or **predicate nominative** of a subordinate clause:

We knew that *they* had arrived early.

We knew that the wealthiest person present was *he*.

An **appositive** that renames a subject:

The two candidates, John and *he*, were both well qualified.

The **object** forms are *me, you, him, her, it, us, you* (plural), and *them*. We use these in any object position:

A **direct object**:

John saw *us*.

An **indirect object**:

Alice told *them* a lie.

An **object of a preposition**:

John knows all about *me*.

An **object of an infinitive**:

He wants to see *me*.

An **object of a gerund**:

He enjoys helping *her*.

An **object of a participle**:

The person taking *them* is responsible for them.

The **possessive** forms are *mine, yours, his, hers, its, ours, yours* (plural), and *theirs*. We use these forms when we need to indicate possession:

The book was *hers*.   [= her book]

I have seen their new car, and I like *theirs* better than *his*.   [= their car better than his car]

Some other pronouns also have separate forms.
Who and *whoever* are subject forms:

Who came early?

They do not know *who* came early.

They will give the money to *whoever* needs it.

In the last example, "whoever" is the subject of the subordinate clause. The entire subordinate clause, "whoever needs it," is the object of the preposition "to."

Whom and *whomever* are object forms:

The lawyer explained to *whom* the document was to be addressed.

They will give out certificates to *whomever* they are not specifically honoring during the ceremony.

In the second example, "whomever" is an object in the subordinate clause (the object of the verb, "are honoring"), and the entire clause is the object of the preposition "to."

What is the meaning of each of the following sentences?

He likes me better than she.

He likes me better than her.

You may have the impression that the first one is incorrect. Actually, both are correct, but their meanings are different:

He likes me better than she likes me.

He likes me better than he likes her.

Thus, two entirely different comparisons are being made—between "he" and "she" in the first example, and between "me" and "her" in the second. The meaning conveyed will match the meaning intended only if the correct form of the pronoun is used.

E X E R C I S E

12-70

Choose the correct form of the pronoun in each of the following sentences.

1. Between you and I/me, it will never work.
2. We sent the package to Joe and he/him.
3. He runs faster than her/she.
4. He asked Joe and I/me to prepare everything.
5. He asked if Joe and I/me would prepare everything.
6. Give the book to whoever/whomever will read it.
7. I knew it was her/she.
8. He is the one who/whom they say did it.
9. It was he/him who had made everything possible.
10. Both my sister and I/me were pleased.

FAULTY PRONOUN REFERENCE

Consider the following sentence:

He arrived at school early so that he could get all the information he needed and still have time to enroll in his classes, which seemed like a good idea.

The meaning here is not clear: "which" can refer to "arrived early," "get all the information," or "have time to enroll." Something specific should be substituted for "which":

> He arrived at school early so that he could get all the information he needed and still have time to enroll in his classes. As it turned out, arriving early was a good idea.   [or: getting all the information he needed was a good idea;   or: having time to enroll in his classes was a good idea]

The pronouns *which, it, they, this, that, these,* and *those* should refer to someone or something specific.

EXERCISE

Rewrite the following sentences so that the pronouns refer to something specific.

1. Many students cannot get the classes they need because they go fast.
2. For many children, television programs relieve their fear of ghosts when they are alone at night.
3. Restaurant owners claim they are now offering more healthful foods. However, they still use too much grease.
4. Their feelings are very strong when they are positive or negative.
5. He enjoys traveling to foreign countries and eating in gourmet restaurants, which can be extremely expensive.
6. The advertising for the film gave potential viewers a specific impression, but it turned out to be quite different.
7. He deposited his check before he went away for the weekend, but this was a mistake.
8. They took pastries along with the sandwiches even though these were quite filling.
9. The rain overflowed the gutter, but it did not damage the sidewalk.
10. Commercials during news broadcasts take time, so they do not have to provide a full hour of news.

EXERCISE

Correct the errors in pronoun form and reference in the following sentences.

1. When a parent takes children to fast-food restaurants, there are no dishes to wash, and the children love them.
2. If traffic is worse at a certain time, the employee can work out a schedule that will comply with it.
3. Opponents of the death penalty argue that it is one crime added to another.
4. Some people feel that they are perfectly happy without a child, and they do not want to put that in jeopardy.
5. Some countries' leaders believe that violence is the only way to enforce their ideas, which motivates them to go to war.
6. Political leaders at times manipulate people by means of religious beliefs and use them to attain what they desire.
7. There are several advantages to attending the local community college. First, they offer a complete range of general education courses.

8. Television shows portraying the use of drugs and alcohol may make children curious to find out what they are really like.

9. Social work and psychology are similar in that they both help people.

10. Joe told Tom that he would not make a good teacher.

FAULTY PREDICATION

Do the following sentences communicate meaning effectively?

> Listening to music is mostly by radio.
>
> Success is when a person has a high income.
>
> An education is done with a lot of hard work.

We have already seen that a linking verb connects the subject of a sentence with something that either renames the subject or modifies it. However, "mostly by radio" cannot logically modify "listening." Similarly, "when a person has a high income" does not modify "success"; and an "education" cannot be "done." Here are some possible restatements of the ideas in the preceding examples:

> People listen to music mostly on the radio.
>
> Many people consider a person with a high income successful.
>
> It takes a lot of hard work to get an education.

E X E R C I S E

Identify and correct the faulty predication in the following sentences.

1. A breakdown is where one cannot cope with all the stress.

2. A person who drives recklessly is the cause of an accident sooner or later.

3. An example of unfair discrimination is the parent who puts a curfew on a daughter but not on a son.

4. A fundamental lesson in history is Dr. Martin Luther King, Jr., who did important work for civil rights.

5. A difficult situation can be a person whose car breaks down on the freeway.

E X E R C I S E

Identify and correct the errors in the following sentences.

1. One of the new employees like to go boating on weekends.

2. Some people do personal grooming while they are driving slowly along a crowded freeway, which may cause an accident.

3. We saw John and he come into the library just before noon.

4. The proposition requires the phasing out of the use of pesticides on food known to cause cancer.

5. He is guilty both of telling lies and trying to damage other people's reputations.

6. He ran for the office and lost, therefore, he decided not to run again.

7. If one wants to learn to play a musical instrument, you have to practice regularly.

8. They enjoyed going out to eat on the weekend; especially for Sunday morning brunch.

9. The rains, melting the new snow, was a disappointment, because they had wanted to go skiing that weekend.

10. He will loan the tape to whomever wants to listen to it.

EXERCISE

12-75

Identify and correct the errors in the following sentences.

1. The keeper not only gave the animals their food but he added something special for each one.
2. A person may be chosen for a job that is not very knowledgeable.
3. He told us the joke and bursts out laughing himself.
4. Lying on top of the computer monitor, Tom found his other glove.
5. There was a knife and a spoon on the placemat.
6. The way to prepare a meal that is both nutritious and easy to make.
7. The real mistake is when we do not face our problems.
8. In the bank, they often have problems serving customers when the computers are down.
9. First he did exercises to warm up, then he began his circuit training.
10. She could take a class in art history if she wants.

Summing Up

You have discovered that sentences communicate their intended meaning when ideas are expressed with grammatical accuracy and correct punctuation and capitalization.

Sentence Boundaries

A sentence must contain at least one main clause. If it contains two or more main clauses, these must be properly connected.

Problems with sentence boundaries:

Run-together sentence: more than one main clause without proper connection

Fragment: less than one main clause, punctuated as if it were a sentence

Correcting Problems with sentence boundaries:

Run-together sentences:

1. Make separate statements, and punctuate with a period or a semicolon.
2. Relate the statements with a coordinating conjunction (*and, but, or, for, nor, so, yet*), and punctuate with a comma, semicolon, or period.
3. Connect the statements with an adverbial conjunction (*however, therefore, then*, etc.), and punctuate with a semicolon or period.
4. Make a statement, and subordinate the other with a subordinating conjunction (*because, when, if*, etc.) and no semicolon or period.

Fragments: Add the missing element

Subject
Verb
Part of the verb
Main clause

Punctuation and Capitalization

Correct punctuation and capitalization help make meaning clear:

Periods end statements, indirect questions, and mild commands.

Question marks end direct questions.

Exclamation points show emphasis.

Semicolons separate two closely connected main clauses.

Commas are used in several structural settings:

After introductory elements (phrases or clauses that come before the subject of the sentence)

Between main clauses joined with a coordinating conjunction

In a series

To separate nonessential or extraneous elements

In dates and addresses

In direct quotations

Colons link explanatory material introduced in the statement before the colon.

Dashes separate an element from the rest of the sentence and call attention to it.

Parentheses separate an element from the rest of the sentence and call attention away from it.

Quotation marks enclose a speaker's actual words or the title of a short work such as a poem, short story, article, or song.

Underlining marks the title of a longer work such as a book, magazine, newspaper, film, television show, or stage work; a term that is being discussed as a term; or a foreign word or phrase. In print, italics replace underlining.

Capitalization is used for various words:

Titles of persons before or in place of a name

Names of particular persons, places, and things

Names of languages, nationalities, ethnic groups, and religious groups

Names of specific courses (appearing with course numbers in college catalogs)

The first word of a sentence

The first word of a direct quotation

The first word and all other words in a title except articles and short connecting words

Modifiers

Correctly used, modifiers add information to other elements in the sentence. Modifiers include adjectives, adverbs, present and past participles, some infinitives, most prepositional phrases, and most subordinate clauses.

Problems with modifiers:

Misplaced modifiers: These add information to the wrong element in the sentence. They need to be repositioned.

Dangling modifiers: These add information to a missing element. The sentence needs to be rewritten to include the missing element.

Vague modifiers: These leave it ambiguous where in the sentence they are supposed to add information. The sentence needs to be rewritten to clarify the purpose of the modifier.

Illogical modifiers: These add information that does not make sense. The modifier should be omitted or changed to one that makes sense.

Inconsistencies

Faulty agreement: This error involves a mismatch of singular and plural forms:

Between subject and verb

Between pronoun and antecedent

Between possessive and possessor

Between adjective and noun

Shifts: These are illogical changes in direction:

In person: an unwarranted change in point of view

In verb tense: an unwarranted change in time reference

Faulty parallelism: This error involves improper coordination of elements that are supposed to be comparable:

With *and* or another coordinating conjunction

With *either . . . or . . .*

neither . . . nor . . .

not only . . . but also . . .

both . . . and . . .

. . . not . . .

. . . rather than . . .

Errors in Function

Faulty pronoun form: when there is an improper choice of subject, object, or possessive form

Faulty pronoun reference: when a pronoun does not clearly refer to someone or something specific

Faulty predication: when a subject and linking verb are followed by something that does not logically rename or modify the subject

Part Three

WORDS

SPELLING

What do the following statements mean?

> A roof with holes may sprout leeks.
> Joe took the fairy to see the Statue of Liberty.

These student sentences were not intended to be humorous; the misspellings were unintentional, and the sentences are therefore misleading.

If you misspell words, you may not successfully communicate your intended meaning. Moreover, it is unfair to expect your readers to figure out what words you had in mind. Overburdening your readers in this fashion can even cost you your audience, thus defeating your purpose for writing in the first place. As a result, if you want to be an adequate or more than adequate writer, your alternatives are either to spell accurately or to have with you and use—whenever you need to write—a dictionary or a machine that provides you with correct spellings. The first solution is obviously the more practical one.

Strategies for Becoming a Better Speller

Most college students have problems with spelling. And, like most poor spellers, they are more or less convinced that there is no solution to their problem. Yet some definite strategies exist that can help writers develop greater accuracy in spelling. Here are some practical ones.

READING MORE—AND MORE SLOWLY

Good spellers usually read a variety of materials. But what may be more important than the amount and type of reading they do is the way they do it. Good spellers read slowly enough to build a visual impression of the words they are seeing. Whether they realize it or not, they are focusing enough on individual words to retain a mental picture of each one. This does not mean that they are reading really slowly. But racing through a text to pick out main ideas or particular items of information does not improve a person's spelling. Consequently, when your purpose for reading is to take in any or all of what you are seeing, try to go at a pace that enables you to get mental pictures of words, and make a point of pausing on a few of the words that you should be able to spell but have never learned.

COPYING WORDS CORRECTLY

Poor spellers frequently make errors in copying words not only from the board in class but even from books and papers right in front of them. If you have this tendency, slow down and practice visualizing what you are writing. Periodically check your work as you go. When you copy incorrectly, you are really forcing a spelling problem onto yourself.

KEEPING A LIST OF WORDS YOU HAVE MISSPELLED

Write down, in list form, the correct version of any word you have written incorrectly in a college paper or elsewhere. In this way, you can more easily focus your attention on the words that are difficult for you personally. An 8½- by 11-inch sheet of paper, folded in columns, is a good place to write the words because you can carry it with you and look at it during idle moments, such as while you are waiting somewhere. By looking at the words frequently, you can help yourself develop that all-important correct mental picture of written words.

If you follow this strategy, you will find that the words you have misspelled will start to repeat. Thus, you may find that you are not misspelling as many words as you thought before you started your personal list. If you find that you have misspelled too many words for a list to be practical, make a list that includes just the most important and most common of your problem words.

You may have had to write the same word several times as part of spelling lessons in elementary school. The idea is a good one because it helps us develop the visual image of each word that is so important if we want to be good spellers. Try applying the same technique to some of the words you currently have trouble spelling. Here again, you can practice writing a word several times during idle moments. It is essential, though, to concentrate on what you are doing, even if it is only for a few minutes, and to make sure that you are spelling the words correctly.

Helpful Spelling Principles

ADDING PREFIXES TO WORDS

When you add a prefix to a word, simply join the prefix to the word without making any changes in the spelling.

dis + approve:	disapprove
dis + satisfied:	dissatisfied
over + turn:	overturn
over + rate:	overrate

E X E R C I S E

13-1

Make single words by joining each of the following prefixes to the accompanying root word.

1. un + certain
2. un + natural
3. mis + place
4. mis + spell
5. inter + change
6. inter + racial
7. re + run
8. re + do
9. with + draw
10. with + holding

ADDING SUFFIXES TO WORDS

A Final *e*

A final (silent) *e* is usually dropped before a suffix that begins with a vowel:

care + ing: caring

The final *e* is kept, however, before a suffix beginning with a consonant:

care + ful: careful

The *e* following a *g* or *c* is kept before suffixes beginning with *a, o, u,* or a consonant to preserve the same sound:

change + able: changeable

notice + able: noticeable

E X E R C I S E

13-2

Combine each of the following root words with the accompanying suffix to form single words.

1. hope + ing
2. hope + ful
3. complete + ed
4. complete + ly
5. coerce + ing
6. write + ing
7. love + able
8. acknowledge + ing
9. manage + able
10. courage + ous

Doubling a Final Consonant

There is an almost foolproof way to figure out whether to double a final consonant before a suffix beginning with a vowel, such as *-ed, -er,* and *-ing.* A good dictionary will spell out the individual words—for example, *occurred,* with two *r*'s, and *offered,* with one *r.* But you can avoid those trips to the dictionary by determining whether or not the base word follows a certain pattern, doubling the final consonant if the word follows the pattern and not doubling if it does not.

Sample base words: *occur* and *offer*
Pattern: CV́C
1. The last three letters of the root word are consonant/vowel/consonant.
2. The accent is on that syllable.

The word *occur* follows this pattern: the last three letters (cur) consist of consonant/vowel/consonant, and the accent in the word is on the second syllable (oc*cur*); therefore, the final *r* is doubled:

occurred,   occurring,   occurrence

The word *offer* does not follow the pattern: the last three letters (fer) do consist of consonant/vowel/consonant, but the accent in the word is on the first syllable (*of*fer), not the second; therefore, the final *r* is not doubled:

offered,   offering

Here are some more examples:

omit:	omit (CV́C)	omitted, omitting
prefer:	prefer (CV́C)	preferred, preferring
swim:	swim (CV́C)	swimming, swimmer
plan:	plan (CV́C)	planned, planning, planner

Which of the following words follow the CV́C pattern?

expel,   admit,   control,   benefit,   complete,   open

Only the first three words follow the pattern, so only they have their final consonant doubled before the suffix.

The pattern is subject to additional clarifications. First, the letters *x* and *w* are never doubled:

tax + ing:	taxing
stow + ed:	stowed

Second, the *u* after a *q* functions as a consonant:

quit + ing:	quitting
equip + ed:	equipped

Third, the final consonant is not doubled if the accent shifts from the final syllable of the root word in the new word.

prefer + able:	preferable
defer + ence:	deference

E X E R C I S E

Combine each of the following root words and suffixes to form single words, using the principle just described.

1. rebel + ed	**11.** regret + able
2. fit + ing	**12.** abhor + ence
3. commit + ed	**13.** hot + er
4. begin + ing	**14.** wrap + er
5. forget + ing	**15.** conceal + ing
6. stop + ed	**16.** patrol + ing
7. jog + er	**17.** get + ing
8. defer + ed	**18.** knit + ing
9. compel + ed	**19.** grab + ing
10. exist + ence	**20.** propel + er

OTHER SPELLING PRINCIPLES

ie/ei

1. After *c,* write *ei:*

receive,   deceit,   ceiling

2. After other letters
   a. Write *ie* if the sound is *ee* as in *we:*

      believe, niece, chief, achieve

   b. Write *ei* if the sound is not *ee:*

      weigh,   foreign,   neighbor,   vein,   height,   their

   Some common exceptions:

   friend,   seize,   either,   neither,   leisure

Words Written Both Joined and Not Joined

Some words are written differently, depending on how they are used.
Everyday is joined only when used as an adjective:

That is an *everyday* occurrence.   ["everyday" modifies the noun "occurrence"]

Compare:

She goes to work *every day*.   ["every day" modifies the verb "goes"]

Maybe is joined only when used as an adverb (meaning "perhaps"):

Maybe he knew the truth.   ["maybe" modifies the verb "knew"]

Compare:

She *may be* saving money by shopping carefully.   ["may be" is the verb]

Nouns Ending in *nts* and *nce*

Do not confuse the plural noun ending in *-nts* with the abstract noun ending in *-nce*.
Examples:

patients/patience,   incidents/incidence,   assistants/assistance,   adolescents/
adolescence,   residents/residence.
The patients in the emergency room must often have a great deal of patience.

American Spellings

Use American spellings consistently when you are writing for American-language
readers:

theater   [not *theatre*]

color   [not *colour*]

connection   [not *connexion*]

license   [not *licence*]

criticize   [not *criticise*]

and so forth.

List of Frequently Misspelled Words

The following words are frequently misspelled by college students. Have someone dictate the words to you, if possible, so that you can identify the ones you have trouble spelling correctly. Then work on the ones you miss.

1. absence	35. disastrous	68. personnel
2. accept	36. disease	69. persuade
3. accommodate	37. embarrass	70. possession
4. acquaintance	38. environment	71. precede
5. adolescence	39. equipment	72. prejudice
6. advantageous	40. especially	73. preparation
7. afford	41. exaggerate	74. privilege
8. afraid	42. existence	75. probably
9. all right	43. explanation	76. proceed
10. a lot	44. financial	77. professor
11. among	45. foreign	78. psychology
12. argument	46. friend	79. pursue
13. athlete	47. fulfillment	80. receive
14. basically	48. government	81. recommend
15. beginning	49. grammar	82. repetition
16. believe	50. height	83. restaurant
17. benefited	51. hoping	84. safety
18. breathe	52. hypocrisy	85. scene
19. budget	53. interesting	86. sense
20. buried	54. irritate	87. separate
21. business	55. license	88. similar
22. cannot	56. loneliness	89. since
23. career	57. lose	90. studying
24. college	58. maintenance	91. succeed
25. coming	59. medicine	92. themselves
26. committee	60. misspell	93. truly
27. conscientious	61. nowadays	94. unnecessary
28. control	62. occasionally	95. until
29. convenient	63. occurrence	96. weather
30. decision	64. omitted	97. whereas
31. definitely	65. opinion	98. whether
32. develop	66. opportunity	99. women
33. disappearance	67. paid	100. writing
34. disappoint		

Summing Up

You have seen that accurate spelling is important in writing. You have also learned some strategies for improving your spelling:

Develop good habits.
>   Read, making a point of seeing words as you go.
>   Copy words accurately.
>   Keep a spelling list.
Follow helpful spelling principles.

What do the following statements mean?

She refuses to talk about her lively hood.

The taxi quickly took them to their destiny.

The United States leads in the production of affective weapons.

The homeless are in die or need.

These statements, like those at the beginning of the last chapter, are misleading. In the first three examples, some wrong words have been used, and in the fourth, a verb (die) has been used as an object of a preposition.

Usage is complex in any language; English, with its high number and varied origins of words, poses an even greater number of usage problems than most languages.

Usage and Appropriate Word Choices

Which sentence in each of the following pairs would you be more likely to use in college writing?

1. The documents will be signed forthwith.
   The documents will be signed immediately.
2. She is a serious numismatist in addition to holding down a regular job.
   She is a serious coin collector in addition to holding down a regular job.
3. During tests, students often scrounge correction fluid off other students.
   During tests, students often borrow correction fluid from other students.
4. He is a whiz at creating computer programs.
   He is an expert at creating computer programs.
5. They did not take all of their things with them when they moved.
   They did not take all of their possessions with them when they moved.
6. He works a lot.
   He works long hours.
7. They go to the theater once in a blue moon.
   They rarely go to the theater.
8. College costs have gone up by leaps and bounds in the last ten years.
   College costs have gone up sharply in the last ten years.

In each case, the second version may have sounded better to you. In fact, the second option for each pair is more appropriate in semiformal writing.

In the first two examples, "forthwith" and "numismatist" are highly formal, whereas "immediately" and "coin collector" are standard terms. Formal language that is not needed to express a specific meaning should be used with caution. Writing that is unnecessarily formal may seem artificial and may even make the reader feel overburdened.

Examples 3 and 4 contain colloquialisms, "scrounge off" and "whiz," that are not appropriate for college papers. Avoid slang and other highly informal terms unless you are discussing their implications as terms (for example, in a social science paper or an English paper on language) or are writing a dialogue in which you are quoting actual slang as it was spoken.

In example 5, the more specific word "possessions" is a better choice than the general term "things." When you write, look for words that express precisely what you mean, avoiding vague words such as *things* or *aspects*.

In the sixth example, "a lot" is vague because it may describe either how long or how intensively he works.

The last two sets contain clichés—expressions that have lost their original meaning through overuse. Clichés may be acceptable in informal conversations, but words and phrases that express specific meanings are better choices in college writing.

Usage and Grammar Function

Some usage errors in English result from problems with grammar functions. The misuse of an apostrophe or the substitution of one grammatical form for another can interfere with the communication of meaning.

POSSESSIVES

An apostrophe turns nouns and some pronouns into possessive adjectives:

Joe's book

somebody's pen

To be certain that you are putting the apostrophe in the right place, identify who or what the possessor is. Consider the following examples:

the boy's bicycle

the boys' bicycles

The first example indicates a bicycle that belongs to a boy, and the second refers to some bicycles that belong to some boys. To place an apostrophe correctly, follow this formula:

1. Identify the possessor.
2. Add the apostrophe after the word indicating the possessor.
3. If there is not an *s* at the end of the word indicating the possessor, add one.

For example, in

the student's backpack

the possessor is the "student." Put the apostrophe after the word "student." Then, since there is no *s* at the end, add the *s*. Compare the following phrase:

the students' backpacks

Here the "students" possess the backpacks; put the apostrophe after the word "students." Since there is already an *s* at the end, no additional *s* is necessary. Compare:

the women's club

Here the "women" have a club; put the apostrophe after the word "women." Then, since there is no *s* at the end, add the *s*.

EXERCISE

14-1

Using the preceding formula, make correct possessives out of the following.

1. The girls car
2. The girls cars
3. The countrys government
4. The countries governments
5. Mr. Johnsons house
6. The Smiths house
7. The Joneses farm
8. The childrens toys
9. The boss secretary
10. The bosses secretary

EXERCISE

14-2

Identify the examples in Exercise 14-1 in which the possessor is plural.

EXERCISE

14-3

Rewrite the following to show the possessor as a modifying adjective.

Example: Joe has a book. = Joe's book

1. The girl has a dress.
2. The girls have dresses.
3. The child has a paint set.
4. The children have paint sets.
5. The bus has windows.
6. The buses have windows.
7. The man has a suit.
8. The men have suits.
9. The city has some parks.
10. The cities have some parks.
11. The book has a cover.
12. The electronic typewriter has a memory.

Would you add an apostrophe in these sentences?

Those tapes are theirs.

The lizard lost its tail.

There is no apostrophe in either of the preceding examples. As these examples indicate, not all possessive forms in English have an apostrophe; some of our possessive forms are "ready made."

TABLE 14-1   *Possessive Forms of Adjectives and Pronouns*

PERSON	POSSESSIVE ADJECTIVES		POSSESSIVE PRONOUNS	
	Singular	*Plural*	*Singular*	*Plural*
First	my	our	mine	ours
Second	your	your	yours	yours
Third	his her its	their	his hers its	theirs

All of the forms listed in Table 14-1 answer the question *whose*. Neither *whose* nor any of the forms in the table take an apostrophe. The words *it's* and *who's* are contractions, not possessives. These are discussed in the "Usage and Vocabulary" section in this chapter.

CONTRACTIONS

An apostrophe is also used in a contraction, where it signifies that one or more letters are missing from the original words:

you're   [= you are]

doesn't   [= does not]

won't   [= will not]

he'll   [= he will]

she'd   [= she would *or* she had]

should've   [= should have]

who's   [= who is *or* who has]

and so forth.

Contractions are not normally used in college writing or in most professional writing. They are appropriate, however, in personal and informal writing.

SOME FUNCTION PROBLEMS

Students often use the wrong form of a word when they write.

It is easy to confuse a possessive with a simple plural or plural possessive, especially if the words sound alike, as in the case of community's/communities/communities':

The *community's* resources were limited.   [The resources of the community were limited.]

The *communities* had limited resources.   [More than one community had limited resources.]

The *communities'* resources were limited.   [The resources of the communities were limited.]

Different forms can be confusing:

They *choose* a different vacation spot each year.

They *chose* Florida for their vacation last year.

The singular and plural forms of the same word should be carefully distinguished:

The *woman* entered a restaurant and took off her coat.

The *women* entered a restaurant and took off their coats.

The distinction between *man* and *men* is the same as the one between *woman* and *women*.

A word may have the same form for different functions:

The *review* was completed ahead of schedule.   [names]

The *review* committee met several times.   [modifies]

The members *review* important policy changes before they go into effect.   [makes a statement]

More often, separate words denote the different functions. Avoid mixing up forms like these:

advise/advice   [verb/noun]

The counselors advise students to take their advice.

breathe/breath   [verb/noun]

When we breathe in, we take a breath.

conscious/conscience   [adjective/noun]

He was conscious of his guilty conscience.

sell/sale   [verb/noun]

They will probably sell everything that is on sale.

Usage and Vocabulary

The large number of words from a variety of sources that we have at our disposal in English gives us many options but also contributes to frequent confusion about words. Our language contains many homonyms—different words that sound alike, such as *its/it's, meet/meat,* and *seen/scene.* In addition, many other words, while not homonyms, are close enough to be confusing.

EXERCISE

14-4

Correct the errors in usage in the following sentences.

1. That was an intentional fowl.

2. He got a head of the crowd.

3. He was worried about his daughter's piece of mind.

4. Waist disposal is a popular concern nowadays.

5. The Dream Team seemed to perform feets of magic.

6. He uses a great deal of fowl language when he talks.

7. Any excessive weight in line made them tend to give up on the rides in the theme park.

8. One of parents' responsibilities is to give their children manors.

9. We are fowling our environment.

10. Packaged products are to be found primarily on the isles in supermarkets.

11. The police are finally taking serious action to find the cereal killer.

12. Air force pilots are known to have cited UFOs.

In order to do the above exercise, you needed to be familiar with several homonyms: *ahead/a head, aisle/isle, cereal/serial, cite/sight/site, feat/feet, foul/fowl, manner/manor, peace/piece, waist/waste,* and *wait/weight.*

EXERCISE

14-5   From among the following homonyms, choose the correct word to fill in each blank: *buy/by, forth/fourth, hear/here, heard/herd, knew/new, knight/night, know/no, one/won, plain/plane,* and *ware/wear.*

1. He chose two _____ doughnuts and _____ chocolate eclair.

2. She will _____ a _____ dress to _____ on her vacation.

3. I _____ for a fact that they have _____ money.

4. The _____ race car went _____ .

5. He _____ he had _____ the _____ trip to Hawaii.

6. The _____ did his rescue work at _____ .

7. I _____ they are _____ .

8. The _____ _____ the noise and stampeded.

EXERCISE

14-6   From among the following homonyms, choose the correct word to fill in each blank: *coarse/course, desert/dessert, do/due, fair/fare, faze/phase, hole/whole, pair/pear, threw/through, way/weigh.*

1. We need to _____ that _____ of suitcases; we want to avoid excess baggage charges on top

   of the _____ .

2. Of _____ , you should _____ the assignment _____ tomorrow!

3. He ate the _____ _____ .

4. He was hurt when he fell into the _____ , but it did not seem to _____ him.

5. The child _____ the ball _____ the window.

6. _____ is the opposite of *fine*.

7. It is not _____ to _____ people who help us.

8. On the _____ to the _____ , we saw a rainbow.

The following homonyms frequently cause problems for writers. You should spend time both on the ones that follow and on the ones in the preceding exercises that give you the most trouble personally.

already/all ready
Already is a time idea:

They had *already* finished when we arrived.

All ready focuses on the idea of being ready. It can mean that all of the people or things are ready:

The packages were *all ready* for mailing.

It can also mean completely ready:

She was *all ready* to leave.

break/brake
Break has several meanings related to the idea of separating:

Be careful not to break any dishes.
He goes on break at 10 o'clock.

Brake refers to a device for stopping something:

It is a good idea to brake if traffic ahead slows down suddenly.

council/counsel
A *council* is an assembly, and a *councilor* is a member of the assembly:

The *council* meets once a month.

Counsel means both "advise" (verb) and "advice" (noun), and the person who gives the advice is a *counselor*:

He *counseled* her to consider all options before making a decision.
She followed his *counsel*.

its/it's
Its is the possessive adjective for *it*:

The puppy was chasing *its* tail.

It's is the contraction of *it is* or *it has*:

> *It's* ready.   [it is]
>
> *It's* been ready for days.   [it has]

passed/past

Passed is the past tense and past participle of the verb *pass*:

> He *passed* all his exams last year.
>
> He has *passed* all of them this year too.

Past can name a time:

> People study the *past* in history classes.   [noun]

or modify:

> We need to understand *past* events.   [adjective modifying events]
>
> The bus went *past*.   [adverb modifying the verb, went]

or connect:

> The bus went *past* the library.   [preposition]

Past is never the verb or part of the verb.

principal/principle

Principal can be an adjective meaning "main, most important":

> Financial gain was the *principal* motivating force behind their decision.

Alternatively, it can be a noun referring to the head of a school:

> The *principal* addressed the student body at the assembly.

A *principle* is a basic truth or guiding rule:

> That heat rises is a well-known *principle* of physics.

right/write/rite/wright

Right means "correct":

> That is the *right* course of action.

or "the opposite of left":

> Most people are more skilled with the *right* hand.

or "a kind of privilege":

> People over 18 have the *right* to vote.

To *write* is to put words or letters on paper.

> Her friends write jokes for a famous comedian.

A *rite* is a ceremony.

> Those churches have different *rites*.

Wright originally meant "worker." It is now used in compounds, such as *playwright* and *wheelwright*.

there/their/they're
There, like *here*, answers the question *where* (notice the similar spelling):

> He went *there* last year.

Their is the possessive adjective for *they*:

> They are ready for *their* departure.

They're is the contraction of *they are*:

> *They're* going to the airport two hours before flight time.

there's/theirs
There's is the contraction of *there is* or *there has*.

> *There's* a circus in town.   [= there is]
> *There's* been a lot of rain lately.   [= there has]

Theirs is the possessive pronoun:

> *Theirs* is brand new.

two/too/to
Two is only the number:

> *Two* groups of researchers invented the laser.

Too means "excessively":

> That suitcase is *too* heavy for me to carry.

or "also":

> They are leaving *too*.

To is used in all other meanings.

whose/who's
Whose is the possessive pronoun or adjective for *who*:

> *Whose* are those books?   [pronoun]
> *Whose* books are those?   [adjective]

Who's is the contraction of *who is* or *who has*.

> *Who's* going with us?   [= who is]
> *Who's* done this before?   [= who has]

your/you're
Your is the possessive adjective for *you*:

Take all of *your* things when you leave.

You're is the contraction of *you are*:

You're late!

Choose the correct form in each case. Have someone dictate the sentences to you, if possible.

1. The *counsel/council* may *break/brake* a voting record at *there/their/they're* next meeting.
2. The *principal/principle* issue *passed/past* by *two/too/to* narrow a margin.
3. *Whose/Who's* to say *whose/who's* idea is *write/right/rite/wright*?
4. *Their/There/They're* *already/all ready* for *their/there/they're* trip.
5. *Its/It's* *already/all ready* *two/too/to* far behind *two/too/to* *break/brake* a record.
6. *Your/You're* bus just went *passed/past*.
7. The *principal/principle* behind *your/you're* decision is sound.
8. The *write/right/rite/wright* was performed differently in the *passed/past*.
9. The puppy has *already/all ready* *passed/past* *its/it's* obedience test.
10. *Their/There/They're* *principal/principle* objection was weak.

The following words are also frequently confused by writers:

accept/except
Accept means "take," whereas *except* means "but":

We *accept* all gifts except money.

affect/effect
Affect is a verb meaning "produce an influence on":

Their decisions always *affect* everyone.

Effect is nearly always a noun meaning "a result" or "an influence":

Their decisions always have an *effect* on everyone.

Use *effect* to name something. Use *affect* to make a statement.

have/of
Only *have* can come after modal verbs such as *should, would,* and *could*:

We *should have* written to them.

He *would have* called if he had had time.

They *could have* helped us finish the project.

lead/led/lead
Lead (rhymes with *fed*) is a metal:

> Pipes for plumbing used to be made of *lead*.

Lead (rhymes with *feed*) is a verb meaning "conduct." **The past tense and past** participle are both *led*:

> The best musicians always *lead* the band.
> Her car *led* throughout the last race.

loose/lose
Loose means "not well fastened."
Lose is the opposite of *win*; it also means "misplace":

> She will *lose* that *loose* button.

personal/personnel
Personal pertains to a *person:*

> He did it for *personal* gain.

Personnel means "staff" or "employees":

> Management sometimes forgets the needs of the *personnel*.

than/then
Than indicates a comparison.
Then indicates either time (it tells *when*) or result:

> They are more powerful now *than* they were *then*.

weather/whether
The *weather* is the atmospheric condition.
Whether indicates a condition or alternative:

> We do not know *whether* the *weather* will be suitable for the event.

EXERCISE

14-8

Choose the correct form in each case. Have someone dictate the sentences to you, if possible.

1. The *weather/whether* is colder in the mountains *than/then* in the valley.
2. No one knows *weather/whether* Joe *lead/led* the riot.
3. They should *of/have* changed the *lead/led* pipes.
4. The *lead/led* will *affect/effect* people's health.
5. *Its/It's affect/effect* may be worse *than/then* people think.
6. The *personal/personnel* will *accept/except* all changes *accept/except* the pay cut.
7. *Lose/Loose* gravel can cause *personal/personnel* injury.

8. He would rather *lose/loose* the title *than/then* ruin his *personal/personnel* life.

9. He could *of/have lead/led* the parade.

10. They should *of/have* foreseen the *affect/effect* of *their/there/they're* decision.

EXERCISE

14-9

Choose the correct form in each case. Have someone dictate the sentences to you, if possible.

1. *Their/There/They're* son could *of/have* said *know/no*.

2. The low morale of the *personal/personnel* was the *principal/principle* problem.

3. He *lead/led* the demonstrators *passed/past* the school.

4. They *passed/past buy/by hear/here* and went *threw/through* town.

5. *Their/There/They're already/all ready two/too/to accept/except their/there/they're* prize.

6. She is really *two/too/to conscious/conscience* of *its/it's affects/effects*.

7. The politician's *advise/advice two/too/to* spend more for our schools is good, of *course/coarse*.

8. The *breaks/brakes* are working better *than/then* they did before.

9. *Its/It's passed/past* record was an indication of future success.

10. They will *lose/loose* unless they *know/no whose/who's* answers are *write/right/rite/wright*.

Summing Up

You have seen that the wrong word or the wrong form of a word can change the meaning of what you write. You should observe the following guidelines:

Choose words appropriately.
    Use the level of language that suits your purpose.
    Use specific words to express your ideas.
Choose the correct form of the word:
    To suit the function:
        To name
        To make a statement
        To modify
        To connect
    To show singular or plural
    To show the correct time element through the appropriate verb tense
Choose words accurately.
    Avoid using homonyms or other similar words that do not express what you mean.

The Dictionary

E X E R C I S E

15-1

Use your dictionary to answer the following questions.

1. What does *demise* mean?

2. How many meanings does *draft* have?

3. How do you spell the word that sounds like "benafishel"?

4. How do you pronounce the word *confidant*?

5. Where should you divide the word *occurrence* at the end of a line of writing?

6. What part of speech is the word *leisurely*?

7. Is *nerd* an appropriate word to use in college writing?

8. What is the origin of the word *dandelion*?

9. What does the abbreviation *GMT* stand for?

10. When was Mohandas Gandhi born?

INFORMATION IN ENTRIES

A dictionary appropriate for college work should contain the information you need in order to answer all of the preceding questions.

Questions 1 and 2 involve definitions of words. For college use, you need a dictionary that gives the different possible definitions of each word.

Look up the word *assumption* in your dictionary. What is the first definition given?

Some dictionaries list definitions for a word in the order in which they arose historically, beginning with the first meaning the word is known to have had. If you found a definition meaning "the taking of a person into heaven" listed first, your dictionary uses this historical order. If you found a definition meaning "the taking of something for granted," your dictionary begins lists of definitions with the one that is most common. Whichever system your dictionary follows, look through all the definitions of a word to find the one that is most appropriate for the context in which the word appears in what you are reading.

In addition to identifying the spelling and pronunciation of a word (questions 3 and 4), a dictionary indicates the word's division into syllables (question 5). This is information you need when you want to divide a word at the end of a line.

College dictionaries specify the part or parts of speech of a word (question 6), enabling users to determine possible functions of words: naming, making a statement, modifying, or connecting. Consider the functions of the following words, all of which come from the same roots.

economy (noun): the management or system of management of resources

economist (noun): the person involved with the management of resources

economics (noun): the science of the production, distribution, and consumption of goods

economize (verb): save resources

economic (adjective): of economics or of an economy

economical (adjective): not wasteful in the use of resources

Question 7 deals with word usage. In a college composition, you would not describe a bankrupt government as *broke*, because this is an informal, conversational term. Nor would you want to use *gyp* in place of *cheat*. Your dictionary should indicate anything that the user needs to know about the current status or level of usage of a word, and it should mark a nonstandard word as being obsolete or slang or limited in some other way. Dictionary entries often include synonyms, antonyms, and examples, as well.

The etymology, or origin of a word, the subject of question 8, can give you a historical perspective that is both interesting and useful. Your knowledge of the English language grows and becomes more meaningful when you can relate words to other words, English and foreign.

A college dictionary contains such additional information as a list of abbreviations (question 9) and geographical and biographical names (question 10). These reference materials are often important in a college setting.

You should familiarize yourself with what your dictionary has to offer. If you examine the explanatory material at the beginning of the dictionary and the entries for the words discussed so far in this chapter, you can truly start to take advantage of this valuable tool.

TYPES OF DICTIONARIES

The size of a dictionary does not always indicate the quality of the book. In general, however, most small portable dictionaries contain limited information. Consequently, a college student generally needs to have a desk dictionary of the English language—one that includes the types of information illustrated in Exercise 15-1.

Specialized dictionaries also exist. These volumes, which serve specific needs in various areas, include technical dictionaries and bilingual dictionaries. These books can usually be found in the reference section of a library.

Students who write extensively may also want to invest in a thesaurus, a dictionary that lists synonyms for words. Writers consult the thesaurus in order to find specific words that express their ideas precisely and in order to achieve variety of expression, with less repetition of the same words. It is easy to make wrong word choices from this type of dictionary, however, and students using a thesaurus often select an inapproporiate word. To understand how that happens, try answering each of the following questions and explaining your answer:

1. You need to give a child a ride home. Would you ask the child where his or her *domicile* is?
2. Do circus acrobats perform on a *tall* wire?
3. You see a cat in a tree. Would you tell someone that you *behold* the cat in the tree? Would you say that you *perceive it*?
4. The people where you work form an organization to protect their interests. Would you say to someone that you had joined the *order* at work?
5. Would you say that your little cousin has *increased* a lot in the past year?

You may have found a problem with the wording in each of the sentences. Yet people using a thesaurus make mistakes like those above. In the first sentence, *domicile* is not the appropriate word. You would probably use *house* instead. But a thesaurus will list *domicile* as a synonym for *house* because both words denote a building where a person lives. In the second example, you would substitute *high*, which denotes "elevated," just as *tall* does. In the third example, the thesaurus gives both *behold* and *perceive* as synonyms for *see*, but they sound strange in the context of the example given. Similarly, the proper word for *order* in the fourth sentence is *union;* and *grown* should be used instead of *increased* in the last example. Yet in each of these examples, the words appear in the thesaurus as synonyms.

Each word in a language has one or more basic, or **denotative**, meanings. But most words have additional associations that make them appropriate only in certain situations. These added ideas are the **connotative** meanings that words have. Since a thesaurus groups words that share the same basic meaning, it is up to the user to find a real synonym—a word with the right connotation for the particular context. This means that writers should use only familiar words from a thesaurus.

Brief History of the English Language

English is an Indo-European language, so it is related in some way to most of the other European languages and to some of the languages of Western and Central Asia.

In prehistoric times, the British Isles were inhabited by Celts and other Indo-European peoples. Centuries later, during the height of the Roman Empire, Latin was first brought to the British Isles. Then, beginning in the fifth century and continuing for several centuries, peoples from what is now Germany and Denmark invaded Britain. During these centuries, their Germanic dialect dominated. This language, Anglo-Saxon, is considered the basis of modern English—even though it accounts for only about 25 percent of modern English words and most of those are not readily recognizable—because an important part of our basic vocabulary and language structure, including most of our pronouns and connectors, comes from this Germanic ancestor.

The Norman invasion of Great Britain in 1066 brought with it the French language. Also, partly because of the influence of the Church, many additional Latin words entered the language. Over the next two centuries, English was transformed from Old English to Middle English, with its Germanic base greatly expanded by the addition of a great deal of Old French and some Latin.

The Renaissance brought additional Latin and Middle French words into English, along with some Greek elements. The language during this time took on its modern form, with over half of the words coming directly or indirectly from Latin.

The past 400 years, marked by the emergence of printed books and periodicals and a huge increase in international travel, have brought many words into the English language from languages the world over. As a result, modern English is an extremely mixed and varied language, and writers in English deal with a truly rich and complex system of words.

College Vocabulary

Do you know the meaning of the word *impasse?* Before you look it up in the dictionary, see if you can figure it out from the following context:

The president proposed the employing of former military personnel in environmental research. The legislature voted the measure down. The president pushed for the creation of new jobs. The legislature turned down the proposal. The president suggested cutting aid to foreign countries. The legislature declined. The president recommended raising taxes on high incomes. The legislators refused to hear of such an idea. The *impasse* was paralyzing the whole country.

From the meaning of the passage, the word *impasse* clearly indicates a deadlock.

See of you can figure out the meaning of *piscatorial* from its use in the following context:

His *piscatorial* feats were a common topic of conversation in the small town where he lived. He held the record for the biggest fish ever caught locally. He regularly prepared an impressive array of fish dishes for any town festive day. And he was famous for his ability to get the most unwilling souls to try their hand at fishing.

The examples of the feats all relate to fish. *Piscatorial* clearly means "pertaining to fish."

How can you understand the meaning of *cartilage* from this next sentence?

The ears are made primarily of *cartilage*—tough, white fibrous tissue attached to bone.

The meaning of the term is obvious from the definition that follows it.

What would you say *verbatim* means, judging from the following sentence?

He repeated his supervisor's comments *verbatim* when he talked to his colleagues, but he reworded them later when he explained the situation to a friend.

"Repeated verbatim" contrasts with "reworded." The contrasting term clarifies the meaning of *verbatim* as "in exactly the same words."

When you find an unfamiliar word in your reading, try to discover its meaning from the context before you consult the dictionary. This good habit will not only help free you from dependence on a dictionary but also aid you in focusing on the meaning of what you read. The four strategies exemplified above are especially useful:

1. Meaning of the passage
2. Examples
3. Definition
4. Contrasting term

In addition to paying attention to context clues, knowing the elements that make up words can help you understand the meanings of words. For example, if the word *soporific* is unfamiliar to you but you know the elements in it, you can make an educated guess about its meaning. The word consists of three basic elements:

sopor = "sleep"
ify = "to make"
ic = adjective suffix meaning "pertaining to"

Putting these elements together, we have an adjective describing something that makes a person sleepy. And this is precisely what *soporific* means.

See if you can discover the meanings of the following words from the elements they contain:

expurgate:
> *ex* = "out of, from"
> *purg* = "to purify, to purge"
> *ate* = verb suffix meaning "to act on"

vociferous:
> *voc* = "voice"
> *fer* = "to carry"
> *ous* = adjective suffix meaning "having the quality of"

xenophobia:
> *xen* = "foreign"
> *phobia* = "fear"

To *expurgate* means to take out material in order to purify something, such as a literary work or a film. Television networks, for example, often present *expurgated* versions of movies. *Vociferous* means having a voice that carries—in other words, loud. *Xenophobia* means fear of foreigners.

Word elements cannot provide you with all the answers to word meanings. In fact, the same element may have more than one meaning. For example, *hom* means both "same" (from a Greek root), as in *homonym*, and "man" (from a Latin root), as in *hominoid*. However, in such cases, the context often makes the meaning clear.

A further complication concerning word elements is that the same element may have different forms in different words. For example, the prefix *ad* meaning "to" or "forward," appears as *ad* in many words (such as *admit*, *adverb*, and *adapt*), but it changes in other words:

> *ac: account, accede*
> *af: affect, affirm*
> *ag: aggression, aggravate*
> *an: annex, annotate*
> *ap: appreciate, application*
> *ar: arrogant, arrears*
> *as: assemble, asset*
> *at: attain, attest*

Notice that in these instances the *d* in *ad* changes to conform to the letter that begins the next element. This type of change is called **assimilation**—a word that itself exemplifies such a change: *ad* + *simil* (="similar").

Many words in English have assimilated elements. For example, the prefixes meaning "with" from both Latin and Greek frequently change through assimilation:

ADOPTION OF PREFIX	COM (LATIN)	SYN (GREEK)
Without assimilation	*combine, compel*	*syndrome, syndicate*
With assimilation	*connect, connote, collide, collocation*	*symmetry, syllable, syllogism*

These and other prefixes may also change simply under the influence of the letter that follows:

	conjugate, conform	*sympathy*

In spite of these complications, you can greatly increase your vocabulary and your reading efficiency by expanding your knowledge of the different elements that are commonly found in words.

Notice the parts that make up the word *prehistoric:*

pre + histor + ic

Pre is a **prefix**, an element attached at the beginning of a word, giving the word a new meaning. *Histor* is the **root** of the word, the part that contains the word's basic meaning. *Ic* is a **suffix**, an element attached at the end of the word. Suffixes often determine the function of the word:

prehistoric: adjective modifying something
prehistorian: noun naming a person whose field is prehistory

Prefixes, roots, and suffixes, like individual words in sentences, have functions of naming, making a statement, or modifying. They are grouped by function in the following subsections.

PREFIXES

Prefixes That Name
auto = "self"
  autocrat: auto + crat ["rule"] = "one who rules by himself/herself; dictator"
  autonomy: auto + nomos ["law"] = "self-government"
Additional words: *automobile, autobiography, automation, automaton*
NOTE: If you are not sure about the meaning or pronunciation of a word, check your dictionary.

Prefixes That Make a Statement
dis = "perform the opposite action"
  dispute: dis + put ["think"] = "debate, argue"
  dissuade: dis + suad ["urge"] = "persuade, or try to persuade, not to do"
Additional words: *dissolve, distrust, dissect, disperse, discourse, disclosure*

EXERCISE

Use each of the words in the two preceding subsections to complete one of the following sentences.

1. Her father, like an _____ , regularly gave orders not only to the children but also to his wife.

2. Those who run state governments usually want their states to have _____ from the federal government.

3. After they drink, it is difficult to _____ them from driving.

4. A famous person who wants to write an _____ usually employs a ghostwriter.

5. Her _____ of people made it difficult for her to make friends.

6. A border _____ has frequently caused a war.

7. Like the airplane, the _____ became a reality following the invention of the internal combustion engine.

8. The public eagerly awaited the _____ of the winners' names.

9. The increasing use of _____ is causing many workers to lose their jobs.

10. The police on horseback attempted to _____ the crowd.

11. Computer images can make it unnecessary to _____ animals.

12. A robot is an _____ .

13. It is usually better to _____ the soap in water before adding the clothes.

14. Her latest _____ on Egyptian art was published in several journals.

Prefixes That Modify

Showing Opposition
a, an = "not, without"
  agnostic: a + gnostos ["known"] = "one who does not claim to know whether or not there is a supreme being"
  apathy: a + pathos ["emotion"] = "lack of emotion or concern"
anti = "against, opposite"
  antipathy: "dislike"
  antibiotic: anti + bio ["life"] = "a substance that acts against a microorganism"
contra = "against"
  countermand: contra + mand ["command, order"] = "recall or revoke by a contrary command"
  contravene: contra + ven ["come"] = "be contrary to something"
in = "not"   (NOTE: **in** also means "in," as in *include*)
  insatiable: in + satis ["enough"] = "not able to be satisfied"
  incorrigible: in + corrigere ["to correct"] = "not able to be corrected"
Additional words: *anarchy, atheist, analgesic, asymmetric, antidote, antagonism, antithesis, antonym, contradict, controversy, intangible, inadvertently*

EXERCISE

15-3

Use each of the words in the preceding subsection to complete one of the following sentences.

1. The constituents' _____ enabled the legislator to ignore the district's real needs.

2. A broad-spectrum _____ is used for many pathological conditions.

3. The new facts _____ their theory.

4. An _____ may visit a church for cultural rather than religious reasons.

5. His _____ toward his supervisor was obvious.

6. They will probably _____ the new order, just as they did the last one.

7. He was known for his _____ curiosity.

8. _____ is absence of government or order.

9. The doctor gave an _____ for the poison.

10. It is not wise to _____ certain people.

11. He _____ pushed the button.

12. _____ is the opposite of synonym.

13. An _____ helps to control pain.

14. He is an _____ liar.

15. An _____ is convinced that there is no supreme being.

16. Comprehension is the _____ of ignorance.

17. The old house had an _____ appeal.

18. _____ designs for clothes became popular in the early 1990s.

19. The constant _____ between the leaders made the trip a nightmare.

20. The _____ centered on religious issues.

Showing Number, Quantity, or Size
uni or **mono** = "one"
    unilateral: uni + lat ["side"] = "one-sided"
    monolith: mono + lith ["stone"] = "a single, massive stone set upright to form a column"
    monolithic: "massive [like the stone]"
bi = "two"
    bilateral: "two-sided"
poly or **multi** = "many"
    polytheistic: poly + theos ["god"] = "believing in many gods"
    multilateral: "many-sided"
omni = "all"
    omniscient: omni + sci ["know"] = "all-knowing, having universal knowledge"
ambi = "both"
    ambiguous: ambi + agere ["drive"] = "having two or more possible meanings"
micro = "small"
    microcosm: micro + cosm ["world, cosmos"] = "a small world or small society that represents a larger whole"
macro = "large"
    macrocosm: "a whole system that contains similar subsystems"
hypo = "less, under"
    hypodermic: hypo + derm ["skin"] = "under the skin"
hyper = "excessively, over"
    hyperactive: "excessively active"

EXERCISE

15-4

Use each of the words in the preceding subsection to complete one of the following sentences.

1. _____ children are often given unnecessary medication.

2. A _____ is a small world that is representative of a larger world, or _____ .

3. There are many _____ religions in the world.

4. Each _____ at Stonehenge weighs many tons.

5. A _____ needle is used for subcutaneous injections.

6. The meaning of the novel is _____ .

7. He wants people to see him as _____ , but they really think he is just a snob.

8. As the meeting progressed, the arguments went from _____ to _____ and finally to _____ ones.

Additional words.: *unify, unicellular, monopoly, monotheism, bicameral, bisect, bilingual, polysyllabic, polyglot, multinational, multitude, omnivorous, omnipotent, ambidextrous, microfiche, macrobiotic, hypothesis, hypocrisy, hyperbole, hypercritical*

EXERCISE

15-5

Use each of the words in the preceding list to complete one of the following sentences.

1. A company that has a _____ on a product can overcharge for the product.

2. To _____ is to cut into two parts.

3. A _____ speaks several languages.

4. A vegetarian is not _____ .

5. There have been many attempts to _____ Europe.

6. Christians hold to _____ .

7. The amoeba is a _____ organism.

8. A _____ of voters signed the petition.

9. A _____ word has several syllables.

10. A _____ person speaks two languages.

11. The United States has a _____ legislature.

12. A great deal of information can be stored on a _____ .

13. _____ means all-powerful.

14. A _____ company operates in several countries.

15. An _____ person is able to use both hands well.

16. A _____ is an intentionally exaggerated statement.

17. Many people nowadays are following a _____ diet.

18. A _____ person constantly finds fault with others.

19. _____ makes relationships between people difficult.

20. A _____ is an idea not yet validated that is based on facts.

Showing Time
ante or **pre** = "before"
> *antecedent: ante + ced* ["go"] = "someone or something that comes before another"
> *precedent:* "something going before that is considered an example for what comes later"

post = "after"
> *postmortem: post + mort* ["death"] = "autopsy"

Additional words: *antebellum, antedate, precocious, precursor, prejudice, presentiment, posterity, postscript, posthumously*

EXERCISE

15-6

Use each of the words in the preceding subsection to complete one of the following sentences.

1. The book was published _____ .

2. We need to clean up the environment for _____ .

3. The propeller plane is the _____ of the jet.

4. The large _____ house was a local landmark.

5. A _____ was performed on the body.

6. She usually adds a _____ to her letters.

7. His _____ turned out to be true.

8. A child who reads at four is _____ .

9. In writing, a pronoun needs to have a specific _____ .

10. The court's ruling set a _____ for similar cases to follow.

11. Adding machines _____ computers.

12. There are many kinds of _____ in human society.

Showing Position

de = "from, away"
   demote: de + mot ["move"] = "move down from a position or rank"
ab, abs = "away from"
   aberration: ab + err ["wander"] = "deviation from the normal"
ex = "out of"
   exonerate: ex + onus ["burden"] = "free from burden, such as guilt or blame"
extra = "outside, beyond"
   extrovert: extra + vert ["turn"] = "person more interested in surroundings than in own thoughts"
intra, intro = "inside, within"
   introvert: "person more interested in own thoughts than in surroundings"
inter = "between, among"
   intervene: "come between"
circum = "around"
   circumspect: circum + spec ["look"] = "cautious"
per = "through"
   pervasive: per + vad ["go"] = "spread everywhere"
trans = "across"
   transcend: trans + scand ["climb"] = "surpass, go beyond"
super = "over"
   superlative: super + latus ["carry"] = "of the highest degree"
sub = "under"
   subjugate: sub + jug ["yoke"] = "conquer, subdue"
tele = "far, distant"
   telekinesis: tele + kinesis ["motion"] = "the moving of objects from a distance without the use of physical means"

EXERCISE

15-7

Use each of the words in the preceding subsection to complete one of the following sentences.

1. The public will probably _____ their leader of blame.

2. An _____ is more likely than an _____ to go to a noisy party.

3. The military service may _____ someone who has behaved unacceptably.

4. The delay was caused by an _____ in one of the computers.

5. The _____ odor of spicy dishes gave the house a distinctive character.

6. *Strongest* is the _____ of *strong.*

7. The Nazis tried to _____ all of Europe.

8. Those questions _____ the limits of the human mind.

9. The magician made things move as if by _____ .

10. A _____ person, she made sound business decisions.

11. A parent should not always _____ in a dispute between children.

Additional words: *deciduous, decadence, desolate, deviate, dehydration, abominable, absolve, abstract, extirpate, expedite, eloquent, extracurricular, extravehicular, intramural, intravenous, intermediary, intermittent, interim, intercede, circumvent, circuitous, circumference, perforate, permeate, perception, transitory, transfusion, superimpose, subsistence, telecommunications*

E X E R C I S E

15-8

Use each of the words in the preceding list to complete one of the following sentences.

1. Evergreen trees are not _____ .

2. Much of the Southwest is _____ .

3. _____ was a serious problem for people crossing Death Valley in wagons.

4. A dictator tries to _____ any opposition.

5. They will do what they can to _____ the claim.

6. _____ activities in school can help a child develop interpersonal relations.

7. Periods of high artistic and literary achievement are followed by periods of _____ .

8. The nurse gave the patient an _____ injection.

9. In the _____ , he found an opportunity to do some work of his own.

10. The _____ light from the shore appeared to be a signal.

11. Someone will have to _____ in that argument.

12. Outlaws _____ from what is generally considered normal behavior.

13. Ideas are _____ whereas things are concrete.

14. The court may _____ the defendant.

15. _____ competition takes place within an organization, such as a school.

16. The _____ of the earth is approximately 40,000 miles.

17. She convinced the people because she was an _____ speaker.

18. The yeti is also called the _____ snowman.

19. Cosmonauts began _____ activities, or space walks, in the 1960s.

20. An _____ helped conduct the difficult negotiations.

21. People on a _____ wage have fewer opportunities in life than those who earn more.

22. _____ refers to communication by means such as radio, telephone, or satellite.

23. The photographer will _____ one image on another to achieve a special effect.

24. A fanatic's _____ of reality is distorted.

25. We need to _____ that eventuality at all costs.

26. No one understands his _____ arguments.

27. The smell of cigarette smoke tends to _____ people's clothing.

28. The patient needed a blood _____ .

29. The cook will _____ the foil to let the steam out.

30. Something _____ does not last indefinitely.

Other Modifying Prefixes

pro = "for, before, forward"
> *proponent: pro + pon* ["put, place"] = "someone who favors a cause or belief"

hetero = "different"
> *heterodox: hetero + dox* ["opinion"] = "not agreeing with a commonly accepted belief"

ben, bon, or **eu** = "well, good"
> *benevolent: ben + vol* ["wish"] = "well-wishing"
> *euphonious: eu + phone* ["voice"] = "pleasant sounding"

mal = "bad"
> *malevolent* = "ill-wishing, spiteful"

re = "back, again"
> *recede* = "go back"

Additional words: *prognosis, profusion, prospective, heterogeneous, benign, beneficiary, eulogize, malcontent, malefactor, retract, revert, revive, recurring, revoke*

E X E R C I S E

15-9

Use each of the words in the preceding subsection to complete one of the following sentences.

1. The United States has a _____ population.

2. A _____ stands to gain from something.

3. It is hard to understand people who constantly _____ what they say.

4. _____ headaches may be a symptom of another problem.

5. The state can either grant or _____ a license.

6. A _____ person is usually friendly.

7. Some people want to _____ a past that never really existed.

8. A _____ tumor can be treated.

9. A _____ is a wrongdoer.

10. A _____ person is dissatisfied with some situation.

11. Dogs that run in packs _____ to their wild behaviors.

12. A _____ home buyer verifies important information about the property.

13. Weeds were growing in _____ on the vacant lot.

14. The people can begin to clean up the mess as soon as the waters _____ .

15. He is a _____ of national health care.

16. A _____ opinion can be a basis for discrimination.

17. According to the doctors, the _____ is favorable.

18. Her _____ look made everyone hesitate to deal with her.

19. She was asked to do the reading because of her _____ voice.

20. People _____ those they admire.

ROOTS

Roots can also name:
bell = "war"
> *belligerent: bell + ger* ["wage, carry on"] = "prone to wage war, aggressive"

or make a statement:
mori, mort = "die"
> *immortal: in + mort* = "never dying"

or modify:
ac, acr = "bitter, sharp"
> *acrimonious* = "bitter, rancorous"

Roots That Name

Referring to People
ego = "I"
> *egoist: ego + ist* ["person"] = "person excessively concerned with own interests"

demos = "people"
> *democracy* = "rule of the people"

anthrop or **hom** = "human"
> *philanthropist: phil* ["love"] + *anthrop* + *ist* = "one who wishes people well and does something accordingly, such as donate money"
> *homicide: hom* + *cid* ["kill"] = "murder"

gen = "class, race"
> *genocide* = "killing of people of a particular race"

Referring to Parts of the Body

corpor = "body"
> *corporeal:* "relating to the body materially, rather than spiritually"

capit = "head"
> *per capita:* ["by heads"] "for each person"

man = "hand"
> *manufacture: man* + *fac* ["make"] = "make (originally, by hand)"

derm = "skin"
> *dermatitis: derm* + *itis* ["inflammation"] = "inflammation of the skin"

E X E R C I S E

Use each of the words in the preceding subsections to complete one of the following sentences.

1. Large companies generally _____ a variety of products.

2. A person who has _____ should see a dermatologist.

3. Her _____ remark made her difficult situation clear.

4. Anyone who listens to him realizes that he is an _____ .

5. _____ nations often overrun neighboring countries.

6. _____ means rule of the people.

7. The popularity of his works has made Shakespeare _____ .

8. Although he was a recluse, he was known as a _____ .

9. The average _____ income falls during a depression.

10. The United Nations has attempted to eliminate _____ .

11. The _____ detective questioned several suspects.

12. One's _____ needs include things such as food and shelter.

Additional words: *rebellious, moribund, mortify, acerbity, exacerbate, acuity, egocentric, demagogue, epidemic, anthropology, anthropoid, misanthropy, Homo sapiens, genus, genealogy, corps, corpse, corpuscle, incorporate, decapitation, capitulate, recapitulate, manuscript, manipulate, emancipate, pachyderm, dermatology, epidermis*

EXERCISE

15-11

Use each of the words in the preceding list to complete one of the following sentences.

1. Teenagers often go through a _____ stage.

2. Things that embarrass us to death _____ us.

3. The wrong medicine can _____ an illness.

4. An _____ person is self-centered.

5. There was an _____ of meningitis in the camp.

6. The newly-arrived patient in the emergency room was clearly _____ .

7. His _____ is evident from the way he talks.

8. People with poor visual _____ often wear contact lenses.

9. A _____ often leads people to believe things that are not true.

10. _____ is the study of the development of human beings.

11. The chimpanzee is an _____ ape.

12. _____ refers to humankind.

13. Some people _____ others because they want to control them.

14. A _____ has a very thick skin.

15. The _____ is the outer layer of skin.

16. A _____ is a dead body.

17. A _____ is a red or white blood cell.

18. To _____ means to surrender.

19. _____ is a form of capital punishment.

20. _____ deals with family history.

21. A _____ is a subfamily of plants or animals.

22. To _____ is to restate the main points of a discussion.

23. The city will _____ next year.

24. A _____ is a body of people who perform some function together.

25. _____ is the study of the skin.

26. To _____ means to free from someone else's control.

27. In the Middle Ages, a _____ was written by hand.

28. _____ is a distrust of human beings.

Other Roots That Name

bio or **viv**, **vit** = "life"

biosphere: bio + sphaira ["ball"] = "the part of our planet on which there is life"

vivify: "make alive, animate"

tempor or **chron** = "time"

contemporary: con + tempor = "belonging to the same time"

chronic: "lasting a long time or recurring"

di = "day"

diurnal: "of the daytime"

ann, **enn** = "year"

biennial: bi + enn = "occurring every two years"

luc = "light"

translucent: "allowing light through"

phon = "sound"

symphony: "a type of complex musical composition or the orchestra that performs it"

terr = "land"

subterranean: "under the ground"

hydr or **aqua** = "water"

dehydration: de + hydr = "loss of water"

aqueduct: "a channel through which water travels"

mar = "sea"

submarine: sub + mar = "vessel that goes under water"

agr = "field"

agrarian = "concerning land or agriculture"

via = way

deviation: de + via = "a departure from what is normal or standard"

urb = "city"

interurban: "between cities"

crat or **arch** = "rule" [*Arch* also means "first" or "ancient," as an *archeology* and *archaism*.]

bureaucracy: bureau ["desk"] + *crat* = "office- or department-based organization"

anarchy: "absence of government or rule"

verb = "word"

verbose: "wordy"

log = "speech, word"

prologue: pro + log = "introduction to a play or poem"

bibl = "book"

bibliophile: bibl + phil = "person who loves or collects books"

phobia = "fear"

agoraphobia: agora ["place of assembly"] + *phobia* = "fear of being in open or public places"

pac = "peace"

pacify: pac + fy ["make"] = "calm, restore to a peaceful state"

EXERCISE

15-12 Use each of the words in the preceding subsection to complete one of the following sentences.

1. A flower garden will _____ a bare yard.

2. In the desert, some animals are _____ and others are nocturnal.

3. There are _____ tunnels under many cities and towns.

4. The Roman _____ , over 2000 years old, was still used to bring water to distant fields.

5. It is easy to suffer from _____ in the desert when it is hot.

6. _____ bronchitis is an annoying problem for many people.

7. Hemingway was a _____ of Faulkner.

8. People who get claustrophobia should not go down in a _____ .

9. _____ buses leave that city every hour.

10. The breakup of the Soviet Union led to _____ in many areas.

11. A _____ to a play sets the mood of the action to follow.

12. _____ writing does not communicate meaning well.

13. The people who lived in the countryside wanted _____ reform.

14. Many different instrumental sounds are combined for a _____ .

15. Bathroom windows are usually _____ , not transparent.

16. At that school, any _____ from the rules can lead to expulsion.

17. The _____ had an enormous library.

18. There is usually considerable administrative inefficiency in a _____ .

19. The organization holds a _____ conference.

20. It is vital for us to take care of the _____ .

21. It was difficult to _____ the frightened child.

22. The recluse suffered from _____ .

Additional words: *biography, autobiography, symbiosis, vitality, revitalize, extemporaneously, anachronism, synchronize, chronological, per diem, annuity, elucidate, phonics, phonetics, terra cotta, terrestrial, hydroelectric, aquatic, maritime, mariner*

Use each of the words in the preceding list to complete one of the following sentences.

1. A motorized vehicle in a film about the Middle Ages would be an _____ .

2. Most people prefer not to speak _____ .

3. The changes in the company should _____ employee morale.

4. Some school children learn to read through _____ .

5. He needed to _____ because his project was not clear.

6. He receives money every January from an _____ .

7. A famous person usually becomes the subject of a _____ .

8. A famous person who writes well may publish an _____ .

9. The six-month-old dog was full of uncontrollable _____ .

10. We should _____ our watches before we go our separate ways.

11. In the research paper, the events are discussed in _____ order.

12. _____ is the mutual dependence of living organisms, generally to the advantage of both.

13. They are paid on a _____ basis.

14. A dam can furnish _____ power.

15. A _____ works on a ship.

16. In science fiction films, _____ beings often associate with extraterrestrials.

17. _____ is a kind of pottery.

18. The study of speech sounds is called _____ .

19. _____ plants may die in a polluted lake.

20. At the _____ museum, we saw various instruments used for navigating on the high seas.

Additional words: *agronomy, viaduct, urban, urbane, autocratic, oligarchy, matriarchal, hierarchy, verbal, verbatim, monologue, neologism, bibliography, claustrophobia, acrophobia, pacifist*

EXERCISE

15-14

Use each of the words in the preceding list to complete one of the following sentences.

1. A _____ does not want to see a country go to war.

2. _____ is an abnormal fear of heights.

3. The _____ goes at the end of a research paper.

4. He repeated the conversation _____ .

5. In a _____ society, women head the clan or tribe.

6. The unsophisticated girl felt awkward around her _____ cousins.

7. _____ deals with soil management and crop raising.

8. People who suffer from _____ may be uncomfortable during a long ride in an elevator.

9. A _____ is a new word for something.

10. A _____ is a soliloquy.

11. A _____ agreement is not always legally binding.

12. In a _____ , there are different levels of authority.

13. _____ is the rule of only a few people.

14. _____ means dictatorial.

15. There is a need for _____ renewal in most large cities.

16. A _____ had been built over the tracks.

Roots That Make a Statement
fac, fec, fic = "make, do"
  effect: ex + fac = "result"
ten = "hold"
  detain: de + ten = "hold"
fer or **port** = "carry"
  transfer: "move from one place to another"
  deport: "force to leave the country"
duc = "lead"
  deduce: "reach a conclusion through reasoning"
tract = "draw (pull)"
  detract: "draw away from"
Additional words: *affect, fiction, facilities, facilitate, efficacy, facsimile, proficient, tenable, tenacious, coniferous, portable, conducive, induction, conduit, retract, protract*

E X E R C I S E

15-15

Use each of the words in the preceding subsection to complete one of the following sentences.

1. His words had an encouraging _____ on everyone.

2. Her company will _____ her to New York next month.

3. Good detectives _____ many facts from a few clues.

4. The policy changes _____ all members of the organization.

5. That preschool attracts many parents because of its excellent _____ .

6. The police may _____ a suspect.

7. The government will _____ those prisoners.

8. The great _____ of that product makes it the most popular one of its kind.

9. His cigarette-stained fingers _____ from his otherwise neat appearance.

10. Some _____ is based on real events.

11. There are many _____ trees in the West.

12. Other problems will ensue if we _____ the issue.

13. They sent the office a _____ of the document.

14. He is _____ at using various kinds of presses.

15. We can _____ the closing of the negotiations by having everything carefully prepared ahead.

16. The belief that humans and apes are unrelated is not longer _____ .

17. A quiet place is _____ to study.

18. To _____ is to draw back.

19. They are _____ in their struggle for human rights.

20. Something _____ can be carried easily.

21. A _____ is a pipe or connecting tube.

22. There is a formal _____ for all new members.

---

　　　　miss, **mitt** = "send"
　　　　　　admit; *ad* + *mitt* = "allow (for), acknowledge"
　　　　jac, **jec** = "throw"
　　　　　　projectile: *pro* + *jec* = "something thrown forward or launched"
　　　　voc, **vocat** = "call"
　　　　　　provocation: *pro* + *voc* = "a calling forth"

graph, **gram** or **scrib** = "write"
> *seismograph: seismos* ["earthquake"] + *graph* = "instrument for measuring the intensity of earthquakes"
> *ascribe: ad* + *scrib* = "attribute to a particular source"

doc = "teach"
> *indoctrinate: in* + *doc* = "uncritically teach certain beliefs"

Additional words: *missile, eject, dejected, trajectory, irrevocable, equivocal, choreography, electrocardiogram, scribe, proscribe, docile*

E X E R C I S E

Use each of the words in the preceding block of text to complete one of the following sentences.

1. To _____ someone is to teach the person to believe something without questioning it.

2. Television viewers in California frequently see the _____ at the California Institute of Technology after there has been an earthquake.

3. _____ means throw or force out.

4. He reacts aggressively only under severe _____ .

5. After failing the test the third time, he felt _____ .

6. The _____ followed the _____ that had been carefully calculated.

7. The doctor ordered an _____ for the patient.

8. The _____ copied several pages each day.

9. The decision, once made, will be _____ .

10. _____ means obedient or tractable.

11. Laws in many countries _____ the sale of drugs.

12. The _____ for the musical was extremely well worked out.

13. A _____ is a type of projectile.

14. They _____ the plot to a medieval author of tales.

15. It is sometimes difficult to _____ that something is true.

16. _____ means ambiguous.

---

vinct, **vict** = "conquer"
> *invincible: in* + *vinct* = "unconquerable"

domin = "master, rule"
> *domineering:* "overbearingly controlling"

cid, **cis** = "kill; cut"
> *incision: in* + *cis* = "a cut, such as one made by a surgeon"

> **frag**, **fract** = "break"
> > *fragile:* "easy to break"
> **claus**, **claud** = "close"
> > *recluse: re + claus* = "one who avoids others"
> Additional words: *vanquish, domain, predominate, excise, incisive, herbicide, frail, infraction, infringe, disclose, preclude*

E X E R C I S E

Use each of the words in the preceding block of text to complete one of the following sentences.

1. The surgeon made a 5-inch _____ in the patient's abdomen.

2. Glass is _____ .

3. The star player will _____ her opponents.

4. The new political party may eventually come to _____ in the legislature.

5. There is an _____ tax on many products.

6. It is dangerous to plant a vegetable garden where a _____ has been used.

7. His record includes a minor _____ .

8. The agreement does not _____ further negotiations.

9. The authorities may never _____ the real facts in the case.

10. People who trespass _____ upon other people's rights.

11. The _____ child could not play contact sports with the other children.

12. His _____ criticism was actually very helpful.

13. The theater is truly his _____ .

14. The _____ rarely talked to anyone.

15. It is difficult to live with a _____ person.

16. The army proved to be _____ .

> **erg** or **labor** = "work"
> > *metallurgy: metal + erg* = "the science of using metals"
> > *laborious:* "requiring much work"
> **sci** = "know"
> > *conscious: con + sci* = "aware, awake"
> **cred** = "believe"
> > *credible:* "believable"
> **vol** = "wish, will"
> > *volition:* "choice"

mon = "warn"

  premonition: pre + mon = "forewarning that is sensed rather than real"

loq = "talk"

  loquacious: "talkative"

dict = "say"

  contradict: "state the opposite of"

Additional words: *ergonomics, collaborate, elaborate, omniscient, credence, incredulity, involuntarily, admonish, elocution, abdicate, indict, jurisdiction*

EXERCISE

Use each of the words in the preceding block of text to complete one of the following sentences.

1. Some studies have shown that, contrary to popular belief, men are more _____ than women.

2. The company hired an expert in _____ in order to increase the efficiency of production.

3. She gave a _____ reason for being late.

4. They make _____ plans for every phase of the event.

5. No one is truly _____ .

6. You should not give _____ to such rumors.

7. The local police have _____ in the case.

8. The king will _____ in favor of his son.

9. People often jump _____ at a sudden loud noise.

10. To _____ means to formally charge with a crime.

11. Many career politicians study _____ .

12. _____ means disbelief.

13. The supervisors constantly _____ the workers for talking.

14. The techniques used in _____ have developed over the course of many centuries.

15. Cleaning a messy house is a _____ task.

16. If we _____ , we can get the work finished much faster.

17. They _____ everything she says, so she almost always keeps her ideas to herself.

18. She had a _____ about the earthquake.

19. He was _____ of his own shortcomings.

20. He did it of his own _____ .

> **veni**, **vent** = "come"
>> *advent: ad + vent* = "arrival"
>
> **vert** = "turn"
>> *divert: di + vert* = "turn aside"
>
> **volv**, **volut** = "roll"
>> *evolve: ex + volv* = "develop"
>
> **cas**, **cad**, **cid** = "fall"
>> *casualty:* "person killed or injured in an accident or war"
>
> **vid**, **vis** = "see"
>> *evidence: ex + vid* = "indications, data"
>
> **spec** = "look at"
>> *retrospect: retro* ["back"] *+ spec* = "a look back"
>
> **aud** = "hear"
>> *inaudible: in + aud* = "incapable of being heard"
>
> **tact**, **tang** = "touch"
>> *tactile:* "relating to touch"
>
> Additional words: *convention, adverse, subversive, vertigo, voluble, cascade, improvise, speculate, conspicuous, auditory, contingent, tangible*

E X E R C I S E

15-19

Use each of the words in the preceding block of text to complete one of the following sentences.

1. The new system has both _____ and intangible advantages.

2. The ear contains the _____ canal.

3. They often _____ about what they would do if they had a vast fortune.

4. Our acceptance of their offer is _____ .

5. They put the suggestion box in a _____ place.

6. _____ means loquacious.

7. She likes to have everything prepared in advance so that she does not have to _____ .

8. A _____ is a waterfall.

9. There was pollution long before the _____ of the automobile.

10. The project may _____ into something rather different from what was originally planned.

11. Dogs can hear many sounds that are _____ to humans.

12. Hundreds of computer experts attended the _____ .

13. Visually disabled people often have very highly developed _____ capabilities.

14. People who suffer from _____ should not work in high locations.

15. They finished everything in spite of the _____ circumstances.

16. She died a war _____ .

17. They will have to _____ traffic in order to repair the bridge.

18. All the _____ supports their conclusion.

19. In _____ , it appears to have been the right decision.

20. At the beginning of the Cold War, people talked a great deal about _____ activities.

SUFFIXES

Some Suffixes That Name

State of Something
-cy, **-ity**: *accuracy, bankruptcy, velocity, agility*

Person Who Does Something
-er, **-or**, **-ist**: *employer, writer, legislator, benefactor, typist, chemist*

Some Suffixes That Make a Statement

To Make
-fy, **-ize**, **-ise**: *verify, rectify, utilize, televise*

Some Suffixes That Modify

-able, **-ible**: *capable, knowledgeable, credible*
-ous: *unanimous, superfluous, ingenious*
-ic: *electric, democratic, altruistic*
-al: *municipal, integral, conditional*
-il, **-ile**: *civil, infantile, tactile*

Summing Up

You have discovered that dictionaries provide much more than just the definitions and spellings of words. Entries in the language dictionary you use for college assignments should contain the following information:

> Definitions
> Spellings
> Syllabification (indicates where words can be divided at the end of a line)
> Parts of speech
> Usage
> Etymology

The thesaurus is a good source of alternative words, as long as you choose only familiar words from among those listed.

When you are reading, you can sometimes figure out the meaning of an unfamiliar word in one of several ways:

From context clues:
    The meaning of the passage
    Examples
    A definition
    A contrasting term
From word elements:
    Roots
    Prefixes
    Suffixes

Part Four

SELECTED READINGS

Elegy for a Hero

DOUGLAS FOSTER

Thick brown dust swirls around my 11-year-old son and me, settling in the layer of sweat on our faces, seeping into our clothes, and coating our city-slick shoes. "It's good we dressed up," Jake says, tromping on. "*Really* good."

After a five-hour drive through the Central Valley of California, we've abandoned our car, because traffic is backed up for miles. We've set off walking, in the blistering heat, to the United Farm Workers of America compound at Forty Acres, just outside Delano.

In the distance, Cesar Chavez lies in an open coffin beneath a mammoth canvas tent. The muffled voice of a priest reciting the rosary wafts our way, the sound blaring one moment, then nearly extinguished.

I've been trying to explain to Jake why we've come. He has an ear cocked, but is also on guard as usual for 60's nostalgia. Jake never met Cesar Chavez, and his childhood in the 1980's lacked great social movements and political heroes.

When I ask if he admires any political leader, Jake says flatly: "Except for sports, nobody. I don't think there are any people like that left any more."

So I tell my son that when I first met Cesar Chavez I was a little older than he is now. It was the edge of summer in 1968 and I was part of a group of junior-high-school kids who had traveled from San Diego to Delano to deliver canned food and clothes we'd gathered for the striking grape harvesters.

As soon as we arrived, we were hurried off to a farm worker picket line, where we had paraded in the dust and heat for hours outside Delano City Council chambers. We marched to protest the jailing of a farm worker who had been beaten by a strike-breaker earlier in the day.

We dodged stones, spittle and epithets from local white teenagers who took special umbrage at the sight of city kids. They gunned past us in dented pickups, shouting "Outside agitator! Commie! Fag!"

Our side prevailed that day. The jailed farm worker was released and there was a little celebration back at the union office. Chavez greeted us in a buoyant mood. As he stepped forward to shake my hand, I remember thinking: But he's so *small*. He was quiet, demure even, speaking in a voice so soft you had to strain to hear him.

After all the shouted, hateful threats that had been aimed at us, Chavez's calm was a salve. He carried himself with dignity, and his embrace that day felt like a benediction.

By the time I met Chavez, most of my other heroes had been shot down. Martin Luther King, Jr., had been assassinated a month earlier, and Robert Kennedy's Presidential campaign would end in a pool of blood a few weeks later.

But Chavez continued on, with his remarkable mix of militancy and nonviolence, using strikes, consumer boycotts and his own punishing fasts to publicize the cause. He would stitch together a global constituency across class and ethnic lines and live to build the first modern farm labor union on United States soil. Chavez became a beacon, drawing volunteers from all over the country to work for social justice in California's agricultural valleys.

I'm struggling to explain this to Jake as we cross to the giant tent, surrounded by hundreds of farm workers and their families. The sun has set, a cool breeze has kicked up and a half moon is rising. Jake has slowed his pace, holding my hand and peppering me with questions.

But there are chunks of the story I've left out, and I push on. I don't want to describe Chavez as a one-dimensional symbol instead of remembering him as a real man. So I keep talking to Jake, stripping away the gloss of nostalgia in search of a fuller memory of the real man.

In the mid-1970's, I turned down Cesar's invitation to join the union and work on its newspaper. I'd decided that I wanted to become a journalist instead of a propagandist for anybody, even him.

As a daily newspaper reporter in the Salinas Valley in the late 1970's, I chronicled the farm workers union's boom—and then its bust. During those years, Chavez cut himself off at his compound in the Tehachapi Mountains. He struck up a friendship with Charles Dederich of the Synanon drug rehabilitation program and adopted some of Dederich's authoritarian methods. When a new generation of farm worker leaders emerged during the strikes of 1979 and 1980, Chavez slapped them down. In a series of purges, he drove many skilled and dedicated members out of the union.

Writing about these controversies was painful. Friends in the United Farm Workers often protested that I was revealing "internal matters" to the enemy. I can still remember Cesar's icy, clipped voice on the telephone, in a conversation in which I was transformed for the first time from "Brother" to "Mr."

Full of trepidation, I tried to report the truth as I understood it, even when that meant angering the hero I admired.

"Do you understand what I'm trying to say?" I ask my son. "Yeah," he replies soberly. "It's like fighting your Dad when you think he's wrong."

On the dais behind Cesar's coffin, an indigenous troupe is dancing during a break between prayers. We're moving down an aisle, surrounded by the cultural cacophony Chavez represented. Rhythmic clapping builds to a crescendo as cries of "Sí, se puede!" "Viva Cesar Chavez!" and "Viva la unión!" alternate with prayers in Spanish and English and a hymn promising Chavez's rebirth. "Resucitó, resucitó," a priest sings. When the Indian dancers replace the priest on stage, they chant, in counterpoint, "Chavez is made from corn! His soul is made of corn!"

Jake hangs back as we approach Chavez's body and I walk on alone. The mourners move closer, and I can smell the sweet sap of hand-cut wood. A middle-aged man in front of me reaches out to rub the pine box's freshhewn seams. He hovers over the short, waxy, well-coiffed man in the coffin.

When my turn comes, I whisper: "Cesar, I miss you. I've missed you for a long time."

Rushing past the honor guard, I hurry to rejoin my son. I'm eager to have his hand in mine again. I'm torn between the urge to say more and the desire to close my mouth. The trip to Delano has been a kind of emotional striptease, and I worry that I've already revealed too much.

In the course of a single day, I've tried to give Jake a quarter century of my experience. Since he doesn't have a hero of his own, I've handed over mine. But before he's had a chance to revel in the thrill of adulation, I've yanked this gift halfway back. Perhaps my insistence on telling a version of the whole truth has stolen from Jake the chance to view at least one person in a heroic light.

Outside the tent, electric generators bleat and huge overhead bulbs pulse in a jet-black night. I'm stumbling in the dark, eager to take one more run at describing the arc that crosses from my experience to my son's.

I'm searching for a way to pass on, as best as I can, the story of a generation that once had many flawed heroes to my heir, whose generation has far too few.

SOURCE: *New York Times Sunday Magazine*, May 23, 1993.
© 1993 by The New York Times Company. Reprinted by permission.

Questions for Discussion and Writing

1. Why does Foster consider Chavez a hero? Who are Foster's other heroes?
2. What are the positive sides to adulation of a hero? What are the negative sides? What do you think Foster means by "flawed heroes"?
3. How would you answer if an 11-year-old asked you who Cesar Chavez was?
4. Chavez used strikes, boycotts, and fasts to achieve better working conditions for farm laborers. In what other situations have these tactics been used? How effective is each strategy? What other recourse do farm laborers or other workers have to attain fair wages and acceptable working conditions?
5. According to Foster, Chavez created a "global constituency across class and ethnic lines." In what ways is a constituency across class and ethnic lines important locally, nationally, and internationally? Why are different interests and points of view so important in our world today?

Would Americans Man Death Camps?

PAUL GALLOWAY

There are undesirable elements in our nation. You know who they are. They are people who are not good Americans. They are an unstable, potentially disloyal and disruptive group.

Recognizing the enormous problems our country faces, our government leaders have decided that these people should be separated from the rest of us.

These people are to be placed in camps. It may be best to eliminate some of them.

This is a time of crisis. It will be necessary for some of us to supervise these camps. It is our duty. This country has been good to us. We have a responsibility to answer our nation's call in time of need.

"Would Americans man death camps?" Stanley Milgram was asked.

"Under certain circumstances, of course they would," he said. "The capacity for destructive actions is in all of us."

Milgram is professor of psychology at the City University of New York's graduate center. In the early 1950s, while he was on the faculty at Yale University, he developed experiments to measure obedience. He wanted to see how far normal people would go in following orders to carry out destructive acts, to comply dutifully to malevolent authority.

Milgram was surprised and disturbed at the results.

"With numbing regularity, good people were seen to knuckle under to the demand of authority and perform actions that were both callous and severe," he wrote about his findings.

"Men who in everyday life are responsible and decent were seduced by the trappings of authority, by the control of their perceptions and by uncritical acceptance of the experimenter's definition of the situation, into performing harsh acts."

NBC presented the *Holocaust*, a four-part television series on the extermination of 6 million Jews by Nazi Germany.

One reviewer of the series was impressed by the depiction of the Nazis, which, he said, departed from earlier movie and TV stereotypes of "heel-clicking automatons."

"In *Holocaust*, most Nazis are seemingly normal people who all too easily answer the call of a racist and fascist government," he wrote.

The characterizations, the reviewer continued, also "force us to wonder whether we might collaborate with an immoral government for the sake of opportunism and self-preservation."

We wouldn't! We say it with vehemence. After all, this is the United States of America! We have consciences! We know right from wrong!

So did the persons who volunteered for Stanley Milgram's experiments.

Writer Philip Meyer described Milgram's test in a 1970 *Esquire* magazine article. A paraphrased account follows. Put yourself in the place of those who participated:

You answer an advertisement for an educational experiment at a university. It will only take about one hour and you will be paid.

When you arrive, the man who will conduct the test introduces himself. His name is Jack Williams. You also meet another "volunteer," a middle-aged man with a paunch. He appears nervous.

Williams tells you about the experiment. He says it has been developed to try to understand the effect of negative reinforcement as a learning technique. Instead of rewarding someone for learning something, which is what positive reinforcement does, this experiment will attempt to determine if punishment for failure to learn is effective.

If the learner doesn't answer a question correctly, Williams says, the teacher will administer an electric shock.

One of you will be the teacher and the other will be the learner. You and the other man draw lots. The drawing is rigged so that you become the teacher and the middle-aged man, who is not a real volunteer, becomes the learner.

Williams leads the learner into another room. You can see them through a glass partition. You watch as the learner removes his coat and rolls up one sleeve of his shirt. He is strapped into a chair. You watch Williams administer paste to the learner's arm, then attach an electrode to it.

The electrode is connected to a wire that leads to a shock generator that you, as the teacher, will operate.

You hear the learner tell Williams that he is concerned. He recently discovered that he had a slight heart condition. He asks if the shocks will be dangerous.

Williams says the shocks may hurt but they won't be dangerous.

Williams returns to your room and explains how the experiment will work. It is like a game, he says. You will read a series of word pairs to the learner. Some examples are blue-girl, nice-day, fat-neck.

After you read the list to the learner, you begin reading only the first word in each pair. Then you read a multiple-choice list, one of them the correct pairing.

The learner answers by pushing one of four switches at his chair. If he's right, you move on to the next word. If he's wrong, you push a switch that gives the learner an electric shock.

The control board of the generator has 30 switches, each labeled according to the degree of voltage. The first switch administers 15 volts, and the intensity is increased 15 volts for each switch until it reaches 450 volts. This switch is labeled:

Danger—Severe Shock. You are told to increase the voltage for each wrong answer.

Williams gives you a 45-volt shock. It's painful. You do not know, however, that no shock will actually be given to the learner, although he will act as if he is being given a shock.

You begin, and according to plan, the learner consistently gives incorrect answers. If you hesitate to administer the shock, Williams coolly tells you to continue.

As the voltage increases, the learner reacts with growing discomfort. He will writhe in his chair, grimace, then moan, shout and scream in pain. After the voltage has gone over 300 volts, he will not respond at all. He will slump in his chair, apparently unconscious.

Go on, Williams will say. Go on.

Would you go on? Would you go to the end of the board?

Milgram tested almost 1,000 persons. What he found, he said, forced "a painful alteration in my own thinking."

He was dismayed.

"More than 60 percent of the subjects went all the way," Milgram said.

"To our consternation, even the strongest protests from the victim did not prevent all subjects from administering the harshest punishment ordered by the experimenter," Milgram said.

The testing initially used Yale students; then volunteers came from the 20-to-50 age group. A balance of unskilled workers, white-collar workers and professional people was achieved.

Subject 0108 defied the experimenter: "The man is banging. He wants to get out. . . . I'm sorry. If the man wants to get out, I'd just as soon stop. . . . I don't want to administer any more (extremely excited). I will gladly refund the check, but I will not harm this man. . . . I'm sorry, but I will not give him any more if he obviously wants to get out. There is no money in the world that will make me hurt another individual."

But from one of the obedient came this:

165 volts. "That guy is hollering in there. He's liable to have a heart condition. Do you want me to go on?"

180 volts. "He can't stand it! I'm not going to kill that man in there! You hear him hollering? He's hollering. He can't stand it. What if something happens to him? . . . I mean, who is going to take responsibility if anything happens to that gentleman?"

The experimenter says he will accept the responsibility. "All right."

240 volts. "Aw, no! You mean I've got to keep going up with the scale? No, sir. I'm not going to kill that man! I'm not going to give him 450 volts!"

But he did.

In his book, *Obedience to Authority*, Milgram writes of one man who was interviewed after he went all the way.

"Great. This is great," he said. "It didn't bother me. I believe I conducted myself well. . . . I did my job."

In a subsequent interview, the man told Milgram of a conversation with his wife. His wife asked whether he had considered that the learner might be dead. "So he's dead," the man said. "I did my job."

Milgram found that defiance increased when the learner was placed in the same room as the teacher. In one situation, the teacher was ordered to force the learner's arm on a metal shock plate to administer the voltage. Nevertheless, 3 of 10 of those in this situation went all the way to 450 volts.

The Milgram experiments were highly controversial. He was sharply criticized for misleading his subjects and placing them in such a position.

"I believe it was a moral experiment," Milgram said recently. "The controversy should not obscure the essential point of the experiment. It shouldn't lose the point of the findings. The subjects could have quit at any time. But we demonstrated the ease with which ordinary human beings can be brought into destructive actions."

He said the experiments have been duplicated by researchers in Munich, Germany, and in Amman, Jordan, with an even higher percentage of obedience than in his experiments.

Milgram emphasizes, however, that a distinction should be made between the laboratory findings and the actual murderous deeds of the Nazis.

Too, we must realize that our history illustrates that Americans have carried out orders from government authority that many individuals would have found repugnant and immoral.

He gives as examples the Indian massacres, slavery, the internment of Japanese-Americans during World War II, My Lai and the free-fire zones of Vietnam.

Milgram said he doesn't want these findings to excuse the horrors of a Holocaust because they show that the capacity to commit evil acts under official orders is a part of human nature. They should instead serve as a warning to us all. He has concluded:

"The results raise the possibility that human nature or, more specifically, the kind of character produced in American democratic society, cannot be counted on to insulate its citizens from brutality and inhumane treatment at the direction of malevolent authority.

"A substantial proportion of people do what they are told to do, irrespective of the content of the act and without limitations of conscience, so long as they perceive that the command comes from a legitimate authority."

"The condition of freedom in any state," Harold J. Laski once wrote, "is always a widespread and consistent skepticism of the canons upon which power insists."

Source: *Chicago Sun-Times*, April 16, 1978. © Chicago Sun-Times, 1978.
Article by Paul Galloway. Reprinted with permission.

Questions for Discussion and Writing

1. Can you recall some examples of obedience to an "authority" that you find objectionable? Consider examples from your personal acquaintances, current events, and historical records.
2. Do people sometimes follow orders for the sake of self-preservation? Explain and give examples.
3. When should people just "do their job," and when should they not? When should they question authority? At what point do individuals become personally responsible for actions they perform at the direction of others?
4. Milgram performed his experiments several decades ago. Would the same experiment performed at the present time yield the same results? Why or why not?
5. What questions should one ask when evaluating the results of a study or an experiment? What do we need to know to judge the accuracy and validity of a study?

A Dilemma

Doan Tran

STUDENT
ESSAY

I often wonder why my family ever came to America. Listening to my parents, anyone would get the impression that the old country was better in every way. But they insist on living in America even though they are not even trying to adapt to the way things are here, whereas I can and want to adapt to the new way of living. Unfortunately, the difference between us is a source of constant conflict in our lives.

The first problem is they think it is possible to live the Vietnamese way this far from Vietnam. That is, they believe they can and should follow all their old traditions. Needless to say, they also expect me to be Vietnamese rather than American. At the same time, however, they expect me to be successful in society here, without understanding that I must learn American ways in order to do well here. This puts me in a bad situation because I cannot get ahead and please them at the same time.

Like parents in the old country, they also expect me to obey them—even though I am 24 years old! In addition, they want to make all of the important decisions for me. For example, according to their plans, I am supposed to finish university, get a degree in business, and then assist my father in managing the family business. The degree brings prestige, in their way of thinking, but it is from my father that I will learn how to handle business matters. It is as if what I do at college does not really matter except for the honor it can bring. As far as college classes are concerned, I am supposed to get very good grades so they can be proud of me. I sometimes wonder how much they care that I am trying to learn. It also does not seem to matter to them that I do not like business at all but I do find several other fields interesting and promising. However, I gave in to their wishes when I signed up for a major because it looked as though I had to choose between college or them.

They also want to make other important choices for me. One concerns my friends. They are almost hostile toward any of my friends who are not Vietnamese. They are so afraid that I may change because of other people's influence. For example, they think it is terrible that some male students have their own apartments and cook and take care of themselves. My parents think it is a disgrace that women are not doing the household work for them. They say that these young men must come from terrible families. I personally think it is a good idea for men to know how to do some of these jobs so they do not have to depend on a woman all the time. As I see it, my parents are keeping me from developing some responsibilities that are practical and are normal in the society we live in.

We also do not agree on the way to resolve our differences. I want to negotiate and compromise, but they want to dictate to me. I try to understand them, but they try to control me. I am tempted to go my own way, but if I do that, they will only consider me a bad son who broke the rules. I really would like to find a solution to my problem.

Questions for Discussion and Writing

1. Why do you think Doan's parents came to the United States?

2. To what extent is it possible to bring a way of life from one country to another? What does such a transfer depend on?
3. What problems do people from other countries encounter when they adapt very little to the ways of doing things in their new country?
4. Should Doan take charge of his own life? Up to what point should a child consider a parent an authority figure?
5. In what ways does acceptance of parental authority conflict with the development of responsibility in a child?

Time to Call a Halt to "The Mutilation of English"

Lois DeBakey

We Are "Subverting the Purpose of Language"

The mutilation of the English language permeates all segments of our society—the educated as well as the semiliterate, the professions as well as business and government. To realize what is happening to language, you need only listen to talk shows. Hosts, celebrity guests and callers often engage their tongues before activating their minds. Talk shows are saturated not only with illiteracies and illogic but with such conversational tags of verbal insecurity as "like," "you know," "I mean" and "Right?"

On television, newscasters often mispronounce and misuse words. A former top anchorman doesn't know the difference between *enormity* and *immensity*. Another doesn't know the difference between *nauseated* and *nauseous*. Some may consider this inconsequential, but every time we blur the distinction between two similar words, we increase the imprecision of the language and, ultimately, the ambiguity. The result is to subvert the purpose of language—communication.

"Illiteracies" from the "Superstars"

We learn language by mimicking what we hear and read. Unfortunately, our models today are not often exemplary. When our youth hear newscasters misusing language, when they hear country-and-Western singers, professional athletes and other entertainers—who are today's "heroes"—using substandard English, they pick it up. My files are overflowing with illiteracies uttered by the "superstars." A well-paid professional athlete says: "I don't gripe about nothing." A celebrated country-and-Western singer reminisces: "I had no nothin'." A movie idol says: "It was like, well, he's got it."

The young assume that since these people are "successful," learning to speak Standard English is unnecessary. But that's a dangerous misconception. When you enter the adult world, you are at a distinct disadvantage if you do not speak Standard English, which is not only more precise than various dialects but is a major unifying force in our pluralistic society.

Problems of unclear expression also abound in the professions. Each has its specialized vocabulary that excludes and awes the uninitiated. Physicians, lawyers and others can establish for themselves a safe distance from challenge by the ponderous trappings of jargon. As for politicians, they usually emit more wind than wisdom. Some have become masters of nonstop nonsense. The same holds for academicians. At professional meetings, my head has reeled from the copious inanities and gibberish I hear couched in ponderous jargon.

"Disintegration of the Family" Hasn't Helped

We become articulate through practice—but there is little conversation in homes today. The disintegration of the family has reduced the opportunities for young people to converse with adults. Consequently, their vocabulary is limited. Few parents today read to their young children or surround them with books. In many homes, people sit catatonically in front of a TV set, receiving messages passively. And what they hear and see on television hardly encourages them to use language thoughtfully.

It is also unfortunate that we do much less writing today, for tying ideas down to written words clarifies our thoughts. Instead of writing letters, however, we now use the telephone.

Our "Underdisciplined, Overtolerant Society"

Underlying this misuse of language lies a change in mores. As a society, we have become underdisciplined and overtolerant. Moreover, we have dismantled the educational system so that young people do not learn to read, write and—more important—reason. A people unable to reason critically is more vulnerable to domination.

By burdening the schools with the full responsibility for social reform, we have prevented them from concentrating on education. In the interest of egalitarianism, we instituted open admissions, grade inflation and social promotion because we did not want to "stigmatize" children. We promoted students uniformly from one year to the next and after the 12th grade handed them diplomas of attendance, not competence. Sadly, the purported beneficiaries of that ill-conceived policy became its victims.

SOURCE: *U.S. News & World Report*, November 7, 1983. Copyright © 1983, U.S. News & World Report, Inc.

Questions for Discussion and Writing

1. Should we expect the spontaneous speech on talk shows and other unrehearsed television programs to be correct? Can speech be both spontaneous and grammatically and logically accurate?
2. Can we expect greater accuracy in writing and rehearsed speech than in spontaneous expression? If so, why?
3. In what ways is Standard English a unifying force in American society? What is the importance of Standard English? Why is it important for a resident of this country to be able to communicate in Standard English?
4. To what extent does conversation indicate communication? When people "make conversation" or gossip, how much real communication is taking place? Do people have a greater opportunity to communicate when they write each other letters or when they talk on the telephone? Explain your answer.

5. Are we an "underdisciplined" society? Should we be trying to get young people to obey rather than to question authority? In what situations is tolerance appropriate? In what ways are we overtolerant? Were people in the past tolerant when they should not have been?

So That Nobody Has to Go to School If They Don't Want To

Roger Sipher

A decline in standardized test scores is but the most recent indicator that American education is in trouble.

One reason for the crisis is that present mandatory-attendance laws force many to attend school who have no wish to be there. Such children have little desire to learn and are so antagonistic to school that neither they nor more highly motivated students receive the quality education that is the birthright of every American.

The solution to this problem is simple: Abolish compulsory-attendance laws and allow only those who are committed to getting an education to attend.

This will not end public education. Contrary to conventional belief, legislators enacted compulsory-attendance laws to legalize what already existed. William Landes and Lewis Solomon, economists, found little evidence that mandatory-attendance laws increased the number of children in school. They found, too, that school systems have never effectively enforced such laws, usually because of the expense involved.

There is no contradiction between the assertion that compulsory attendance has had little effect on the number of children attending school and the argument that repeal would be a positive step toward improving education. Most parents want a high school education for their children. Unfortunately, compulsory attendance hampers the ability of public school officials to enforce legitimate educational and disciplinary policies and thereby make the education a good one.

Private schools have no such problem. They can fail or dismiss students, knowing such students can attend public school. Without compulsory attendance, public schools would be freer to oust students whose academic or personal behavior undermines the educational mission of the institution.

Has not the noble experiment of a formal education for everyone failed? While we pay homage to the homily, "You can lead a horse to water but you can't make him drink," we have pretended it is not true in education.

Ask high school teachers if recalcitrant students learn anything of value. Ask teachers if these students do any homework. Ask if the threat of low grades motivates them. Quite the contrary, these students know they will be passed from grade to grade until they are old enough to quit or until, as is more likely, they receive a high school diploma. At the point when students could legally quit, most choose to remain since they know they are likely to be allowed to graduate whether they do acceptable work or not.

Abolition of archaic attendance laws would produce enormous dividends.

First, it would alert everyone that school is a serious place where one goes to learn. Schools are neither day-care centers nor indoor street corners. Young people who resist learning should stay away; indeed, an end to compulsory schooling would require them to stay away.

Second, students opposed to learning would not be able to pollute the educational atmosphere for those who want to learn. Teachers could stop policing recalcitrant students and start educating.

Third, grades would show what they are supposed to: how well a student is learning. Parents could again read report cards and know if their children were making progress.

Fourth, public esteem for schools would increase. People would stop regarding them as way stations for adolescents and start thinking of them as institutions for educating America's youth.

Fifth, elementary schools would change because students would find out early that they had better learn something or risk flunking out later. Elementary teachers would no longer have to pass their failures on to junior high and high school.

Sixth, the cost of enforcing compulsory education would be eliminated. Despite enforcement efforts, nearly 15 percent of the school-age children in our largest cities are almost permanently absent from school.

Communities could use these savings to support institutions to deal with young people not in school. If, in the long run, these institutions prove more costly, at least we would not confuse their mission with that of schools.

Schools should be for education. At present, they are only tangentially so. They have attempted to serve an all-encompassing social function, trying to be all things to all people. In the process they have failed miserably at what they were originally formed to accomplish.

SOURCE: © 1977 by The New York Times Company. Reprinted by permission.

Questions for Discussion and Writing

1. What factors besides the attempt to educate everyone contribute to the problems in the public education system?

2. To what extent does the attempt to educate everyone undermine the system? What positive influences does this policy have on children's education?

3. Many people, including Einstein and Edison, have done poorly in the school system but have excelled in other areas. How might abolition of compulsory schooling have affected these individuals? How might society then have been affected?

4. Sipher does not define the term *education*, but he indicates that it is not "an all-encompassing social function" or "day-care centers" or "indoor street corners." What areas do you think a public school education should encompass?

5. Sipher brings up the idea of community institutions "to deal with young people not in school." Does the lack of detail about the nature and practical operation of these institutions weaken Sipher's assertion that young people should not be required to go to school? Do you have any ideas regarding the structure and operation of such institutions?

Skool Daze

Wess Roberts

Once upon a time, a teacher and her first-grade students spent a school year together in a little red schoolhouse. The teacher wanted her students to learn all of the material prescribed for the year. And so it was that she had spent the summer vacation reviewing new curriculum materials, writing lesson plans, preparing student handouts, developing tests, outlining homework assignments, and planning field trips.

Her students had spent the summer with their families doing the kinds of things that five and six year olds did in their town.

On the first day of school, the students and teacher met in their classroom. "Who would like to learn how to read better?" the teacher asked her class, for these were students who were just learning to read.

"Can we learn to read sports magazines?" asked Kevin, who liked to watch and talk about professional baseball and basketball.

"I don't like reading. Can't you just read us a story?" asked Robert.

"Can we read stories about animals?" asked Megan, who liked to visit the zoo.

"Why can't we just have a longer recess instead?" asked Rod, who showed no initial interest in reading.

"I'm hungry!" said Amanda, who was always munching on something.

"My stomach hurts. Can I go see the nurse?" asked Bruce, who seemed to be ill.

"I like to read," said Louise, who appeared to be the class brain.

And the teacher taught her class to read at the first-grade level.

On the second day of school, the class and the teacher met again in their classroom. "Who would like me to teach arithmetic today?" she inquired.

"I don't need to learn how to count," said Kevin. "I'm going to have a computer when I get big."

"Counting doesn't seem like much fun," said Robert.

"I'll never be very good in arithmetic!" Megan exclaimed.

"I don't want to learn how to add and subtract things," stated Rod. "Let's play kickball instead."

"How long before lunch?" Amanda inquired.

"Arithmetic gives me a headache," said Bruce.

"I like arithmetic!" shouted Louise. "Can we learn how to use computers, too?"

And the teacher taught arithmetic to her class.

On the third day of school, the class and the teacher met in their classroom. "Who would like to learn how to write?" she asked her class.

"I want to learn how to sign autographs," said Kevin. "I'm going to grow up to be a basketball player when I grow up."

"Can we have music time? Writing doesn't sound like fun," said Robert.

"Yeah!" shouted Megan. "I'll write notes to everyone in the class. Can I get extra credit if I write the principal a letter?"

"Why do we need to learn how to write?" asked Rod. "We're only in the first grade."

"Can we write a note to the cooks in the cafeteria, and tell them what we want for lunch?" asked Amanda.

"Writing makes my hand hurt," said Bruce.

"I'd like to learn how to write," said Louise.

And the teacher taught the children how to write.

On the fourth day of school, the teacher assembled her students in their classroom.

"Who has their homework ready to hand in?" the teacher asked.

"I was playing with my friends last night. Is it okay if I turn it in tomorrow?" asked Kevin.

"I couldn't find my homework assignment sheet," said Robert.

"I didn't have time to do my homework. I was talking to my friends until I went to bed last night," reported Megan.

"I don't like homework," said Rod.

"I think I left my homework in the cafeteria yesterday," said Amanda.

"Homework makes me want to throw up," mumbled Bruce.

"Thanks for sharing that with us, Bruce," someone said as the class groaned in unison.

"Here's my homework; I hope it is what you wanted," said Louise.

And the teacher graded the class on their homework assignments, giving F's to all the children who failed to hand in their work.

On the fifth day of school, the students met the teacher in their classroom. "Who is ready for the test?" asked the teacher.

"I don't want to take a test, but thanks just the same," said Kevin.

"Test? What test?" asked Robert, who hadn't paid attention earlier in the week.

"Do the boys have to take it too?" Megan asked.

"I'm not very good at tests," Rod said.

"Can we go to lunch first?" asked Amanda.

"Can I go to the bathroom?" asked Bruce.

"I studied last night. I'm ready," said Louise.

And so the teacher gave her students their test.

After a while, the teacher sent home a note with each student inviting the parents to parent-teacher conferences. "Whose parents will be coming to the parent-teacher conferences?" asked the teacher.

"My dad is coaching his baseball team tonight, and my mom is working in the snack bar," reported Kevin.

"My parents are taking me to a concert tonight," said Robert.

"I left the note at one of my friend's houses," said Megan. "My parents don't know about it."

"My parents don't like parent-teacher conferences," said Rod.

"We're going out to dinner tonight. Mom and Dad want to know if they can come another time," said Amanda.

"My mom and dad said to tell you that they're not feeling well," said Bruce.

"My parents will be here," said Louise.

And the teacher held a parent-teacher conference with Louise's parents.

A few years later, the teacher went to visit her former students who were now in the twelfth grade. "How's everyone doing?" the teacher asked.

"I hurt my knee playing soccer last summer. The doctor says I can't play sports anymore," said Kevin.

"I'm in a band," said Robert.

Megan wasn't present. She was married and had a year-old baby.

No one knew where Rod was. He just stopped coming to school one day.

"I've been on a diet," said Amanda.

"I like school now," said Bruce.

"I'm going to college next year," said Louise.

And the teacher looked forward to her next visit with her former students.

A few years passed, and they met again. "How's everyone doing?" the teacher asked.

"I own a sporting goods store," said Kevin.

"My band is doing well," said Robert.

"I'm doing much better," said Megan. "I took the GED (General Education Development) exams, and now I'm enrolled in college. Although it is, at times, a little frustrating taking care of the family and studying too."

"I couldn't find any work I liked, so I'm going to a vocational school where I'm learning how to be an electrician," said Rod, who had returned for the class reunion.

"I'm a dietitian," said Amanda.

"I'm a doctor," said Bruce. "Now whenever I get sick, I just prescribe myself some medicine."

"I'm a schoolteacher," said Louise.

And the story began anew.

SOURCE: From *Straight A's Never Made Anybody Rich* by Wess Roberts. © 1991 by Wess Roberts. Reprinted by permission of HarperCollins Publishers, Inc.

Questions for Discussion and Writing

1. Does Roberts see the role of public schools as Sipher (in the previous reading) does?
2. What positive influence can public schools have on children who are not especially oriented toward traditional academic learning?
3. Would abolishing compulsory schooling have made an important difference in the lives of the seven people in the story?
4. What negative effects can result from forcing traditional academic learning on all children?
5. Who should be responsible for a child's learning?

King—From Martin to Rodney

HARRIET R. MICHEL

President Neff, members of the faculty, students and friends, I am so honored to be with you today as you celebrate the life and achievements of the Rev. Dr. Martin Luther King, Jr. Even though this is only the second year for this event, it sends an important message to the college community and the community of Huntingdon that you formally recognize Dr. King's place in history.

During the past few weeks Dean Taylor called my office several times to request the title of my speech and later to request authorization to release the transcript and video tape to the media.

I must admit all that made me a bit nervous, since I knew I'd be composing my remarks right up to the minute I entered the auditorium. It should give some comfort to any of my former professors sitting out there to realize that some things never change.

My comments today are not a scholarly treatise on race relations in the United States, but rather, they are personal observations and thoughts of an African-American who's spent her life on a journey guided by the unseen star of justice, fairness, equality and hope.

Juniata's observance of Dr. King's birthday holds personal meaning for me because 28 years ago I, with a few activist faculty members, led a small band of frightened, but committed students from this campus to Selma, Alabama to join Dr. King's fight for racial justice.

As one of the very few blacks on campus, I spent endless hours during my 4 years here, both in and out of the classroom trying to sensitize my classmates, and some faculty I might add, to the hopes, fears and aspirations of black people . . . trying to make us seem more familiar and less exotic.

I was constantly challenging the status quo and insisting on the validity of the black perspective. I'm certain I was considered dogmatic by some, and a pain in the neck by many others, but I saw myself as an agent of change.

The decision to take off for Selma was overwhelmingly *unpopular*, especially to the administration, who worried, understandably, about our safety.

There were pleas and threats from classmates, faculty, President Ellis and our parents. One story that has never been told concerns my own mother's response to my actions. I never gave it a thought that she would disapprove of my going, but since I was a first generation college graduate in my family and I was a senior close to graduation my mother, when I called to tell her, insisted that I not go. For the first time in my life, I openly defied my mother, and I said, "Mom I gotta go," and go we did.

And when we got there our participation was vividly recorded in several pages of *Life* magazine and on television newscasts as men on horseback chased us down and beat us with vicious billyclubs.

I can't speak for my fellow travelers, but the experience of packing into stifling hot churches nightly, hearing the majestic voice and message of Dr. King, while outside lurked men who would threaten our lives because we were peacefully demanding justice, was something I shall never forget.

The collective action of thousands of students like us, combined with others . . . black and white, men and women, young and old, jew and gentile, clergy and laymen . . . moved America to action, resulting in the most progressive civil rights legislation passed in this century.

President Johnson initiated new social programs to remedy inequities, benefitting not just blacks, but many other oppressed groups as well. The civil rights movement, in which we students from Juniata were but a small part, provided the blueprint and impetus for women, hispanics, gays and lesbians, the elderly and disabled to organize and fight for their own special interest and needs.

No one can deny that there were some solid accomplishments of that period. Groups which had been ignored or purposely locked out were suddenly provided access through affirmative action programs.

But that golden age of civil rights had two major shortcomings, both of which impact on the attitudes of today.

First, it was too short lived, lasting less than 20 years. Nonetheless, society assumed that, in the case of blacks, the effects of 350 years of slavery and legal discrimination could be overcome by the new laws and new programs. As far as the broader society was concerned this period of attention to racial issues would exonerate America, allowing its long standing debt to blacks to be stamped *"Paid in Full."* That is why many whites ask today with annoyance, "What *do* blacks want?" We gave them their civil rights; the rest they must earn on individual merit. It appears that few white Americans feel an obligation to make any further sacrifices on behalf of the nation's black minority.

The second shortcoming of that era was, despite the claim of conservatives that Great Society programs robbed people of initiative and created what they call a victim mentality, the monies committed to training the poor and providing opportunities for jobs and businesses, *were never sufficient.* Somehow we justified the expenditure of billions of dollars to develop weapons like fighter planes which were redundant in an age of nuclear warheads, but we haggled about the dollars necessary to develop human capital. If social programs were over budget or failed to produce expected results in a limited period of time, we scrapped them as useless. Such standards were not applied to the massive bailout of the savings and loan industry or the bailout of the Chrysler Corporation. We declared those situations critical to our national interest and the money kept flowing.

In addition to the shortcomings already mentioned, the civil rights movement also produced new problems which continue to plague us.

A backlash of resentment developed among many whites who became anxious and threatened by the challenge to their traditional position of advantage and privilege. Unfortunately, those feelings provided fertile ground for recruiters of the new conservatism of the '80s.

Finally, while the new laws and programs through affirmative action provided institutional access, they did nothing to challenge the traditional standards, values and definitions that institutions used to judge, promote or reward their members. Most of the conventional thinking and behavior of institutions remained intact. Therefore, the majority culture continued to define each minority group based on existing prejudices and misconceptions. An example of this problem is illustrated in a *New York Times* article on the racial brawl that shut down Olivet College in Michigan last spring. I quote,

> "The college is a sociological test tube, mixing white students from mostly rural Michigan towns who have little or no contact with blacks and a tiny minority of blacks mostly from Detroit, isolated in a remote and alien setting. It has no black professors or administrators and only one black employee out of 132, the minority recruitment officer, who is frequently on the road."

Olivet College like many colleges was desegregated but not integrated. One analyst on race relations says,

> "The remedial steps society took to deal with racism have been desegregation steps. We've mixed black students in white institutions without doing anything about the attitudes of whites and the culture of the institutions. As a government and a society we put them there and went home."

So even with greater access to traditional institutions there was little room for the "added value" of the new entrants who were admitted or promoted through affirmative action. Therefore in those traditional institutions, women who wanted to succeed behaved like men, racial ethnic minorities worked frantically to sublimate ethnic differences, the disabled struggled to prove they could succeed with little or no special assistance and gays and lesbians, except for certain industries, stayed in the closet.

Regrettably before the demands for institutional change could really take hold, in 1981, Ronald Reagan's administration began its assault on the rights of minorities and women by focusing on the existing policy of affirmative action.

But the attack on affirmative action was only a small part of Reagan's campaign against the hard won rights of blacks, hispanics, women and other groups that have suffered inequities. Since 1964 the country had developed and refined a body of constitutional, statutory, and regulatory approaches designed to exorcise the existence and effects of the racism, sexism, and homophobia so deeply entrenched in our society. From that time until 1981 all of our presidents, to greater or lesser extent, contributed to this effort, even when, like Richard Nixon, they were less than enthusiastic. Recent Republican administrations broke with this tradition and in many instances represented a 180 degree shift from the position of their predecessors.

The swift rise of the conservative right during the Republican years tapped into, at the most visible level, the growing number of whites who expressed misgivings over how blacks were conducting themselves. Along with complaining about welfare dependency and violent crime, more and more whites have come out against preferential programs, and increasingly condemn blacks for casting their race as victims who have no control over their condition. In the same vein, white Americans are more frank to admit their support for barriers, all the while denying that they have gained any advantages because they are white. More typically whites describe themselves as bystanders who must watch while their country is held hostage by a demanding minority. In this view, the behavior of blacks is a major explanation for what ails America.

Accompanying the rise of the conservative right was the reintroduction of racial politics. During the past 12 years racial politics was developed into a high art form. Apart from some blatant Willie Horton episodes, racial references tended to be conveyed in nuances and codes including allusions to crime and comments on quotas. Nowhere was this more evident than last summer's Republican convention.

Who can forget Pat Robertson's call for America to return to its "true Christian roots" or Marilyn Quayle's inveighing against women who forget or abandon their "true natures." Or Patrick Buchanan's face filling our television screens with rage demanding that we must take back our cities, take back our country, take back our culture.

I think we could all agree that in the United States today, even with the promise of a new administration, these are mean spirited times marked all too often by the loss of civility and understanding.

Where once Americans felt locked into what Martin Luther King called "a network of inescapable mutuality," today there is a danger of the balkanization of American culture—the loss of a clear, collective sense of common cultural and social goals. Rather than an ecumenical spirit there is only tribal hostility.

The black-white problem is not the only ethnic flashpoint in America. Other ethnic tensions pervade our society and must be addressed. The problems between blacks and Asians in New York, or Hispanics and Asians in Los Angeles, or whites and Hispanics in the southwest suggest that misunderstandings riddle the relations between all ethnic groups in America.

Regrettably, race has made America its prisoner since the first slaves were landed on these shores.

We are hardly the only nation to perpetrate racial prejudice and ethnic bigotry. Witness the abominable stories of the ugly rise of nazism in Germany and Scandinavia, ethnic cleansing in the former Yugoslavia and the growing popularity of the National Front party in France whose motto is "France for the French."

Yet of all the world's nations, the United States speaks most eloquently of universal justice and equal opportunity so it must set a higher standard for human life and racial harmony.

And further it must do so quickly for those citizens with whom it has had the most complicated relationship and greatest failure rate . . . black Americans.

To be sure the 20th century has seen profound, powerful and encouraging changes in race relations and the status of black Americans.

Yet despite all the changes and advances, W.E.B. DuBois's troubling observation in 1903 remains true in his book, *The Souls of Black Folk*, that the problem of the 20th century is the problem of the color line—87 years later: the color line still divides us. At a time when the black middle-class is expanding and black politicians are gaining new influence and power, racial misunderstanding and conflict seem to be growing. Blacks and whites perceive and experience the world in radically different ways, and except for an increasingly integrated workplace, society remains largely divided in housing, schooling, and socializing. The problem is especially severe in America's cities, where racial tensions too often flare up into ugly, indeed, violent incidents. Complicating the situation is the crisis of the urban underclass, which defies easy solutions, feeds racial stereotypes, and further divides black and white options on how to achieve racial progress.

While economic and social trends account for much of the recent deterioration in race relations, another reason looms large: there is no national consensus on race issues today. No consensus exists, for example, on what to do with the real and pressing problems of poverty and institutionalized racism. National leaders offer little more than platitudes about racial justice and are deeply divided over the role of government in rectifying the consequences of discrimination.

This stalemate at the national policy level created increasing levels of anger and fear in black communities across the country.

It matters less to blacks that 30 percent of them had "made it" into the middle class; what mattered more was the nearly 30 percent who were stuck in a morass of poverty, crime and drugs known as the *underclass*. Moreover, even the most successful blacks understand that in this currently racially charged climate, middle class or underclass a nigger is still a nigger and more whites are emboldened to say so.

The riots last summer in Los Angeles, while shocking, were predictable to anyone attuned to the black community.

The outrage and indignity of the Rodney King jury verdict ignited hostilities which had long been simmering just below the surface, not only in Los Angeles, but in other cities like Kansas City, Milwaukee, Seattle and Toronto, Canada, where racial strife was far less apparent.

The increasing incidents of violence against blacks by police and average white citizens, the growing sense of vulnerability among blacks as evidenced by diminishing quality of life factors like increased infant mortality rates, decreased life expectancy rates, shrinking college enrollment and completion rates, limited access to credit, loans, mortgages and on and on has forced the black community at all levels to search even deeper for solutions which are designed, driven, and yes increasingly funded by themselves. It is generally held that blacks don't know anything about self help. We're one community that doesn't hang together and we don't help one another. I'd just like to say to you that self help is a long and noble tradition in the black community. There is hardly any black church in this country, any black organization that has not scraped their pennies together and made sure that its youngsters are able to go to college, to raise scholarship funds, to provide day care centers, do whatever they can—so it is a misnomer, it is inaccurate to believe that it has never been there, that we are not prepared, and willing, and able to help ourselves.

But blacks *cannot* and *should not* solve these problems alone. Race is America's problem, one that has been too long ignored by most of her citizens, one that will lessen her moral authority on the world stage, one that will limit her ability to compete in the global economy.

We must build a new national consensus on race relations.

And to do that we must create the national will for social change—search for a way to do better. Much of this hope rests with the new administration and the new Congress. Even with all the competing needs Clinton, like Johnson, can do much to create the national will to change.

We must change whites' racial attitudes, especially toward blacks, because the American racial dilemma is a problem created by whites. Any significant improvement in race relations depends on changing white attitudes.

While it is true that both white and black attitudes currently feed on each other and contribute to today's escalation of racial misunderstanding, one cannot deny that the source of the problem remains the white community's continuing inability to understand the peculiar situation of blacks in America.

We must fight white misperceptions that:

1. Discrimination is a thing of the past;
2. Our nation's civil rights problems were solved 20 years ago;
3. The minority poor are wholly responsible for their own plight;
4. Past racial discrimination has no effect on the opportunities that blacks have today;
5. Poverty and the social pathology that often accompanies it are a black or minority problem;
6. Government programs have not worked because many blacks are still in poverty;
7. Blacks and whites have the same opportunities in obtaining jobs, housing, and employment;
8. Blacks are angry because they haven't been able to succeed like Asians and other minorities;
9. Affirmative action gives undeserving blacks opportunities at the expense of whites;
10. Blacks blame racism for everything.

I have spent all of my professional life, all of my career since leaving Juniata, working in various ways and in various settings to overcome the misperceptions and suspicions ethnic and racial groups have of one another.

I continue to speak out against injustice and press for change because I believe purpose without passion lacks power.

Dr. King said,

> "The measure of a man is not where he stands in moments of comfort and convenience, but where he stands at times of challenge and controversy."

Well, with regard to race relations these certainly are times of challenge and controversy. But times of challenge and controversy are also times of extraordinary opportunity . . . a time when fresh perspectives and new ideas are most needed.

The question for each of you today—students, faculty, administrators, the college community as a whole—is where will you stand? What will you do to bring this society back together?

Unlike other social problems—homelessness, drugs, poverty—where we may be concerned but feel overwhelmed and unable to fashion solutions, better race relations *is* something each one of us can do something about.

It won't be solved in the laboratory like cancer or AIDS, it will only be solved with each of us taking ownership for making it better. For ensuring a better common destiny.

I'd like to leave you with a quote from the late Whitney Young, president of the National Urban League.

> "I do have faith in America not so much in a sudden upsurge of morality nor in a new surge toward greater patriotism.
>
> "But I believe in the intrinsic intelligence of Americans.
>
> "I don't believe that we forever need to be confronted by tragedy or crisis in order to act.
>
> "I believe that the evidence is clear.
>
> "I believe that we as a people will not want to be embarrassed or pushed by events into a posture of decency.
>
> "I believe America has the strength to do what is right because it is right.
>
> "I am convinced that, given a kind of collective wisdom and sensitivity, Americans today can be persuaded to act creatively and imaginatively to make democracy work.
>
> "This is my hope, this is my dream, this is my faith."

Ladies and gentlemen, thank you very much.

SOURCE: Speech delivered at Juniata College, Huntingdon, Pennsylvania, January 18, 1993. Reprinted by permission of City News Publishing Company.

Questions for Discussion and Writing

1. Michel says that as a student at Juniata College she endeavored to make blacks seem "more familiar and less exotic." How can contacts between people of different races lead to improved relations?

2. What laws, ordinances, and policies have been enacted with the purpose of creating familiarity between races?

3. Michel states that in spite of affirmative action, "women who wanted to succeed behaved like men." Yet new points of view have been expressed by women, by blacks, and by people in other groups that have benefited from the civil rights movement. To what extent should we continue to follow the dominant European male viewpoints? How extensively should we consider new ideas and perspectives?

4. What do you feel should be done about poverty in America? What measures are likely to help? What can the poor themselves realistically do to help their own situation?

5. Several ideas are quoted from Whitney Young at the end of the reading. On what does Young base these beliefs? Do you agree with them?

The Hard Way Out

Martin Rocha

STUDENT ESSAY

In today's society, divorce is a fact of life. Half of all marriages in this country end up in a divorce. People who have children often make a great effort to avoid splitting up because they believe it is better if the children have a two-parent family even if the family does not get along. But this is not the only reason people with children stay in a bad marriage. In reality, it takes a lot of courage for a parent to divorce because most single parents have to deal with some really serious difficulties.

Financial stress is the most obvious problem in the new family setting. Most of the time, the children end up living with their mother. The woman who takes sole or even just primary responsibility for the care of the children is assuming a tremendous financial burden. It is difficult nowadays for a family to live on one income, and it is even more difficult, in most cases, if the mother is the one that is providing the income. It is estimated that the man's income goes up 70% after a divorce, while the woman's goes down 45%. Even if the father is paying child support, since most men who pay it give much less than is really needed for the children, the family often lives in poverty.

Shortage of time is another serious problem for the single parent. When one person is providing most or all of the income as well as taking care of the time-consuming work and responsibilities around the home, it is very difficult for the parent and children to spend enough time together. They may be able to attend to necessities only. This is a shame because parents and children need to spend time together sharing and doing things for fun, not just things that have to be done.

Another problem is that children in single-parent homes tend to be burdened with a lot of responsibilities. Although it is a good idea for children to learn to take care of themselves at a fairly early age, when they have to depend on one parent who cannot be there as much as two parents could, the children may have to take on responsibilities that frighten them. These can include staying home alone, fixing food, and knowing what to say to strangers on the telephone. Since the children are not ready to handle so much and there may be no alternatives, single parents have to work extra hard to help their children through these difficulties. With all the parent's help, the children may still be forced to grow up too soon.

Last but not least is the problem of criticism from other people. Single parents are treated like outcasts by many adults, with the excuse that they did not know how to make a marriage work. Their children are also snubbed by other children in the neighborhood and at school. It is as if they were bad people. This kind of unfair criticism hurts adults and children alike.

Couples that stay together "for the sake of the children" are usually causing more harm than good. But that still may seem like the easy way out because the parent who takes on the burden of running the family alone has such a hard road to travel.

Questions for Discussion and Writing

1. What are the negative effects on a child when the parents do not get along but do not get divorced? What are the real concerns of people who stay together "for the sake of the children"?

2. The writer gives statistics on men's and women's incomes after divorce. Do these figures, if they are substantially accurate, have a bearing on the high number of unmarried mothers on welfare?
3. What other burdens besides those mentioned in the essay does the single parent generally have to bear?
4. What responsibilities besides doing homework should children take on regardless of their single-parent or two-parent situation?
5. What can a single parent do to minimize the social criticism aimed at his or her children? How can a single-parent family maintain the sense of family?

Homeless Families: How They Got That Way

Families are the fastest growing segment of the homeless population, and most homeless families are headed by single women, according to a University of Southern California (USC) researcher who has conducted an in-depth study of homeless families.

"These women are not crazy," says family sociologist Kay Young McChesney, director of the Homeless Families Project at USC. "They aren't substance abusers, either. Even though most of them were very poor, they had managed to keep a roof over their children's heads until something happened to upset their already precarious economic balance."

McChesney and her research team interviewed eighty-seven mothers of children under the age of eighteen in five Los Angeles County shelters. The women's median age was twenty-eight, their median number of children, two. A disproportionate number were black. About 30 percent had male partners; the rest were single mothers.

About 40 percent of the women became homeless when threatened with eviction or legally evicted, McChesney found. "In Los Angeles, the median rent for a one-bedroom apartment is $491 a month," she says. "The average monthly AFDC [Aid to Families with Dependent Children] payment to a mother with one child is $448. So these women face a choice: they can buy food and diapers, or they can pay the rent. Some months, they decide to eat."

Money had been stolen from about 33 percent of the women, or they simply ran out of money after moving to Los Angeles. Many of the married couples interviewed were in this group. Often the husband had lost his job in another state. When his unemployment benefits ran out, the family moved to California. "They're the Okies of the eighties," says McChesney. "Even if the man finds a job, the family doesn't have enough money to cover the high cost of moving into an apartment."

Approximately 25 percent of the mothers found themselves with no place to live when they left, or were thrown out by, male partners—some of whom had abused them. "Many of these women were being supported in a reasonable fashion when they suddenly found themselves in the street," McChesney says. "In trying to set up a household on their own, they were crippled by the fact that, in general, women don't make as much money as men—only about 48 cents to the dollar. What's more, they couldn't afford to pay someone to care for the kids while they were at work or looking for work."

McChesney found that a large number of women had been physically abused by their natural parents, then placed in foster homes where foster fathers or brothers sexually abused them. "They ran away in their teens and had been doing what they could to survive," she says. "Some had been homeless, except for short periods, for years. Then they got pregnant, and as one said, 'I can make it by myself. But what do I do with my baby?'" McChesney added. "So they wind up in Los Angeles County shelters, where they can stay for a month at most. Then they're back in the street—this time with their babies."

McChesney's study also revealed that homeless families have something in common besides poverty: they are unable to turn to parents, brothers, or sisters for help because their families are either dead, out of state, or estranged. "Considering the median age of the women in the sample, they had a surprisingly high number of deceased parents," says McChesney. "Thirty percent of the women had deceased mothers, with three women not knowing enough about their mothers to know whether they were alive or dead," she writes, "making about a third of the women with no mother to turn to.

"Thirty-five percent of the women's natural fathers were dead, and another six women knew so little about their fathers that they didn't know whether they were alive or dead, making a total of 43 percent effectively with no father. . . . Fully 16 percent of the women were orphans, with both parents dead. Five were not only orphans but also had no living siblings."

Of mothers who had living parents, many had families too far away to be of any help. Only 50 percent had a mother in the Los Angeles area, and only 35 percent had a father who lived there. Almost half had no brothers or sisters in the Los Angeles area.

Those who had living kin in the area were often unable to turn to their family for support. Forty-three percent of the mothers in the sample had been runaways or in foster or institutional care when they were children or teenagers. Many of these women had been abused, physically and/or sexually, by their biological parents, then abused again by foster parents.

"The difference between the poor who wind up homeless and those who don't seems to be a matter of having relatives to turn to when problems come up," McChesney suggests. Yet when families are homeless, society has a tendency to blame the victims themselves, instead of searching for the underlying causes of the problem.

McChesney argues that the primary cause of the current crisis in homelessness is an acute shortage of affordable low-cost housing. "Numerous studies document that, while the number of families living in poverty has increased in the eighties, the number of low-cost housing units available has decreased," she explains. "Nationally, for every unit available, we estimate there are two households in need of low-cost housing. Increasing the number of beds in emergency shelters is not going to solve the problem. More low-cost housing must be provided if we are to stem the rising tide of homelessness."

SOURCE: Reprinted by permission of Transaction Books.

Questions for Discussion and Writing

1. This study gives statistics on single-mother homeless families only. How do you think the situation of other homeless persons compares?

2. What factors contributed to the homelessness of the women discussed in the article? What factors besides these may have contributed? What additional contributing factors may be relevant for other homeless persons?
3. What are the positive sides of government involvement in the problem of homelessness?
4. What are the negative sides of government involvement in the problem of homelessness?
5. Some people who come from extremely negative, unsupportive environments have managed to turn their lives around. Is it fair to use such examples to criticize those who do not manage to progress in spite of their difficult situation?

Abortion

PAT WARNER

STUDENT ESSAY

The current rage over abortion is really frustrating. Many of the people who oppose abortion call themselves pro-lifers in order to make abortion sound like murder. But in doing so, they are giving a misleading impression of the abortion issue.

In the vast majority of abortion cases, only the woman concerned is portrayed as bearing responsibility for the situation even though it takes both a man and a woman to produce an embryo in the first place. This blame that focuses on the woman alone is just one more example of gender discrimination. In addition, the man who does not choose to be impacted by the situation may succeed in staying completely out of the picture. Even if both parents decide to abort, it is the woman that the pro-lifers accuse of murder.

The term *murder* also gives a false impression. Most reputable dictionaries define *murder* as the killing of a person, and a *person* is a member of human society, not a collection of cells inside a person's body. That this concept of murder is what people generally go by can be seen from the fact that someone who murders a pregnant woman, even if she is carrying a possibly viable fetus, is not accused of a double homicide.

Just as murder means the killing of a person, life, for most people, means more than just a heartbeat. Life has come to imply some kind of quality existence, not one of abject poverty, ignorance, pain, and misery. People cannot thrive on thin air. Many women who consider having an abortion cannot foresee any way of providing bare necessities for a child. They often turn to abortion because they are desperate. Many so-called pro-lifers will criticize a woman heavily for going on welfare in order to support unplanned children. But this is a no-win situation because if the mother works, she has to somehow earn enough to support herself and her baby plus pay for child care while she is at work, and it is very difficult to earn that kind of money. Actually, there is a certain amount of hypocrisy and quite a bit of discrimination in this criticism, which is really founded on the assumption that the woman can and must depend on a man—husband or boyfriend—for her support. But it is this pressure on a woman to "have someone" that contributes to so many unwanted pregnancies in the first place. Empowering women so that they feel they can be useful, productive members of society beyond a role as wife and mother, that is, making women feel that they have a right to exist on their own, would help to keep women from putting themselves so easily at risk of getting pregnant.

Another misrepresentation is that putting the unplanned child up for adoption is an easy solution to the problem. This idea is especially popular among people who have never been in the situation. What they do not know or seem to care about is that to keep a creature for nine months, experiencing the growing bond as the pregnancy advances, then to give away the child that has come to mean so much, has to be plain torture. It is a terrible thing to ask a person to do. Many women who early in their pregnancy decide to give up the baby for adoption find that when the time comes, it is unbearable. Whether they go through with the decision or somehow keep the baby, coping with life is incredibly difficult.

Most pro-choice advocates, contrary to popular belief, have very negative feelings about abortion. Most of them feel that avoiding an unwanted pregnancy is the best choice. In the majority of cases they feel that the government should not move in and add a responsibility to women and women alone for a child that a woman has no reasonable way of taking care of. In reality, the abortion question is an incredibly complex and difficult one. Making it out as something simple can only make the dilemma worse.

Questions for Discussion and Writing

1. What has been the effect on the abortion rate of anti-abortion legislation enacted in various American states and foreign countries?
2. Should the government have the right to legislate against behaviors that affect only the individual performing the behavior?
3. Would the anti-abortion movement change radically if fathers became subject to prosecution in abortion cases?
4. The writer mentions the pressure on a woman to "have someone" as a factor contributing to the high number of unwanted pregnancies. Who puts this pressure on a woman? At what age do girls begin to be pressured in this way? What forms does this pressure take?
5. The writer suggests that "empowering women" would help to keep them out of situations conducive to unplanned pregnancies. What are many women doing to gain control of their own lives?

Official Stories
Media Coverage of American Crime Policy

Robert Elias

Promises, Promises

Crime, it seems, will always be with us. A dozen years ago, Ronald Reagan launched new, "get tough" policies on crime which unleashed police departments across the nation. These policies were rationalized in the name of crime victims; more law and order—a tougher official stance—would protect victims and end the scourge of crime. Seven years later, George Bush defeated Michael Dukakis after painting him as "soft on crime" with his notorious Willie Horton ads. During the

Bush administration, a federal crime bill was enacted, further escalating our violent response to crime.

Almost four years after Bush's election, Los Angeles exploded in riots—the result of years of official neglect toward the social victims of American culture. The riots were sparked by yet another incident in a long pattern of police brutality, itself a product of the American government's promotion of official violence. Rather than convict the offending officers (whose videotaped beatings so conclusively proved their guilt), the Simi Valley jury instead saw in Rodney King their worst fears: Willie Horton redux, another black man terrorizing white cops and white communities. As the city erupted, George Bush solemnly deplored the violence he had helped incite to win an election.

The "decade of the crime victim," launched by Ronald Reagan's 1981 presidential task force and continued by the Bush administration, produced more victims than ever—more crime, more fear of crime, more racism and sexism, more desperation. Despite all the promises of the last dozen years, Americans are still the victims of crime in unprecedented numbers, and further from any real solutions than ever before.

In the face of each succeeding crime wave, we get the same old answers, from Democrats and Republicans, liberals and conservatives alike. There's only one way to confront it: with force. We need more police, greater firepower, and harsher punishments, even though we already lead most nations in exercising this kind of force. Conservative Republicans like Reagan and Bush are not the only ones supporting get-tough strategies against crime. In 1991, liberal Democrat Joseph Biden successfully sponsored a Senate crime bill; Biden proudly announced that it was the "toughest ever." The bill provided no new strategies; instead, it merely intensified what had already been tried and shown to fail: building more prisons, curbing defendants' rights, stiffening penalties, and so on. Yet despite such draconian measures, crime rates continue to rise, and the fear of crime has reached staggering levels. Nor does the Clinton administration's crime bill, recently passed by the U.S. Senate, offer any fundamental changes; instead, it will put hundreds of thousands of new police officers on the street and may even extend the death penalty to 50 new crimes.

Is this truly the best we can do?

Media Amnesia and Crime

> The press corps is like a pool of stenographers with amnesia.
>
> —I. F. Stone

> Read *Time* and understand.
>
> —TV commercial for *Time* magazine

Over the years, U.S. crime policy has remained remarkably consistent, with get-tough strategies used to fight periodic "crime wars." Just as consistently, these strategies have failed. Yet policymakers continue to support them, shunning the systemic changes needed to undo the adverse social conditions which generate most crime and most victimization. These policymakers are understandably reluctant to admit the historic failure of U.S. crime policy, for which they are in no small part responsible.

How can they perform this sleight-of-hand? As with most public policy, Americans learn about government crime policy largely through the media. The press provides our window on public problems, on the government's strategies to solve them, and on how well those strategies succeed (or fail). If Americans were to read the criminological literature, the failure of our crime policy would be clear enough. Since most of us don't have the time or the inclination for such study, we rely upon the mass media to do it for us.

Yet, with few exceptions, the media have uncritically reproduced official, conservative, "law-and-order" perspectives with little fundamental analysis of their success or failure. They have also repeatedly covered and promoted "crime wars" and "drug wars" which inevitably fail but which are periodically resuscitated (with the media's help) as if these wars had never been fought—and lost—before. The media fail to hold policymakers responsible for strategies which *predictably* don't work. Indeed, they help make the problem worse; the media's amnesia, unwitting or not, encourages people to support policies which actually promote the growth of crime.

One telling example of this is the coverage devoted to crime policy by the three major newsweeklies—*Time, Newsweek,* and *U.S. News and World Report*. When they are not getting their news from network television, millions of Americans rely upon these magazines for information about their world. To determine just what kind of information about crime and society Americans have received from the newsweeklies, I examined every general crime story appearing in *Time, Newsweek,* and *U.S. News and World Report* from 1956 to 1991. The result of this study is a comprehensive picture of crime in America, as well as the government's policies to address it. This picture has much to tell us—albeit in ways the newsweeklies didn't intend.

Defining Crime

The bias of the headlines, the systematic one-sidedness of the reporting and the commentaries, the catchwords and slogans instead of argument. No serious appeal to reason. Instead a systematic effort to instill conditioned reflexes in the minds of the voters—and for the rest, crime, divorce, anecdotes, twaddle, anything to keep them distracted, anything to keep them from thinking.

—Aldous Huxley

First, the newsweeklies faithfully reproduced government definitions of crime, despite abundant evidence that officials define crime discriminatorily: focusing primarily on lower- and working-class behavior, and excluding harms (such as corporate wrongdoing) which are far more costly, both in lives and in property lost or damaged. Thus, the newsweeklies helped to promote—and also legitimize—the official definition of the crime problem, its seriousness, and its cure.

This bias produces some insidious distortions. Without a crime, there can be, officially, no victimization. Only those behaviors defined as crime are eligible to be treated as victimizations; and among those victimizations, only those pursued seriously by law enforcement get their due attention. Thus, we are obsessed with drunk drivers, even though far more accidents are caused by safety defects and shoddily engineered automobiles; and we are obsessed with child abductions (though quite rare), while slighting the immensely larger problem of child abuse. Because the media prefer not to question official crime categories, many genuine victims and victimizations are ignored—cast out of the public's consciousness and out of the realm of public assistance.

Even when the newsweeklies covered white-collar crime (as the endless scandals of the late 1980s made it almost impossible to avoid), the biases remained.

White-collar crime was never portrayed as a structural or systemic problem but, rather, only as a matter of deviant individuals like Michael Milken or Charles Keating. And while the newsweeklies advocated tougher punishments for street criminals, for corporate criminals just getting caught was punishment enough. *Newsweek*, for example, repeatedly argued that drug dealers and other common criminals must be "mercifully destroyed" yet claimed that, for white-collar criminals, the "harshest penalty is the one they inflict on themselves"—and this despite the fact that white-collar and corporate criminals produce far more economic and human damage. In fact, unlike their coverage of crime in the streets, the newsweeklies' coverage of crime in the suites was bland and restrained: no pictures of tearful victims, no outraged editorials, no fanciful theories about how Milken's or Keating's laziness or bad upbringing caused his criminal career.

Government and law-enforcement officials also criminalize behavior which arguably produces no direct harm to others. For example, enforcement of "vice" laws drains valuable resources (about one-half in most urban police departments) that could be put to better use on crimes producing real victimization. These priorities do a disservice to actual crime victims and to the community, and the media only compound this disservice by legitimizing rather than questioning them.

Aside from victimless crimes, the newsweeklies, like the government, conceptualize crime as one-on-one offenses committed by strangers, even though most violent crime—and much property crime—actually occurs between people who know each other. Within that realm, the newsweeklies stress the exceptional over the commonplace: sensational but unusual crimes get far more attention, even though this distorts the nature of most crime that occurs. Alternatively, crimes like mass murder or serial killing get extensive play by the newsweeklies even as they miss the real story: that is, that most mass murderers and serial killers are men, and most of their victims are women. Finally, the media typically treat crime in simplistic, Manichaean terms: victims are innocent good people and offenders are guilty bad people, even though many offenders have themselves been victimized—by specific crimes such as child abuse, and often by the unremittingly harsh environment of their past.

Who gets defined as a criminal relies, in the first place, upon how we have bounded our understanding of crime. We consider as criminals only those kinds of people committing the behaviors officially defined as "crime." But within this already biased sample, do we really consider as criminals *all* the people who commit these acts or only some of them?

Not surprisingly, the newsweeklies conceptualize as criminals only a *portion* of those committing official crimes. In this, they take their cues from law enforcement, reporting only on those people who police departments define and pursue as criminals, whether or not they are responsible for most of the official crime. Nonwhite minorities, for example, are the ones arrested in most drug busts, even though whites consume more illegal narcotics. Drug laws and crackdowns have historically followed the changing drug-use patterns of minorities, not the seriousness of the drugs themselves; criminality is largely manufactured for certain groups. The newsweeklies also periodically (and condescendingly) lament the high level of "black-on-black" crime while ignoring not only its causes but also the higher level of "white-on-white" crime. In short, the media do practically nothing to second-guess or correct our conventional (and inaccurate) conceptions of crime and criminality.

Who do we find portrayed as criminals in the newsweeklies over the last 35 years? Well, it's changed some: first it was Negroes, then it was blacks, and now it's African-Americans. Blacks and other nonwhite minorities were described and pictured in the newsweeklies' crime coverage most frequently, even though these groups *do not* commit the majority of crimes (even as selectively defined). In contrast, the newsweeklies described and pictured victims mostly as white people. Consider the sensational coverage of the Carol Stuart murder case, as the media cheered on the Boston police's "search and destroy" mission to hunt down the allegedly black assailant. Never mind that she was actually murdered by her husband Charles Stuart, a far more likely suspect, who made up the story of the black assailant; never mind, too, that the real story here was yet another female victim of domestic violence.

What emerges from my study of the newsweeklies is a pattern of discrimination in which criminals are conceptualized as black people and crime as the violence they do to whites. Yet this didn't prevent *Newsweek*, for example, from running a post–L.A. riot story which claimed to discover that the public, the media, and politicians have all been engaged in a "conspiracy of silence" by *refusing* to admit they associate crime with blacks. Given the way the media have regularly contributed to and reinforced such racist notions of crime, is it any wonder there are such terrible race problems in our country?

Who confronts this scourge of alleged African-American crime? Accurately enough, the newsweeklies show white police officers on the front lines. But do they lament the suspicious racial confrontation this represents? Do they question what pits black offenders not only against white victims but also white cops? No— instead they lament the institutional constraints that are imposed on the police. Police officers themselves are frequently portrayed as victims—first of government bureaucrats who never give them enough resources (even though law-enforcement appropriations actually keep rising), then of liberal courts which hobble the police and allow civil-rights "technicalities" to create a "revolving door" in the system. This message gets transmitted into the public consciousness despite abundant evidence to the contrary: for example, a General Accounting Office study showed that less than 2 percent of the convictions in criminal cases in the 1970s and early 1980s were reversed because of civil-rights violations.

Yet the media routinely omit other perspectives on the relationship between the police and crime. For example, despite persistent cases of police brutality and misconduct over the years, almost no reports claim that the police cause victimization. Even the videotaped beating of Rodney King by Los Angeles police produced only mild (and safe) rebukes from the newsweeklies at the time. Rather than examine King's beating as a symptom of a systemic problem, the media focused instead on deviant officers and the frustrations of police work: if good cops "occasionally" get out of hand, it's just the inevitable result of the losing battle they're being asked to fight.

Experts Right and Wrong

> In ways which journalists themselves perceive only dimly or not at all, they are bought, or compromised, or manipulated into confirming the official lies: not the little ones, which they delight in exposing, but the big ones, which they do not normally think of as lies at all, and which they cannot distinguish from the truth.
>
> —Andrew Kopkind

According to the newsweeklies, crime is caused by evil people, often abetted by misguided do-gooders. Bad characters inevitably exist; some people are naturally

evil or are led down the path of wrongdoing by permissiveness and bad upbringing. Thus, we'll always have criminals; all we can do is to remain vigilant against
them. But beware! We cannot leave this task to the "bleeding-heart liberals" in our
society. According to the newsweeklies, it is these fuzzy-headed do-gooders who
subvert the tough measures required to get the job done. Instead of the "revolving
door," we need more draconian penalties, including the death penalty (the only
language the "savages" and "monsters" among us understand)—*not* compassion
and a concern for human rights.

Yet the newsweeklies never really examine the "causes" or "sources" of crime
at all; even when they use such words, they consider (at most) only crime's symp-
toms. Rather than examining whether something might be wrong with our laws,
our society, or our fundamental institutions, the newsweeklies conceptualize
crime as an entirely individualized problem: everyone has the opportunity to avoid
becoming a criminal. It's your choice—except, of course, for those irretrievably
evil people among us who simply must be put away.

To reinforce these ideas, the newsweeklies consulted a variety of law-enforcement "experts." In the last 35 years, they printed dozens of anti-crime speeches
and lengthy interviews with people who supposedly have the answers. Yet in my
examination of these interviews, I found the experts often unqualified and the
expertise routinely dubious. To start with, the ideologies presented were almost
unremittingly right-wing. In the more than 85 interviews completed by the newsweeklies over the last 35 years, only one expert—Alan Dershowitz—fell left of the
middle of the political spectrum (a man, no less, who's regarded as increasingly
conservative himself). Indeed, these interviews hardly revealed anyone we
might call even a moderate on crime policy; virtually all the interviews were
conducted with people who had strongly conservative (if not reactionary) "law-
and-order" views on crime control. Ideology aside, almost all of the experts
consulted held government positions, usually in some aspect of law enforcement; only 11 percent weren't working for the government at the time they
were interviewed.

What government officials, specifically, do we hear from? We hear the most
from various heads of the FBI, led prominently by one interview after another
with the ubiquitous J. Edgar Hoover. We hear from a variety of conservative sen-
ators, particularly John McClellan, who fueled an entire career based upon get-
tough crime policies. We hear from several U.S. attorneys-general, with the
notable omission of the only genuine liberals in the last 35 years—Ramsey Clark
and Bobby Kennedy. Instead, we read interviews with Richard Kleindeinst, William French Smith, and repeatedly with John Mitchell (before his own imprisonment for violating the law). Somehow, the only presidents having sufficient
law-and-order expertise to warrant interviews were Richard Nixon, who resigned
from office to avoid impeachment, and Ronald Reagan, who presided over the
most criminally indicted administration in U.S. history.

The newsweeklies also interviewed numerous police superintendents and
battle-weary police sergeants, various hard-line district attorneys from America's
largest and most crime-ridden cities, and a sampling of conservative judges (invariably condemning their own weak-willed colleagues), ranging from local judges
like Seattle's William Long to Supreme Court justices like Warren Burger. Interviews were routinely conducted with the heads of various Department of Justice
divisions like the Criminal Division and Law Enforcement Assistance Administration, with affiliated agencies such as the Customs Bureau and Civil Aviation Security, and with various drug enforcers like the Drug Enforcement Administration,

the National Institute on Drug Abuse, the Federal Bureau of Narcotics, and the State Department's International Narcotics Bureau.

Who counters the overwhelmingly uniform and conservative government perspective provided by these official experts? Those interviewed from outside government included a handful of psychiatrists, lawyers, law professors, sociologists, college presidents, and clergy. Virtually without exception, they echoed instead of challenged the official line. The psychiatrists attributed crime to evil individuals; the sociologists claimed we were too soft on crime; and the clergy decried our society's permissiveness and declining moral fiber.

Yet most of those interviewed by the newsweeklies would be hard-pressed to demonstrate their expertise on the crime problem they were so eager to discuss. Expertise is somehow conferred by virtue of one's political appointment, status in society, or hard-nosed views on the subject, even if that person actually has little or no background in the field. Moreover, the few experts who did possess such qualifications were clearly selected for their willingness to endorse the status quo. The newsweeklies repeatedly interviewed conservative or reactionary criminologists like James Q. Wilson and Fred Inbau, yet criminologists with a liberal, progressive, or humanistic critique to make of current policies, such as William Chambliss and Elliott Currie, are never allotted space in their pages. By suppressing such alternative views, the media reproduce—indeed, embody—the consistently unsuccessful crime policies we've used for most of this century.

Crime Wars as Propaganda

> In our country people are rarely imprisoned for their ideas because we are already imprisoned by our ideas.
>
> —Marcus Garvey

We can see even more glaring examples of old ideas paraded as brilliant new solutions when we examine the newsweeklies' coverage of the "wars" on drugs and crime launched by the Reagan and Bush administrations. With few exceptions, the newsweeklies eagerly embraced these wars, running story after story breathlessly reporting the escapades of our anti-drug warriors—so much so that even the mainstream media eventually began to wonder whether it had overdosed on drug-war coverage. The drug war and crime war were both presented as bold new approaches: since we had *never tried* declaring war on these problems before, here was a chance to pull out all the stops and finally get them resolved.

Unfortunately, we *have* launched drug and crime wars before, repeatedly—at least a few in each of the last three decades. And when we examine the newsweeklies' coverage since the 1950s, we discover that they have functioned faithfully as cheerleaders for these policies, reporting each new drug war or crime war as if they hadn't been around for the previous one a few years earlier. As in George Orwell's *1984*, inconvenient information gets tossed down the memory hole, to be replaced by official stories. So formulaic has the newsweeklies' coverage become that crime stories are repeatedly recycled; contents and headlines have been almost interchangeable, both within and among the newsweeklies, for more than three decades. (*U.S. News and World Report* even ran the *identical* picture of a Los Angeles narcotics arrest twice—10 years apart!) The extraordinary (and willful) duplicity of this coverage has helped conceal the fact that each of these wars has failed, and failed miserably. The media's institutional amnesia robs us of our own history, as well as the ability to learn from past mistakes.

In our repeated wars on drugs and crime, "war" is not merely a strategy, it is a cultural psychology. "Declaring war" is a sign that we take the problem seriously. We are a culture of violent solutions, even if our violence—from the Persian Gulf to our city streets—solves nothing. In fact, we "solve" the violence of crime by committing more violence, however counterproductive—and when random official violence won't suffice, only the organized violence of war will do.

Analyzing our language of "crime prevention" shows how deeply seated our war psychology is. Consider the following words and phrases, repeatedly used in the newsweeklies' coverage: *war, arms race, drastic measures, dead zones, boot camp, plague, wimp, feel the noose, slaughter, trenches, battle strategies, up in arms, target, clampdown, taking aim, menace, punishment, smashing, counterforce, scores, battle, battle cry, frontal assault, strikes back, harden hearts, firing line, front lines, attacking, get tough, busting, mission, enemy, crackdown, struggle, dead on arrival, crushing, curse, invasion, shoot, hard-line, all-out attack, cutting, search and destroy, bombs, kills, monsters, meltdown, force, scourge, savages, confrontation, fighting crime, fights back, fighting the war, big guns, striking, stings, enveloping evil, potshots, peril, alert, curb, armed forts, blood,* and *war at home.*

(At the same time, law-enforcement officials and policymakers have taken steps to coopt the language of peace. For example, the police routinely bear the title of *peace officers* even as they become progressively more violent.)

Judging just from this language, much less our attendant behavior, what kind of lessons are we teaching about violence? What kind of response are we encouraging? When the media reproduce our warlike language, they reflect the violence of official strategies and behavior; but they also invent and embellish that language, searching for new ways to represent the violence upon which we so routinely rely. Given this cultural bombardment, it is not surprising that opinion polls repeatedly show the general public calling for blood—a sham of democracy paraded as "the voice of the people," without any acknowledgement of how that voice is manipulated and shaped by the media's representations of crime policy.

Since, according to the newsweeklies, "the people" are ultimately responsible for preventing crime, these magazines also featured articles on what ordinary citizens have been doing to "fight back." Most of these articles shared a similar narrative strategy. First, the public's heightened fear of crime is stressed (although the question of whether or not the newsweeklies' own coverage artificially enhances that fear is never addressed). Next, citizens are portrayed as being at the "end of their tether," usually disgusted by the criminal-justice system's unwillingness to get tough on criminals. Finally, we learn how citizens have taken matters into their own hands.

How then, according to the newsweeklies, do people take control of the crime problem? Well, one thing they *never* do is to resort to vigilantism, since that would be going too far—even if the newsweeklies have repeatedly created the environment for just such a response. Instead, citizens adopt various self-protection strategies or buy various security measures, including guard dogs, armed guards, lighting systems, foolproof locks, walkie-talkies, and dozens of other crime-control gadgets. They must also take self-defense classes and learn "avoidance" behavior— that is, learn how to substantially reshape their lives and life-styles to avoid crime. Citizens form or join crime-control organizations such as Crime Stoppers and Neighborhood Watches, and they must systematically monitor judges, police, and other officials to make sure they're being tough enough on criminals. All this the newsweeklies tell us is not only what citizens are doing but what they *must* do to check crime.

Never mind that vigilantism does routinely emerge from this environment, or that crime-control gadgets are either too expensive or too inefficient (despite creating huge profits for the security industry). Never mind that these strategies do nothing to address and eliminate crime's fundamental sources and ask us instead to adapt to an inevitably criminal society. Never mind that most citizens' organizations are created and run by officials as public-relations gimmicks to supplement their traditionally unsuccessful crime-fighting strategies. Never mind that Crime Stoppers and Neighborhood Watches have little or no impact on reducing crime, or that we already have the world's toughest criminal-justice system. With the newsweeklies' encouragement, "the people" do fight back—but without the knowledge they need to actually address the problem. Instead, they are merely enlisted as footsoldiers in the on-going (and endless) official war on crime.

Wars, however—even if we entertain the possibility of "just wars"—are inherently immoral and routinely counterproductive. Declaring "war" on drugs or crime teaches lessons that directly contradict our most cherished values. A peace movement against crime would reflect a significantly different culture—one dedicated to justice and human rights, the absence of which stimulates most crime and violence. A society which takes victimization seriously is best equipped to take crime and crime's victims seriously; such a society would not routinely promote war and then enlist the wounded in a new round of violence.

People can and should take back crime control and prevention from an establishment which has historically shown itself unwilling or unable to take crime seriously. People can and must fight back. But to be successful, they must adopt alternative strategies which address crime's actual sources. Successful crime reduction requires a fundamental change in American culture—not merely the minor tinkering of a Bill Clinton but, rather, a substantial reform of our inequitable and unjust political, economic, and social structures. People can launch that change in their own communities—but only through organizations controlled by them, not by officials who have everything to lose from such changes.

In the next issue of *The Humanist*, I will discuss what a "peace movement" against crime would look like.

SOURCE: *The Humanist* January/February 1994. Reprinted by permission of the American Humanist Association.

Questions for Discussion and Writing

1. What adverse social conditions contribute to both crime and victimization?
2. Elias asserts that media reporting of crime usually focuses on individual acts by people from lower or middle classes. Why is it important for the public to know about corporate crime as well?
3. Are people who are convicted of crimes simply "bad" and the rest of the population "good"?
4. What is the importance of getting accurate information through the media?
5. The article cites several examples of terms of violence used in different situations. Suggest alternative, nonviolent terms in each case, and explain what they communicate.

Why Students Must Be Held Accountable for Their Writing

Sherry Sherrill

Not long ago, a colleague stopped by my office to bemoan the quality of his students' writing; in his hands were several research papers. As I recall, one paper had 52 misspelled words on one page; another contained about 100 words—written in large script to "fill the page"; another was written in incomplete sentences. Inherent in my colleague's comment was the often unspoken, but nevertheless believed, notion that the English department is not doing its job, that students cannot write because we have not taught them.

My main comment in response, defense, retaliation to my colleague was that he has every right not to accept any paper of poor quality for a passing grade and has the right to reject a paper that obviously did not meet his standard for competence. I must admit to sputtering these remarks and not making a very coherent response in defense of all of us who (whether we like this terminology or not) are in the trenches.

You probably can guess the rest. Once alone, I thought of a dozen better, more cogent, more useful responses that I should have given and, even more tardily, I felt angry at myself and at my colleague. So here it is—my response to all of you out there who *require* writing in your classes but are not adamant about demanding competent writing and holding students accountable for what they put on paper and how they put it there. Yes, spelling should count.

The concept of writing across the curriculum (or writing to learn) works only if the required writing is evaluated in some way and at some level of expertise. I am referring to any type of writing: essay questions, short answer, term papers, book reports, research projects, and the like. The standards of writing competence by which papers are judged may vary among instructors, but if students are not shown that the quality of their writing eventually counts in the classroom, they never will be concerned about quality. They will learn to value quantity over quality, and they will learn minimum effort will earn a passing grade. In short, they will have learned well what you taught them—e.g., that correctness does not really matter and that they will be forgiven for not knowing much about spelling, or punctuation, or sentence structure, or style, or any other element used to present their ideas.

Failing to evaluate students' writing undercuts, cheats, and demeans every party involved in the educational process. It cheats students because it teaches them the lesson that incompetence in their language is acceptable and that English teachers are the only ones who care about the quality of their writing. I am reminded of a recent conversation with a business communications student who, as an accounting major, was taking an upper-level accounting course. Her writing for me was very inconsistent, a B here, a D there. Her accounting instructor had assigned a research paper, but as the student so happily put it, "He don't mind about spelling mistakes and all them other things like you do." Perhaps *he don't* mind, but *I do;* and I think others in this student's career path also will mind. What lesson has been taught here? Clearly, it is that only the picky people in English instruction care about standards, that poor usage, written or spoken, only counts against you in English classes.

If only English teachers are perceived as caring about matters of style and correctness, then we become the villains in the educational sequence. We cannot win because we cannot get students beyond the idea that we are demanding, that our requirements are seriously out of touch with their other educational realities. Once this idea is entrenched, it subtly undermines all other faculty who use writing in their classes: "Don't take X's class because you'll have to do a term paper or write essay questions on your test."

Finally, requiring writing without holding students accountable for the quality of that writing violates the whole notion of educating students. As we send out more and more graduates who have never been made to master basic skills, we powerfully undermine their ability to function as workers, as parents, as social beings, as constituents of their world. We graduate people who *will* be held accountable as soon as the ink on their application is dry. Many of them will not be prepared to meet the basic demands of the work place; some may not even be successful in filling out the job application. All surely will be examined in light of the institution granting them their degree, and blame will be assigned. The true measure of a college's success is not how many graduate, but how *qualified* those graduates are. Thus, not making students responsible for the quality of their work undermines the value of the student, the teacher, and the college. We cannot afford to continue sending the schizophrenic signal that students should write but should not bother about the competence of their writing.

These are strong words, perhaps strong enough to evoke these responses: "Fine, I'll just stop requiring writing of any sort," or "Okay, I'll mark all that writing, but everyone will fail my class." As for the first response, you must not move backward in educating your students. We are late enough in picking up the writing-to-learn concept, and we simply cannot afford to lose more ground. You must keep using writing. It is the right thing to do. To the second response, you are correct. There may be more bad grades. That is part of what holding students accountable for their writing means. They must prove to you through writing that they understand accounting, or taxes, or economics, or pipe fitting, or marketing. The English faculty's task is to teach the language of language; your task is to teach students to use that language to write about your content area. If they cannot demonstrate competence in that skill, why is it that they deserve a college degree? Will an employer require less competence? Do law enforcement officers "tell" a final accident report? Does a real estate appraiser give an oral final estimate? Can any of us "call in" our taxes?

Questions for Discussion and Writing

1. Should instructors in other subjects give poor grades on papers that are written in poor English?
2. Many students feel that spelling is not important because computers and dictionaries are widely available. Do you agree?
3. Stories and novels are examples of creative writing. Is the quality of the writing important in creative works? Do creative writing students need to be concerned with revision?
4. Whose responsibility is it to make sure a student becomes competent in writing?
5. The writer refers to uses of English beyond the classroom. What are these uses? Why is competence in English important outside the English classroom?

Source: Innovation Abstracts (March 4, 1994). © 1994 by NISOD at the University of Texas at Austin. Reprinted by permission of the author.

APPENDICES

ARTICLES: A/AN AND THE

Count Nouns

SINGULAR

Count nouns in the singular require an article because a person is talking about either **a particular one** or **no particular one**.

For **a particular one**, use *the*:

The clock in *the* classroom is slow.

The sun is shining in *the* sky.   [one sun, one sky]

The book on *the* table belongs to *the* teacher.

For **no particular one**, use *a* before a consonant sound and *an* before a vowel sound:

A car has *an* engine.

An elephant is *a* big animal.

A perfume is supposed to have *a* nice fragrance.

His neighbor is *a* doctor.

A noun becomes a particular one when it is mentioned again:

She found *a* flute at *a* garage sale. *The* flute was actually in working condition.

Driving carelessly, he knocked down *a* mailbox. You can see *the* mailbox lying on the ground.

PLURAL

Since *a* and *an* are related to the idea of "one," they are used only for no particular one. There is no plural for this idea:

Singular: *a* dog

Plural: dogs   [no article]

Therefore, we use an article in the plural only for particular ones:

I like apples.   [no particular ones, so no article]

The apples on *the* neighbor's tree are ripe.   [particular ones]

Working students are busy people.   [no particular working students]

The working students in *the* night classes at this school look tired.   [particular working students]

Noncount Nouns

SINGULAR

There is no *a* or *an* before a noncount noun because a person cannot talk about no particular one of something that does not have one at all:

Meat and whole-grain bread are nutritious foods.

Honesty and good communication are important in *a* friendship.

Most people work for money.

The definite article, *the*, is possible in a specific situation or for a particular quantity of something:

> *The* honesty **of that candidate** was obvious.
>
> Did you take *the* money **that was on the table?**

PLURAL

There is no plural for noncount nouns because if we cannot talk about one of something, we cannot have two of it.

Notice that the use of the article in idiomatic expressions does not always follow the principles just outlined. Notice, too, that the same noun may be used in more than one way, and the use of the article changes accordingly:

> The flute was in good *condition*.   [noncount noun without an article]
>
> Bronchitis is *a* pathological *condition*.   [count noun indicating no particular one]

Keep in mind that we use *the* for something that both the speaker (or writer) and the listener (or reader) identify as the same one or ones.

E X E R C I S E

A-1

Using the principles explained and illustrated in the preceding discussion, add articles where necessary in the following sentences, and justify your answers. If you use *the*, identify what makes the noun particular.

1. _____ dog has _____ tail.

2. _____ nurse that you met yesterday works at _____ hospital on First Street.

3. _____ books on _____ bottom shelf are his.

4. Most people are afraid of _____ death.

5. _____ death of _____ famous person is usually reported on _____ front page of _____ newspaper.

6. She likes _____ fruit or _____ salad and _____ cup of _____ coffee for _____ lunch.

7. I see _____ cat climbing _____ tree. Now _____ cat is at _____ top of _____ tree.

8. There is _____ apple on _____ kitchen table. I will eat _____ apple while I make _____ dinner.

9. I went to _____ dinner given in honor of _____ new mayor of Riverview.

10. _____ women do not always like _____ housework.

11. He has had both _____ gastritis and _____ pneumonia during _____ past year.

12. Agatha Christie wrote _____ mystery stories.

13. We use _____ chalk to write on _____ chalkboards.

14. _____ metal is usually stronger than _____ plastic.

15. _____ oak and _____ pine are _____ kinds of _____ wood.

16. _____ photographer uses _____ camera.

17. It takes _____ money to get along in _____ life.

18. _____ heavy food gives _____ older people _____ indigestion.

19. _____ unemployment is _____ problem in _____ large cities.

20. She is _____ professor.

E X E R C I S E

Examine the use of the article, according to the preceding principles, in various selections in books and in magazine and newspaper articles (not advertisements, because these use some telegraphic language, with words omitted).

Forms of Other

The forms of _other_ can be adjectives (_another, the other, other, the other_) or pronouns (_another, the other, others, the others_). The use of the article with them is normal, except that _a/an_ is joined to _other_ (_another_):

1. She bought _another_ couch.   [She bought _a_ couch—a second one.]
   She already had _a_ couch, and she bought _another_.
2. _The other_ couch is a queen sleeper.
   The other is a queen sleeper.
3. She has had _other_ couches.   [Count noun _couches_ is in plural but signifies no particular ones, so no article.]
   She has had _others_.   [Count pronoun is in plural but signifies no particular ones, so no article.]
4. _The other_ couches were more expensive.   [_the ones_ she had before]
5. We have to go _another_ two miles.

In this last example, "two miles" is a singular idea representing a total distance, not two separate miles. The form _another_ (_an + other_) makes sense because the meaning is "an additional two miles" (an additional distance of two miles). Compare: "Two miles _is_ far to go when a person is not feeling well."

Expressions of Quantity

Watch the use of the article with expressions of quantity. The same principles apply:

Many students work at night.   [no particular students]

Many of *the* students at her college work at night.   [particular students]

Most children do not go to school in summer, but most of *the* children in fast-growing communities go to year-round school.

They generally eat little bread, and they ate little of *the* bread at dinner last night.

Notice in the preceding examples and in the next set of examples that *of* is used only with a particular quantity or particular ones. Keep in mind that a possessive adjective (*my, your,* and so on) or a demonstrative adjective (*this, that, these, those*) makes a noun particular:

Few *of* her books are in English.

Some *of* those items are on sale.

One student cannot speak for everyone, but one *of the* students at this school claims to do so.

Each student needs books and materials, and each *of the* students at that school also carries an assignment notebook.

Personal pronouns do not carry any distinction between particular and not particular:

Most of *it* comes in powder form.

All of *them* go to school.

Almost can modify an expression of quantity. The same article principles apply:

Almost all people do work of some kind.

Almost all of *the* people who were at *the* meeting speak Spanish.

Notice the following misuse of *almost*:

Almost presidents in the world are men.

The meaning, if any, is that real presidents are women!

Avoid using *a* or *an* or plural forms with noncount nouns. Some difficult ones are *information, advice, knowledge, homework, furniture,* and *equipment*:

He is always giving *advice* on things about which he has no *knowledge*.

There is a great deal of *information* in the college catalog.

There is a lot of *homework* for that class!

They bought some *furniture* and *equipment* for their new office.

PREPOSITIONS

The former rule against ending a sentence with a preposition no longer has much force. However, in writing, it is better to avoid placing the preposition at the end unless the sentence is overly formal otherwise. The sentence

> They did not understand what he was talking *about.*

communicates more effectively than

> They did not understand *about* what he was talking.

Avoid adding extra prepositions. Do not write sentences like this one:

> The archeologist opened the box *in* which the jewels had been kept *in.*

Omit the *in* at the end.

List of Common Prepositions

Some of the words in the following list of prepositions are not always prepositions:

> He is walking *around* the house.   [preposition]
>
> He is walking *around.*   [adverb modifying walking]
>
> She works *as* an interpreter.   [preposition]
>
> He ate everything in sight, *as* he usually did.   [conjunction starting a subordinate clause]
>
> He bought a car *like* hers.   [preposition]
>
> *Like* beginnings do not always lead to *like* endings.   [adjectives]

The word *like* has not been consistently accepted as a conjunction. Use *as, as if,* or *as though* instead:

> You can learn the guitar just *as* he did.   [not *like*]

PREPOSITIONS

about	beyond	onto
above	by	out
across	despite	outside
after	down	over
against	during	past
along	except	since
among	for	through
around	from	to
as	in	toward
at	inside	under
before	into	until
behind	like	up
below	near	upon
beneath	of	with
beside	off	within
between	on	without

PHRASAL PREPOSITIONS

according to	by way of	in place of
along with	due to	in spite of
apart from	except for	instead of
as to	in addition to	out of
because of	in front of	up to
by means of	in lieu of	

VERBS

There are three principal parts to an English verb:

1	2	3
go	went	gone
write	wrote	written

For regular verbs, the second and third parts are alike:

call	called	called
talk	talked	talked

The first part has several uses:

Infinitive: to go, to call
Present tense: I go, I call
Past negative and interrogative: I did not go. I did not call. Did I go? Did I call?
With modal auxiliaries: I may go. I may call.
To form the gerund and present participle: going, calling

The second part is used only for the simple past affirmative:

I *went* there yesterday.

I *called* at 8 o'clock this morning.

The third part is used with *have, has, had,* and *will have*:

They *have gone* to that restaurant several times.

He *has written* three letters so far this morning.

They *had called* before I left.

He *will have written* many letters by closing time.

Since the third part is the **past participle**, it is also used as a modifier:

The beautiful sunset, *gone* after just a few minutes, still made everyone feel better after the difficult day.

Her sister, *called* for jury duty, had to report to the courthouse early in the morning.

Present participles are active modifiers, whereas past participles are passive modifiers (see also the explanation of **active/passive** in Chapter 11):

The movie was *boring*.

Everyone was *bored* by the movie.

The past participle can be part of the verb in a passive sentence:

The letter *was written* by the secretary.

Some verbs are **transitive** (they have a direct object):

He buys old books.   ["books" is the object of "buys"]

Others are **intransitive** (they do not have a direct object):

The dogs are barking.

Others can be both:

> Airplanes fly.   [intransitive]
>
> Pilots fly airplanes.   [transitive, with "airplanes" as the direct object of the verb, "fly"]

Verbs that are intransitive only cannot be used for passive sentences. Avoid writing sentences like

> An important event was happen.   [*or:* "was happened"]

Some verbs have similar—and confusing—forms for their transitive and intransitive meanings:

1	2	3	Type
lie	lay	lain	intransitive
lay	laid	laid	transitive
sit	sat	sat	intransitive
set	set	set	transitive
rise	rose	risen	intransitive
raise	raised	raised	transitive

> They *lay* around the pool all day yesterday.
>
> They *laid* their napkins on the tray when the waiter came by.
>
> They *sat* near the window watching the sunset.
>
> They *set* their backpacks under a tree.
>
> They *rose* to applaud the performer.
>
> They *raised* many questions during the meeting.

Modal auxiliaries—*can, could, may, might, must, have to, should, ought to, had better*—are part of the verb. Notice that they are not followed by *to* except in the cases of *have to* and *ought to.*

The only modal that has a complete range of past, present, and future forms is *have to.*

Irregular Verbs

TABLE C-1   *Principal Parts of Common Irregular Verbs*

1	2	3
arise	arose	arisen
awake	awoke/awaked	awoke/awaked
be	was/were	been
bear	bore	borne/born
beat	beat	beat/beaten
become	became	become
begin	began	begun
bend	bent	bent
bet	bet	bet
bid	bid	bid
bind	bound	bound
bite	bit	bitten
bleed	bled	bled
blow	blew	blown
break	broke	broken
breed	bred	bred

bring	brought	brought
broadcast	broadcast	broadcast
build	built	built
burn	burnt/burned	burnt/burned
burst	burst	burst
buy	bought	bought
cast	cast	cast
catch	caught	caught
choose	chose	chosen
cling	clung	clung
come	came	come
cost	cost	cost
creep	crept	crept
cut	cut	cut
deal	dealt	dealt
dig	dug	dug
dive	dove/dived	dived
do	did	done
draw	drew	drawn
drink	drank	drunk
drive	drove	driven
eat	ate	eaten
fall	fell	fallen
feed	fed	fed
feel	felt	felt
fight	fought	fought
find	found	found
fit	fit	fit
flee	fled	fled
fling	flung	flung
fly	flew	flown
forbid	forbade	forbidden
forecast	forecast	forecast
forget	forgot	forgotten
forsake	forsook	forsaken
freeze	froze	frozen
get	got	gotten
give	gave	given
go	went	gone
grind	ground	ground
grow	grew	grown
hang	hung	hung
have	had	had
hear	heard	heard
hide	hid	hidden
hit	hit	hit
hold	held	held
hurt	hurt	hurt
keep	kept	kept
know	knew	known
lay	laid	laid
lead	led	led
leave	left	left
let	let	let
lie	lay	lain
light	lit/lighted	lit/lighted
lose	lost	lost
make	made	made
mean	meant	meant
meet	met	met
mislay	mislaid	mislaid
mistake	mistook	mistaken
pay	paid	paid
put	put	put
quit	quit	quit
read	read	read
rid	rid/ridded	rid/ridded
ride	rode	ridden
ring	rang	rung

rise	rose	risen
run	ran	run
say	said	said
see	saw	seen
seek	sought	sought
sell	sold	sold
send	sent	sent
set	set	set
shake	shook	shaken
shed	shed	shed
shine	shone	shone
shoot	shot	shot
show	showed	shown
shrink	shrank	shrunk/shrunken
shut	shut	shut
sing	sang	sung
sink	sank	sunk
sit	sat	sat
slay	slew	slain
sleep	slept	slept
slide	slid	slid
slit	slit	slit
sow	sowed	sown
speak	spoke	spoken
speed	sped/speeded	sped/speeded
spend	spent	spent
spin	spun	spun
spit	spit/spat	spit/spat
split	split	split
spread	spread	spread
spring	sprang	sprung
stand	stood	stood
steal	stole	stolen
stick	stuck	stuck
sting	stung	stung
stink	stunk	stunk
strike	struck	struck
string	strung	strung
strive	strove	striven
swear	swore	sworn
sweep	swept	swept
swim	swam	swum
swing	swung	swung
take	took	taken
teach	taught	taught
tear	tore	torn
tell	told	told
think	thought	thought
throw	threw	thrown
thrust	thrust	thrust
tread	trod	trod/trodden
understand	understood	understood
undertake	undertook	undertaken
upset	upset	upset
wake	woke/waked	woken/waked
wear	wore	worn
weave	wove	woven
weep	wept	wept
win	won	won
wind	wound	wound
withdraw	withdrew	withdrawn
wring	wrung	wrung
write	wrote	written

NOTES: Some British forms are different from the standard American forms.
The verb *hang* is regular in the meaning of *execute*.
The verb *lie* is regular in the meaning of *say something untrue*.

Verb Forms

TABLE C-2

Verb Forms for a Sample Regular Verb

AFFIRMATIVE	NEGATIVE	INTERROGATIVE
Simple Present		
I talk	I do not talk	Do I talk?
You talk	You do not talk	Do you talk?
He talks	He does not talk	Does he talk?
We talk	We do not talk	Do we talk?
You talk	You do not talk	Do you talk?
They talk	They do not talk	Do they talk?
Present Progressive		
I am talking	I am not talking	Am I talking?
You are talking	You are not talking	Are you talking?
He is talking	He is not talking	Is he talking?
We are talking	We are not talking	Are we talking?
You are talking	You are not talking	Are you talking?
They are talking	They are not talking	Are they talking?
Simple Past		
I talked	I did not talk	Did I talk?
You talked	You did not talk	Did you talk?
He talked	He did not talk	Did he talk?
We talked	We did not talk	Did we talk?
You talked	You did not talk	Did you talk?
They talked	They did not talk	Did they talk?
Past Progressive		
I was talking	I was not talking	Was I talking?
You were talking	You were not talking	Were you talking?
He was talking	He was not talking	Was he talking?
We were talking	We were not talking	Were we talking?
You were talking	You were not talking	Were you talking?
They were talking	They were not talking	Were they talking?
Simple Future		
I will talk	I will not talk	Will I talk?
You will talk	You will not talk	Will you talk?
He will talk	He will not talk	Will he talk?
We will talk	We will not talk	Will we talk?
You will talk	You will not talk	Will you talk?
They will talk	They will not talk	Will they talk?
Future Progressive		
I will be talking	I will not be talking	Will I be talking?
You will be talking	You will not be talking	Will you be talking?
He will be talking	He will not be talking	Will he be talking?
We will be talking	We will not be talking	Will we be talking?
You will be talking	You will not be talking	Will you be talking?
They will be talking	They will not be talking	Will they be talking?
Present Perfect		
I have talked	I have not talked	Have I talked?
You have talked	You have not talked	Have you talked?
He has talked	He has not talked	Has he talked?
We have talked	We have not talked	Have we talked?
You have talked	You have not talked	Have you talked?
They have talked	They have not talked	Have they talked?
Present Perfect Progressive		
I have been talking	I have not been talking	Have I been talking?
You have been talking	You have not been talking	Have you been talking?
He has been talking	He has not been talking	Has he been talking?
We have been talking	We have not been talking	Have we been talking?
You have been talking	You have not been talking	Have you been talking?
They have been talking	They have not been talking	Have they been talking?

Past Perfect

I had talked	I had not talked	Had I talked?
You had talked	You had not talked	Had you talked?
He had talked	He had not talked	Had he talked?
We had talked	We had not talked	Had we talked?
You had talked	You had not talked	Had you talked?
They had talked	They had not talked	Had they talked?

Past Perfect Progressive

I had been talking	I had not been talking	Had I been talking?
You had been talking	You had not been talking	Had you been talking?
He had been talking	He had not been talking	Had he been talking?
We had been talking	We had not been talking	Had we been talking?
You had been talking	You had not been talking	Had you been talking?
They had been talking	They had not been talking	Had they been talking?

Future Perfect

I will have talked	I will not have talked	Will I have talked?
You will have talked	You will not have talked	Will you have talked?
He will have talked	He will not have talked	Will he have talked?
We will have talked	We will not have talked	Will we have talked?
You will have talked	You will not have talked	Will you have talked?
They will have talked	They will not have talked	Will they have talked?

Future Perfect Progressive

I will have been talking	I will not have been talking	Will I have been talking?
You will have been talking	You will not have been talking	Will you have been talking?
He will have been talking	He will not have been talking	Will he have been talking?
We will have been talking	We will not have been talking	Will we have been talking?
You will have been talking	You will not have been talking	Will you have been talking?
They will have been talking	They will not have been talking	Will they have been talking?

English Verb Tenses: A Clarification for Nonnative Speakers

English verb tenses actually make sense. They are oriented around past, present, and future time (*tense* means "time"), and they are based on three key concepts: time period represented, focal point in time, and action in progress or not in progress.

TIME PERIOD REPRESENTED

If we are talking about something we did last month, the **time period** represented is "last month," including the entire month. Whether we say one thing happened or two things happened or many things happened, the time period remains that one month in the past. The time period can be very long (for example, an entire century) or very short (for example, ten seconds). The time period can be past, present, or future time, or it can be the time preceding one of these three.

FOCAL POINT IN TIME

If someone says he or she has always spoken English, the person is talking about the time period that goes from infancy to the present (when the person makes the statement). In other words, the reference is to what has happened so far—that is, up to the present—and the **focal point in time** is the time up to the present. Accordingly, we have six possible focal points in time:

1. **past**: used for something that happened during a specific time period in the past
2. **present**: used for something that happens during the present time
3. **future**: used for something that will happen during a specific time period in the future

4. **up to the past**: used for something that had happened before a specific time in the past
5. **up to the present**: used for something that has happened before the present time
6. **up to the future**: used for something that will have happened before a specific time in the future

In items 4, 5, and 6 on the preceding list, the important time is the focal point before the past, present, or future. The starting time may be at any point before that, and it need not be known. If a person says, for example, "I have owned several houses," we do not learn when the situation of the statement started (that is, when the person first became the owner of a house).

Our focal point in time can also be a period of time in the past (item 1), a period of time including the present (item 2), or a period of time in the future (item 3).

ACTION IN PROGRESS OR NOT IN PROGRESS

If we say, for example, "we are writing," we are talking about an action in progress at the present moment (the moment when the statement is made). If we want to indicate something that we do from time to time, we say "we write." Similarly, speaking of a time in the past, we can use "we were writing" to indicate an action in progress at a specific time in the past; in contrast, "we wrote" indicates something we did one or more times during some specific time in the past. In the same way, "we will be writing" indicates something in progress at a specific time in the future, but "we will write" shows something we will do one or more times during some specific time in the future.

All six time periods (past, present, and future, and the time preceding each one) have one form for an action not in progress (numbers 1 to 6 in Table C-3) and one for an action in progress (numbers 7 to 12 in Table C-3).

As shown in Table C-3, each of the three basic time divisions (past, present, and future) has two possible focal points: one **during** the time, and one **before** the time. This is why we have six (three time periods × two focal points for each one) verb tenses in English. Using the same numbering that we used in Table C-3 and in the preceding explanations, we have the following simple forms of the six verb tenses:

1. **Past** (also called simple past or preterite)
2. **Present** (also called simple present)
3. **Future** (also called simple future)
4. **Past perfect** (also called pluperfect)
5. **Present perfect**
6. **Future perfect**

We also have the following progressive forms of the six verb tenses:

7. **Past progressive**
8. **Present progressive**
9. **Future progressive**
10. **Past perfect progressive**
11. **Present perfect progressive**
12. **Future perfect progressive**

Here are some additional examples, each of which uses a different tense of the regular verb *talk*. The sentence numbers correspond to the numbers of the verb

TABLE C-3   *Verb Tense Chart*

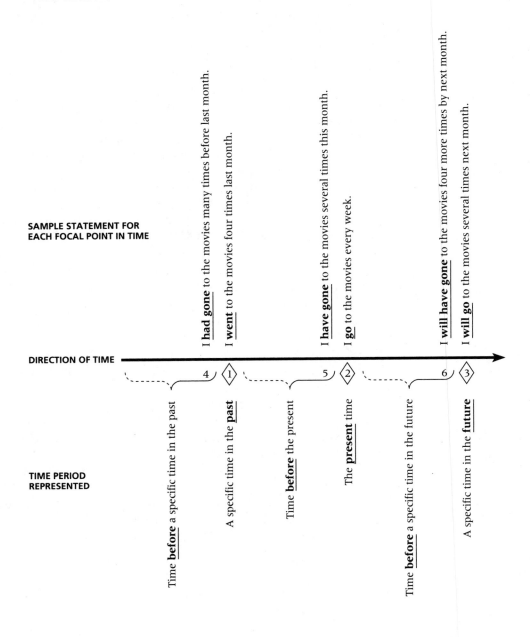

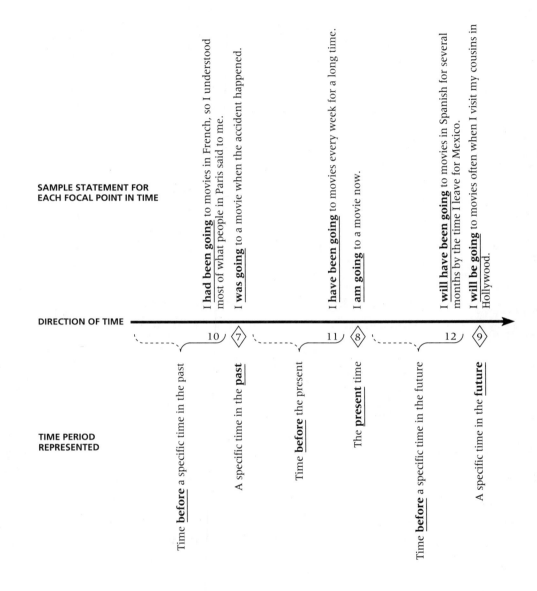

SAMPLE STATEMENT FOR EACH FOCAL POINT IN TIME

I **had been going** to movies in French, so I understood most of what people in Paris said to me.

I **was going** to a movie when the accident happened.

I **have been going** to movies every week for a long time.

I **am going** to a movie now.

I **will have been going** to movies in Spanish for several months by the time I leave for Mexico.

I **will be going** to movies often when I visit my cousins in Hollywood.

DIRECTION OF TIME

10 ⟨7⟩ 11 ⟨8⟩ 12 ⟨9⟩

Time **before** a specific time in the past

A specific time in the **past**

Time **before** the present

The **present** time

Time **before** a specific time in the future

A specific time in the **future**

TIME PERIOD REPRESENTED

tenses in Table C-3 and in the preceding explanations. As you read the examples, refer to the table to identify each time period represented and each focal point of the statement.

1. I talked to my supervisor yesterday.
2. I talk to people every day.
3. I will talk to some students tomorrow.
4. I had talked to the musician on the phone before I met him.
5. I have talked to several people today.
6. I will have talked to each member individually before the committee meets.
7. I was talking to a neighbor when the phone rang.
8. I am talking right now.
9. I will be talking to someone at this time tomorrow.
10. I had been talking on the phone for over an hour when someone knocked at the door.
11. I have been talking on the phone for over an hour.
12. I will have been talking for over an hour by the time I finish.

E X E R C I S E

Using the numbering system in Table C-3, number the following sentences according to the time period represented, the focal point of the statement, and action in/not in progress.

1. I always write letters to friends during the holidays.
2. I am writing a letter now.
3. I wrote to a friend last week.
4. I was writing when the timer sounded.
5. I will write to my grandmother next week.
6. I will be writing when they get here.
7. I have written several letters today.
8. I have been writing since 9 o'clock.
9. I had written two letters before the mail came.
10. I had been writing for a long time before the mail came.
11. I will have written five letters by the end of the day today.
12. I will have been writing for seven hours by the time I stop.

SOME COMMON WORD COMBINATIONS

The word combinations in the following list can be used as formulas. For example, we can say that we worry about *somebody* or *something*. This means that we can substitute another form that names:

He worries about *money*.

He worries about his *girlfriend*.

He worries about *doing* difficult assignments.

He worries about *gaining* weight.

to be accustomed to *something*

to be acquainted with *somebody/
something*

to admit doing *something*

to take advantage of *something/somebody*

to give advice to *somebody* about
something

to advise *somebody* about *something*

to advise *somebody* to do *something*

to affect *somebody/something*

to agree to do *something*

to allow *somebody* to do *something*

to arrive *in/at*

to pay attention to *somebody/something*

to avoid doing *something*

to begin doing *something*

to begin to do *something*

to be bored with *something*

to bring about *something*   [cause]

to bring up *somebody*   [raise]

to bring up *something*
    [introduce a topic]

to be capable of doing *something*

to take care of *somebody/something*

a change in *something/somebody*

to be composed of *something*

to consider doing *something*

to consist of *something*

to continue doing *something*

to continue to do *something*

to convince *somebody* of *something*

to convince *somebody* to do *something*

to be convinced of *something*

to count on *somebody/something*

to decide on *something*

to decide to do *something*

to depend on *somebody/something*

to deserve *something*

to deserve to do *something*

different from *somebody/something*

to discriminate against *somebody*

to dislike doing *something*

to distinguish *somebody/something* from
    somebody/something

to have an effect on *somebody/something*

to enjoy doing *something*

to be equipped with *something*

to escape from *something*

to excel in *something*

to excuse *somebody* from doing *something*

to have an excuse for *something*

to expect *somebody* to do *something*

to be exposed to *something/somebody*

to fail to do *something*

to be familiar with *somebody/something*

to feel like doing *something*

to feel like *something*

to finish doing *something*

to forget doing *something*
[not remember having done it]

to forget to do *something*   [not do it]

to hope for *something*

to hope to do *something*

to influence *somebody*

to insist on doing *something*

to intend to do *something*

to be interested in doing *something*

to be interested in *something/somebody*

to be involved in *something*

to keep doing *something*

to be known for *something*

to lack *something*

a lack of *something*

to like to do *something*

to like doing *something*

to listen to *something/somebody*

to look at *something/somebody*

to look forward to *something*

to look forward to doing *something*

to manage to do *something*

to mention doing *something*

to mention *something*

to mind doing *something*

to mind *something*

to be motivated to do *something*

to be opposed to *somebody/something*

to be opposed to doing *something*

to participate in *something*

to permit *somebody* to do *something*

to prefer doing *something*

to prefer to do *something*

to pretend to do *something*   [to give out
   a false impression of doing *something*]

to prevent from *something*

to prohibit from *something*

to provide *somebody* with *something*

to reach *something*

to be related to *somebody/something*

to be relevant to *something*

to rely on *somebody/something*

to remember doing *something*   [recall]

to remember to do *something*
   [not forget]

to be responsible for *something*

to result in *something*

to be satisfied with *something*

to start doing *something*

to start do to *something*

to stop doing *something*

to stop *somebody* from doing
   something

to succeed in doing *something*

to be supposed to do *something*

to thank *somebody* for *something*

to understand *somebody*'s doing
   something

to be used to *somebody/something*

to want *somebody* to do *something*

to worry about *somebody/something*

A N S W E R   K E Y

Chapter 1

1-1 The sentences should be arranged in the following order: 4, 7, 6, 9, 5, 8, 2, 3, 10, 1.

People approach the task of writing a composition in different ways. First of all, there are those who panic. The blank page stifles their creative powers. As a result, they find it difficult to get any words on paper. Next, there are those who "just start writing." These writers often feel that they only lose time if they try to organize their ideas first. And they also hope, all too frequently, that by simply going back and making a few corrections and changes, they can produce good writing. Finally, there are those who list ideas in order to gather a body of relevant information. They take time to think about their subject and write down everything that comes to mind about it. These writers can then structure their ideas and write a coherent composition.

1-2
1. People's *approaches* to writing
2. That they are *different*
3. Sentence 4
4. Sentence 4 is more general than the others, and it brings up an idea that is developed in all the other sentences.
5. The idea that people's approaches to writing are *different*
6. The three different approaches discussed are (1) "list ideas"; (2) "just start writing," and (3) "panic."
7. Sentences 3, 5, and 7
8. 7, 5, 3
9. The transitions "first of all," "next," and "finally" make the order clear.
10. They are also distinguished by the parallel wording: "there are those who." Furthermore, each of the three sentences is a *general* statement that *brings up* an approach.
11. They go from the approach that produces no writing, through the approach that produces something, to the approach that is most likely to produce good writing—that is, from negative to positive, or from no results to good results.
12. More details and explanations are given on each approach.

13. It explains *why* many people panic.
14. It tells *what* typically *results* from the panic. Notice the transition "as a result."
15. They explain *why* people "just start writing." Notice the transition "and," which connects two comparable ideas: the two *reasons* for the "just start writing" approach.
16. They explain *how* a person who follows this approach proceeds.
17. Both describe beliefs of those who "just start writing." The transitions "and" and "also" relate "these writers often *feel that . . . and . . . they also hope* that . . . ."
18. It acts as a transitional device to refer to the writers mentioned in sentences 3 and 5, respectively.

1-3
1. Latin
2. There are *reasons* for bringing Latin back into the school.
3. A knowledge of Latin helps people (1) build their vocabulary in English, (2) understand English grammar, and (3) develop language awareness.
4. No. The topic, Latin, reappears in the concluding sentence, and so does the controlling idea, stated in other words: the "*reasons* for bringing Latin back into the school" in the topic sentence becomes "*should* have its place in the classroom" in the conclusion. Notice also that the words "Latin . . . is very much alive in English" *summarize* the reasons, and "it should have its place in the classroom" is the logical conclusion. The paragraph describes reasons, or causes; and the conclusion, beginning with "Thus," states the effect, or result.
5. Latin: reasons for bringing it back into the school
   - I. Helps one build vocabulary in English
     - A. Over half of English words derived from Latin
     - B. New words created primarily from Latin elements
   - II. Helps one understand English grammar
     - A. Example: Understanding of noun cases helps with subject/verb agreement

III. Helps one acquire language awareness
  A. Different levels of language appropriate in different situations
  B. Sense of words is developed with study of language such as Latin
IV. Conclusion: It should have its place in the classroom

In informal outlining it is often appropriate to use a single subtopic (as with II. A. in the preceding example) to indicate an example, definition, or further explanation.

1-4
1. There are no explanations or illustrations to enable the reader to understand what is stated in the main supporting sentences. The controlling idea, "dislike," is not developed with reasons. The paragraph communicates very little meaning; it more nearly resembles a list than a paragraph.

1-5
1. This paragraph is much better because it gives the necessary reasons.
2. The tone of the paragraph is generally less formal than that of most college writing. Also, the case against these types of shows would be stronger if they were presented as objectionable to many television viewers rather than a matter of personal dislike to the writer alone.
3. The conclusion contains the topic, "TV shows," and the word "these" indicates "the ones the writer *dislikes*"—the controlling idea. The *result* of what is explained in the paragraph appears in the form of *action taken*: the writer changes channels.
4. TV shows: dislike
  I. Violent police dramas
    A. Senseless violence
    B. Lead children to accept violence as normal
  II. Soap operas
    A. Situations forced
    B. Actors and actresses lack genuine emotions
    C. Stories pointless
  III. Game shows involving couples
    A. Contestants are baited
    B. They reveal inappropriate personal information
    C. Programs degrade participants and insult viewers
  IV. Conclusion: Change channels

Your outlines may vary somewhat from the sample outlines given. For example, in the preceding outline for the paragraph on TV shows, the subentries for soap operas can also be broken down as follows:
  II. Soap operas
    A. Lack of reality
      1. Situations forced
      2. Actors and actresses lack genuine emotions
    B. Stories pointless
5. A paragraph showing greater objectivity could be written on shows that are frequent targets of viewers' objections. Such a paragraph could begin with the following topic sentence: "Many people find several types of television shows objectionable." Specific examples involving actual shows would also make the paragraph more convincing.

1-6
1. The paragraph is unsatisfactory because some of the sentences are off the subject.
2. They are all about the writer and his or her personal situation rather than the need for familiarity with the college catalog.
3. The sentences giving personal information about the writer would be appropriate in writing for readers who know the writer personally (the writer, relatives, or friends). Thus, these sentences would be acceptable in a diary, a journal, or a letter to someone close.
4. Yes. If we take out the "I"-oriented sentences, the remaining ones develop the reasons why students should be familiar with the college catalog.
5. The topic ("catalog") is stated, and the word "knows" reminds us of the controlling idea, "should become *familiar*." The concluding statement also shows the effect, or result, of familiarity with the contents of the college catalog: the student will "save frustration."
6. Take out the "I"-oriented sentences that do not add anything useful, such as those about the dorm room and the sister. Reword the sentences about interesting subjects and about wasting time so that they relate to students as a class of people rather than to the writer alone. Add detail to explain the "wealth of other information."

1-7
1. Owning a car
2. There are *reasons* for preferring *not* to own one.
3. Owning a car involves "expense," "liability," and "putting up with requests for rides."
4. "First"; "another problem"; "last"
5. The major costs of owning a vehicle are listed and described.
6. The extent of the liability is explained, and an example of some possible consequences is given.
7. The explanations indicate *why* giving rides can be a problem.
8. They *summarize* the problems of owning an automobile: expense, liability, and putting up with requests for rides.
9. The *result* is that owning a car can be "a mixed blessing."

1-8
1. The *overcrowding* of classes
2. It *has negative effects* on student learning.
3. Overcrowded classes are "more difficult to teach"; they are "difficult to arrange"; the students in them "are less well served."
4. "First of all"; "another disadvantage"; "a final problem"
5. Each key idea is supported with information showing *why* there is a problem.
6. Learning is sacrificed.
7. Because we are facing keen international competition, cutting education budgets may be false economy.
8. It would be better not to cut education budgets.

1-9
1. Parent-oriented child raising
2. This approach *has* a number of long-lasting *negative effects* on children.
3. Children grow up with a distorted self-image; they do not learn to communicate; it is difficult for them to learn to trust anyone.
4. Each key idea is contained in the topic sentence of a separate body paragraph.
5. It provides a *summarizing idea* for the key supporting ideas: "victims": people who in childhood have acquired a low self-image and lack of ability to communicate and trust are victims of their childhood. The *result* of the parents' misconception is also identified: the children do not show real caring.

1-10
1. T: reforestation projects; C.I.: Government *should sponsor* these.
   Development: The reasons for sponsoring reforestation projects
2. T: entertainment habits; C.I.: changed by VCRs
   Development: In what ways VCRs have changed the habits
3. T: eating disorders; C.I.: greater awareness
   Development: What awareness has developed, or in what ways greater awareness is evident
4. T: shared custody; C.I.: detrimental
   Development: Ways in which shared custody is detrimental
5. T: legislation; C.I.: giving *greater opportunities* to persons lacking power
   Development: What legislation being passed gives greater opportunities
6. T: articles in news magazines; C.I.: contain *misleading* information
   Development: What misleading information has appeared in articles
7. T: big city; C.I.: noisy
   Development: Ways in which the big city is noisy
8. T: essay writing in nonacademic subjects; C.I.: appropriate
   Development: reasons for including essay writing
9. T: movements; C.I.: indicate growing concern
   Development: Ways in which the movements indicate a growing concern.
10. T: knowledge of history; C.I.: *valuable* in journalism
    Development: Ways in which a knowledge of history is valuable in journalistic work
11. T: teaching children not to waste materials; C.I.: *can* be done
    Development: How children can be taught
12. T: teaching children not to waste materials; C.I.: *should* be done
    Development: Why children should be taught
13. T: shopping mall; C.I.: *more* than a group of stores
    Development: In what ways it is more than a group of stores

14. T: slavery; C.I.: still exists
Development: In what ways slavery still exists
15. T: adjustment to life in a foreign country; C.I.: difficult
Development: Ways in which adjustment is difficult

Chapter 2
2-1 Ideas will vary.

2-2
1. *Switzerland;* the others are (European capital) cities.
2. *Wages;* the others are fringe benefits.
3. *Skillet;* the others are oven dishes.
4. *Effort;* the others are synonyms. An effort is what is usually required to attain a goal, aim, or objective.
5. *Hope;* the others are negative feelings. Hope is positive.
6. *Abuse;* the others are positive ways to treat someone or something. Abuse is negative.
7. *Can opener;* the others are general-purpose tools. A can opener is a kitchen utensil.
8. *Disadvantaged;* the others are positive character traits in a person. Disadvantaged, a negative idea, describes a person according to circumstances, not character.
9. *Similarity;* the others are synonyms. Similarity names a kind of relationship, not the abstract idea of relationship.
10. *Hear;* the others are active processes. Hearing is passive. The active idea related to *hear* is listen.

2-3
1. *Cook* is more general; it includes the others.
2. *Art* is more general; it includes the others.
3. *Pollution* is more general; it includes the others.
4. *Projectile* is more general; it includes the others.
5. *Pay* is more general; it includes the others.
6. *Work* is more general; it includes the others.
7. *Toys* is more general; however, it does not include the others.
8. *Curtains* is more specific.
9. *Clothing* is more general; it includes the others.
10. *Education* is more general; it includes the others.

2-4 Group 1: 1, 2, 5, and 6
Group 2: 3, 4, and 7

2-5 Why: 3, 4, and 7
How: 1, 2, 5, and 6

2-6 Why: 3, 4, 8, and 9
What: 5, 6, and 10
How: 1, 2, and 7

2-7 What: 1, 2, and 6
How: 3, 7, and 9
Why: 4, 5, and 8

2-8 Riverview Community College: advantages
I. High academic standards
 A. Small classes taught by highly motivated instructors
 B. Wide variety of transferrable courses
II. Well-planned facilities
 A. Large, well-stocked library
 B. Ample, affordable cafeteria
 C. Sufficiently large, well-lit parking lots
III. Convenient location
 A. Near freeway exit
 B. Near major shopping center

2-9 Answers will vary. Some possibilities:
Group 1: Benefits of [or "Reasons for doing" or "Advantages of"]
 Entertaining
 Relaxing
 Educational
 Learn skills
 Enjoy life
 Motivation to improve skills
 Stimulate imagination
 Bring out of bad mood
 Discover interests
 Money-making potential
Group 2: Reasons for doing or advantages of would include the same ones as benefits of
Group 3: Description of a particular hobby
 How to do a particular hobby
Group 4: Description of a particular hobby
 Comparison of different hobbies
Group 5: Affect life
 Enjoy life
 Bring out of a bad mood
 Entertaining
Group 6: Affect life
 Learn skills
 Money-making potential

2-10 Some possible answers:
1. More fresh food, more vegetables, more whole grains, more fiber, more lean meats, less fat, less sugar, less salt, etc.
2. More books on healthful diet in bookstores, more diet-oriented treatment programs, more emphasis on healthful aspects of food products in media advertising and on packaging, etc.
3. To avoid health problems, to feel better, to look better, etc.

2-11 Some possible answers:
1. Students can be classified by degree goal, age group, attitude toward college, reasons for attending, motivation, study habits, school status, social status, finances, participation in extracurricular activities, etc.
2. Automobiles can be classified by type of body, size, comfort, cost, quality, target market, resale value, features, where made, safety record, repair record, etc.

2-12 Some possible answers:
Group 1: Conditions (= what conditions)
  Salary
  Hours
Group 2: Search (= how)
  How to get
Group 3: Search (= why)
  Money
  Survive
Group 4: Frustration (= causes of frustration)
  Boring
  Don't use potential
Group 5: Opportunities
  Meet people
  Challenges
  Creative ones
  Rewards
  Independence
  Self-esteem
Group 6: Coworkers
  Bosses
Group 7: Goals
  Independence
  Money
  Job that fits abilities
  Self-esteem
Group 8: Importance
  Why needed

Group 9: Why people change (negative—causes)
  Frustrations (as in group 4 above)
  Pressures
  Conditions
  Bosses
  Sacrifices
Group 10: Why people change (positive—effects desired)
  Enjoy/earn
  Rewards
  Goals (as in group 7 above)
  Opportunities (as in group 5 above)
  Status

2-13 See explanations in text.

2-14 See explanations in text.

2-15 Effects of water pollution are dangerous.
 I. Killing or harming life forms in the water itself
    A. Kills through direct toxic effects
    B. Kills indirectly by destroying food sources
       1. Disrupts ecosystem
    C. Causes genetic mutations
 II. Endangering health of humans and animals that drink it
    A. Introduces dangerously toxic substances directly into body
    B. Contributes to buildup in body of substances that would be harmless in small quantities
    C. Destroys resistance
    D. Adds to body's work in eliminating waste products
 III. Evaporating, it pollutes atmosphere, creating vicious circle
    A. Rises during evaporation, contributing to air pollution problem
    B. Combines with other pollutants in air, bringing them down with rain

Chapter 3

3-1 See explanations in text.

3-2 1. b
2. d
3. a

3-3 See explanations in text.

3-4 1. There is no statement indicating the purpose of the paragraph. The sentences give a series of recommendations.

2. There is a topic but no controlling idea; no statement about freeways is developed in the paragraph.

3. There is no statement indicating the purpose of the paragraph. Instead, the writer presents a chronology.

4. There is no statement indicating the purpose of the paragraph. Instead, there is a chain of causes and effects.

5. The purpose of the paragraph is not stated. There seems to be more than one point.

3-5   Only paragraph 3 has appropriate support for a statement. A possible statement: "The tourists had some unique experiences on their first day in Paris." Paragraph 1 consists of a series of unsupported arguments. Paragraph 2 presents random information on freeways. Paragraph 4 lacks necessary explanations. Paragraph 5 has points that go in different directions.

3-6   Some possible answers:
1. Teachers use widely differing methods in presenting information to students.
2. The VCR has brought new entertainment opportunities to the home.
3. A variety of visitors show up in the park on any nice afternoon.

3-7   Statements 2 and 4 are convincingly supported.

3-8   1. What has happened to the writer does not necessarily indicate that the rising tuition costs are creating a hardship for students in general.
2. One example does not prove a general statement.
3. The writer should be illustrating *what* opportunities are not being utilized, not *why* they are not being utilized. The information is also outdated.
4. The department of fisheries in a state with an important fishing industry may be more concerned with the sale of fish than with its food value.

3-9   1. a. What is the laser?
b. Who invented it?
c. Where was it invented?
d. When was it invented?
e. Why was it invented?
f. How was it invented?
2. a. What kind of instrument is the flute?

b. How is it played?
c. What differences are there between flutes?
3. a. How did the French Revolution start?
b. What led to the outbreak of the revolution?
c. What was the result?

3-10   Answers will vary. Some possibilities:
Street lighting has been reduced.
Police protection has been reduced.
Streets are swept less frequently.

3-11   Answers will vary. Some possibilities:
Preread
Read straight through
Skim

3-12   Answers will vary. Some possibilities:
Nostalgia for the past
Desire for adventure
Appeal of a close, communicating family

3-13   Answers will vary. Some possibilities:
Gain additional knowledge that is beneficial in and out of school.
Discover interests and aptitudes.
Develop habit of using spare time in a positive way.

3-14   Answers will vary. Some possibilities:
Lubricating the vehicle
Checking tire conditions and pressure
Checking brakes
Checking battery
Checking fluids

3-15   Answers will vary. Some possibilities:
Being careless with fire
Improperly cutting trees
Interfering with water runoff patterns
Littering

3-16   Answers will vary. Some possibilities:
Both show addictive behaviors.
Both have problems getting along with those around them.
Both are in denial of reality.

3-17   Compare your definition with the one in your dictionary.

3-18   See explanations in the text.

3-19   Key supporting ideas will vary.
1. *what:*
   Stand and Deliver
   Dead Poets' Society

2. *why:*

> More involved in school
>
> Can learn skills useful in later school work and adult life
>
> Can discover personal interests and abilities through exposure to various computer programs

3. *how:*

> Eat a lot of vegetables.
>
> Season with herbs, spices, and low-calorie dressings.
>
> Eat fish and lean, skinless chicken and turkey.

3-20 1. Key ideas should indicate *why.*
   a. Good
   b. Good
   c. The fact that more people could carpool does not explain *why* the city needs a rapid transit system. It is a separate problem.
   d. *What* should be done to buses does not explain *why* the city needs a rapid transit system.
   e. Not good; this is what *would happen* if the city had an efficient system.

2. Key ideas should indicate *why.*
   a. Good
   b. Good
   c. That reservations for the theater are necessary does not explain *why* New York City is a good place to go for a vacation.

3. Key ideas should indicate *why.*
   a. Good
   b. Good
   c. Not good; the need to conserve resources is an environmental issue, not a financial one.

4. Key ideas should indicate *why.*
   a. Indicates *how,* not *why*
   b. Indicates *how,* not *why*
   c. Indicates *how,* not *why*
   d. Good

5. Key ideas should indicate *what.*
   a. Good
   b. Good
   c. Good
   d. This explains *how* to reduce costs, not *what* is expensive.

3-21 1. a. Not good; better: "Many people do not have any other means of transportation."
   b. Not good; better: "Many people cannot afford cars."

2. a. Not good; too many bosses does not necessarily mean too few lower-level employees; better: "If money is going for bosses instead of lower-level employees, efficiency is impeded."
   b. Good

3. a. Good
   b. Good
   c. Good
   d. Not good; we are concerned with the words that stay, not with those that go; better: "Even though trends come and go, some of the words they bring stay in the language."

4. a. Good
   b. Good
   c. Not good; *when* children use them does not explain *why* they should be banned; better: "Children using them on the Fourth of July are often injured." This could be used as a detail to explain the problem brought up in item b.
   d. Not good; that manufacturers state fireworks are safe does not indicate why they should be banned; better: "Users of fireworks often ignore the manufacturers' safety recommendations."

3-22 1. a, c, d, b
   2. e, b, a, c, d
   3. c, b, a, d

3-23 1. a, b, d, c
   2. d, c, b, a

3-24 1. a, c, d, b; concrete–abstract
   2. b, d, f, c, e, a, g; chronological
   3. d, a, b, c; order of importance
   4. d, c, f, b, a, e; spatial
   5. b, d, c, a; general–particular

3-25 1. spatial
   2. chronological
   3. order of importance
   4. general to particular, also considering order of importance and abstract to concrete
   5. concrete to abstract, also considering order of importance and particular to general

Chapter 4

4-1 1. T: plan

CI: important part of the prewriting process

KSIs: easier to evaluate content of composition in outline

outline shows relationships between ideas

easier to make changes in outline, saving time and frustration

2. T: college budget cuts

CI: making goal of post-secondary education difficult

KSIs: students not able to get classes—need extra years

greater financial burden on students

3. T: slaves

CI: declared free by President Lincoln

KSIs: enthusiastically received

will not affect all slaves

4. T: life

CI: has more to offer now

KSIs: longer

offers more than just working, eating, and sleeping

more communication

4-2 See explanations in text.

4-3 Sample outlines:

1. Tasks in learning to drive—difficult

I. Learn to control the car

A. Find correct pedal without looking

B. Step on pedal not too hard or too lightly

C. Steer

D. Do all of the above at the same time

II. Keep track of situation on road

A. Normal driving plus potential emergency situations

III. Get used to following rules of road

A. Learn signs in handbook

1. Look different on road

B. Master conventions for changing lanes, turning, stopping

IV. Conclusion: No wonder some give up on learning

2. Ways of conducting class—different

I. Lecture—traditional

A. Teacher has information students need to learn.

B. Students must listen, take notes, memorize as much as possible.

C. Student progress measured by how much information students can reproduce on tests.

II. Group discussion

A. Teacher suggests ideas for groups to consider.

1. Periodically recapitulates and synthesizes

B. Teacher provides limited information.

C. Little assessment

III. Structure so that students arrive at understanding of certain concepts

A. Teacher guides students to understanding of content.

1. Suitable materials

2. Appropriate questions

B. Teacher tests students' active comprehension of concepts.

IV. Conclusion: So different but all common

3. Factors—have contributed to hostilities in Yugoslavia

I. Several ethnic groups

A. Eastern-oriented Serbs—Russian alphabet

B. Western-oriented Croats—Western alphabet

C. Moslems

II. Historical differences

A. Different parts have belonged to various foreign powers.

1. Little feeling of loyalty toward country

2. Tendency toward separatism

a. Example: Fought against one another in World War II

III. Recent historical events

A. Breakup of Soviet Union

B. Drive for self-determination in other parts of the world

IV. Conclusion: Need to resolve differences and take place in interdependent world

4. Purposes of department store customers—different

I. Buy something in particular

A. Something they need or want or something on sale

B. Find and purchase with minimum of complication

C. In a hurry or do not like to shop

II. Just to buy

    A. Wealthy or spending because it gives a sense of power

    B. Accumulate packages, often with little real idea of what or how much

  III. Bargain hunt

    A. Beat store out of something

    B. Show deal to friends

  IV. Buy little or nothing

    A. No money, so spend time instead

    B. Cannot make up mind

    C. Store owes something for nothing

  V. Conclusion: Whatever the purpose, clerk knows

4-4 See explanations in text.

4-5 The person learning to drive has to master the difficult tasks of controlling the car, keeping track of the road situation, and following the rules of the road.

4-6 Sample summaries:

One sentence:

For our health, it is important to have a proper diet that provides nutritious foods and contains a minimum of unhealthful foods and food additives.

All information:

It is important to have a proper diet. First, our bodies require healthful foods. We need the nutrition provided by fruits and vegetables, protein, fiber, and vitamins and minerals. We also need to minimize our intake of foods high in fat, which causes not only excess weight and the problems associated with high cholesterol levels but also cancer; sugar, which causes weight problems; and salt, which can cause high blood pressure. Second, our bodies should not be getting harmful additives. Substances such as pesticides, herbicides, and growth hormones used in the production of food and the preservatives, emulsifiers, and coloring used to treat and conserve food can be detrimental to our health.

4-7 More public awareness is presently focused on the growing number of homeless people. The problem has complex causes that go far beyond substance abuse and lack of responsibility. One cause is our system of self-reliance. We are accustomed to getting help not so much from the government as from volunteers. When circumstances change, however, people who are needy may thus be left out in the cold. Another major factor is the worsened economy. Jobs are harder to get now, and the buying power of most paychecks is less, so fewer people can afford housing. Another cause is the budget cutting in education. More people are failing to acquire the education and skills necessary for an adequate job. A further cause is the closing of many state mental hospitals. This has left on the streets people who cannot be looked after at home. A final cause is the drug problem. Drugs bring quick money but destroy a person's sense of reality. The homeless problem is one which needs a solution.

4-8 Evaluate your own summary according to the following criteria; then compare yours with those of your classmates.

Does it give an accurate idea of the essay to someone who has not read the original composition?
Does it cover the most important information?
Is it coherent?
Is it in your own words?

4-9 See explanations in text.

4-10
1. This is based on the assumption that what this person considers food should be considered food by everyone.
2. This is based on the assumption that the presence in the stomach of both lemon and milk is harmful to the body—a cultural rather than a scientific idea.
3. This is based on the assumption that it is right to limit individuals to whatever station—by wealth, or gender, or race, etc., they are born into. According to this belief, in other words, all people should not be equal.
4. This is based on the assumption that men, not women, need to earn money. According to those who hold this view, in other words, women can and should depend on men for money.
5. This assumes that English as it is spoken by Americans, Canadians, and other non-

English native speakers is only a dialect or substandard version of the language.

6. This generalization about the behavior of a whole category based on that of a part of the category is illogical.

7. This is another generalization of highly questionable accuracy. The assumption that formal education makes a person "smart" is also questionable.

8. This is based on a religious belief. Someone who does not share that belief does not accept the premise of the statement and is therefore not convinced by it.

4-11 1-D, 2-C, 3-A, 4-B, 5-E

4-12 See explanations in text.

4-13 1. Simply *looking* will not bring in money.
2. Jobs do not hire; people do.
3. Television does not try to emphasize anything; people do.
4. The warranty is a piece of paper that cannot fix anything.
5. The vehicle should not be fined; the owner should.

4-14 1. A family is not a reason. The need to provide for a family may be one.
2. A major is not a reason. The reason he chose that particular school may be that it has a good program in his major.
3. Workers are not a consideration. The quality of the relationships with fellow workers may be.
4. Bad grades are not a conflict. They are a problem that adds to the student's conflicts.
5. Working is work! Working on an assembly line is hard, or strenuous, or nerve wracking.

4-15 1. "Murder" and "mischief" are at opposite extremes of misconduct. "On adventure shows, children see negative behaviors that range from simple mischief all the way to murder."
2. "Important" and "populated" are not comparable. "Because people are becoming increasingly aware of the importance of a college education, more people are enrolling."
3. "Kills" and "makes sick" do not go together. It does not make sense to talk about making

a life form sick after talking about killing it. "Toxic waste is making fish sick and even killing them."

4. "Profitable" and "violent" do not go together. Many people make large profits in the drug business, and some have resorted to violence to establish themselves in it."

5. They "have" something, "do" something, and "have" something! A better statement: "Many young people today working minimum wage jobs live on their own and raise children."

4-16 1. The concrete colors and shapes do not go with the abstract patience. A better statement: "A puzzle can teach a child not only to recognize colors and shapes but also to work on something patiently."
2. We need to acquire something before we can build on it.
3. The extreme (= fatal) AIDS and murder do not go with the possibly trivial friction in the family. "Drug abuse can lead to problems that range from friction in the family to murder or death from AIDS."
4. "Journalists" and "publications" do not make a good parallel because a comparison is being made between people and things. Furthermore, journalists work for publications. "Concerned journalists working for independent publications are revealing much inaccurate information that we are being led to accept as true."
5. The abstract idea of "frightening" and the concrete idea of "destructive" are not comparable.
6. "Conserving resources" is concrete and "making sense" is abstract.
7. "Cultures" and "personalities" are not comparable. Moreover, one finds people, not cultures and personalities.
8. "Drugs," a concrete thing, and "shootings," an event, do not go together. "Some police dramas have too many episodes involving shootings, drug dealing, and drug use."
9. "Vulgarity," "idolization," "imagination," and "violence" are not logically parallel. Imagination is essentially positive, and the others are negative.
10. "Relatives" (people) and "property" (things) are not comparable losses.

11. "All ages, sexes, and backgrounds" does not work because there are only two sexes.

12. "Purchased" should come before "used."

13. "Kill" and "restrict the growth" are backward. "Smog can restrict the growth of plants or even kill them."

14. "Unhealthful" and "carcinogenic" do not fit together because "unhealthful" includes "carcinogenic."

15. Should be "neither hope *for* nor aim *at*."

4-17 1. People should have equal educational opportunities, and the systems in place are supposed to provide equal opportunities. But the opportunities, in reality, are not equal.

2. Graduating from college offers no guarantee that a person will never easily be tricked into believing false claims.

3. In many families with both parents working outside the home, there is quality time for the children. The absolute statement about "no quality time" is an inappropriate exaggeration.

4. A person cannot do just anything. This is another exaggeration.

5. Dogs come in many sizes, but not all. For example, none are as big as horses or cows.

4-18 1. The figure, $500, is inappropriate. Some people save only a small amount by carpooling, while others save much more than $500.

2. "People" includes "everybody else."

3. "Pronunciation" is not an example of language.

4. Traffic tickets do not make a good example of vehicle expenses, since many people who drive vehicles do not get tickets. Expenses such as gas and maintenance make better examples.

5. Colleges do not provide services "from children to seniors;" these are not examples of services.

4-19 1. Writing skills do not lead to careers. They are a necessary part of the preparation for many careers.

2. Having the skills is not a way of doing something. "A person who has good writing skills can more easily get a point across."

3. Poems and stories are not examples of "being" a writer.

4. "Through television" is not a way.

5. "Television" is not a place.

6. "Paintball" does not think.

7. A "place" is not an example of an advantage.

8. Something cannot be "jammed" with something abstract.

9. "Reasons" are not "advantageous."

10. Japan is part of the world, so the parallel between the world and Japan is illogical. Notice also that the term *shocked* is inappropriate because it can be understood in the concrete sense of movement caused by a blow (so true in this particular case) as well as in the [presumably] intended sense of emotional shock.

4-20 1. Homes are part of cities, so the parallel is illogical.

2. "Responsibilities" are not a benefit. In addition, "enhanced career opportunities" can be interpreted as part of a better life.

3. "Organization" is likely to include "preparation."

4. An abstract idea ("education") cannot tend to do anything.

5. The car and the clothes cannot "do" anything.

6. Such a result is so improbable that the statement is ineffective.

7. The "program" does not do the deducting of the money.

8. The stated transition from "volunteers" (people) to "defense" (an abstraction) does not make sense. "Our nation went from a volunteer system to the military defense we know today."

9. They *are* something and they *do* something—not a good parallel. Also, they are inappropriately described as putting "interests" (an abstraction) before "children" (people). Better: "These parents, usually wealthy, put their business interests before their children's needs."

10. "Television" and "people" are not comparable.

Chapter 5

5-1 Some possible answers:
1. Mary wanted to drive from California to New York, *but* she could not get enough time off to make the trip.
2. She had carefully prepared everything for her presentation. *Moreover*, she was psychologically ready.
3. Joe forgot to bring his glasses, *so* he was not able to follow what was happening in the movie.
4. College students should give careful thought to the choice of a major before they enter college. *Otherwise*, they may lose years by not taking prerequisite courses right away.
5. Speakers of one Romance language may be able to understand a great deal of what is said in another Romance language. *For example*, Spanish speakers understand much of what they hear in Italian.

5-2 Some possible answers:
1. The professor explained and illustrated the principle involved. *In addition*, she gave the students some practice exercises.
2. At the end of the year, she had to pay $280 more in federal income tax. She *also* had to pay almost the same amount in state taxes.
3. More and more people are carpooling. *First*, they want to save money. *Second*, they recognize the need to save fuel. *Last*, they are concerned about the environment. (Notice that *above all* is not a good choice before this last item because it indicates the most important one in a series of items. The primary concern of most people who carpool is to save money rather than to help the environment. In other words, the environmental issue may be the most important one from society's point of view, but it is generally not the key issue for the people who do the carpooling, and it is their point of view we see here.)
4. VCRs have changed people's entertainment habits. *First of all*, people can entertain themselves much more economically. *Next*, they have a much wider choice of films than what is available in the theaters and on television. *Finally*, they can socialize while they watch films.

5-3 Some possible answers:
1. The vacationers left town without a map. *As a result*, they got lost.
2. *Since* Joe was careless about following directions, he failed the exam.
3. The child was playing very roughly with the dog, *so* the animal bit the child.

5-4 Some possible answers:
1. To the visitor, Southern California appears to be a model of multicultural diversity. *For instance*, many signs are only in a language other than English.
2. People who are no longer young often feel critical of parents today. They complain, *for example*, that children in stores are no longer supervised by their parents.
3. Some astronauts returning to Earth have not touched down in water. *For example*, those who have flown in the shuttles have not landed in the ocean. *Or*: Some astronauts, *such as* those who have flown in the shuttles, have not touched down in water.

5-5 Some possible answers:
1. Students are required to take physical science classes to develop their general educational background. *Similarly*, they have to take social sciences.
2. Far from the stabilizing influence of the Pacific Ocean, the deserts of the Southwest have temperatures that often rise to extreme heights during the day. These temperatures *likewise* drop dramatically at night.

5-6 Some possible answers:
1. Writers need to explain their key supporting ideas. *In other words*, they need to provide examples, illustrations, and definitions.
2. Many people avoid giving beggars money because they are afraid it will be used for the wrong purposes. *That is*, the beggar may use it to buy alcohol or drugs.

5-7 Some possible answers:
1. We prepared the food. *Meanwhile*, they got the sleeping equipment together.
2. *As soon as* they learned of their grandfather's death, they made arrangements to attend

the funeral. (Notice that when *as soon as* is used, *immediately* is omitted.)

3. Sue toured the United Nations buildings. *Then* she took a leisurely stroll around Greenwich Village.

5-8 Some possible answers:

1. The new airport had every modern convenience. *Nearby*, there was a heliport with direct flights to several city buildings.

2. The cliff dwelling was built in the depression in the rock. *Above*, the cliff dropped off sharply.

5-9 Some possible answers:

1. Prisons are supposed to be places where criminals are rehabilitated. *Yet* there is a great deal of criminal activity taking place inside them.

2. In Paris, the tourists saw the Eiffel Tower, the Arc de Triomphe, and Montmartre. *In addition*, they visited several museums.

3. People are finding it difficult to buy homes *because* they cannot qualify for loans.

4. Mary wanted her child to learn the responsibilities involved when one has an animal, *so* she bought her a dog.

5. Many people want to get into the field of computers. *However*, they may not have the necessary math skills.

6. Some inconsiderate shoppers leave their carts next to display bins. *Therefore*, it is difficult for other shoppers to get by.

7. Some supermarkets have lowered their prices on certain staples. *For example*, one chain has cut the price of a pound of butter to $1.30.

8. We need to teach children to conserve. *That is*, we must show them how to preserve the world they will inherit.

9. Sirens occasionally wake them. *However*, nothing else disturbs their sleep.

10. The students in her class listen carefully. *As a result*, they learn a lot.

5-10 1. *relationship* and *association*

2. *repair person, mechanic, employee,* and *garage worker; customer, owner of the vehicle,* and *car owner; car* and *vehicle*

5-11 1. *person learning to drive a car, driver, new motorist, learner,* and *novice*

2. *children, individual, young person, student, son or daughter, recent graduate,* and *teenagers; college, school,* and *higher education*

5-12 Some possible answers:

1. *photograph: picture, illustration, shot, print, image, representation*

2. *tabloid: magazine, periodical, scandal sheet, journal, publication*

3. *poverty: lack of money, lack of funds, lack of means, lack of income, poorness, destitution, financial difficulties, privation, penury, indigence, straitened circumstances*

4. *selfish: egoistical, self-centered, self-absorbed, concerned with own interests, wrapped up in himself/herself/themselves*

5. *prove: demonstrate, validate, give evidence for, substantiate, back up*

6. *shield: screen, shelter, guard, safeguard, preserve, keep out of harm*

5-13 1. "These inconveniences" summarizes the key ideas: it is expensive to have a car; vehicle ownership brings legal liability; and a person who has a car must put up with requests for rides.

2. "These types of classroom management" summarizes the key ideas: traditional teachers use the class time to lecture to the students; other teachers use most of the class time for group discussions; and other teachers structure class time so that the students will arrive at an understanding of certain concepts.

3. "An individual matter" summarizes the key ideas: a religious holiday; a time of togetherness for family and friends; and a time to stop and appreciate a special beauty.

5-14 Some possible answers:

1. Various bulky items in landfills

2. Worldwide problems

3. Advantages of a particular car

4. Negative emotions

5. Tourist activities

5-15 1. "These power utensils" *summarizes* the ones named: mixers, sharpeners, and can openers; "moreover" is an *addition* signal.

2. "However" is a *contrast* signal; "these manifestations of ESP" *summarizes* telepathy, clairvoyance, and precognition.

3. *Synonyms:* "children" and "young people"; "zoo" and "animal park." *Summarizing words:* "how animals behave" summarizes the behaviors listed. *Result* signal: "thus."

4. *Synonyms:* "Soviet Union" and "Russia"; "shopper," "buyer," and "purchaser"; "item" and "article." *Time* signals: "first," "then," and "finally."

5-16   1. "are expensive . . . moreover . . . often break down"   [two inconveniences of the tools]

2. "have been studied a great deal . . . however . . . little understood as yet"   [contrast idea because something that has been studied a great deal is usually more than a little understood]

3. "observe . . . thus . . . learn"

Chapter 6

6-1   Some possible answers:

1. They bought a new lawn mower, and they looked at various landscaping tools.

2. They looked at an edger, but they did not buy it.

3. She was expecting an important phone call, so she avoided tying down both phone lines.

4. They may use their vacation time to take a trip, or they may stay home and do some remodeling.

5. Many people do not recognize Columbus' discovery of America because it was a discovery only from the European point of view, and we are Americans, not Europeans.

6. We will not leave until the others come.

7. Many people do not believe there is a problem with the ozone layer even though abundant evidence shows that such a problem with the ozone layer exists.

8. The band, leaving the field, was being honored with a standing ovation.

9. The cord, tied in a tight knot, needed to be undone in order to be usable.

10. The students bringing their lunches from home save money and eat better food.

11. She needed the paper on the bottom of the pile.

12. Many students took part in the awards ceremony before the game.

13. She gave her daughter a picture book of animals to help her learn about nature.

14. He bought a sturdier backpack to carry several heavy books.

15. His dog, a Siberian husky, likes to eat the plants in people's gardens.

16. Some parents seem to be unaware that *discipline*, a Latin word that means instruction, is supposed to be a learning experience rather than merely punishment.

17. The banana, a tropical fruit, is a good source of potassium.

18. Some of our country's most famous novels and short stories were written by Nathaniel Hawthorne, an unconventional thinker and writer.

6-2   1. There is ferry service from La Paz, at the southern end of Baja California, to Mazatlan.

2. Mazatlan, an Indian name for deer, has the world's highest lighthouse.

3. The player named rookie of the year comes from her home town.

4. The lady working the cash register is bilingual.

5. They will spend their vacation in Egypt to see the pyramids.

6. She bought several pieces of matching furniture, to be placed in her living room.

7. When we recycle paper, we save trees, a valuable resource.

8. The deposits collected on recyclable materials provide an incentive for people to conserve.

9. Their broom closet, located in the kitchen, is a convenient place to store a number of items.

10. The people sitting around the table were watching the children eat strange new foods.

6-3   Some possible answers:

1. She bought the plane ticket, and she made a reservation for a hotel room. She bought the plane ticket in addition to making a reservation for a hotel room.

2. He consulted an expert on his problem, yet he still could not find a solution to it. In spite of consulting an expert on his problem, he still could not find a solution to it.

3. She bought a new umbrella, for the rain had been predicted to last at least a week. She bought a new umbrella because the rain had been predicted to last at least a week. Since the rain had been predicted to last at least a week, she bought a new umbrella.

4. Joe was saving money because he needed a new camera. Needing a new camera, Joe was saving money.

5. The weather was finally starting to warm up, so Joe opened all the windows.

6. Small appliances, such as coffee makers and juicers, are often given to newlyweds.

7. Mustangs, like Volkswagens, are still popular cars.

8. The less expensive means of transportation in Europe, in other words, the bus and the train, tend to be crowded.

9. To learn how to repair his own vehicle, he bought a repair manual for his truck. He bought a repair manual for his truck in order to learn how to repair his own vehicle. He bought a repair manual for his truck so that he could learn how to repair his own vehicle.

6-4 Some possible answers:
1. The girls got their tennis rackets, and they went to the park. After getting their tennis rackets, the girls went to the park.

2. They were going to play in a tournament, and they were going to watch the national championships on television in the recreation room to learn something from the professionals. Even though they were going to play in a tournament, they were going to watch the national championships on television in the recreation room to learn something from the professionals. After playing in a tournament, they were going to watch . . . . Since they were going to play in a tournament, they were going to watch . . . .

6-5 Some possible answers:
1. Marie had never worked with the public before, yet she got a job as a receptionist.

2. Joe did not have time to study for the final, yet he did well on it, to his great surprise.

3. Since Julie did not understand restaurant menus in most European countries, she usually ended up ordering spaghetti.

4. Because it had stopped raining, Joe did not take his umbrella with him.

5. Sue could tell that there was a garage sale going on down the street because cars were going by one after another.

6. Many people do not know that the tax changes of the 1980s hurt the lower and middle classes.

7. The tourists drove across the Golden Gate Bridge, and they took the elevator to the top of Coit Tower.

8. The explorer, covered with snow, crawled into the tent.

9. A candidate who has an excellent record of public service does not necessarily win the election.

10. Shakespeare, the author of some of the best plays ever written, would have won many literary prizes had he lived in our century.

11. I knew I would need my watch during the test, yet I forgot to bring it with me to the test.

12. She read the important letters carefully, dumping the junk mail into the recycle bin.

13. City parks, such as green belts, provide much-needed space for urban dwellers.

14. Joe, whose car had broken down on the freeway, was standing at a call box.

15. The man about whom the professor spoke went on an archeological expedition to Yucatan last year.

16. We visited San Francisco, where we bought some sourdough bread, in the summer of 1989.

17. They have been enjoying cooking dinners together, and they like eating what they prepare.

18. They spent the whole day looking in vain for just the right tool, so they decided to try a different model.

19. She bought the red one, but she was not happy with it after she got it home.

20. The bulletin board, always messy, was a constant eyesore.

6-6   Some possible answers:
1. Resisting the temptation to add color to her handouts, she had all of her printing done on white paper in order to avoid contributing to environmental pollution.
2. Eager to get as much as possible out of the class, Joe attended regularly and made friends with other highly motivated students, with whom he discussed the class work.
3. People were unhappy with the new mayor, who allowed taxes to be raised on low-income housing and did nothing to stop businesses from moving to areas where labor was cheaper.
4. Some environmentalists, who may actually be hurting what they stand for by doing things such as tying themselves to trees, seem to be more concerned with participating in a cause than in helping the environment.

6-7   Some possible answers:
1. Some people flock to college writing classes to improve their writing skills because they realize that it is up to writers, not readers, to clarify meaning.
2. People in Los Angeles, where there were riots in 1992, are working to make the city they rebuild a better one.
3. There were only two promising programs on television that evening, neither of which she finished watching because one was unnecessarily violent and the other was a rerun of something she had already seen.
4. Born in Salem, Massachusetts, the scene of witch hunts in the 1600s, Hawthorne uses the supernatural extensively in his short stories and novels.
5. Students who major in a foreign language have to take linguistics, the study of the structure of the language, and philology, the study of the historical development of the language.

6-8   Sentence groups: 1–3, 4–9, 10–13, 14–16
The term *critical thinking* goes far back, at least to the early part of the century. One of the early critical thinking scholars, Edward Glaser, published *An Experiment in the Development of Critical Thinking* in 1941 and had already developed, in collaboration with Watson, the *Watson-Glaser Critical Thinking Appraisal*, a test of students' ability to reason. Critical thinkers endeavor to figure things out, backing their assertions with strong evidence and carefully considered reasoned judgments. Teachers who follow the principles of critical thinking associate knowledge with real understanding, not with the rote memorization of facts.

Chapter 7

7-1   Sample introductions:
1. A college education has become an important goal for more and more people. Not only do graduating high school seniors and their parents focus on college, but adults who have been out of school for years are flocking back to the college classroom. This push for higher education in our society is no accident. In reality, a college education is worth the effort because in several important ways it helps prepare a person for life.
2. A child whose parents get a divorce is greatly affected by the breakup of the home. The child may be placed in each of the two new home settings for several months of the year in order to have an opportunity to bond with both parents. However, this shared custody actually creates some very serious problems for the child.

7-2   1. The topic, "television," is introduced in the first sentence; and the controlling idea, "has had a strong positive influence," appears in the last sentence. The other side is reported: notice of the blame television has received for violence, lack of education, and low intelligence, and acknowledgment of the potential harm of television broadcasting. All of the preceding ideas are likely to draw the reader's attention because they are much-discussed current issues that involve people both logically (and illogically) and emotionally.
2. The topic, "people who exaggerate the importance of one possible factor in a complex problem," and the controlling idea, "are trying to avoid the responsibility of dealing with the actual causes of problems," both appear in the final sentence of the introduction. Examples of the types of

statements these "single cause" people make are given (blaming television for violence, lack of education, and low intelligence, and blaming single mothers for the high crime rate), illustrating the opposite of the reality the writer proposes to discuss. These emotionally charged statements are also likely to draw the attention of the reader, whether the reader agrees or disagrees with them.

7-3 See explanations in text.

Chapter 8

8-1 1. Topic: "ways—types"; controlling idea: "different"; summarizing words: "these types of classroom management" summarizes the key ideas.
2. Topic: "dieting—diet"; controlling idea: reflected in "it takes long-term methods to get long-term results"; "long-term methods" also summarizes the key ideas.
3. Topic: "pressuring"; controlling idea: "disservice" reminds the reader that the insistence is not good; result: "disservice"
4. Topic: "problem of homelessness"; "Is growing" is the result of the controlling idea: "has complex causes"; result: "is growing"; suggestion: "all of us need to take a closer look"

8-2 1. Topic: "community college"; summarizing words: "useful institution"; result: "here to stay"
2. Topic: "community college"; summarizing word: "life"; result: "one can make life happen"
3. Topic: "community college"; summarizing word: "everyone" (reminds the reader of the variety of people who can be served by the community college in the ways brought up in the key ideas); results: "improve as a person" and "advance in society"
4. Topic: "it" (refers to "community college"); summarizing words: "something worthwhile"; "depriving themselves" is the negative reflection of the controlling idea: those who do not take advantage of the important functions are depriving themselves.
5. Topic: "convenience store"; summarizing word: "visit" (reminds the reader of the key supporting ideas focusing on the inconve-

niences that the visitor encounters); result: "frustrating experience"
6. Topic: "earthquake" (and "one"); summarizing words: "disastrous effects"; suggestion: "should prepare . . . in order to reduce the disastrous effects."
7. Topic: "earthquake"; "normality" reflects the opposite of the key ideas (in other words, summarizes the opposite situation); result: it takes a great deal of human energy and money to bring life back to a semblance of normality"

Chapter 9

9-1 Fragment: "Like one that is not stressful."
Run-together sentence: "When you get home . . . you still have some energy left."
Modifier error: "a job with a college education" and "education like becoming a executive, doctor, or even a professor"
Shift in person: "[You] Compare the fast-food wages" and "When you get home"
Faulty parallel: "than without one"   [illogical comparison]
Faulty statement: "a degree can get a person a better paying job" and "compare the fast-food wages to a doctor" and "a degree can get a person a more pleasant job"
Incorrect verb form: "*compare* to a job"
Incorrect article: "*a* executive"
Misspelling: "desent"

9-2 1. Lacks controlling idea, key supporting ideas, and appropriate supporting information. Rambles. Repetitious wording (first and second sentences; fourth and fifth sentences; "popcorn, candy, and all kinds of snacks": popcorn and candy are snacks); unclear wording ("a little of nothing"); and wording that needs to be more specific ("a *great* place"). The expression "full-action packed" should be "action-packed." Not all of the ideas seem relevant, and not all have good transitions, although this is difficult to analyze because of the lack of a controlling idea and key ideas. The second-person point of view (you) is inappropriate because the writer seems to mean "people in general." There is also a shift to the first person ("Let's not forget"). In addition to the general lack of support for anything, there is the unsupported general statement that "Its very economical . . . ." The third sentence needs a comma ("If you like, you . . . ."), as does ". . . one evening, remember . . . ." Agreement error: "There's popcorn, candy . . . ." and "there's always the movies." Usage error: "When *your* searching" and "*Its* very economical . . . ." Contractions inappropriate. Fragment: first sentence. Misspelling: "to" [much], "convience," "[went] their."

2. Lacks key ideas and supporting information. The third sentence repeats the topic sentence. Ineffective wording: "to *look* for a movie to *see*," "to *distinguish* what movie to see," and "the listings are specified . . . ." Faulty statement: "One . . . is through a newspaper," "Going . . . is a hard way," and "way . . . is thru a newspaper." The *Los Angeles Times* is not an example of a calendar section. The word *are* in "who are the leading actors and actresses" should come at the end of the phrase. Contractions. The words "because it's a waste of time" are given as an explanation of why it is better to know what is playing at the movies, but it does not explain; rather, it brings up a point that needs explaining (but is not explained). Abbreviated spelling: thru. Paragraph repeats instead of explaining and supporting.

3. Key ideas not clear, and supporting information scarce and disorganized. Unsupported general statement: "It doesn't cost very much . . . ." Faulty statement: "Meeting new people always happens . . . ." Agreement error: "movies is." Use of *you* to indicate people in general. Contractions. Modifier error: "when going . . . ." Run-together sentence: "So whenever . . . entertainment and company." Needs comma after "much" and after "because of this." Spelling error: "alot." Faulty reference ("it") in several places.

9-3 1. Lacks controlling idea. Series of unconnected statements (without transitions) that go in different directions. Lacks support for whatever was supposed to be supported. Statement "For some, watching television is a waste of time" implies that someone considers it a waste of time; since

different people do not agree on what constitutes a waste of time, it would be better to say "Some people consider watching television a waste of their time." "Thus," at the beginning of the concluding statement, should indicate a result of what precedes, but it does not in this case. Run-together sentence: "Some watch . . . interrupts." Fragment: "The people who feel that television is a waste of time." Spelling error: "fined."

2. Direction not clear: the first half tells *what*, and the second half tells *why*. The first half also lacks transitions. Fragment: "Swimming . . . benefits." Run-together sentence: "They need it . . . energy level." Incorrect verb form: "involve." Needs comma after "brisk walking."

9-4 1. The first sentence appears to be the topic sentence, leading in the direction of *why* choosing the right career is necessary. But the only information in support of this is the idea that we will be sorry for the rest of our lives (which needs extensive, specific explanations!); and the paragraph continues with the idea of choosing not a career (as in the first sentence) but a major. The rest of the paragraph then discusses *how* to avoid choosing the wrong major. The question (sentence 2) is ineffective. The third sentence is a fragment, as is the fifth. There is a shift to *you*. *He* is used to mean a person, implying that only a man needs to make a choice regarding a major (or was it a career?). The concluding sentence does not conclude anything; it also contains the pronoun *it*, which does not refer to anything specific.

Ideas for revision: Focus on either career or major. Choose as the controlling idea either that a person *should* make a careful choice or that a person *can* make a good choice. Bring in much more specific detail. Structure and connect ideas logically.

A sample revision:

It is important for people to choose a career carefully. Doing a job that is in some way fulfilling can make a great difference in a person's life. For one person, satisfaction may come from helping others. For someone else, the opportunity to make use of individual creativity may be crucial. Some people have a strong preference for indoor work; others would rather have an outdoor job. Some like to deal constantly with difficult challenges, whereas others like to have their decisions made for them. Many individuals would rather work alone, while others need to be surrounded by people. The person who misses out on a career that is in some way personally fulfilling and therefore rewarding will definitely be less content with life in general than he or she would be with the help of some kind of job satisfaction. Another important factor in a person's choice of a career is the prospective job situation. Anyone who needs to earn a living from a job should avoid a field in which there is little or no demand for new workers. Another point to consider is that when a career requires extensive preparation, that preparation constitutes a substantial investment of time and money. Thus, the individual needs to make a careful choice so that with a little luck the choice will pay off.

This revised version focuses on why a person should be careful about choosing a career (hinted at in the original) and uses the two factors brought up in the original (picking something interesting and being realistic) as sources of supporting information.

2. Topic sentence at end; topic and controlling idea are not clear early in the paragraph. Supporting explanations do not emphasize *how* the resource persons can help. Teens are mentioned at the beginning, but then persons aged 15 to 24 are included. Misleading impression that the paragraph is about the leading causes of death among teenagers; then the subject switches to resources. The second sentence has a colon between linking verb and predicate nominative, and the fourth sentence has a colon between the verb and the direct object. In

the same sentence, the word "resources" is used to include both people and organizations (illogical parallel). The next sentence states that "social workers are *agencies*" (in other words, that people are organizations). It also has an agreement error: "conflicts is." There should be no capital letter in "Psychiatric hospital." In the next sentence, "other's" is a simple plural, so it should not have an apostrophe. In the same sentence, "when it is thought" is vague; the source of the judgment should be indicated specifically. There is a shift to *you* at the end. The paragraph is wordy, with several awkward sentences, such as those beginning "Another type of aid is . . . ." The statement that "the family is one of the most valuable resources" is highly debatable because the disturbed teenager usually has serious problems with the family; generally, a great deal of professional therapy (and a great deal of explanation in this paragraph) would be necessary to justify counting on the family as part of the teenager's positive support. Telling what the family "must" do does not explain *how* the stated recommendations can actually be achieved. In the last sentence, there should be a comma after "see."

Ideas for revision: Make focus clear at the beginning, and word the key ideas so that the structure of the paragraph becomes clear. Add detailed explanations.

A sample revision:

Suicide is a leading cause of death among teenagers, many of whom take their lives without letting anyone know of their desperation. Yet a number of resources are available to these troubled young people. First, professional help can put teenagers in crisis back on track. Social workers deal with family conflicts and thus can create a better home environment for a youth in need of outside help. Other professionals in a position to aid disturbed young people are the private therapists, who help their clients develop important coping skills and better communication. Teenagers likely to harm themselves or others can also get help through counselors at psychiatric hospitals. A second potential source of aid for the troubled teen is any nonprofessional person who knows and interacts with the unstable adolescent. A family member, a friend, or even a teacher who learns to communicate well with the troubled individual and accepts some responsibility for the teenager's problems can be an invaluable resource person. Greater public awareness of these potential resources is essential if we are to reduce the number of these tragic deaths.

3. Lacks a controlling idea and structure; there are only random comments about election campaigns. The second sentence has the word "things," which does not refer to anything specific; the same is true of the pronouns "it" and "this" in sentences 2 and 3. The statement that "it lets the public know *everything*" is an inaccurate absolute, as is the idea that "the public votes for the *best* candidate." There is a change in direction with "bring out scandals," and this statement is placed before the more general remark that there are "a few bad things about campaign advertising." "A candidates advertising" needs an apostrophe, as do "a candidates personal," "the candidates life," and "his families reputation" (which should be his or her family's reputation). The contraction "does'nt," which should not be used in the first place, has the apostrophe in the wrong place. In the next sentence, "discredit" and "put down" are too close in meaning to be used in parallel. In the two sentences that follow, "things" and "This" need to be replaced by terms with specific meaning. "Life" and "are" do not agree. The "Not only . . . but also" phrases are not parallel. The concluding statement indicating the writer's personal opinion does not contribute anything of value to the composition, especially since it brings up new issues ("necessary and helpful"), which should be developed (in the body of the writing) or left out. The last sentence also has "wasn't" in place of "were not," and "it" (campaigning) is being both "used" and "misused." "Weapon or . . . game" is an illogical paral-

lel. This paragraph is contradictory and confusing. The lack of specific words makes some of the meaning ambiguous.

Ideas for revision: Settle on a controlling idea and find key supporting ideas that are strong points. Then develop them with specific detail.

A sample revision:

Election campaigns, supposedly conducted to help voters make intelligent political choices, in reality provide little useful information about candidates. First, a politician's stand on important issues may not be clarified at all. Campaign discussions sometimes barely touch on the matters of greatest interest to the public. The voters need to know the candidates' real intentions concerning the economy, education, health care, and other vital concerns, but these important issues may be discussed only superficially. The voters, furthermore, are frequently misled by the statements the candidates do make. Another serious problem with election campaigns as they are usually conducted is their negative focus. Many candidates expend a great deal of energy trying to discredit their opponents. They get far too involved in finding potential scandals involving other candidates and sometimes not even the candidates themselves but rather their families. In other words, the public may hear more gossip than useful information about the people running for office. People would be better served if candidates focused on what really matters.

Chapter 10

10-1 1. Honesty is the best policy.
2. A man with a cane crossed the street and went into a store.
3. Many apples had fallen from the tree at the top of the hill beyond the barn.

10-2

1. ADJ ⌒ N ⌒ ADV
   New cars run efficiently.

2. ADJ ⌒ N ⌒ ADV
   Many people read widely.

ADJ   N   ADV   PREP   N
3. Most teenagers often go to the movies.

ADJ   N   PREP ADJ   N
4. Large airplanes can fly to distant places.

ADJ   N   ADV   PREP   N
5. Restaurant owners often work in the evening.

10-3

ADJ   ADJ   N   ADV
1. Television talk shows frequently present

ADJ   D.O. N
important topics.

N   D.O. N   PREP   N
2. The children were watching the men on the roof.

ADJ   N   ADJ   D.O. N PREP N
3. Local architects have drawn a new set of plans

PREP   N
for the project.

ADJ   N   ADJ   D.O. N
4. Instant replays provide valuable information

PREP ADJ   N
during athletic events.

ADJ ADJ   N   ADJ ADJ   D.O. N
5. Most city dwellers dread heavy morning traffic.

10-4

PRON   ADV CONJ PRON
1. We stayed home because it was raining.

PRON   PREP   N CONJ PRON
2. They will go to the game if they get tickets.

PRON   CONJ PRON   N
3. They will wait until they hear the news.

N PRON PRON   PREP   N   ADV
4. The movie that we saw on television yesterday has

ADJ   D.O. N   PREP   N PREP N
caused considerable controversy about the idea of life

PREP   N
after death.

N PRON   ADV PREP PRON ADJ   D.O. N
5. The lady who came in at 7 p.m. presents workshops

PREP   N
on writing.

10-5

ADJ   N   PRED. NOM.
1. Their neighbor is a doctor.

ADJ   N   PRED. ADJ.
2. Their neighbor is intelligent.

PRON   ADJ   PRED. NOM.
3. He is an interesting person.

PRON   ADJ   PRED. NOM.
4. He was a good student.

PRON   PRED. ADJ
5. He was studious.

10-6

N   CONJ   N   ADV
1. Birds fly, but chickens only flutter.

PRON   PRED. NOM.   CONJ PRON ADV   PRED. NOM.
2. He is a doctor, and he is also a golfer.

N   PREP   N PREP
3. The students may enroll in classes in Paris

PREP   N   CONJ PRON   ADV
during the summer, or they may just travel

PREP   N
around France.

PRON   D.O. PRON PREP   N   CONJ PRON   ADJ D.O. N
4. He ate all of the pasta, and he had a big serving

PREP N
of dessert.

PRON   ADJ   D.O. N   CONJ PRON ADV   ADV
5. He knew his neighbors, but he almost never talked

PREP PRON
to them.

10-7

ADJ   N PREP   N   D.O. N
1. The big dog under the tree watched the cat

PREP   N   PREP   N
in the window of the mansion.

ADJ   N   ADV
2. The inexperienced travelers unwisely took

ADJ   D.O. N   PREP ADJ   N PREP   N
several suitcases on their trip to Europe.

ADJ   ADJ   N CONJ   ADJ   ADJ   N
3. The crafty elderly lady and the clever young man

ADV   D.O. N   PREP   ADJ   N CONJ
quietly hid the microchip in the cigarette case and left

PREP   ADJ   N
through the back door.

ADJ   N   PREP   ADJ   N
4. The smaller children in the school playground were

PREP   N PREP   N
running toward the swings near the cafeteria.

5. The tall tree on the hillside was swaying wildly in the wind.

10-8 1. tree/watched
2. travelers/unwisely
3. man/quietly
4. playground/were
5. hillside/was

10-9
1. The English of all social classes drink tea when they need consolation.

2. The girls who have finished school sometimes work for the local storekeepers as clerks or bookkeepers.

3. Retired people in the country gladly spend their spare time in their vegetable gardens because they want produce that has not been sprayed with insecticides.

10-10 1. to go [infinitive]
2. to visit [infinitive]
3. to improve [infinitive]
4. to get [infinitive]
5. driving [participle]
6. trying [participle]; to get [infinitive]
7. struck [participle]
8. stored [participle]
9. working [participle]; to finish [infinitive]

10-11 1. decorating [gerund]
2. decorating [present participle]
3. decorating [gerund]
4. composing, playing [gerunds]
5. composing, performing [gerunds]
6. playing [present participle]
7. trying [present participle]
8. opening [gerund (it is the object of the preposition about)]

10-12

1. We drove home yesterday.

2. People and their pets have things in common.

3. Joe reads and writes Spanish.

4. We are in the twentieth century.

5. There are many museums in Los Angeles.

6. There is a vase on the shelf.

7. One of the supervisors comes to class.

8. She will have been typing for five hours by the time she finishes her research paper.

9. Your book must have been taken by your roommate.

10. Walking toward the dugout, the injured pitcher was cheered by everyone.

11. I will go out to shop when it stops raining.

12. He read the book that had been recommended by his instructor.

10-13

1. Children and young animals play.

2. Horses can carry riders and pull carts.

3. Bicycles and scooters are used for transportation.

4. There was an interesting movie at the local theater last night.

5. I like to swim when I go to the beach.

6. There are too many bosses in most companies.

7. The employees wanted to leave early to see the

   holiday parade.

8. Their relatives would have liked to visit Disneyland.

9. All of the apples were eaten.

10. There should have been more people

    in the history class.

Chapter 11

11-1 The words needed to complete the meaning of
the subject and verb are in boldface.

1. He passed.

2. He passed the **salt**.

3. He passed **her** the **salt**.

4. She named her pet **alligator Nosey**.

5. Her other pet is a **tortoise**.

11-2

1. People speak.

2. Many people speak fast.

3. Many people in a hurry speak fast.

4. Many people who are in a hurry speak fast.

5. Many people speak fast when they are in a hurry.

6. Students in large lecture halls must listen carefully.

7. During the winter, dusk comes in the afternoon.

8. It is raining.

9. It is raining hard.

10. It rains often in tropical zones.

11-3

1. The puppy dug a hole. *D.O.*

2. The older puppy furiously dug

   an impressively deep hole. *D.O.*

3. The puppy in the neighbors' backyard quickly dug a

   big hole behind a tree. *D.O.*

4. The puppy that the neighbors had just bought dug a

   hole because he smelled something in the ground. *D.O.*

5. The neighbors take the puppy on a walk *D.O.*

   whenever they can.

6. Joe took the silverware from the drawer. *D.O.*

7. Some people eat too many sweets. *D.O.*

8. Mary should have filled the gas tank *D.O.*

   before she entered the freeway.

9. The mother of the nine neighbor children is taking

   karate lessons. *D.O.*

10. More people are now getting regular exercise *D.O.*

    because they are thinking more about their health.

11-4

1. Mary showed Joe the photographs. *I.O.* *D.O.*

2. She also showed him the souvenirs that she had *I.O.* *D.O.*

   bought.

3. She did not tell him the reason for her trip to Florida. *I.O.* *D.O.*

4. She had already shown her neighbors everything. (I.O. / D.O.)

5. Joe gave Mary some advice. (I.O. / D.O.)

6. She brought him a gift that she had bought in Florida. (I.O. / D.O.)

7. He gave her flowers for the first time. (I.O. / D.O.)

8. She passed him the plate of cookies. (I.O. / D.O.)

9. The president of the school gave the graduating students their awards. (I.O. / D.O.)

10. Extracurricular activities in high school can teach students of all backgrounds many valuable lessons. (I.O. / D.O.)

11-5
1. Instructor renames Joe.
2. Rich modifies Joe.
3. Vegetarian renames neighbor.
4. Busy modifies Mary.
5. Executive renames Mary.
6. Good modifies food.

11-6
1. The salesman called the car a bargain. (D.O. / O.C.)
2. The customer later called the car a lemon. (D.O. / O.C.)
3. The club elected Joe treasurer. (D.O. / O.C.)
4. That instructor found the class well prepared for the test. (D.O. / O.C.)
5. The students found the discussion stimulating. (D.C. / O.C.)
6. She finds him sensitive and shy. (D.O. / O.C. / O.C.)
7. The sportswriters named the player rookie of the year. (D.O. / O.C.)

8. The government declared the earthquake a natural disaster. (D.O. / O.C.)

9. The committee nominated Mary chairperson. (D.O. / O.C.)

10. From her position of power, Mary called everyone lazy and incompetent. (D.O. / O.C. / O.C.)

11-7
1. Her father is a doctor. (S.C.)
2. He is extremely busy. (S.C.)
3. Her mother is a chemist. (S.C.)
4. She is very creative. (S.C.)
5. Mary was an honor student. (S.C.)
6. She looked intelligent. (S.C.)
7. She was very talented in music. (S.C.)
8. Dan became a computer expert in his spare time. (S.C.)
9. He became quite adept at programming. (S.C.)
10. All of them often felt tired. (S.C.)

11-8
1. Horses can sleep while they are standing.
2. Mary's cat used to walk the three dogs in the morning. (D.O.)
3. Cows give their calves milk. (I.O. / D.O.)
4. Everybody considered the proposal outrageous. (D.O. / O.C.)
5. The sunset was an enormous splash of rich colors. (S.C.)
6. Everyone called the sunset spectacular. (D.O. / O.C.)

7. The car salesman sold the customer a lemon. [I.O. / D.O.]

8. Elephants work hard ~~for people in India.~~

9. Elephants, because they are so strong, can lift very heavy objects. [D.O.]

10. Animals can be extremely useful ~~to people~~ [S.C.] ~~in many ways~~.

11-9 1. birds fly [main clause]
2. birds fly [main clause]; fish swim [main clause]
3. birds search for food [main clause]; while they fly [subordinate clause]
4. when the cat appeared [subordinate clause]; the birds flew away [main clause]; the dogs started barking [main clause]

11-10 1. the beginnings of some movies are confusing [main clause]; simple sentence
2. the VCR has made it possible to watch both recent and older films at home [main clause]; fewer people are going out to the movies [main clause]; compound sentence
3. teenagers and young adults often prefer to go out to the movie theater [main clause]; while people in other age groups tend to watch more movies at home [subordinate clause]; complex sentence
4. when the public shows an interest in a particular kind of film [subordinate clause]; movie producers are quick to notice [main clause]; similar films soon appear [main clause]; compound-complex sentence
5. the clouds above the mountains resemble the head of a dog [main clause]; simple sentence
6. the students and their parents enjoyed the trip to the park [main clause]; simple sentence
7. one of the students took pictures [main clause]; another wrote an article about the trip for the school newspaper [main clause]; compound sentence

8. fruits and vegetables should not be sold to the public [main clause]; if they have been sprayed with dangerous chemicals [subordinate clause]; complex sentence
9. growers need to be especially careful about using pesticides [main clause]; because people nowadays are exposed to so many other environmental pollutants [subordinate clause]; complex sentence
10. as the sun came up [subordinate clause]; a layer of mist seemed to hug the ground [main clause]; a faint chill pervaded the air [main clause]; compound-complex sentence

11-11 1. The subject, mechanic, is performing the action.
2. The mechanic is performing the action on the subject, car.
3. The subject, mayor, performed the action.
4. The mayor performed the action on the subject, ball.
5. The subject, child, performed the action.
6. The child performed the action on the subject, keys.

11-12 1. teacher [active]
2. teacher [passive]
3. host [active]
4. host [passive]
5. people [passive]
6. people [active]
7. hurricanes [active]
8. earthquakes [passive]
9. Vikings [passive]
10. peoples [passive]

11-13 1. The couple ordered omelettes.
2. In high school, most students take math. *Or:* Most students take math in high school.
3. The producers canceled the play. [*Note:* If the action taken by the producers is less important than the fact that the play was canceled, a better version is: The play was canceled.]
4. The patient tolerated the medicine well.
5. The gods launched thunderbolts at the invaders.
6. The government should pass more legislation to control environmental pollution.

7. A highly qualified person who is turned down for a job experiences negative feelings.

8. Hank Aaron set a new record for home runs.

9. The wind has blown the leaves all over the lawn.

10. Those lucky enough to get tickets eagerly awaited the opening night of *The Phantom of the Opera*.

11-14 1. finish [subjunctive]
2. finishes [indicative]
3. push [imperative]
4. pushes [indicative]
5. return [subjunctive]
6. returns [indicative]
7. Return [imperative]
8. did . . . return [indicative]
9. Will . . . go [indicative]
10. go [subjunctive]

Chapter 12

12-1 Periods and semicolons are grammatically interchangeable. The following possibilities are suggestions only:

1. Bookstores sell books; libraries loan them.

2. It had rained heavily the night before. The grass looked fresh and green the next day.

3. Books take time to publish; magazines may have more up-to-date information.

4. He did not understand accounting; he sometimes fell asleep in class.

5. People who are busy with their jobs all week sometimes enjoy cooking on the weekends. Cooking is a creative occupation.

6. The contestants all arrived at the finish line. The first three were awarded prizes.

7. Smog is a combination of fog and atmospheric pollutants. It now covers much more than our cities.

8. The car came to a stop; it had run out of gas.

9. People tend to raise their children the way they were raised; they feel more comfortable with what is familiar to them.

10. Successful students have often learned good study skills; unsuccessful students typically waste much of their time.

12-2 1. The first airplanes flew, but they went slowly compared to today's jets.

2. On their trip to Los Angeles, they visited several museums, and they went to the theater every evening.

3. The children fell asleep in the car after leaving Disneyland, for they were tired.

4. The student needed to review the material carefully, or she would fail the course.

5. She studied hard, so she passed.

6. Joe did not care for the food at the reception, but he liked the champagne.

7. Joe knew he had drunk too much at the reception, yet he got behind the wheel of his car.

8. Joe stopped the car, and he showed the officer his license.

12-3 Some possible answers:

1. They painted the entire house. In addition, they redid the roof.

2. The student wrote the essay very carefully. As a result, it came out well.

3. The tape broke; thus, the audience missed the rest of the song.

4. The boxes were empty; therefore, they were easy to carry.

5. The ticket prices had gone up; consequently, the travelers could not afford to fly.

6. The converter box was not working properly; however, they managed to get a picture by bypassing it.

7. The tourists brought back an entire suitcase of souvenirs. As a result, they had problems getting through customs.

8. A recent study has shown coffee to be no more harmful to the health than tea or caffeinated sodas. Consequently, many avid coffee drinkers are happier now.

12-4 The semicolons in the following sentences can be replaced with periods:

1. All of the books Joe needed for his research paper were checked out; consequently, he had to change his topic.

2. Dan wanted to hear the group's latest tape; therefore, he bought it.

3. Mary stopped to buy some take-out food; then she went home.

4. Some of the first-year students spent their money without thinking; thus, they ran out.

5. The rental movie lasted four hours; however, everyone watched it twice.

6. We set up the camp; meanwhile, they prepared dinner.

7. The team played extremely well last season; nevertheless, they did not win the pennant.

8. At first, the new director was afraid he could not handle everything; then he found he could manage very well.

9. She is a really careful driver; therefore, she has never gotten a ticket.

10. Some college instructors travel a great deal; as a result, they have many interesting experiences.

12-5 1. Whenever it rains, the streets get flooded.
2. no punctuation needed
3. no punctuation needed
4. Although the contestant accumulated several thousand dollars, she did not win the game.
5. no punctuation needed
6. no punctuation needed
7. no punctuation needed
8. no punctuation needed
9. I knew her history professor, who was an extremely knowledgeable person.
10. Since the rain would spot his recently detailed car, Dan decided to postpone his trip to the store.

12-6 1. subordinate clause already comes first
2. If it costs too much, few people can afford to buy it.
3. Because our plane came in late at the airport, all of us got home late.
4. subordinate clause already comes first
5. After everything had been set up, the man at the entrance began admitting people.
6. Before he phoned his aunt, he sent her a telegram.   [Notice that "aunt" is moved to the first clause and "her" replaces it in the second clause.]
7. Ever since they came to live in the United States, they have been using English.
8. cannot be reversed
9. cannot be reversed
10. subordinate clause already comes first

12-7 Some possible answers:

1. To those in the areas severely damaged, it was not just another earthquake. It was a major disaster.

2. Six members of the team were coaches from the local schools, and most of the others were athletes who competed locally.

3. The only people who will register guns are law-abiding citizens; criminals will not register theirs.

4. Registering guns would not eliminate the danger as accidents would still happen.

5. Those against gun control claim a Constitution-based right, whereas those for control emphasize the danger factor.

6. It is not enough for some to own a house; their house must be nicer than their neighbors' homes.

7. The team ran the length of the field. Then they scored a goal.

8. The game was long; however, we stayed until the end.

9. The team travels out of town several times during the season. Therefore, they have high operating costs.

10. They have won all their games so far this season; thus they have a good chance to win the championship.

12-8 Some possible answers:
1. Peter may not graduate because his grades are not good.
2. He has also been having trouble getting the classes he needs because he has to fit them around his work schedule.
3. Many advanced classes are now offered only every fourth semester. This scheduling makes it more difficult for some people to graduate.
4. Some people can study with the stereo on, whereas others cannot do two things at the same time.
5. Mary was not interested in a career when she got out of high school. Then she changed her mind.
6. no change
7. no change
8. He did all of the assignments; nevertheless, he did not get credit for the ones not done correctly.

9. He was also taking a Russian class. He found it especially difficult.

10. He goes to the beach to relax because he is under so much stress.

12-9 Some possible answers:

1. They are going on vacation. Then they are enrolling in some classes.

2. Mary is taking a British literature class. She finds it highly challenging.

3. Joe likes physics whereas Mary prefers English.

4. Mary was interested in the cliff dwellings of Mesa Verde, so she went there during spring break.

5. She had read up on the culture of the Indians who built them. Thus she was able to appreciate what she was seeing.

6. They had built their dwellings right in the depressions in the cliffs. As a result, their enemies could not destroy their homes.

7. Mary is thinking about changing her major to archeology. She is also considering a double major.

8. She is fascinated with ancient civilizations. In fact, she hopes to go to Yucatan before the end of the year.

9. She cannot afford to fly there. However, she may go by bus.

10. She is looking for a traveling companion. Otherwise, she will have to pay the full expense for lodging.

12-10 Some possible answers:

1. The taxpayers will pay off the national debt.

2. No one got effective environmental protection laws enacted.

3. Someone in a dream invented a truly safe passenger automobile.

4. George Lucas will create a new *Star Wars* series.

5. The first customer of the day ordered ham on rye.

12-11 Fragments:

"Traveled through . . ."; "Also became . . ."; "Then stopped . . ."; "And were . . ."; "Half walked . . ."; "Certainly hoped . . ."; "And told . . ."; "Then coasted . . ."; "At that point. . . ."

Possible revised paragraph:

The most enjoyable trip can become a nightmare when something goes wrong with the car. While driving across the state last year, my friend and I unexpectedly found ourselves negotiating curves along a mountain road. We traveled through one dense grove of trees after another for a long time, with no sign of civilization. The sun had gone down, and our lights were on. Finally, the road began to straighten out somewhat. It also became less hilly. Then, suddenly, the car began to slow down—on its own. Then it stopped altogether. We had run out of gas! And we were most likely stranded, as no cars had gone by in either direction for miles. We sat for some time in silent frustration over our predicament. Finally, I, being the more athletic of the two, decided to start off in search of help, going in the direction in which we had been headed. I half walked, half ran down the road until I came to a place, a mile or so from the car, where the road dropped down into a valley. There, to my relief, I saw what I had been hoping to see: lights. I did not know what was there but certainly hoped it was a gas station. I ran back to the car and told my friend that there was salvation after all. Since it was downhill, we were able to push the car to where the lights were visible. Then we coasted the rest of the way down. At that point we discovered, to our delight, that we had come upon not only a gas station, at which we were able to fill the tank, but also a cafe, where we wound down over a hot drink, and a convenience store, where we bought a road map in the hope of never making the same mistake again.

12-12 Some possible answers:

1. People who borrow things but never return them should be castigated.

2. The astronauts who were the first to see the other side of the moon had an incredible experience.

3. The airplane that just landed on the runway has a flat tire.

4. Formulating a clear topic sentence with several key supporting ideas is an important part of the prewriting process.

5. The last person to leave the room is supposed to turn off the lights.

6. The tourists in the first car behind the engine choked on the smoke.

7. The benefits, most of which are very important to those who choose such a career, are described in detail in the company's brochure.

8. Depression, so common that it is considered to be one of the major health problems in this country today, is still not covered by many health plans.

9. The steps to follow in order to bake potatoes, which are in any beginner's cookbook, are simple.

10. His truck, since it would stall even though he had just had the carburetor worked on, still needed some repairs.

12-13 1. The game has taken over three hours already.   [or: had taken]

2. The student is writing research papers for several classes.   [or: was writing;   or: will be writing;   etc.]

3. He had done everything that he was supposed to do.

4. They have always striven to succeed.   [or: had always striven]

5. Those tourists have flown to Mazatlan nearly every year since 1977.   [or: had flown]

6. The race had begun before we got to the track.

7. Their neighbors had come to see what all the noise was about.

8. People were coming from everywhere just to see what the police were doing about the incident.

9. They had grown up in a small town in Colorado.

10. They are riding in the Calgary Stampede next year.   [or: will be riding]

12-14 Some possible answers:

1. Since it had been raining for days, many streets were flooded.

2. After she bought the new curtains, she decided she did not like them.

3. While they were at their friends' house for dinner, there was an earthquake.

4. He was walking as if he knew where he was going.

5. Even though it was a hot day, they were wearing wool sweatshirts.

6. Unless the government implements a realistic solution to the state's financial problems, the current crisis will get worse.

7. Nobody knows yet where all of the trash will go in the next century.

8. That is the book that he has been talking about all along.

9. Whichever solution they adopt, it will take a miracle to make it work.

10. The homeless are people whose needs are being overlooked.

12-15 1. Joe, wanting to make a large down payment on a car, was saving money.

2. Alice did all of the problems in the chapters assigned, including the extra-credit ones.

3. She called early for an appointment to get a convenient time.

4. She packed all of her things carefully the night before to be ready for an early morning departure.

5. We enjoy walking all around the town in the evening.

6. Many people have voiced complaints about the practice of keeping animals in captivity in zoos and other kinds of animal parks.

7. He forgot to buy some of the ingredients he needed for the pizza, even the mozzarella.

8. He is always extremely well prepared and carefully dressed for his speeches.

9. Erin and Pete enjoy training dogs, particularly those belonging to movie stars.

10. They like to spend time in the movie stars' homes, to have the run of dream houses.

12-16 Some possible answers:

1. They ate out often on Friday nights, especially when there was nothing at home that could be prepared quickly and easily.

2. Whenever they go to their friends' house for dinner and invite us as well, we all have a good time.

3. If it costs too much and nobody can afford to pay for it, nobody will buy it.

4. They made a point of leaving before the traffic got too heavy so that they would not risk being late for their plane.

5. The members of the band often meet on their own to practice the music.

6. Most teenage girls give up dieting sooner or later, either when they have reached their desired weight or when they come to realize that they need food.

7. If there are too many negative ions in the air we breathe, the excess will cause health problems.

8. That book explains how one can learn a foreign language without going to the country where the language is spoken.

9. Since they had all agreed to meet at Pete's house and then they all got there late, Pete was angry.

10. Volunteer groups often run into problems because if the leader does not know what is going on at all times, some confusion may arise in the organization.

12-17 Some possible answers:

1. Erin and Pete checked out more than a dozen books from the library in hopes of having all of the information they needed for their new job as dog trainers.

2. Joe's supervisor needs to learn to deal with people in positive ways instead of being sarcastic so much of the time.

3. Decontrol means that oil producers can charge a higher price per barrel of oil, thus increasing profits.

4. There were no special requirements for joining the Penitentes, although novices usually came from Penitente families.

5. Computers often limit verbal communication among people in places such as offices and banks. In this way, they contribute to the communication gap.

6. Steinbeck's *The Pearl* shows that people in small towns are not necessarily more warm and caring than their city counterparts; they are envious, in fact, of the good fortune of another villager.

7. The people of the small town follow the family to the doctor, staring with brazen curiosity that does not come from human compassion, as do many of the people on our big-city freeways who slow down to stare at an accident scene.

8. People in small towns also combat boredom by gossiping a great deal, often saying disrespectful things about their neighbors.

9. The benefits of that job are the good pay, the convenient location, and the daytime hours. All of these factors are important to most people.

10. Convenience stores sell many highly processed foods that are not good for people, not to mention the fact that these foods are overpriced.

12-18

Many students graduating from high school find it worthwhile to continue their education at the local community college. A two-year college, first of all, can offer them a start in higher education, preparing the students until they feel ready for a four-year university. Also, going to the local college is financially advantageous. They can normally continue to live with their families, without needing to pay rent for an apartment. They can also take public transportation to school. This usually makes it unnecessary to buy a car, unless the student needs the car to go to work. The experience of going to the community college also gives the recent high school graduate an opportunity to become more independent and mature. For example, it is entirely up to the student to attend class. Students in college are more likely than those in high school to take this responsibility seriously, partly because they are usually the ones paying for their classes. A final advantage to attending the local community college is that students have an opportunity to make friends at school with people of different ages and backgrounds, in this way further enriching their learning experience. For many, it is thus a wise decision to include in their lives some time at the community college.

12-19 Some possible answers:

1. You do not have to pay for it now. All you need is a deposit.   [RT]
2. He turned in his exam without looking it over carefully. Thus he made some mistakes.   [RT]
3. The students finished the group project for their history class. Those who were better in English checked it over.   [RT]
4. We need to finish painting the house this weekend. Otherwise, it will not be ready in time for our coming guests.   [RT]
5. There are three important advantages to attending Riverview Community College: the wide variety of courses, the convenient class times, and the excellent instructors.   [FR]
6. Joe plays baseball, and he also enjoys soccer.   [RT]
7. They put up a fence; however, the neighbors' dogs get in under it.   [RT]
8. Joe finished writing the letter; then he sent it.   [RT]
9. I like Italian food. Mel does too.   [RT]
10. He wanted to learn to play the organ, although he did not know how to read music.   [FR]

12-20 Some possible answers:

1. He likes physics even though it is difficult.   [FR]
2. The grass was green the day of the field show tournament because it had rained intermittently for several days preceding the event.   [FR]
3. The local band performed well in the event, and they won several sweepstakes awards.   [RT]
4. Although they did well in all categories and won awards in several, they still were not satisfied with their performance.   [FR]
5. They prepared carefully; thus they did well.   [RT]
6. They performed in the field show tournament. Then they left for the Hollywood Christmas Parade.   [RT]

7. Many of them are serious musicians. Therefore, their music sounds good.   [RT]
8. While everybody was busy trying to find out what had happened, the thief got away.   [FR]
9. Mary was wearing gloves in spite of the fact that it was quite warm.   [FR]
10. She thought that everything had been left for the last minute, whereas in reality everything had been prepared well in advance.   [FR]

12-21 Some possible answers:

1. correct
2. Mel will change the oil on his truck. Then he will check the air filter.   [RT]
3. He does not have to pay for the ticket right away. All he needs is a deposit.   [RT]
4. Borodin was a famous musician who was also a chemist.   [FR]
5. Since it had been raining all morning, the traffic was moving slowly.   [FR]
6. She did not have confidence in the dentist because he was keen on astrology.   [RT]
7. It is hard to get up Monday mornings, especially if one has gone away for the weekend.   [FR]
8. Joe tried to fix his own car. The result was that it would not even start.   [FR]
9. They will clean up everything in their backyard, and then they will do the front.   [RT]
10. Some people can do two things at the same time, whereas others are not so lucky.   [RT]

12-22 Some possible answers:

1. First you brainstorm a topic until you run out of ideas. Then you organize your thoughts.   [RT]
2. He likes to travel; however, it is expensive.   [RT]
3. He always reads for an hour after dinner. He watches television later.   [RT]
4. correct
5. Her relatives went to Balboa Park yesterday, and they will go to Sea World tomorrow.   [RT]
6. If you go to Europe, you should take an umbrella with you.   [FR]
7. They enjoyed Paris the most; however, we liked Rome better.   [RT]

8. To the people in the areas hardest hit, it was not just another hurricane. It was the worst nightmare of their lives.   [RT]
9. correct
10. In his time, there was not the air pollution that exists today, not to mention the technological advances that have played a major role in creating that pollution.   [FR]

12-23 Errors:

"To live . . ." [FR];   "Never having . . ." [FR]; "I had another . . ." [RT];   "The chance . . ." [FR];   "I was curious . . ." [RT];   "Although I was . . ." [FR];   "Clouds which . . ." [FR]; "They hide . . ." [RT];   "To see . . ." [FR]; "That give us . . ." [FR];   "In spite of . . ." [FR]; "Giving life . . ." [FR]

Many of life's dreams go unfulfilled. Yet we continue to let them occupy an important part of our lives. One of my great but as yet unfulfilled desires is a simple one: to live close to the sea. I have always felt I have missed something important, never having had the experience of waking up to the sound of the waves. I had another childhood dream that came to me often. I dreamed of the chance to fly in a glider. I was curious to know what it would be like, and I also could imagine how beautiful the ground below might be. However, I was always afraid of heights. And I was also bothered by the idea that visibility is poor, at times even reduced to nothing, when the sky is cloudy. Clouds, which are beautiful to look at but frightening to fly through, hide the land and block out the sun. My final dream was to travel, to see the Taj Mahal, the Swiss Alps, and Tierra del Fuego. All of these dreams are as yet unfulfilled. Perhaps it is our continuing desires that keep us motivated in life and give us a reason to go on in spite of all of the difficulties, giving life a meaning it would not otherwise have.

12-25
1. Who invented the laser?
2. Do you know who invented the laser?
3. The instructor did not know who invented the laser.

4. The eruption of Vesuvius in A.D. 79 destroyed the cities of Pompeii and Herculaneum.
5. Ms. Belmont was born in St. Cloud on May 1, 1950, at 4 P.M.
6. Don't touch that wire!
7. Cows, horses, sheep, etc., are common farm animals.
8. Julius Caesar was born in 100 B.C.
9. Our flight will leave for Washington, D.C., at 10 A.M.
10. Dr. Martin Luther King, Jr., is an important figure in the history of human rights.

12-26
1. Most printing is done on white paper; the colors used to color paper add to environmental pollution.
2. We like the old-fashioned theaters; they prefer the modern cinema complexes.
3. Mary had found everything she needed for her sociology paper; however, she had not yet checked out any materials.
4. Ann briefly visited London, Paris, and Rome; then she went on to Moscow.
5. Manny brought the speakers, the amplifier, the turntables, the mixer, and several crates of records; but he forgot to bring some country music, even though it was sure to be requested.
6. One of the players hurt his hand; another sprained her ankle.
7. The recipe calls for lamb, chicken, and beef, which are best if they are rubbed with spices and cooked in the oven; vegetables, especially carrots, onions, green beans, and garbanzos, cooked in a spicy tomato sauce; and a special pasta, over which the meat and vegetables are served.
8. People continue to be interested in new frontiers; the popularity of science fiction shows this fascination with the unknown.
9. Animals tend to draw people's attention; therefore, television advertisers are using them more and more in commercials.
10. People are dumping waste in storm drains; it is then turning up on the beach.

12-27

1. For the marathoners, <u>running</u> <u>is</u> a career.

2. In the army, dogs are trained to attack

   the enemy.

3. In the past, conglomerate mergers were

   subject to antitrust laws.

4. Until all of the people had exited, the doors

   were kept unlocked.

5. After Mary had calculated everything, she

   figured her tax.

6. By the way, the mayor is coming to dinner.

7. If you know Latin, you can understand many

   more words in English.

8. Although he killed the insect, he failed to

   destroy its nest.

9. When we go to San Francisco in December,

   we will visit the Golden Gate Park museums

   and Alcatraz Island.

10. On her way to Texas, Mary flew over the

    Colorado River.

12-28

1. We carefully prepared everything for the

   experiment, and the results came out as we

   had expected.

2. The animal control officer caught the stray

   dog, but then she could not find the owner.

3. Joe especially liked the movie *Gandhi*, so he

   saw it a second time.

4. There would be less concern over the

   scarcity of natural resources if solar energy

   were more widely used, and oil could be put

   to other uses.

5. He will do the dishes, or she will be

   very angry.

6. They will not paint their house this year,

   nor will they replace the missing boards in

   the fence.

7. The new candidate promised to give the

   economy top priority, and he said he had a

   plan that had met with the approval of

   many economists.

8. Mary had run out of money by the end of

   November, yet she managed to finish the

   school year.

9. She took extra units each semester and

   went to summer school, so she finished

   college in three years.

10. <u><u>It</u> <u>was</u></u> a frightening event, but <u>he</u> <u><u>made</u></u> it a

learning experience.

12-29 1. Doctors recommend a low-fat diet, the elimination of smoking, and stress management.
2. The people who took the all-day tour saw Runnymede, Stonehenge, and Bath.
3. Hawthorne's novels are *The Scarlet Letter, The House of the Seven Gables, The Blithedale Romance,* and *The Marble Faun.*
4. On the mountain pass, driving is dangerous when rain pours down, gusty winds blow, and dense fog covers the roadway.
5. They had tea, coffee, cake, and sandwiches at tea time.   [or: tea, coffee cake, and sandwiches]
6. They had orange juice, bacon and eggs, toast, and coffee for breakfast.
7. The telephone book contains a calendar of events, local points of interest, and zip codes.
8. Mary has not taken chemistry, physics, or biology.
9. The tool set on sale contained screw drivers of different sizes, pliers, and wrenches.
10. Sentence errors include run-together sentences and fragments, dangling and misplaced modifiers, agreement errors, shifts, and faulty parallelism.

12-30 1. Yellowstone National Park, her favorite vacation place, was struck by a major earthquake in 1959.
2. Her father's father, who was a storekeeper, lived in several different states.
3. Hawthorne wrote *The Blithedale Romance,* which shows life in a socialistic community.
4. Hawthorne's first novel, *The Scarlet Letter,* is an interesting study in human nature.
5. correct
6. Some of the principles of the French Revolution had already been tested during the American Revolution, which had been fought several years earlier.
7. correct
8. Christopher Columbus, who traveled to America, could communicate with sailors from different countries.

9. correct
10. Addressing our serious environmental problems, which are getting more public attention now than they did a few years ago, has become an important part of every politician's agenda.

12-31 1. You know, Joe, that you really need to study more.
2. That means, among other things, spending more time reading the textbook and thinking about the information it gives.
3. correct
4. Mary's father, whom I met by chance at a luncheon, is one of the trustees.
5. Joe found out, moreover, that there would be a long delay.
6. Tom, you should try to get your work finished before we have to close.
7. Our current idea of benefiting from the taxes we pay to the government goes back to the American Revolution, which started in 1776.
8. *Moby Dick,* a novel by Herman Melville, is thought by some critics to be America's finest novel.
9. He knew, however, that the design would not turn out well.
10. Mary Kelly, whose sister lives in San Francisco, travels a great deal around the country.

12-32 1. correct
2. correct
3. The local librarian, who was the first person to be invited, is the guest speaker.
4. The chairperson, whose speech is always prepared by someone else, puts everyone to sleep.
5. correct
6. She did not tell the audience, however, exactly which countries she had visited.
7. Her own field of study, psycholinguistics, is one she feels will become extremely important in the near future.
8. She believes, furthermore, that worldwide television broadcasting will revolutionize many cultures.
9. Airplanes, which are about as old as automobiles, became feasible after the invention of the internal combustion engine.

10. Take the books back, people, or you will have to pay a fine.

12-33 1. Mary's grandmother moved to Chicago, Illinois, on March 10, 1948.
2. She lived there until April 1973 or April 1974, I am not certain which.
3. She then moved to 426 Chapman Avenue, Santa Ana, California 99802.
4. She lived there until August 1, 1977, when she moved to Rancho Cucamonga, California.
5. Mary has lived in Tucson, Arizona, Las Vegas, Nevada, and Orange, California.

12-34 1. Joe asked, "When will they get here?"
2. Mary answered, "They still have not let me know."
3. Barbara replied, "They will let us know when they are ready."
4. She said, "If you really want to go on the expedition, you will have to take the class first."
5. "If you really want to go on the expedition," she said, "you will have to take the class first."
6. "If you really want to go on the expedition, you will have to take the class first," she said.

12-35 Suggested answers:
1. Friendship is a two-way relationship: each person must give to the other a little of himself or herself.
2. You need several ingredients to make bread: flour, shortening, milk, salt, sugar, and yeast.
3. Joe has already passed his exams in the following subjects: English, art, geology, anthropology, and Italian.
4. Napoleon made one disastrous error in judgment: he decided to invade Russia.
5. Television—he had grown up on the adventure programs and documentaries offered by cable—had been his real link with the world outside his own community.
6. Most sections of the required classes at community colleges—English and math—fill very quickly.
7. The Civil War (1861–1865) was fought over both economic and human rights issues.

8. The frequently performed (various stage versions and films) story of the phantom of the opera touches some of our deepest feelings.

12-36 1. Mary said, "I really like that dress!"
2. "I really like that dress!" Mary said.
3. Mary asked, "Do you like it too?"
4. "Do you like it too?" Mary asked.
5. Joe's commented after the election, "The President really has his work cut out for him!"
6. Mary said, "My mother will be arriving at six o'clock."
7. "My mother will be arriving at six o'clock," Mary said.
8. Did she shout, "Stop!"?
9. "I know," he said, "that you were a big help."
10. "I also know," he continued, "that we can count on your help in the future. We have a lot of faith in you."

12-37 1. I read the novel *Pride and Prejudice*.
2. He was studying the following: psychology, American history, and German.
3. Robert Louis Stevenson, a famous Scottish poet and novelist, lived in Monterey, California, before he moved to the Samoan Islands.
4. She was born on the first Wednesday in June in O'Connors Hospital, on San Carlos Avenue, San Jose, California.
5. The Mojave River flows north from the San Bernardino Mountains.

12-38 1. William Faulkner, who wrote *The Sound and the Fury*, won the Nobel Prize in 1949.
2. Did the contestant yell, "I won!"?
3. I read the last chapter of Balzac's novel *Eugenie Grandet*. It is entitled "So Goes the World."
4. The last chapter of Balzac's novel *Eugenie Grandet* is entitled "So Goes the World."
5. The song "Old Man River" is from the musical *Show Boat*.
6. She was born on July 10, 1950, in Portland, Oregon, and now lives in Idaho.
7. The teacher shouted, "Hurry up, children, or you will be late!"
8. Ann spent all morning visiting the Tower of London. Then she went on to Greenwich in the afternoon.

9. Ann voted for the incumbent for one reason: he was strong on environmental issues.

10. The Emancipation Proclamation was written during the Civil War.

12-39
1. Her grandfather moved to 860 Stevens Creek Road, San Jose, California, on June 20, 1964.
2. The poem "Autumn Leaves" is in the book *Collected Poems*.
3. We will see the Statue of Liberty, the World Trade Center, and the Hudson River when we fly over New York City.
4. She asked, "What time are you leaving?"
5. Chicken, fish, meat, and eggs are good sources of protein.
6. My aunt's doctor died last summer.
7. "What sort of person would hurt an animal?" her son asked.
8. I am due to leave from San Francisco at 9 A.M. and will arrive in Chicago at 2 P.M. at O'Hare International Airport.
9. We enjoyed the play; moreover, we saw it a second time.
10. We were convinced, moreover, that they were right.

12-40
1. We used tomatoes, onions, garlic, and spices to make the sauce.
2. "You know, Barbara, that you need to do well in that class," he reminded her.
3. The appointment on Wednesday, July 10, is theirs.
4. Shakespeare, who was born in 1564, was a famous English playwright and poet.
5. She bought the house for one simple reason: it was a bargain.
6. They stayed, I believe, to see the entire movie; therefore, they got home late.
7. George Washington, who led the colonial forces during the American Revolution, did not write the Declaration of Independence.
8. I sent the package to Professor John Smith, 348 North Union Street, Salem, Massachusetts.
9. Working all night and attending classes all morning, Joe usually felt tired.

10. The last chapter of Agatha Christie's novel *Passenger to Frankfurt* is entitled "Journey to Scotland."

12-41
1. He asked, "Why did you do that?"
2. "Why did you do that?" he asked.
3. "Why," he asked, "did you do that?"
4. Gogol's story "The Nose" is in the book *Petersburg Tales*.
5. We read the book *Star Trek* before we saw the movie.
6. My neighbor, Professor Smith, teaches art at Riverview Community College.
7. "They have already decided," he said, "to postpone the job until summer."
8. He said that they had already decided to postpone the job until summer.
9. "More and more people are becoming aware of environmental problems," he noted. "They are also starting to take action on them."
10. "Unless you take Latin, you will have a difficult time with scientific terminology," the instructor told Joe.

12-43

1. The large tiger ~~in the cage~~ paced impatiently while the keeper fed the other animals.

2. The keeper opened a panel and threw a chunk ~~of meat~~ in.

3. Lying ~~on a ledge~~, the hungry animal quickly ate the food.

4. The paper used ~~for newspapers~~ is often recycled.

5. He needed the class to fulfill a requirement.

12-44
1. *Error:* "sitting" modifies "we"
Corrected version: We saw a rare bird sitting on the chimney.

2. *Error:* "in a bad mood" modifies "vegetables"
   Corrected version: In a bad mood, he went out in the freezing wind and picked the vegetables.

3. *Error:* "in their chemistry class" modifies "discovered"
   Corrected version: In their chemistry class, the students heard the stories of how the new elements were discovered.

4. *Error:* "rolling" modifies "the hiker"
   Corrected version: The hiker saw the bottle cap rolling under the stone.

5. *Error:* "on the way [to the mall]" modifies "squirrels"
   Corrected version: On the way to the mall, their new neighbors saw some squirrels.

6. *Error:* "leaving the store" modifies "power mower"
   Corrected version: Leaving the store, Joe noticed a large power mower.

7. *Error:* "that did not agitate very well" modifies "lady"
   Corrected version: Sue bought a washing machine that did not agitate very well from her new neighbor lady.

8. *Error:* "badly burnt" modifies "guests"
   Corrected version: The guests did not enjoy the badly burnt roast.

9. *Error:* "on Thursday night" modifies "cheating"
   Corrected version: On Thursday night, the new faculty members received a copy of the school's statement on cheating.

10. *Error:* "such as the United States" modifies "weapons"
    Corrected version: Powerful countries such as the United States waste money on nuclear weapons.

12-45 1. *Error:* "such as store owners and local employees" modifies "losses"
   Corrected version: During the Los Angeles riots of 1992, many people, such as store owners and local employees, suffered enormous losses.

2. *Error:* "by Gogol" modifies "fraud"
   Corrected version: *Dead Souls* is a novel by Gogol about a tax fraud.

3. *Error:* "like Dickens" modifies "characters"
   Corrected version: Gogol, like Dickens, uses humorous names for his characters.

4. *Error:* "that was very valuable" modifies "museum"
   Corrected version: We donated an artifact that was very valuable to the museum.

5. *Error:* "that do not have a good academic preparation" modifies "universities"
   Corrected version: Many athletes that [or who] do not have a good academic preparation are accepted into universities.

6. *Error:* "almost" modifies "visited"
   Corrected version: The tourists visited almost all of the museums in Paris.

7. *Error:* "annoyed" modifies "legislators"
   Corrected version: Many legislators received letters from constituents annoyed by their lack of action.

8. *Error:* "aside from the newspaper" modifies "world"
   Corrected version: Aside from the newspaper, radio was the main source of information about what was going on in the world.

9. *Error:* "in expensive clothing" modifies "cars"
   Corrected version: Young people are influenced by other youths who *wear* expensive clothing and *drive* around in luxury cars.

10. *Error:* "in the home" modifies "drugs"
    Corrected version: In the home, parents should make clear to their children the dangers of drugs.

12-46 1. *Error:* "watching" modifies "reading"
   Corrected version: When one watches television for long hours, reading enough becomes difficult.

2. *Error:* "frustrated" modifies "move"
   Corrected version: Since we were frustrated by the situation, our next move was to leave.

3. *Error:* "when getting" modifies "learning"
   Corrected version: When a novice gets someone's help, learning to play the piano can be a rewarding experience.

4. *Error:* "when studying" modifies "information"

Corrected version: The information given in class may be invaluable when students are preparing for a test.

5. *Error:* "before discovering" modifies "puddle"
   Corrected version: Before the mechanic discovered the hole in the pan, a puddle of oil had already formed on the garage floor.

6. *Error:* "treated" modifies "clinics"
   Corrected version: Many medical clinics charge patients a fee for treatment.

7. *Error:* "when comparing" modifies "differences"
   Corrected version: There are several important differences between CDs and tapes.

8. *Error:* "while driving" modifies "they" [= children]
   Corrected version: Safety windows are a desirable feature in a car in which small children ride: the children cannot fall out while the car is moving.

9. *Error:* "stalled" modifies "hours"
   Corrected version: Many stress-related complaints develop when people spend hours in stalled traffic.

10. *Error:* "capitalizing" modifies "mini-markets"
    Corrected version: Capitalizing on the convenient location, entrepreneurs generally build mini-markets near gas stations or large housing tracts.

12-47 In each sentence in the exercise, the present participle erroneously modifies "it." Here are some better versions of the intended ideas:

1. It could be seen twenty years ago that there was a need for environmental regulation.

2. It is not possible for children who watch television for long hours to read enough.

3. Having lost everything in the fire, they found it difficult to face the future.

4. As we sailed along the coast, we could see clearly the mountains beyond the coastal lowlands.

5. The evidence makes it obvious that these are the right conclusions.

6. Since she came from a family of doctors, it was natural for her to go into medicine.

7. The characteristics of the disease make it evident that there is risk of contagion.

8. It is easier to figure out what to wear when we listen to the forecast.

9. After I stirred the boiling hot coffee, it was not too hot to drink.

10. If we weigh the two sides, it should be easy to arrive at a sensible decision.

12-48 1. The modifier "nothing" is inaccurate. Opinions differ as to whether "little" or "a great deal" is appropriate.

2. The modifier "never" is inaccurate. *Corrected version:* Riots historically have seldom brought great change.

3. *Corrected version:* Homeless people frequently turn to addictive substances to escape from their desperate reality.

4. *Corrected version:* Most college students have to juggle classes and part-time jobs.

5. *Corrected version:* A student should always write legibly when taking lecture notes.

6. *Corrected version:* Most students have financial problems.

7. *Corrected version:* He is a humorist. [*or:* He is a humorous person.]

8. *Corrected version:* The verdict was unjust. [because "justice" cannot be "unfair"]

9. *Corrected version:* The play was really well choreographed.

10. *Corrected version:* On hearing the news, we acted quickly.

12-49 1. The hikers found the stream inviting, as it burbled along.

2. Since we went camping every year, the park's best-known bear became the favorite subject of our pictures.

3. The child, dragging his feet, brought the car to a stop.

4. Because we had finished all the sauce, we could not serve the spaghetti to the guests.

5. The hike left Joe, who had smoked several cigarettes, out of breath.

6. My original impression changed when I arrived.

7. After Mary had run hard for most of a long block, the bus pulled away just as she was reaching it.

8. Feeling sleepy during the long lecture, the participants had difficulty following the speaker.

9. Taking his statement at face value, we were shocked by it.

10. She promised on the telephone to treat all of her friends to dinner.

12-51 1. goes
2. were
3. comes
4. number . . . were
5. were
6. speaks
7. were
8. is
9. are
10. predicts

12-52 1. were
2. are
3. goes
4. is
5. are
6. number . . . were
7. learns
8. were
9. are . . . contain
10. makes

12-53 1. *Error:* "anyone . . . they"
Corrected version: Anyone who wants a ticket has to go to the box office to get it.   Anyone wanting a ticket has to go to the box office to get it.

2. *Error:* "one . . . they"
Corrected version: People can enroll in the local college and take as many classes as they want.   One can enroll in the local college and take as many classes as one wants.

3. *Error:* "person . . . they"
Corrected version: People graduating from high school often do not know what career they want to pursue.   A person graduating from high school often does not know what career he or she wants to pursue.

4. *Error:* "anybody . . . they"
Corrected version: Anybody who crosses the line is out!   Anybody crossing the line is out!

12-54 Some possible answers:
1. All of the students passed their finals.
2. All of the students brought their own books to class.
3. All of the people in the office use good English in their letters.
4. Each of the boys has his own room.
5. Each child has a room. All of the children have their own rooms.
6. None of the people remembered to bring their keys.
7. Have any of you picked up your tickets yet? Have any of them picked up their tickets yet?
8. Neither of the players turned in his [*or* her *or* a] uniform.
9. One of the members of the orchestra brought her [*or* his *or* a] music stand from home.
10. Someone's notebook is still here.

12-55 1. fewer
2. less . . . less
3. few
4. little
5. few
6. much
7. much
8. fewer
9. fewest
10. least

12-56 1. *Error:* "one . . . have"
Corrected version: One of her most important goals for the next few years has always been to get a degree.

2. *Error:* "estimate . . . seem"
Corrected version: The repair shop's estimate for some of the repairs seems high.

3. *Error:* "Jim and he . . . was"
Corrected version: He said that Jim and he were absent that day.

4. *Error:* "scientist . . . make"
Corrected version: Scientists make mistakes too.

5. *Error:* "amount . . . notices"
Corrected version: The number of notices sent to customers was larger last month.

6. *Error:* "horse . . . minds"
Corrected version: Neither the horse nor the cows mind the rain.

7. *Error:* "neither . . . are"
   Corrected version: Neither of those jobs is easy.
8. *Error:* "is . . . number"
   Corrected version: There are a number of problems to solve.
9. *Error:* "terrier . . . are"
   Corrected version: Neither their collie nor their neighbors' terrier is going to win the prize.
10. *Error:* "child . . . them"
    Corrected version: Try to share thoughts with your child by sitting down together and talking about school activities.

12-57 1. *Error:* "amount . . . locations"
   Corrected version: Ansel Adams found Yosemite to have a vast number of excellent locations for photographs.
2. *Error:* "one . . . show"
   Corrected version: One of his most famous pictures shows the play of light and shadow on Half Dome.
3. *Error:* "child . . . knows"
   Corrected version: Neither the child nor the puppies know how to sit still.
4. *Error:* "ecologist . . . are"
   Corrected version: The book was written by ecologists who are concerned about the Amazon Basin.
5. *Error:* "either . . . are"
   Corrected version: Either of those videos is worth renting.
6. *Error:* "amount . . . people"
   Corrected version: Many feel that we need a national health care system to reduce the number of uninsured people.
7. *Error:* "neither . . . were"
   Corrected version: Neither of her sisters was present.
8. *Error:* "is . . . less . . . accidents"
   Corrected version: There are fewer accidents when people avoid drinking and driving.
9. *Error:* "anyone . . . they"
   Corrected version: When students want to drop a course, they have to process a drop.
10. *Error:* "teenager . . . themselves"
    "responsibility . . . are"
    Corrected version: Working teenagers learn to understand how important responsibility to themselves and others is.

12-58 Some possible answers:
1. A person who wants to go abroad needs to save money.
2. A student who misses too many classes may fail a course.
3. One first reads an essay over and then goes back and rewrites it.
4. They always watch television programs that keep them from sleeping.
5. A person who wants to go to a very popular restaurant makes reservations.
6. In elementary school, the teacher would punish the students if they did not have their homework.
7. I like working with someone I can talk to openly.
8. After completing an application, the prospective employee should check it over carefully.
9. People going to their first job interview feel nervous.
10. Before electricity came into use, people had to carry candles from room to room.

12-59 1. Soon after they left on their hike, they came to a river that they could not cross.
2. Mary worked in the store all summer, but then she found out, to her disappointment, that she could not stay on the job part-time during the school year.
3. The shoplifter was moving toward the door when suddenly the clerk shouted.
4. They said they would come home early.
5. If she goes to New York for her vacation, she can visit the United Nations buildings.
6. If he goes to Mexico City for two years, he will become fluent in Spanish.
7. Her uncle always liked to discuss the changes that had taken place in his line of work.
8. The teacher said she would not be able to help the students a great deal unless they helped themselves.
9. They could use the interlibrary loan if they wanted.
10. Shakespeare includes ghosts in several of his plays, such as *Hamlet*, in which Hamlet's father appears in the form of a specter. [Notice that the present tense is

used in discussions of works of literature or art.]

12-60 1. *Error:* "was hoping . . . starts"
Corrected version: Joe was hoping to go to the game, but then it started raining.

2. *Error:* "gave . . . forgets"
Corrected version: Mary gave us the materials and then forgot to tell us how to use them.

3. *Error:* "could do"   [with a real, not a hypothetical situation]
Corrected version: With a 1.5% blood alcohol level, people may do things they would not normally do.

4. *Error:* "student . . . you"
Corrected version: A student who wants to succeed has to work hard.

5. *Error:* "person . . . you"
Corrected version: A speaker has to make sure the audience can hear.

6. *Error:* "were watching . . . go"
Corrected version: We were watching a murder mystery on television when all of a sudden the lights went out.

7. *Error:* "make . . . would gain"
Corrected version: Many people make money from a war by selling arms; others gain by selling results of research to develop new weapons.

8. *Error:* "put . . . has"
Corrected version: Cagliostro put her in a trance and then had her jewels removed.

9. *Errors:* "need . . . will cheat"   "tourists . . . you"
Corrected version: When traveling abroad, tourists need to know the value of money, or people cheat them.

10. *Error:* "likes . . . could ride"
Corrected version: If she likes, she can ride with us.

12-61 1. *Error:* "students . . . you"
Corrected version: In high school, students have to take the classes the counselor gives them.

2. *Error:* "is . . . would have to"
Corrected version: The local college is convenient because students do not have to drive far.

3. *Error:* "is . . . would happen"
Corrected version: The death penalty is a re-

minder of what might happen if a person kills someone.

4. *Error:* "took . . . have . . . try"
Corrected version: In *Animal Farm*, the animals take over the farm, but they have many problems as they try to run it.   [present tense for discussion of literary work]

5. *Error:* "did realize . . . has changed"
Corrected version: Mary did not realize that Joe had changed jobs.

6. *Error:* "was leading . . . catches"
Corrected version: Mary was leading the race when Barbara caught up.

7. *Error:* "person . . . you"
Corrected version: A person who likes working with the public should not become a laboratory technician.

8. *Error:* "completed . . . reopen"
Corrected version: After the workers completed the construction project, they reopened the freeway.

9. *Error:* "want . . . could study"
Corrected version: If they want, they can study French during the summer.

10. *Error:* "called . . . says . . . will see"
Corrected version: Her friend called her and said he would see her later.

12-62 1. In Florida, people can go to theme parks, visit Cape Canaveral, and enjoy the beaches.

2. They are scholars, educators, and authors.

3. They hope to move soon and to enjoy their new home.

4. Her name regularly appears in magazines and newspapers, and she is often mentioned in trade journals.

5. He is a young pianist of great talent who hopes some day to perform professionally.

6. The problem with those cars is their noise and their tendency to overheat.

7. They enjoy talking, listening, and even criticizing.

8. She was an intelligent but impractical person.

9. The student decided to schedule her study time and to avoid parties, or she would be unhappy once again with her final grades.

10. Fast-food restaurants are creating a heavier and lazier population.

12-63
1. He refused to read, discuss, or sign the document.
2. She is interested in anthropology, archeology, and history.
3. He borrowed all the books, magazines, and newspapers that gave information on the subject.
4. He is a poet, gourmet, and world traveler.
5. She has worked in education, in the travel business, and with a major food producer.
6. She sold her stereo, her bookcases, and her lawn mower.
7. She did not eat many apples or oranges or much pineapple.
8. He is an architect, engineer, and athlete.
9. When they went on vacation, they took their tent, camp stove, and canoe.
10. They like boating, fishing, and looking for seashells.

12-64 Some possible answers:
1. An excellent artist, he sells many paintings.
2. Mary works in an office and as a notary public.
3. They were intelligent children who appeared frequently on quiz shows.
4. Joe has a tractor that he rents out.
5. Basketball is a game that encourages social interaction, develops in the player a sense of responsibility, and provides a way of releasing emotions.

12-65
1. Off-road vehicles not only disturb the peacefulness of the desert but also harm nature's balance.
2. He wanted either to study French or, better yet, to go to Paris.
3. He wanted to get the job by qualifying for it rather than by using someone's influence.
4. Recycling both conserves resources and helps solve our trash disposal problem.
5. They neither smoke nor drink.
6. He prefers to work out at a health club instead of spending all the money it would take to buy his own equipment.

12-66
1. Tim wants to become a lawyer, an inventor, or a businessman.
2. He either reads the materials he wants right in the library or photocopies them and takes the photocopies home.
3. She not only swims well but also dives like an expert.
4. They sell neither books nor instruction manuals in that electronics store.
5. He went to Europe both to see famous places and to eat the various national dishes.
6. To lose weight, eat less food, consume fewer calories, and walk a lot.
7. The advantages of a warm climate are that people have lower heating bills, need less clothing, and can enjoy more outdoor activities.
8. She got good grades by always attending class, taking notes carefully, and reviewing her notes as soon as possible after class.
9. He likes to swim first, hike next, and then eat after the other activities.
10. We are destroying our planet by wasting materials and polluting our air and water, and yet we pretend that everything is all right.

12-67
1. Basketball is good for those who appreciate the game as well as for those who play it.
2. Five people who have never played together and who do not know each other can immediately become a team.
3. They do so by relying on signals, making quick decisions, and establishing order with one another.
4. Joe speaks French and Spanish, and he understands Italian.
5. The author is comparing living conditions in the United States to those in other countries.
6. When we conserve materials, we help the situation on our planet by not exhausting our resources and by giving them time to replenish themselves.
7. A busy person can have something to eat more quickly by going to a fast-food restaurant than by cooking at home.
8. Public transportation is an inexpensive, convenient, and safe way to travel.
9. If more people used public transportation, there would be fewer cars on the road,

and people would save money and waste less time in transit.

10. The proposed program would be not only helpful to the people but also economical for the government.

12-68 1. Athletes who smoke are slower than nonsmoking athletes, and they also lack stamina and suffer from shortness of breath.

2. Until another source is developed that will provide energy at a price comparable to that of petroleum, all industrialized nations will continue to depend on oil.

3. Employers tend to hire people with good educational backgrounds.

4. The alcoholic's situation gets worse until the drinker either goes bankrupt or gets help.

5. Leonardo da Vinci was an engineer, a painter, and an inventor.

6. My neighbor is addicted not only to drinking but also to gambling.

7. An increase in global temperature will melt the polar ice caps, the water from which will flood many valleys and thus disturb nature's balance.

8. The public sometimes forgets that people want to find adequate employment rather than stay on welfare.

9. The cost of a community college education is reasonable compared to that of a private university education.

10. The difference in cost is important for those who want an education but cannot afford to pay the higher amount.

12-70 1. me [both "you" and "me" are objects of the preposition "between."]

2. him

3. she

4. me

5. I

6. whoever

7. she

8. who

9. he

10. I

12-71 1. Many students cannot get the classes they need because these classes fill fast.

2. Television programs relieve the fear of ghosts that many children alone at night have.

3. Restaurant owners claim they are now offering more healthful foods. However, many of these foods still contain too much grease.

4. Their feelings, whether they are positive or negative, are very strong.

5. He enjoys traveling to foreign countries and eating in gourmet restaurants, activities which can be extremely expensive.

6. The advertising for the film gave potential viewers a specific impression, but the film itself turned out to be quite different.

7. His decision to deposit his check before he went away for the weekend turned out to be a mistake.

8. Even though the sandwiches were quite filling, the picnickers took pastries along as well.

9. The rain overflowed the gutter, but the water did not damage the sidewalk.

10. Commercials during news broadcasts take time, so the broadcasters do not have to provide a full hour of news.

12-72 1. When a parent takes children to fast-food restaurants, there are no dishes to wash, and the children love the restaurants.

2. If traffic is worse at a certain time, the employee can work out a schedule that makes it possible to avoid the heavy traffic.

3. Opponents of the death penalty argue that execution is one crime added to another.

4. Some people are perfectly happy without a child, and they do not want to put that happiness in jeopardy.

5. Some countries' leaders believe that violence is the only way to enforce their ideas, and this conviction motivates them to go to war.

6. Political leaders at times manipulate people by means of religious beliefs that these leaders use to attain what they desire.

7. There are several advantages to attending the local community college. First, the school offers a complete range of general education courses.

8. Television shows portraying the use of drugs and alcohol may make children cu-

rious to find out what these substances are really like.

9. Social workers and psychologists are similar in that they both help people.

10. Joe felt that Tom would not make a good teacher and told him so.

12-73 1. *Error:* "breakdown" = "where one cannot cope"
Corrected version: A person who cannot cope with all the stress may have a breakdown.

2. *Error:* "person" = "cause"
Corrected version: A person who drives recklessly may cause an accident sooner or later.

3. *Error:* "example of unfair discrimination" = "parent"
Corrected version: The parent who puts a curfew on a daughter but not on a son is unfairly discriminating.

4. *Error:* "lesson" = "Dr. King"
Corrected version: We can learn a fundamental lesson in history if we become familiar with the work of Dr. Martin Luther King, Jr., who was an important civil rights activist.

5. *Error:* "situation can be a person"
Corrected version: A person whose car breaks down on the freeway can be in a difficult situation.

12-74 1. *Error:* "one . . . like"   [AG]
Corrected version: One of the new employees likes to go boating on weekends.

2. *Error:* "which"   [REF]
Corrected version: Some people do personal grooming while they are driving slowly along a crowded freeway, but the distraction may cause an accident.

3. *Error:* "he"   [PRON]
Corrected version: We saw John and him come into the library just before noon.

4. *Error:* "food known to cause cancer"   [MO]
Corrected version: The proposition requires the phasing out of the use on food of pesticides known to cause cancer.

5. *Error:* "both of telling . . . and trying"   [PA]
Corrected version: He is guilty both of telling lies and of trying to damage other people's reputations.

6. *Error:* [RT]
Corrected version: He ran for the office and lost; therefore, he decided not to run again.

7. *Error:* "one . . . you"   [SH]
Corrected version: One who wants to learn to play a musical instrument has to practice regularly.

8. *Error:* [FR]
Corrected version: They enjoyed going out to eat on the weekend, especially for Sunday morning brunch.

9. *Error:* "rains . . . was"   [AG]
Corrected version: The rain, melting the new snow, was a disappointment, because they had wanted to go skiing that weekend.

10. *Error:* "whomever"   [PRON]
Corrected version: He will loan the tape to whoever wants to listen to it.

12-75 1. *Error:* "not only gave . . . but he"   [PA]
Corrected version: The keeper not only gave the animals their food but added something special for each one.

2. *Error:* "job that is not very knowledgeable"   [MO]
Corrected version: A person that [or who] is not very knowledgeable may be chosen for a job.

3. *Error:* "told . . . bursts"   [SH]
Corrected version: He told us the joke and burst out laughing himself.

4. *Error:* "lying on top of the computer monitor, Tom"   [MO]
Corrected version: Tom found his other glove lying on top of the computer monitor.

5. *Error:* "was . . . knife and spoon"   [AG]
Corrected version: There were a knife and a spoon on the placemat.

6. *Error:* [FR]
Corrected version: That book shows busy housekeepers the way to prepare a meal that is both nutritious and easy to make.

7. *Error:* "mistake" = "when we do not face our problems"   [PRED]
Corrected version: Not facing our problems is the real mistake.

8. *Error:* "they"   [REF]
Corrected version: In the bank, tellers often have problems serving customers when the computers are down.

9. *Error:* [RT]
   Corrected version: First he did exercises to warm up. Then he began his circuit training.
10. *Error:* "could take . . . wants" [SH]
    Corrected version: She can take a class in art history if she wants.

Chapter 13

13-1
1. uncertain
2. unnatural
3. misplace
4. misspell
5. interchange
6. interracial
7. rerun
8. redo
9. withdraw
10. withholding

13-2
1. hoping
2. hopeful
3. completed
4. completely
5. coercing
6. writing
7. lovable
8. acknowledging
9. manageable
10. courageous

13-3
1. rebelled
2. fitting
3. committed
4. beginning
5. forgetting
6. stopped
7. jogger
8. deferred
9. compelled
10. existence
11. regrettable
12. abhorrence
13. hotter
14. wrapper
15. concealing
16. patrolling
17. getting
18. knitting
19. grabbing
20. propeller

Chapter 14

14-1
1. The girl's car
2. The girls' cars
3. The country's government
4. The countries' governments
5. Mr. Johnson's house
6. The Smiths' house
7. The Joneses' farm
8. The children's toys
9. The boss' secretary
10. The bosses' secretary

14-2 #2, #4, #6, #7, #8, #10

14-3
1. The girl's dress
2. The girls' dresses
3. The child's paint set
4. The children's paint sets
5. The bus' windows
6. The buses' windows
7. The man's suit
8. The men's suits
9. The city's parks
10. The cities' parks
11. The book's cover
12. The electronic typewriter's memory

14-4
1. That was an intentional foul.
2. He got ahead of the crowd.
3. He was worried about his daughter's peace of mind.
4. Waste disposal is a popular concern nowadays.
5. The Dream Team seemed to perform feats of magic.
6. He uses a great deal of foul language when he talks.
7. Any excessive wait in line made them tend to give up on the rides in the theme park.
8. One of parents' responsibilities is to give their children manners.
9. We are fouling our environment.
10. Packaged products are to be found primarily on the aisles in supermarkets.
11. The police are finally taking serious action to find the serial killer.
12. Air force pilots are known to have sighted UFOs.

14-5
1. He chose two plain doughnuts and one chocolate eclair.

2. She will buy a new dress to wear on her vacation.
3. I know for a fact that they have no money.
4. The fourth race car went forth.
5. He knew he had won the plane trip to Hawaii.
6. The knight did his rescue work at night.
7. I hear they are here.
8. The herd heard the noise and stampeded.

14-6 1. We need to weigh that pair of suitcases; we want to avoid excess baggage charges on top of the fare.
2. Of course, you should do the assignment due tomorrow!
3. He ate the whole dessert.   [*or* pear]
4. He was hurt when he fell into the hole, but it did not seem to faze him.
5. The child threw the ball through the window.
6. *Coarse* is the opposite of *fine*.
7. It is not fair to desert people who help us.
8. On the way to the fair, we saw a rainbow.

14-7 1. council, break, their
2. principal, passed, too
3. Who's, whose, right
4. They're, all ready, their
5. It's, already, too, to, break
6. Your, past
7. principle, your
8. rite, past
9. already, passed, its
10. Their, principal

14-8 1. weather, than
2. whether, led
3. have, lead
4. lead, affect
5. Its, effect, than
6. personnel, accept, except
7. Loose, personal
8. lose, than, personal
9. have, led
10. have, effect, their

14-9 1. Their, have, no
2. personnel, principal
3. led, past
4. passed, by, here, through
5. They're, all ready, to, accept, their
6. too, conscious, its, effects
7. advice, to, course

8. brakes, than
9. Its, past
10. lose, know, whose, right

Chapter 15

15-1 After finding the answers in your dictionary, see the explanations in the text.

15-2 1. autocrat
2. autonomy
3. dissuade
4. autobiography
5. distrust
6. dispute
7. automobile
8. disclosure
9. automation
10. disperse
11. dissect
12. automaton
13. dissolve
14. discourse

15-3 1. apathy
2. antibiotic
3. contravene
4. agnostic
5. antipathy
6. countermand
7. insatiable
8. anarchy
9. antidote
10. contradict
11. inadvertently
12. antonym
13. analgesic
14. incorrigible
15. atheist
16. antithesis
17. intangible
18. asymmetric
19. antagonism
20. controversy

15-4 1. hyperactive
2. microcosm, macrocosm
3. polytheistic
4. monolith
5. hypodermic
6. ambiguous
7. omniscient
8. unilateral, bilateral, multilateral

15-5
1. monopoly
2. bisect
3. polyglot
4. omnivorous
5. unify
6. monotheism
7. unicellular
8. multitude
9. polysyllabic
10. bilingual
11. bicameral
12. microfiche
13. omnipotent
14. multinational
15. ambidextrous
16. hyperbole
17. macrobiotic
18. hypercritical
19. hypocrisy
20. hypothesis

15-6
1. posthumously
2. posterity
3. precursor
4. antebellum
5. postmortem
6. postscript
7. presentiment
8. precocious
9. antecedent
10. precedent
11. antedate
12. prejudice

15-7
1. exonerate
2. extrovert, introvert
3. demote
4. aberration
5. pervasive
6. superlative
7. subjugate
8. transcend
9. telekinesis
10. circumspect
11. intervene

15-8
1. deciduous
2. desolate
3. dehydration
4. extirpate
5. expedite
6. extracurricular
7. decadence

8. intravenous
9. interim
10. intermittent
11. intercede
12. deviate
13. abstract
14. absolve
15. intramural
16. circumference
17. eloquent
18. abominable
19. extravehicular
20. intermediary
21. subsistence
22. telecommunications
23. superimpose
24. perception
25. circumvent
26. circuitous
27. permeate
28. transfusion
29. perforate
30. transitory

15-9
1. heterogeneous
2. beneficiary
3. retract
4. recurring
5. revoke
6. benevolent
7. revive
8. benign
9. malefactor
10. malcontent
11. revert
12. prospective
13. profusion
14. recede
15. proponent
16. heterodox
17. prognosis
18. malevolent
19. euphonious
20. eulogize

15-10
1. manufacture
2. dermatitis
3. acrimonious
4. egoist
5. belligerent
6. democracy
7. immortal

8. philanthropist
9. per capita
10. genocide
11. homicide
12. corporeal

15-11
1. rebellious
2. mortify
3. exacerbate
4. egocentric
5. epidemic
6. moribund
7. acerbity
8. acuity
9. demagogue
10. anthropology
11. anthropoid
12. Homo sapiens
13. manipulate
14. pachyderm
15. epidermis
16. corpse
17. corpuscle
18. capitulate
19. decapitation
20. genealogy
21. genus
22. recapitulate
23. incorporate
24. corps
25. dermatology
26. emancipate
27. manuscript
28. misanthropy

15-12
1. vivify
2. diurnal
3. subterranean
4. aqueduct
5. dehydration
6. chronic
7. contemporary
8. submarine
9. interurban
10. anarchy
11. prologue
12. verbose
13. agrarian
14. symphony
15. translucent
16. deviation
17. bibliophile

18. bureaucracy
19. biennial
20. biosphere
21. pacify
22. agoraphobia

15-13
1. anachronism
2. extemporaneously
3. revitalize
4. phonics
5. elucidate
6. annuity
7. biography
8. autobiography
9. vitality
10. synchronize
11. chronological
12. symbiosis
13. per diem
14. hydroelectric
15. mariner
16. terrestrial
17. terra cotta
18. phonetics
19. aquatic
20. maritime

15-14
1. pacifist
2. acrophobia
3. bibliography
4. verbatim
5. matriarchal
6. urbane
7. agronomy
8. claustrophobia
9. neologism
10. monologue
11. verbal
12. hierarchy
13. oligarchy
14. autocratic
15. urban
16. viaduct

15-15
1. effect
2. transfer
3. deduce
4. affect
5. facilities
6. detain
7. deport
8. efficacy

9. detract
10. fiction
11. coniferous
12. protract
13. facsimile
14. proficient
15. facilitate
16. tenable
17. conducive
18. retract
19. tenacious
20. portable
21. conduit
22. induction

15-16
1. indoctrinate
2. seismograph
3. eject
4. provocation
5. dejected
6. projectile-trajectory
7. electrocardiogram
8. scribe
9. irrevocable
10. docile
11. proscribe
12. choreography
13. missile
14. ascribe
15. admit
16. equivocal

15-17
1. incision
2. fragile
3. vanquish
4. predominate
5. excise
6. herbicide
7. infraction
8. preclude
9. disclose
10. infringe
11. frail
12. incisive
13. domain
14. recluse
15. domineering
16. invincible

15-18
1. loquacious
2. ergonomics
3. credible
4. elaborate

5. omniscient
6. credence
7. jurisdiction
8. abdicate
9. involuntarily
10. indict
11. elocution
12. incredulity
13. admonish
14. metallurgy
15. laborious
16. collaborate
17. contradict
18. premonition
19. conscious
20. volition

15-19
1. tangible
2. auditory
3. speculate
4. contingent
5. conspicuous
6. voluble
7. improvise
8. cascade
9. advent
10. evolve
11. inaudible
12. convention
13. tactile
14. vertigo
15. adverse
16. casualty
17. divert
18. evidence
19. retrospect
20. subversive

Appendix A

A-1
1. *A* dog has *a* tail.
2. *The* nurse that you met yesterday works at *the* hospital on First Street.
3. *The* books on *the* bottom shelf are his.   [a particular bookcase is understood]
4. Most people are afraid of death.
5. *The* death of *a* famous person is usually reported on *the* front page of *the* newspaper.   [*or* a newspaper]   ["the" if the local paper is understood]
6. She likes fruit or *a* salad and *a* cup of coffee for lunch.

7. I see *a* cat climbing *a* tree.   [*or* the tree]   Now *the* cat is at *the* top of *the* tree.   ["cat" and "tree" are mentioned again]

8. There is *an* apple on *the* kitchen table.   [the writer has a particular kitchen in mind]   I will eat *the* apple while I make dinner.   ["apple" is mentioned again]

9. I went to *the* dinner <u>given</u> in honor of *the* new mayor of <u>Riverview</u>.

10. Women do not always like housework.

11. He has had both gastritis and pneumonia during *the* <u>past</u> year.

12. Agatha Christie wrote mystery stories.

13. We use chalk to write on chalkboards.

14. Metal is usually stronger than plastic.

15. Oak and pine are kinds of wood.

16. *A* photographer uses *a* camera.

17. It takes money to get along in life.

18. Heavy food gives older people indigestion.

19. Unemployment is *a* problem in large cities.

20. She is *a* professor.

Appendix C

C-1
1. 2
2. 8
3. 1
4. 7
5. 3
6. 9
7. 5
8. 11
9. 4
10. 10
11. 6
12. 12

INDEX